NF

INTERNATIONAL CAPITAL AND SERVICE FLOWS

ECONOMISTS OF THE TWENTIETH CENTURY

General Editors: Mark Perlman, *University Professor of Economics, University of Pittsburgh* and Mark Blaug, *Professor Emeritus, University of London, Professor Emeritus, University of Buckingham and Visiting Professor, University of Exeter*

This innovative series comprises specially invited collections of articles and papers by economists whose work has made an important contribution to economics in the late twentieth century.

The proliferation of new journals and the ever-increasing number of new articles make it difficult for even the most assiduous economist to keep track of all the important recent advances. By focusing on those economists whose work is generally recognized to be at the forefront of the discipline, the series will be an essential reference point for the different specialisms included.

A list of published and future titles in this series is printed at the end of this volume.

International Capital and Service Flows

Theory and Measurement for Economic Policy
Volume II

Herbert G. Grubel

Professor of Economics
Simon Fraser University
British Columbia

Edward Elgar

Published by
Edward Elgar Publishing Limited
Gower House
Croft Road
Aldershot
Hants GU11 3HR
England

Edward Elgar Publishing Company
Old Post Road
Brookfield
Vermont 05036
USA

338.973
G88t
v. 2

British Library Cataloguing in Publication Data
Grubel, Herbert G.
  Theory and Measurement for Economic
  Policy. – Vol. 2: International Capital
  and Service Flows. – (Economists of the
  Twentieth Century Series)
  I. Title II. Series
  337

ab

Printed in Great Britain at the University Press, Cambridge

ISBN 1 85278 905 0 (Volume I)
     1 85278 906 9 (Volume II)
     1 85278 907 7 (Volume III)
     1 85278 787 2 (3 volume set)

Contents

v

Acknowledgements

The publishers wish to thank the following who have kindly given permission for the use of copyright material.

American Economic Association for articles: Herbert G. Grubel and Anthony D. Scott (1966), 'The International Flow of Human Capital', *American Economic Review*, **LVI**(2), May, 268–74; Herbert G. Grubel and Anthony D. Scott (1976), 'The Characteristics of Foreigners in the U.S. Economics Profession', *American Economic Review*, **LVII**(1), March, 131–45; Herbert G. Grubel (1968), 'Internationally Diversified Portfolios: Welfare Gains and Capital Flows', *American Economic Review*, **LVIII**(5), December, 1299–1314.

Banca Nazionale del Lavoro, Rome, for articles: Herbert G. Grubel (1983), 'The New International Banking', *Banca Nazionale del Lavoro Quarterly Review*, **146**, September, 263–84; Herbert G. Grubel and Michael A. Walker (1991), 'The Dominance of Producers Services in the US Economy', *Banca Nazionale del Lavoro Quarterly Review*, **176**, March, 57–68.

Basil Blackwell Ltd for article: Herbert G. Grubel (1987), 'All Traded Services are Embodied in Materials or People', *The World Economy*, **10**(3), September, 319–30.

Canadian Journal of Economics for article: Anthony Scott and Herbert G. Grubel (1969), 'The International Movement of Human Capital: Canadian Economists', *Canadian Journal of Economics*, **II**(3), August, 375–88.

Financial Analysts Federation for article: Herbert G. Grubel (1979), 'The Peter Principle and the Efficient Market Hypothesis', *Financial Analysts Journal*, November/December.

Fraser Institute for article: Herbert Grubel (1992), 'The Economic and Social Effects of Immigration', Chapter 5 in Steven Globerman (ed.), *The Immigration Dilemma*, 99–127.

Helbing & Lichtenhahn Verlag AG Basle for article: David L. Hammes, Jean-Jacques Rosa and Herbert G. Grubel (1989), 'The National Accounts, Household Service Consumption and its Monetization', *Kyklos*, **42**(1), 3–14.

Institute of Southeast Asian Studies for articles: Herbert G. Grubel (1985), 'Multinational Banking', *Research Notes and Discussion Paper No. 56*, 1–21; Herbert G. Grubel (1989), 'Liberalization of Trade in Services: A Taxonomy and Discussion of Issues', 1–18.

Macmillan Ltd for article: Herbert G. Grubel (1982), 'The Theory of International Capital Movements' in John Black and John H. Dunning (eds), *International Capital Movements: Papers of the Fifth Annual Conference of the International Economics Study Group*, 1–21.

J C B Mohr (Paul Siebeck) Tübingen for articles: Herbert G. Grubel (1979), 'Towards a Theory of Two-Way Trade in Capital Assets' in Herbert Giersch (ed.), *On the Economics of Intra-Industry Trade: Symposium 1978*, 71–82; Herbert G. Grubel and Michael A. Walker (1989), 'Modern Service Sector Growth: Causes and Effects' in Herbert Giersch (ed.), *Services in World Economic Growth: Symposium 1988*, 1–34.

Pergamon Press Ltd for article: H.G. Grubel (1984), 'Economics of the Brain Drain', *International Encyclopedia of Education*, 517–23.

Springer-Verlag for article: Herbert G. Grubel (1992), 'Profitable Currency Speculation: Service to Users or Destabilizing?' in Herbert Giersch (ed.), *Money, Trade, and Competition: Essays in Memory of Egon Sohmen*, 23–37.

University of Chicago Press for articles: H.G. Grubel and A.D. Scott (1966), 'The Immigration of Scientists and Engineers to the United States, 1949–61', *Journal of Political Economy*, **LXXIV**(4), August, 368–78; Herbert G. Grubel (1974), 'Taxation and the Rates of Return from Some U.S. Asset Holdings Abroad, 1960–69', *Journal of Political Economy*, **82**(3), May–June, 469–87.

University of Wisconsin Press for article: Herbert G. Grubel and Anthony D. Scott (1966), 'The Cost of U.S. College Student Exchange Programs', *The Journal of Human Resources*, **I**(2), Fall, 81–98.

Introduction *author*

The purpose of this Introduction is to put the articles in this volume into the intellectual, institutional and policy context within which they originated. It also affords me the opportunity to reflect on the professional attention received by the selection, to indicate where I have changed my views and to acknowledge debts of gratitude to sponsors, co-authors and collaborators.

1.–2. After the Soviet Union successfully launched Sputnik in the late 1950s, the United States embarked on a massive programme designed to boost scientific research and higher education. This policy produced a large increase in demand for scientists in the US and stimulated a massive inflow of scientific manpower. This phenomenon raised much concern among policy-makers abroad, especially in the developing countries, since it was seen to interfere with their plans for economic development. In addition, it was considered to be inequitable that the United States, the richest country of the world, should benefit from the educational investment which the poorer countries had made in their citizens.

Chapter 1 in this volume, co-authored with A.D. Scott, applies standard neoclassical price theory to the analysis of the brain drain, as the phenomenon was called. We conceived the paper after we had read a discussion paper by Harry Johnson on the same subject while Scott and I were on the faculty of the University of Chicago. Our paper was published in the *American Economic Review*, has been cited widely and is associated with the 'internationalist' view of the brain drain. I was asked to write the second paper in this volume for publication in the *International Encyclopedia of Education*. It contains a digest of the conventional wisdom about the brain drain that emerged from research during the 1960s and 1970s.

The basic message of these two chapters is as simple as it is unacceptable to those who disagree with neoclassical price theory. The brain drain migrants raise their own welfare since they act freely. Except for the relatively minor gains for a few from increased opportunities to engage in exchange, the welfare of those in the receiving country is unchanged since the migrants contribute to output what they claim through their earnings. In the country of emigration the remaining population analogously does not lose since the migrants take away both their contribution to and claim on output.

Individuals who are educated at public cost typically repay this public investment by paying taxes that go to the education of their own children. Emigrants take away both their children and tax payments, leaving unchanged the tax burden and costs of education of those left behind. By analogy, there are no gains in the country of immigration.

Externalities through cultural and scientific work similarly have little effect on the countries receiving and losing the migrants. Most research activity results in knowledge capital that is appropriated by the agents sponsoring it. Pure research which does not have these characteristics, on the other hand, is a world public good and its benefits accrue to all peoples, including those in the countries where the scientists have been educated. If brain drain migrants perform basic research in the country of immigration which they would not have undertaken at home because of a lack of facilities or any other reason, the country losing the migrant enjoys a net gain as a result of the scientists' emigration.

Very few policy recommendations to stop the brain drain or deal with its consequences have ever been made. The most prominent proposal by Jagdish Bhagwati – to tax migrants in the receiving country and transfer the funds to the sending country – has not been considered seriously by any government. Like all other proposals, it involves costs which are not worth the benefits, which the internationalist model suggests in any case are very small.

3.–6.   Chapters 3 through 6 were co-authored with Scott and contain empirical work designed to establish the magnitude of the brain drain and more generally the international circulation of human capital due to foreign education. National data on migration turn out to be an unreliable measure of the brain drain since they report only when individuals enter a country but not when they leave it. This has been important because highly skilled manpower is very mobile internationally. Considering all US immigrants as being permanent has therefore resulted in a serious upward bias in estimates of US brain gains.

A more accurate estimate of the brain drain can be obtained by the examination of registers of professionals. In our research we used the membership list of the American Economics Association and the Register of Scientific Personnel maintained by the National Science Foundation for demographic information on the stock of manpower in the US. The results of our investigations show that the foreign born and educated represent a small fraction of US scientific manpower, though there are important differences between fields and in age-groups. The data also reveal that these individuals constitute very small percentages of the stocks of foreign science manpower, especially from India, which was one of the main countries concerned with the effects of the brain drain.

Canada was especially concerned about the brain drain because of the close integration of its economy and educational system with that of the US. Using estimates of human capital values we found that the value of educational services obtained by Canadians studying in the US and brought back to Canada exceeded the value of the human capital lost through the permanent emigration of Canadians. The free circulation of people and human capital thus resulted in a net gain for Canada by the reckoning of standard human capital accounting procedures.

The methodologies developed in Chapters 3–6 will be of considerable use to analysts interested in the study of the effects of migration and international education on the stock of human capital in individual countries. Such estimates, much like those of physical capital, are important for an assessment of the causes of economic growth and the effectiveness of educational and other government policies.

7.   Chapter 7 in this volume was prompted by a growing concern over immigration

policies by the government of Canada discussed widely during the 1980s and 1990s. The paper presents the standard neoclassical analysis of the effects of immigration. In addition it considers the concept of optimum population size relevant to immigration policies in the long run.

In the discussion of externalities associated with immigration, the study presents data on the ethnic composition of immigrants during the post-war years. These data show that until the 1970s about 90 per cent of Canada's immigrants came from Europe. Since then, this percentage has fallen steadily to about 30 per cent in recent years. If these trends continue, in the longer run, the historic ethnic and social mix of the Canadian population will be altered drastically.

Sociologists and other social scientists have different opinions about the consequences of these changes for the welfare of Canadians in the future. The study reviews the opinions of those who are optimistic and of those who are pessimistic about the economic and social implications of the possible new ethnic composition of the population. I conclude from this review that the possibility of significant negative externalities justifies including the ethnic implications of immigration in the overall benefit-cost calculus of different policies. Scholarly discussion of these issues should not be stifled on the grounds of racism.

8.   During the late 1960s I was teaching in the Finance Department of the Wharton School at the University of Pennsylvania where much research effort was devoted to the development of the Markowitz-Tobin model of portfolio management. Stimulated by a luncheon discussion with Douglas Vickers, I decided to apply the model to a study of the benefits of the international diversification of assets.

The key ingredient of my research was the use of historic foreign stock-market indices and dividend yields, adjusted for exchange rate changes, as the investment alternatives to be compared with holding a fully diversified portfolio of US stocks, as measured by a popular stock index and associated dividends. The assembly of the data and the calculations were difficult relative to the ease with which these tasks can be completed in today's world of efficient computers and software.

The results of my calculations showed that the international diversification of portfolios can result in substantial welfare gains for wealthholders. The paper was published in the *American Economic Review* and was reprinted in several books of readings for university students and investment analysts. In many papers published over the following years, my methodology was refined, extended and applied to different data sets. The manager of one very successful US mutual fund told me that my findings had significantly influenced the design of his investment strategy.

9.   One of the implications of the model of international portfolio diversification is that capital can flow in both directions between two countries whether returns are equal or different in either country. The value of reduced risk from diversification can outweigh the loss of expected yield. This result was used to explain the two-way flow observed in the real world and long considered puzzling in the context of traditional models in which rates of return alone motivate international capital flows.

Chapter 9 considers a range of other explanations of such two-way flows of capital between countries, the international diversification model being one. Others are the modern theory of direct foreign investment and the existence of taxation. The paper was presented at a conference at the Institute for World Economics at Kiel devoted to the economics of intra-industry trade. The similarities of the phenomena of two-way trade in goods and assets are obvious. However, explanations are very different.

10.   As a result of my interest in international capital flows, John Dunning invited me to write a review of the theory of international capital movements, with some consideration of promising areas for future research. The paper was presented at a conference at the University of Reading and is published as Chapter 10 in this volume. Several of the areas for promising research identified in it remain to be tackled in the early 1990s.

11.–12.   Since the late 1960s banks have begun to open large numbers of foreign offices. The growth of this international investment by banks is documented in Chapter 12, which also shows the extent to which banks from different countries have invaded each other's territory. The motives and welfare effects of this new type of banking are discussed in Chapters 11 and 12.

The paper suggests a taxonomy of motives: serving domestic firms and travellers abroad, exploiting opportunities for the differentiation of services in a foreign market, and participating in international consortium banking and wholesale markets. While each type of activity is driven by slightly different motives, the dominating determinant is the low marginal cost of using knowledge banks have acquired for other purposes. Such activities therefore increase efficiency and welfare since they permit the amortization of a fixed cost over a larger output. Consumers gain from increased variety of service characteristics and lower average costs.

13.   Many attempts have been made to 'explain' the large fluctuations in nominal and real exchange rates since the early 1970s. One of these explanations attributes the fluctuations to the speculative activities of banks. At the same time, the analysis documents that these same banks make large profits from their speculation.

Chapter 13 confronts this conclusion with the logically powerful proposition that speculators can earn profits only if they buy when the price is low and sell when it is high. Such behaviour must drive up low and drive down high prices and therefore reduce fluctuations. My analysis also questions the validity of other institutional information about the behaviour of speculating banks.

I conclude that speculation by banks probably does not cause increased exchange rate fluctuations but instead narrows them. Without the speculation by banks, exchange rate instability would be even greater as wealthholders around the world react massively and rationally to news which affects expected returns from foreign asset holdings. The large profits from bank speculation represent returns to the provision of increased exchange rate stability to exporters and importers of goods, services and long-term assets.

As one commentator on my paper has said, it remains an important challenge for economists to reconcile evidence on profit-making speculation with the view that such speculation is also destabilizing. I agree.

14. During the year 1970 I worked in the research department of the US Treasury. There I encountered a little known data base concerning the earnings and taxes paid by US firms abroad. I used this data base to estimate the after-tax rates of return on US investment in many different countries. The findings of this study are extremely important in any assessment of the merit of foreign investment for both sending and receiving countries.

From a private point of view, only before-tax yields determine the decision to invest at home or abroad because existing international double taxation agreements ensure that all taxes paid to foreign governments can be fully used to offset US tax obligations. This incentive structure secures the efficient allocation of capital in the world. However, from the point of view of the United States or any capital exporting country, it can result in a social loss since the tax-revenue on this investment accrues to a foreign country.

My analysis considers conditions under which there are no such social losses from privately profitable foreign investment. In fact, the empirical results suggest that there are none. These findings imply in turn that countries hosting foreign investment gain through these taxes, and that these gains far outweigh those considered in the standard neoclassical analysis of the welfare effects of foreign investment.

15. People are born with different talents useful in athletics, the arts, sciences and also investment analysis. People with extraordinary talents need time to develop them and persuade the world of their existence before they gain appropriate recognition.

The modern theory of portfolio management and the derived efficient market hypothesis both abstract from the existence of people with different talents and the time-consuming process of developing them. Yet, this characteristic of human beings can actually resolve the bitter dispute between academic proponents of the efficient market hypothesis (who claim that no analysts can beat the market) and investment analysts (who believe they can or know someone who does so regularly).

In Chapter 15 I describe the process which makes talented analysts earn extraordinary returns for a number of periods; however, as this success leads to increased responsibilities or higher pay, they reach the limits of their talent. The Peter principle is reflected in this process whose momentum carries some to a position where just a little too much is expected of them.

I remain convinced of the merit of this analysis, even though the lack of data on the performance of individual investment managers has prevented its empirical evaluation. The challenge remains to find and test such information.

16.–17. The Canadian and US economies went through massive industrial restructuring during the 1980s which saw a significant rise in the service sector at the expense of manufacturing. This development led to the prediction of 'deindustrialization', loss of competitiveness, the vanishing of the middle class and all kinds of other dire consequences. A number of influential analysts used these predictions to support their recommendations for more economic planning, calling it 'industrial policy'.

In response to these developments, the Canadian government commissioned the Fraser Institute to undertake a massive study of the service industries. I acted as the academic director of this project and Chapters 16 and 17 contain its most important general findings written up in co-authorship with Michael Walker.

Using an innovative methodology, these papers employ the national income account statistics of Canada and the US to divide service sector output into consumer, government and producer services. Our main findings contradicted common expectations and were inconsistent with the basic premise of the analysts seeing service sector growth as a serious policy issue. In both countries since the 1960s, in real terms and as a per cent of national output, the government service sector declined, the consumer service sector remained about constant and the producer service sector rose.

We interpret the growth of the producers' service sector to be the outcome of human and knowledge capital deepening in the economy, accompanied by increased specialization of the services sold by new and growing firms to the producers of goods and other services in the economy. These producers' services are responsible to a considerable degree for the growth of productivity in manufacturing and elsewhere since they are the vehicle through which the rapidly growing base of scientific, engineering and management knowledge is introduced into the productive sector of the economy.

The policy implications of these ideas are important. A country's manufacturing sector may be shrinking, but the output of this sector embodies increasing qualities of the country's skilled labour force. There is no need for an industrial policy to preserve manufacturing. In addition, the results imply that regional development subsidies, which have traditionally focused on real capital formation, might be more effective in the form of subsidies to producer service inputs. According to this view, for instance, the productivity of Canada's fishing industry might be increased more per dollar of subsidy by scientific marketing and product improvement advice than by the construction of a new wharf or boats.

18.   Econometric measurement of the determinants of the demand for consumer services yields unsatisfactory results when income and a relative price variable are the only independent variables considered. The introduction of the variable female labour force participation rate corrected this deficiency, as is reported in Chapter 18 published jointly with David Hammes and Jean-Jacques Rosa.

The statistical importance of the female labour force participation rate suggests that a significant proportion of the demand for consumer services since the 1960s has been the result of women joining the work force and using commercially provided services to replace the work they would otherwise have done in the home. These findings have interesting implications for the future of consumer service industries as the limits of female labour force participation are reached or growth is reversed. They also permit inferences about the extent to which economic growth recorded in conventional national income accounts has been due, not to the real expansion of economic activity, but to the shift of unrecorded housework into the formal sector.

19.–20.   Insights about the important role of producer services in the economy also have some interesting implications for the understanding of issues in negotiating the liberalization of international trade in services. Thus, Chapters 19 and 20 suggest that all such trade can take place only after services have been embodied in goods or people. From this analytical perspective, service trade involves issues that are no different in kind from those in goods trade. The only differences lie in the relative magnitude and ease of detection during border crossing.

'People service' trade requires individuals to cross borders to absorb services like tourism or education and to deliver services like those of entertainers or engineers. 'Factor service' trade takes place through the conventional exchange of capital and labour services, but importantly also when the output of human capital crosses borders after embodiment in books, films, reports or electronic messages. The bulk of service trade involves goods, with varying degrees of embodied producer service inputs. This new taxonomy concerning the nature of international trade in services provides a number of analytically useful insights and new perspectives on negotiations over liberalization.

THE INTERNATIONAL FLOW OF HUMAN CAPITAL*

By HERBERT B. GRUBEL, *University of Chicago*
and ANTHONY D. SCOTT, *University of British Columbia*

I

We have been drawn to the subject of this paper by recent strong manifestations of public interest in two major problems in international relations: first, the migration of highly skilled individuals to the U.S.—often referred to as the "brain drain"—and, second, the large-scale program of training foreign students in the U.S. Both of these problems have in common that they involve an international transfer of resources in the form of human capital that goes completely unrecorded in any official balance-of-payments statistics. This common feature clearly defines our field of analysis and excludes problems associated with the transfer of human capital services, such as occur in connection with the Peace Corps, programs of technical assistance through governmental agencies, technical and scientific advice by private corporations, etc.—all of which are reflected in official balance-of-payments statistics.

We have prepared some empirical estimates of the U.S. balance of trade in human capital from foreign student exchange and the immigration of scientists and engineers, which will shortly be published. These studies, while involving interesting conceptual problems of measurement, produced no startling results and suggest that in comparison with the size of the U.S. economy these capital flows are quite small. We present here only a few summary statistics to give an impression of the nature of the empirical results we have obtained. First, it turns out that the total U.S. program of foreign college student exchange, involving 58,000 foreign students in the U.S. and 11,000 American students abroad, resulted in a maximum net U.S. cost of only $17 million in 1962, after appropriate adjustment of the gross cost for the human capital value of students electing to remain in the U.S. Second, the total human capital value of scientists and engineers immigrating to the U.S. during the thirteen-year period from 1949 to 1961 came to $1.0 billion. Third, the role of foreigners in the American economics profession estimated on the basis of the National Science Foundation survey statistics is as follows: 12 percent are foreign born, 9 percent had also foreign high school training, but only 3 percent earned their

* This paper is part of a larger study concerned with the international migration of highly trained people, financed by the Rockefeller Foundation and directed by Harry G. Johnson, whom we thank for his support, both intellectual and financial.

268

1

highest professional degree abroad. Fourth, the shares of annual output of first-degree engineers lost by emigration to the U.S. by some major individual countries were found to differ widely between countries and tended to be surprisingly high in some instances. For example, Norway lost 24.1 percent, Greece 20.9 percent, Germany 9.5 percent, and France 1.2 percent of their annual output of first-degree engineers to the U.S. Finally, scientists and engineers are from six to twelve times as likely to emigrate to the U.S. as people in other professions, judging from the occupational composition of all immigrants and that of the labor force in the migrants' native countries.

While such empirical work sheds light on the quantitative importance of issues which all too often are argued in complete ignorance of any facts, we have found that nearly all discussions of the brain drain and exchange student programs suffer most seriously from the absence of any theoretical framework. The main part of this paper is devoted to a theoretical analysis of issues surrounding the international flow of human capital embodied in highly skilled migrants to the U.S. and in foreign students electing not to return to their native countries.

II

The argument that a country "loses" by the emigration of highly skilled individuals is most nearly always valid when we consider the "country" to be a nation state whose national objective is to maximize its military and economic power. From this point of view, a person's emigration absolutely reduces his country's mobilizable manpower, and its national output is lowered by the amount the emigrant contributed to it.

While this view of national losses is held quite widely, it is sorely outmoded in our age. The identification of military power with the number of a country's inhabitants, even if they are highly skilled, is very vague and precarious. Wealth, science, and technology dominate modern warfare, and it is quite easy for most nations to purchase military equipment on the world market at costs much below those that would have to be incurred in the development of individual national weapons systems. Economic power, in turn, depends not so much on aggregate national output as it does on per capita income, which may or may not be affected by an individual's emigration.

In place of this outmoded nationalist concept of a country, we suggest the use of another one, according to which a country is an association of individuals whose collective welfare its leaders seek to maximize. While the level of individual welfare is determined by many factors, including items of collective consumption such as military might and foreign economic influence, the most important determinant of human welfare in the long run is the standard of living; that is, the quantity of goods and services available for consumption. Therefore, in the following analysis we will focus our attention on the changes in income brought about by the emigration of highly skilled individuals.

If a country wishes to maximize the income available to all its people, then emigration should be welcomed whenever two conditions are met. These are, first, that the emigrant improves his own income and, second, that the migrant's departure does not reduce the income of those remaining behind. The first condition is normally met when emigration is voluntary. Specification of the circumstances under which the second holds true will occupy the rest of this paper.

III

According to the traditional analysis of the migration of labor, the departure of a person normally raises the long-run average income of the people remaining, because it results in an increase in the nation's capital-labor ratio. In the case of the migration of a highly skilled person, however, this conclusion does not hold if the human capital embodied in the emigrant is greater than the country's total per capita endowment of human and physical capital, assuming perfect substitutability of the two forms of capital in the long run. In this case the emigration of a highly skilled person reduces the total income to be distributed among the residents of a country and it follows that in societies where this distribution occurs through planning or other nonmarket means the remaining population suffers a reduction in welfare.

In a market economy where persons are paid their marginal product, however, such a reduction in per capita income is only a statistical phenomenon which has no influence on the welfare of the remaining people: the emigrant removes both his contribution to national output and the income that gives him a claim to this share, so that other incomes remain unchanged. There may be income redistribution effects through changes in the marginal products of the remaining people, but since the brain drain involves rather small numbers of people, these effects are likely to be small enough to be safely considered negligible.

Thus it follows that in a market economy any effects that the emigration of a highly skilled person is likely to have on the welfare on those remaining behind must be sought either in short-run adjustment costs or in market failures.

The short-run costs are due to production losses—specifically those created by the unemployment or inefficient employment of factors of production whose effectiveness depends on cooperation with the skills the departing person takes along. The size of these costs depends on two elements. First, the greater the short-run substitutability of other factors of production or skills for those that have emigrated, the smaller the inefficiencies and loss of output. Second, the more rapidly a replacement for the emigrant can be trained, the smaller the losses. It is difficult to generalize about the characteristics of individual professions or national education systems in regard to these qualities, but it seems reasonable to expect that the emigration of a well-established, experienced professional will cause greater frictional losses than would the emigration of a common laborer or the decision of a student not to return home. Also, we would expect that bursts of heavy emigration alternating with periods of low emigration rates present more difficult adjustment problems than do steady flows, even if the latter represent a greater long-run average than do the former, because of the economy's likely structural adjustments to predictable changes.

Of greater analytical interest than these short-run costs of adjustment to emigration are the long-run effects on welfare associated with failures of the free market to allocate resources efficiently. There are two main sources of such inefficiencies which appear to underlie most of the arguments about losses from the emigration of highly skilled persons.

The first category of losses has to do with genuine externalities, where the market fails properly to compensate the individual for the contributions he makes to society. It is important to note that these externalities must be directly associated with the personal characteristics of the emigrant and not his profession. Thus, if a typical doctor's work contains a large measure of social benefits for which he does not get compensated, these benefits are lost to society only for the length of time required to train another person to take his place as a doctor. It therefore follows that in many of the well-known instances of genuine external effects in consumption or production, emigration imposes only short-run frictional costs to society which disappear in the long run.

While it is difficult enough to find genuine cases of economically significant externalities in the real world, it is even more difficult to find cases which have the added limitation of being associated with a specific person. Examples coming to mind are the external diseconomies from alcoholism or the nonmarket benefits accruing to others from a person's propensity to engage in political or charity work without monetary compensation. The difficulty of finding meaningful examples may legitimately be taken as an indication of the relative unimportance of most externalities given the size of the resources allocated through properly functioning markets.

The second category of losses stems from market failure remedied through activities of the government. It is alleged that the emigration of highly skilled persons affects others most significantly through changes in the cost of providing such government services.

In this connection, it is frequently suggested that public education is a social investment in individuals which emigrants fail to repay, and that therefore the highly trained in particular ought to be forced to repay this investment before they are allowed to leave the country. Such suggestions and the entire idea of a "debt to society" due to publicly-financed education appear to be based on misapprehension.

Society is a continuing organism, and the process of financing education represents an intergeneration transfer of resources under which the currently productive generation taxes itself to educate the young, who in turn upon maturity provide for the next generation of children and so on. What is relevant for our purposes of analysis is that the average burden of financing education falling on the emigrant's generation is not changed by his departure, because he takes along not only his contribution to tax revenue but also his children, on whom this share of revenue would have been spent.

Analogous arguments can be made for the financing of other government services such as defense, police protection, judicial services, etc. However, in all of these instances, including education, the conclusion that no adverse welfare effects result from a person's emigration is valid only if the incidence of taxes is equal to the incidence of benefits from government services.

There is evidence that the enjoyment of the quantitatively most significant services provided by governments is largely proportional to the taxpayers' income, which includes return on human capital. Defense—the largest item in the budget of many nations—benefits more those persons who, as a result of foreign conquests, would lose sizable stocks of assets than those who do not. Roads are used more by those who drive cars than those who walk. The amount of education demanded by the offspring of the highly educated is likely to be above that demanded by the children of people with average education. Only relatively few government services, such as public parks and those related directly to the welfare of the poor, contain elements of subsidy by high-income taxpayers. Therefore, the presumption is strong that the government can reduce many of the services it provides by nearly the same proportion by which tax revenues decline when a highly skilled person emigrates, changing the tax burden or income of the remaining people only marginally and certainly by much less than the gross reduction in tax revenues suggests.

It is true that if government services are provided through lumpy investment projects, reductions in government services may not be possible without increases in average cost. However, such increased burdens from reduced population are short run and last only until either a new, optimum-scale plant replaces the old or as population returns to its old level. At any rate, in most countries complaining of the brain drain the problem is not one of possible excess capacity in public projects but rather one of overcrowding.

It is often argued that a country loses because the highly skilled emigrants would have worked on projects of great importance to the development of the country had they stayed at home. This argument is valid either if we take the nationalistic view of the country or if the person's work would have been associated with large external effects. In this case, also, the nationalistic view is to be rejected for the reasons presented earlier. While it is popular to argue that external effects are frequent in market economies, we have ben unable to discover economically significant instances where individuals provide social services associated with their person rather than profession for which they are not paid—including in work fostering economic development.

Another frequently heard allegation is that the emigration of the highly educated is equivalent to a Darwinian process of selecting the best, which causes a reduction in the genetic "quality" of the country's human stock and influences national welfare in the long run. This is probably a valid argument in principle but its empirical significance is likely to be quite small, given the small relative size of the migratory flows and the population stocks. It should also be noted that the transmission of human characteristics through the genes is a rather unreliable process, and that the offspring of many intellectually distinguished emigrants never achieve their parents' level of attainment.

IV

While our analysis so far suggests that the emigration of highly skilled persons reduces the welfare of the remaining people only under rather rare circumstances, we can make a good case for the proposition that these types of emigrants in fact tend to increase the welfare of their former countrymen in several important ways.

Historically, emigrants have been known to raise significantly the incomes of their families at home through remittances. In more subtle ways emigrants can influence policies in the country of their new residence towards their native country, and often the emigrants retain an interest in their home countries' affairs, giving counsel and advice, which carry great weight because of the positions of independence and prestige they hold in the foreign country. Furthermore, the very act of emigration may be beneficial to those remaining behind just because of the public attention given to the individual's departure, which can lead to critical reappraisals of institutions and procedures and their ultimate modernization and improvement.

The potentially largest benefit to the people remaining behind, however, may accrue through the pure research of scientists and engineers in the foreign countries, contrary to the often heard allegation that the emigration of people in these fields is the source of greatest material losses. The product of basic research, knowledge, is a free good becoming available to all as it is published. Since most scientists move to countries where conditions of work are better for them, either because the new country is better able to furnish research equipment or because of stimulating colleagues, the probability is great that such moves increase the scientists' overall productivity. As a consequence of such emigration by scientists, the native countries not only obtain the scientific knowledge free, but they are actually likely to get more than they would have had the men stayed at home. Applied research also tends to benefit countries other than the one in which it is first put to use. Reductions in the cost of production or new product developments tend to spread through the world as a result of competition. As far as national prestige from scientific achievements is concerned, the scientists' native countries are perfectly free to claim these men as native sons, which in no way reduces the host-country's right to be proud that the work was done within its borders.

V

We conclude from this analysis that the transfer of human capital occurring when highly skilled people emigrate between countries always reduces the economic and military power of the migrant's native country, though by a smaller amount than it is often alleged. We have argued, however, that such concern with the effects on economic and military power is anachronistic and that a concern with the individual welfare of the population ought to take its place. From this point of view it was seen that the emigration of highly skilled persons is likely to cause economic losses in the short run until replacements for the emigrants can be trained. Long-run losses in a market economy are likely to be small and are primarily associated with externalities and with elements of income redistribution, in the government's tax and expenditure policies. Benefits to the native countries of the emigrants may be sizable, primarily because much of the output of highly skilled persons, especially scientists and engineers, tends to benefit the people of all countries. A good case can therefore be made for a continuation of present policies and the free movement of human capital throughout the world.

2

Brain Drain, Economics of the

This article presents the economics of the brain drain by first giving a definition of the concept and explaining why it is of such great political and emotional importance. Next, the motives of brain drain migrants are analyzed and problems of measurement are discussed. The final parts consist of a study of the welfare effects of the brain drain and some policy proposals for dealing with it. The material presented here draws heavily on scholarly books dealing with the economics of the brain drain by Adams (1968) and Grubel and Scott (1977) and on scholarly books with an emphasis on the economics of human capital and migration more generally by Myers (1972) and Psacharopoulos (1973). Blume (1968) and Dedijer and Svenningson (1967) are bibliographies of early writings on the brain drain.

1. Definition and Historical Background

Popularly the concept of the brain drain is used to refer to the migration of highly skilled individuals who are trained in one country and take up residence and work in another. Such migration has taken place throughout history, but it became the focus of public attention during the early 1960s when the United States embarked on a major increase of expenditures on science and engineering in order to meet the Soviet challenge symbolized by the launching of Sputnik. These expenditures created an excess demand for highly skilled manpower that was met by immigration. United States immigration laws strictly limit the inflow of foreigners generally but were most liberal in granting visas to highly skilled persons.

At the same time, developing countries launched major efforts to industrialize and other industrial nations attempted to catch up with United States technological and scientific standards. The loss of highly skilled manpower frustrated these countries' economic development efforts and the brain drain became a widely discussed political issue. During the late 1960s and 1970s the brain drain from developing countries to Western Europe and multinational organizations also became sizable and the phenomenon was recognized as a more general problem.

For economic science the brain drain is a component of two separate traditional fields of study: migration and human capital. In the terminology of these fields it involves the crossing of international borders by human capital embodied in and owned by migrants and not recorded in conventional international balance of payments statistics. By this definition, the crossing of borders by highly skilled people on contract to provide human capital services on a project in a country other than their home country does not involve a brain drain. Payment for these services enters balance of payments statistics. On the other hand, when individuals study abroad and return to their home countries, unrecorded human capital crosses borders and involves a form of brain drain.

The preceding considerations suggest that the economics of the brain drain might be called less emotively the economics of international human capital flows. However, the use of the term brain drain is so well-established that it is advantageous to continue its use here in the study of the broader phenomenon of unrecorded migration of human capital.

2. Motives for Migration of Highly Skilled Workers

Motives for migration generally and of students and highly skilled workers are complex. However, four main considerations dominate the decision to migrate: income, professional (or study) opportunities, living standards, and working conditions. The migrant considers each of these four elements by comparing conditions between pairs of countries. Personal tastes and circumstances as well as costs of transaction and travel enter individuals' decision-making calculus. The basic calculus is known to many people from personal experience or can be readily envisaged. In practice it is made very difficult by uncertainties surrounding all decision variables and the need to discount future prospects. It is facilitated by the fact that migration can usually be reversed if uncertain events turn out unfavorably. Formal models of the decision-making calculus are found in the literature noted below.

2.1 Survey Studies

One set of empirical studies of motives of brain drain migrants tend to be based on questionnaires designed and administered by sociologists. For a massive study using this approach see Glaser (1973). These studies have tended to find that respondents put professional opportunities as their primary motive, while earnings and living conditions are relatively unimportant. Scepticism has been expressed about the meaning of these findings since respondents may well have been rationalizing their motives and have been conditioned to do so by social pressures in their home

countries. It simply is not socially acceptable to leave one's home country and the source of finance for one's education in order to enjoy a higher living standard abroad. Going abroad for better research opportunities, on the other hand, is a more socially acceptable motive.

2.2 Economists' Studies

Economists who have studied migratory patterns have found that wage rate and income differences between countries of migration can explain statistically derived differences in propensities to migrate. The results reconfirm the validity of the basic economic models applicable to all migration, which postulate that people move to maximize the present value of their expected earnings net of costs of moving and adjustment.

These economists' findings about the motives for the brain drain point to difficulties of solving it in the short run except through costly direct controls on international travel or the creation of inefficient and inequitable income gaps between trained and untrained people in losing countries. In the longer run, however, income gaps may be expected to narrow and reduce motives for the brain drain.

3. Magnitude of Brain Drain Flows

Initially during the 1960s evidence on the magnitude of the brain drain was primarily episodal. Newspapers provided a treasure of allegedly representative stories. Efforts by scholars to quantify the phenomenon were stymied by the lack of readily accessible and suitable data. The most readily available data for any kind of quantification were those of the United States immigration and naturalization service. They showed that indeed there were large numbers of highly skilled migrants who acquired United States immigration visas. In some fields such as nursing and medicine the numbers represented sizable proportions of total United States production of such skills. For skills other than medical, however, the flows by and large represented relatively small proportions of both stocks and flows of newly trained personnel in the United States and most of the countries of emigration.

Using the United States statistics on flows and multiplying the number of migrants by the estimated present value of their earnings due to higher education, that is their human capital value, resulted in figures that were large relative to United States foreign aid, especially that to India. This fact was used by some politicians to dramatize the problem of the brain drain and to demand United States or collective world action to remedy the resultant injustices. As will be seen below, it is highly misleading to compare flows of foreign aid and migrating human capital in order to make inferences about welfare effects and moral debt relationships.

3.1 Problems with United States Immigration Statistics

Later research, as summarized by Friborg (1975) and discussed in the Committee in Foreign Affairs (1974), revealed that the United States immigration statistics and their early uses failed to reflect three important aspects of the brain drain. First, a substantial proportion of the United States immigrants were individuals who had obtained part or all of their higher education in the United States and were financed by United States funds or their own work. In fact, these individuals left their home countries as unskilled laborers and therefore, if anything, reflected a policy of United States immigration that was welcome by most people. To obtain information on the educational background of brain drain migrants, it was necessary to analyze biographic information on the stock of United States scientific and technical personnel. Such analysis showed that a foreign Ph.D. was held by only one-third of foreign-born United States scientists. In all likelihood, brain drain flows during the postwar years had similar characteristics.

Second, the United States statistics failed to record return flows of highly skilled people to their native or third countries. Since no major countries keep records of returning natives classed by education levels and there are no data collected on people leaving the United States, again information on net flows could be obtained only from statistics on stocks. The use of military and church records in some European countries permitted inferences to be made about net versus gross migration. For the countries and professions surveyed during the 1960s, emigration to the United States tended to be matched by return migration to such an extent that the net averaged only about 30 percent of the gross. Analogous data for developing countries are not available.

Third, the United States immigration data contained no information on the number and human capital value of migrants returning to their home or native countries after study in the United States. Since the brain drain is just one aspect of the international circulation of human capital and is in an important sense a part of the cost of foreign student training, the value of student capital should be compared with the value of the genuine brain drain capital. A special survey of Canadian economists in Canada and in United States positions revealed that even though Canada suffered a deficit on conventional brain drain account, her overall human capital account was positive by a large margin because many Canadians obtain graduate degrees in the United States.

The continuous and accurate measurement of presently unrecorded international human capital flows remains an elusive goal whose attainment is considered desirable because it would permit more rational discussion of and policies for control of the brain drain. However, since existing data do not permit the construction of such statistics and the cost of new data collection procedures is very high in relation to the expected benefits from their use, quantitative information on the magnitude of international human capital flows is likely to continue to come in the future from isolated efforts providing bench mark information and using data collected for other purposes.

4. Welfare Effects: Short-run Output Effects

When a country unexpectedly loses through emigration a highly skilled person there are likely to be short-run adjustment costs since technologically optimal efficiency is achieved by the cooperation of human capital with physical capital and labor in a mix determined by the state of knowledge and relative prices of the three types of inputs. Thus when a supervising engineer suddenly leaves a plant, in the extreme case where he is totally indispensable, machines and labor have to remain idle until a replacement is found. Typically engineers are not totally indispensable and output efficiency of capital and labor drops only somewhat, depending on the nature of the technology. The temporary losses can be reduced for any given technology if the departure of the engineer is known in advance. In the extreme, there need be no adjustment costs at all.

The argument just presented in the context of an individual firm or plant also applies in its basic outline to society as a whole, except that replacements of skilled persons cannot simply be hired from another job but require time-consuming education and therefore may involve longer periods of inefficient operating procedures. However, if emigration can be predicted, then it is possible to plan education in such a way that there are never any short-run shortages of skilled people and the economy operates at all times with the technologically optimal mix of human and real capital and labor.

In the real world, short-run adjustment costs are likely to be minor and human capital losses have been quite predictable. Some analysts argue that in some countries, such as India, political processes or planning errors have resulted in an excess production of human capital for given knowledge and physical capital and labor. In the case of such countries short-run losses are nil since emigrating human capital was unemployed.

5. Long-run Output Effects

Long-run output effects of the emigration of human capital can usefully be analyzed with the help of what is known as the generalized theory of capital. According to this, model society can invest its stock of capital in knowledge, and human and physical capital. Markets, competition, and patent laws result in a tendency for the marginal productivity of each capital form to be equal and society's output to be maximized. The three forms of capital can be added up to find the overall endowment of labor with capital.

Now consider that a country in efficient equilibrium with respect to the distribution of the stock of the three types of capital loses a certain amount of human capital and labor through emigration. A reallocation of society's remaining capital stock is likely to be necessary and may be assumed to take place. In the new equilibrium that country's total output will be lower than before the loss of the labor and capital. However, under relatively simple and usual assumptions about the nature of the production function, total output per worker in the country may be raised or lowered or remain unchanged. It will be lowered if the amount of human capital taken along by the average emigrant is greater than the original overall capital per worker simply because under these conditions the postemigration stock of capital per worker in the country is lowered. Since productivity and output are an increasing function of the overall capital–labor ratio, the smaller ratio brought about by the emigration leads to lower labor productivity and average income.

It is easy to see that average output remains unchanged if the emigrants' capital per person equals the country's initial overall stock of capital per worker and that it will be raised if emigrants take along less than the average. The emigration of unskilled workers according to this model must always raise output per capita of the remaining workers. This fact may well explain why there is so rarely opposition to the emigration of unskilled workers.

In a very rough calculation it was found that in the mid-1960s the human capital value of two years' university training in India was about equal to the average of human and physical capital per Indian worker. This result suggests that the loss of university graduates somewhat lowers, and of beginning university students somewhat raises, India's capital stock per worker and income per person.

The preceding model of the real output effects of the brain drain over-simplifies a complex process in many ways but provides a useful focus and directs attention to the essential aspects of the migration of highly skilled persons.

6 Welfare Effects

6.1 The Nationalist Model

The brain drain became the source of much public concern in the 1960s and continues to occupy discussions at the United Nations Commission for Trade and Development (UNCTAD) and other UN agencies because of the following perception of the welfare effects and inequities. The population of a country taxes itself to finance the operation of institutions of higher learning or the study of citizens abroad. This collective investment in education is made in expectation of general returns to society: the country's total output is raised, the productivity of cooperating factors of production is increased, a greater tax base permits raising more revenue to be spent on further development and on welfare projects, and the country as a whole moves into the modern age improved by science and technology and accompanying externalities. Moreover, competitive selection processes of education tend to provide education to the most gifted and dynamic young people who are sources of leadership generally and carriers of desirable genetic material.

Given these expectations of return from investment in the education of young people, their emigration or failure to return from study abroad represents a serious loss. Basically, the investment has been wasted and what makes this waste particularly hard to take is that it involves great inequities. For example, in developing countries people with low and average incomes have lowered their incomes to finance education, the benefits of which now accrue to the emigrants who live in the lap of luxury in industrial countries and add to the further growth and tax base of peoples who have incomes that are a multiple of those who financed the migrants' education. Projects for the provision of very basic technology and medical services in developing countries suffer or have to be abandoned because of the lack of skilled manpower while those brain drain migrants make possible technical and medical projects in industrial countries that represent basically unnecessary luxuries.

Under this nationalistic view, the effects of the brain drain are often quantified by measuring the value of income earned by brain drain migrants in their countries of new residence. This sum is then considered to represent the inequitable transfer of resources from poor to rich nations.

6.2 The Internationalist View

Economists have approached the analysis of the welfare effects of the brain drain by building logically rigorous models based on simple and widely accepted principles of economics. The resultant model and conclusions have become known as the internationalist approach for reasons that will become obvious. The basics of this model are as follows.

Consider a world of nation–states in which all people are paid an income equal to the value of their contribution to the nation's output. This assumption reflects one of the cornerstones of modern price theory and is known as the marginal productivity theory of factor incomes. It implies that there are no externalities from work so that a skilled person provides no benefits to society other than those for which payment is received. This assumption is unrealistic and will be relaxed below. As a second basic initial assumption consider that in this hypothetical world all education is financed privately by parents.

In a world without externalities and government-financed education the emigration of one or a small number of highly skilled persons leaves unchanged the welfare of those left behind because the migrants take along an equal valued contribution and claim to output. Thus, the emigration of Indian scientists who earned x rupees in their home country lowers that country's national output by x rupees but does not affect the income of those remaining behind.

In the country of immigration, the brain drain migrants contribute to output exactly what they are paid and use as claim on the output. Therefore they do not alter the incomes of the people there. The migrants, however, raise their own incomes. Under the assumption that welfare is an increasing function of income, we reach the important fundamental conclusion that the migration raises world welfare since that of the migrants is raised and that of the population in the receiving and sending countries is unchanged.

6.3 Role of Education Financing

Under a system where education is financed by parents, basically any debt obligations are between members of a family and should not be of concern to the state. However, it is useful to consider two polar views of the nature of the intergenerational obligation arising through the financing of childrens' education within families because most people can relate to this situation and it provides good insights into the nature of obligations arising out of publicly financed education systems.

Under one basic view children and their education are considered to be an investment good which yields returns when the children look after the welfare of their parents in old age. When children emigrate they may renege on their obligations to parents but they may also end up making better provision for them out of higher incomes than they would have if they had not emigrated.

Under the second basic view children are a consumption good and parents have a moral obligation to raise and educate their offspring just like their parents and every generation of parents have done. The obligation of every productive generation is not to their parents but to their own children. Under this view educated emigrants leave no obligations behind because they take along their offspring.

These two views of the nature of the obligation can readily be translated into the more realistic situation where education is financed by public education. Under the investment view, emigrants owe repayment through taxes to finance pensions and welfare expenditures. Emigration therefore involves a clear-cut reneging on a moral obligation and lowering of welfare of those left behind. Under the consumption view of children, on the other hand, those left behind

do not suffer a reduction in welfare since the emigrants take along both their contributions to taxes used for financing education and their children on whom this tax money would have to be spent.

It is probably true that the investment view of children and education dominates attitudes in developing countries while the consumption view dominates attitudes in industrial countries. If this judgment is correct it can help to explain why concern over the inequities of the brain drain is so much more prevalent in developing than industrialized countries.

6.4 General Government Taxes and Services

The preceding argument over the financing of education can be generalized to tax payments and all government services generally. Emigrants reduce tax revenue and demand for all government services simultaneously, leaving unchanged tax burdens on those remaining behind. By analogy, there are no gains to taxpayers in countries of immigration. There may be some secondary effects on welfare if the taxes paid exceed the value of benefits received and if government services provided are lumpy such that expenditures remain unchanged regardless of how many people are served. Typically, however, educated high-income taxpayers also demand high levels and quality of services, as for example legal, police, pension, and education programs. Lumpiness of expenditures on such items as defense and roads tends to be invariable only in the short run.

6.5 Externalities from Work of Migrants

Highly educated people are believed to provide societies with many positive externalities through leadership and contributions to arts, sciences, and culture generally. To the extent that this is true, the emigration of highly trained individuals lowers the welfare of those left behind. Undoubtedly, the loss of such externalities represents a valid and important flow of welfare from losing to gaining countries.

However, it is easy to overestimate the importance of these externalities. Most artistic, scientific, and technical contributions are rewarded through salaries or the sale of copyrighted publications and patents, typically leaving uncompensated only contributions to strictly nationalistic feelings of pride. The production of pure knowledge that cannot be patented is usually an international good, the benefits of which accrue to the world as a whole including the home country of the brain drain emigrant. The real benefits of a scientific breakthrough leading to a cancer cure, for example, accrue to Indians whether an Indian scientist does the research in the United States or his native country.

It is also misleading to consider the scientific and other achievements of brain drain migrants in their new countries of residence and infer that the real benefits or glory of their achievement would have accrued to their home countries if they had not emigrated. In many instances, these achievements would not have been possible in the home countries because of the lack of scientific support facilities and colleagues.

Highly skilled persons could also be considered to sometimes provide negative externalities, not just positive leadership qualities. Historically, academics generally and the academic proletariat of under-employed intellectuals have at times provided the stimulus for civil unrest and revolutions that turned out not to have been in the longer run interest of countries. The emigration of such highly skilled potential revolutionaries can have positive exter-nalities for their home countries.

6.6 Nonmarginal Flows

The preceding analysis of welfare effects assumed implicitly that migration involved small numbers and therefore could be treated as marginal. In fact, brain drain flows have been and are marginal by almost all standards. However, economic models of nonmar-ginal changes have also been constructed. They pro-duce the following need for modification of the above conclusions.

If large numbers of unskilled workers leave a country, the capital–labor ratio and therefore the marginal productivity of the remaining labor are raised while the return to capital falls. In the receiving country the opposite effect takes place. Thus, large-scale general labor migration has income redis-tribution effects that are considered to be desirable by many people. However, if such large-scale migration involves highly trained individuals, the accompany-ing changes in the overall capital–labor ratio reduce and may reverse this income redistribution effect. In the country of emigration wage rates rise less or may even fall and in the country of immigration they fall less or may even rise.

6.7 Benefits from Mobility

In the technical and quantitative discussion of the economic effects of the brain drain sight is often lost of the fact that it is part of the general phenomenon of the international circulation of human beings that includes travel for business, recreation, and study, all of which involve stays abroad of varying length. As was noted above, some of the seemingly permanent brain drain migration involves stays of limited dura-tion and there is some practical ambiguity between study, advanced training, and permanent migration.

The international circulation of people generally provides enormous benefits to humanity. The edu-cational experiences of travel are recognized widely. Most of today's leaders in all fields of human endeavor have studied or worked abroad temporarily during their careers. Contacts among people from different nationalities raise tolerance and under-standing and thus lower the risks of international conflict. There is no doubt that without the interna-tional circulation of people the world would be a much less attractive place. The brain drain, which involves some people extending or making per-manent their stay abroad, may usefully be considered as part of the cost, much like the cost of trans-portation, that has to be incurred in order to derive these benefits.

7. Policy Recommendations

Given the public concern over the brain drain and the political rhetoric about it in international organi-zations, there have been surprisingly few solid policy proposals on either how to reduce it or how to deal with its consequences. There are three types of policy recommendations.

First, there are those policies that would reduce the incentives without interfering with the flow of students and professionals in any way. The basic objective of these policies is to raise the incomes and working conditions of highly skilled people in countries that suffer from the brain drain. These policy recommendations are unrealistic in that given the scarcity of resources and many different develop-ment objectives of most countries, raising highly skilled peoples' incomes and expanding research facilities is not one of the most important priorities. Moreover, it would lead to inequities and inefficiencies. The creation of international research institutes where scientists from developing countries can go for temporary work and updating of skills has been proposed but failed to find sponsors.

Second, there have been proposals to change immi-gration policies of brain drain gaining countries to make them less discriminatory in favor of highly skilled people and to make it more difficult for stu-dents and temporary visitors to obtain permanent resident status. United States and Canadian policies in this regard have been tightened during the 1960s as part of a general move towards admissions pro-cedures that discriminate on the basis of time of application rather than national origin, wealth, and other allegedly discriminatory criteria. However, the governments of industrial countries have resisted all pressures from more radical elements in developing countries to initiate easy procedures whereby foreign students and other highly skilled persons can be extradicted on request of native countries' govern-ments. There has been concern about the abuse of such procedures for political purposes. Developing countries have attempted generally to use legal tech-niques to assure return of students sponsored by official sources, but they have no effective leverage to assure the return of students sponsored privately. Except for countries of the socialist bloc, none have introduced prohibitions on travel to prevent the brain drain.

The third set of proposals is aimed at redressing the inequities which are alleged to arise under the nationalistic view from the debt on educational outlays owed to the losing countries. One set of proposals suggests bilateral intergovernmental compensation agreements. Such an approach might encourage the development of international specialization in the production and export of human skills.

Another widely discussed set of proposals requires that brain drain migrants be assessed for a special tax surcharge which is transmitted to the countries in which they were educated, either directly or through some international organization. Neither of these proposals has been adopted, though the tax scheme has been discussed widely among academics mainly through the initiative of J. Bhagwati (1976).

See also: Migration (Internal) and Education

Bibliography

Adams W (ed.) 1968 *The Brain Drain.* Macmillan, New York

Bhagwati J N (ed.) 1976 *The Brain Drain and Taxation,* Vols. 1 and 2. North Holland, New York

Blume S 1968 "Brain drain": A look at the literature. *Univ. Q.* 22: 281–90

Committee on Foreign Affairs. US House of Representatives 1974 *Science, Technology and American Diplomacy: Brain Drain, A Study of the Persistent Issue of International Scientific Mobility.* US Government Printing Office, Washington. DC

Dedijer S, Svenningson L 1967 *Brain Drain and Brain Gain: A Bibliography on Migration of Scientists, Engineers, Doctors and Students.* Research Policy Program, Lund

Friborg G (ed.) 1975 *Brain Drain Statistics: Empirical Evidence and Guidelines.* Swedish Research Council Committee on Research Economics. Report 6. NFR, Stockholm

Glaser W A 1973 *The Migration and Return of Professionals.* Bureau of Applied Social Research, Columbia University, New York

Grubel H G, Scott A D 1977 *The Brain Drain: Determinants, Measurement and Welfare Effects.* Wilfrid Laurier University Press, Waterloo. Ontario

Myers R G 1972 *Education and Emigration: Study Abroad and the Migration of Human Resources.* David McKay, New York

Psacharopoulos G 1973 *Returns to Education: An International Comparison.* Elsevier, Amsterdam

UNCTAD 1979 The reverse transfer of technology: A survey of its main features, causes and policy implications. Publication Sales No. E.79.II.D.10, United Nations, New York

H. G. Grubel

[3]

THE IMMIGRATION OF SCIENTISTS AND ENGINEERS TO THE UNITED STATES, 1949–61*

H. G. GRUBEL AND A. D. SCOTT

University of Chicago and University of British Columbia

I. INTRODUCTION

FEW policy issues have stirred as much emotional reaction and as little empirical work as the alleged large-scale migration of scientists and engineers from the rest of the world to the United States during the last decade. This paper is an attempt to put together various available scraps of empirical information on the basis of which an informed picture of the magnitude of the "brain drain" to the United States can be formed.

We have considered the theoretical implications of the emigration of the highly skilled for the welfare of the remaining population elsewhere (Grubel and Scott, 1966). In this paper we will exploit the data which the U.S. National Science Foundation, with the help of the U.S. Immigration and Naturalization Service, has recently collected and published in three pamphlets (National Science Foundation, 1958, 1962, 1965). In these sources are contained the numbers of scientists and engineers who emigrated to the United States between 1949 and 1961. For the years 1957–61 the data indicate the countries of last residence of these migrants; for 1961–62 the data distinguish the immigrants' countries of birth and of last residence.

* This paper is part of a larger study concerned with the international flow of human capital. We thank Harry G. Johnson, the director of a Rockefeller Foundation research project at the University of Chicago, for his financial and intellectual support. Richard Parks, Gregg Lewis, Albert Rees, and Louis Parai have made helpful comments on an earlier draft of this paper.

We have combined this latter information on emigrants by countries with newly available data on the stocks of scientists and engineers and numbers of first degrees in these fields granted by individual countries (Organization for Economic Co-operation and Development, 1964). In the next section we present time series on total U.S. immigration of scientific manpower, relate them to statistics on the U.S. output of first degrees in the various disciplines and compute the capital value of these migrants to the United States. In Section III we present time series on the losses experienced by some individual countries and relate these to their current output and existing stock of scientists and engineers. In Section IV we examine the emigration of scientists and engineers in the context of general migration.

II. THE INFLOW TO THE UNITED STATES

Table 1 shows the number of natural scientists and engineers who emigrated from the rest of the world to the United States during the period 1949–61. As can be seen from column (1), the annual inflow increased steadily from the beginning of the period, reached a peak of 5,823 immigrants in 1957, and declined thereafter. While in this paper we are not primarily interested in the development of flows through time, it should be noted that the 1957–58 immigration figures are inflated by the influx of refugees from the Hungarian revolution in October, 1956, and that the period

368

1957–61 marked a period of strong economic growth in Europe and of relative economic stagnation in the United States.

The economic importance of these flows to the United States can best be seen by relating the figures on annual immigration to the annual output of first-degree scientists and engineers of the U.S. educational system. Column (2) gives the absolute numbers, and column (3) expresses the number of immigrants as a percentage of the total U.S.

output. The time pattern of the last series follows closely that of the basic statistics on immigration: the peak year occurred in 1957, at which time immigrants added 8.1 per cent to the number of scientists and engineers becoming available to the U.S. economy through the U.S. education system.

The magnitude of this inflow can be visualized quite readily by considering that in 1960–61 there were a total of 1,311 institutions conferring four-year Bachelor's degrees. That year, the for-

TABLE 1

FLOW OF SCIENTISTS AND ENGINEERS TO THE UNITED STATES
NUMBER AND VALUE, 1949–61

YEAR	No. of Scientists and Engineers			Educational Resource Cost per Student (U.S. $)				Earnings Foregone per Man* ($)	Social Value of Immigrants ($000)		
	Immigrants	U.S. Graduates	(2)÷(1) ×100	12 Years Basic	4 Years College	1 Year Graduate	Total		Total Resource Cost	Total Earnings Foregone	Total
	(1)	(2)	(3)	(4)	(5)	(6)	(7)	(8)	(9)	(10)	(11)
1949...	1,234	93,715	1.3	3,192	1,928	1,181	6,301	9,338	7,775	11,523	19,298
1950...	1,519	115,464	1.3	3,468	2,152	1,302	6,922	10,030	10,515	15,236	25,751
1951...	1,561	93,793	1.7	3,745	2,380	1,423	7,548	10,895	11,782	17,007	28,789
1952...	2,297	72,646	3.2	3,898	2,456	1,459	7,813	11,586	17,946	26,613	44,559
1953...	2,718	60,834	4.5	4,067	2,532	1,494	8,093	12,105	21,997	32,901	54,898
1954...	3,200	57,883	5.5	4,297	2,704	1,602	8,603	12,105	27,530	38,736	66,266
1955...	2,862	57,066	5.0	4,512	2,876	1,709	9,097	13,143	26,036	37,615	63,651
1956...	3,790	62,534	6.1	4,865	3,008	1,859	9,732	13,661	36,884	51,775	88,659
1957...	5,823	71,594	8.1	5,233	3,332	2,009	10,574	14,180	61,572	82,570	144,142
1958...	5,190	79,677	6.5	6,231	3,424	2,081	11,736	14,353	60,910	74,492	135,402
1959...	5,081	86,474	5.9	7,244	3,512	2,153	12,609	15,218	64,066	77,323	141,389
1960...	4,326	89,443	4.8	7,597	3,624	2,210	13,431	15,564	58,103	67,330	125,433
1961...	3,922	93,000	4.2	7,950	3,692	2,267	13,909	15,910	54,551	62,399	116,950

* For 17 years of school.

Source: Cols. (1)–(3): National Science Foundation (1962, Table 2); all years are fiscal; social sciences are excluded; data for 1961 graduates are estimated; includes professors and instructors. The estimates of col. (1) are a compilation made by the Immigration and Naturalization Service using occupation classifications of the Bureau of the Census. The occupations are reported by the applicants for visas; generally no independent checks are made by consular or immigration authorities with regard to the professional qualifications of the applicants. The estimates of col. (2) were supplied by the U.S. Department of Health, Education, and Welfare, Office of Education, and include "earned bachelor's degrees in sciences and engineering." The estimate for 1956 agrees approximately (within 2 per cent) with the number of Bachelor's degrees granted in agricultural, biological, and physical sciences, and engineering and mathematics according to U.S. Department of Commerce (1958). Col. (4): The figure for 1956 was taken from Schultz (1961); the time series is based on an index of expenditure per student published regularly by the U.S. Department of Health, Education, and Welfare in various issues of the *Biennial Survey of Education in the United States*. Cols. (5), (6): Our own estimates, based on student enrolment and expenditures by institutions of higher learning as reported in various issues of *Digest of Educational Statistics* (U.S. Dept. of Health, Education, and Welfare). We followed in general the approach used by Schultz (1961) but made various adjustments to eliminate institutional expenditures on public service and organized research and to account for the generally lower student-faculty ratio in graduate education. The computations are documented in detail in Grubel and Scott (mimeographed). Col. (8): Estimate for 1956 from Schultz (1961); the time series is based upon *Economic Report of the President, 1965* (Table B29). Col. (9): col. (1) × col. (2); col. (10): col. (1) × col. (8). It should be noted that our social-value calculations assume that the immigrants were of the same age and had a quality of training equal to that of U.S. scientists and engineers entering employment. This assumption was necessary because we lacked information on the age of immigrants and the quality of their education.

eign immigration was equivalent to the science and engineering Bachelor's degrees granted by fifty-three "average" U.S. universities. The expenditure of resources involved in the maintenance of such a number of educational institutions is quite large, but knowledge of the size of these expenditures would not allow us to draw any meaningful inferences about the "value" accruing to the United States from this inflow of highly educated persons.

Instead, what is required for this purpose is a more complicated computation of the human-capital value of these migrants. The concept of "human capital" and its measurement has recently been developed by Schultz (1960), Becker (1964), and others.[1] It involves the basic idea that education is acquired through spending resources for instruction of the individual as well as by sacrificing the output the person could have produced had he worked instead of gone to school. Maintenance and other costs of living have to be incurred regardless of whether someone attends school or not and therefore are not part of the investment in him.

We have used the estimates of acquisition cost to approximate the value of the human capital brought into the United States by immigration. Since our concern is with the gains to the United States, it is appropriate to use U.S. prices, so that our computations amount to estimating what it would have cost to bring a native American to the level of education held by the average immigrant at the time he arrives.

The information required for such

calculations comprises, first, the educational attainment and age of the immigrants; second, the resources spent on instructing a person in the United States until he reaches that level; and, third, the amount of earnings foregone by the individual during his school attendance. On the first item, because we were unable to obtain direct information, we made the assumption that the average immigrant had completed four years of college plus one year of graduate instruction and was twenty-three years old. This assumption is subject to revision when new evidence is accumulated. The data provided in Table 1 permit an easy estimate of the sensitivity of the final results to changes in the assumption.

The second and third sets of information are shown in columns (4)–(8) of Table 1, and their derivation is documented in the notes to the table.[2] The average annual educational cost per student for seventeen years and the average earnings foregone by a person completing seventeen years of schooling that year are found in columns (7) and (8), respectively. Each of these columns is multiplied by the number of immigrants and the resulting values are recorded in columns (9) and (10) and totaled in column (11).

As can be seen, the inflow of embodied human capital into the United States, completely unrecorded in an official statistics, has been as high as $144 million in 1957 and came to $1,055 million for the thirteen-year period. The 1957 figure was equivalent to 13 per cent of U.S. merchandise imports and 8 per cent of net new non-military U.S. government foreign aid grants for the same

[1] In some studies "on-the-job training" is included as an input into the formation of human capital. Since we do not have information on this aspect of the immigrants' education we are forced to disregard it, although to do so tends to result in an underestimate of the capital values.

[2] Readers interested in greater details of computation are referred to Grubel and Scott (mimeographed).

year.[3] Yet, while these values are a significant magnitude relative to some U.S. external accounts, they are of negligible importance relative to the size of the U.S. stock of human and material wealth and the capacity to produce current output. It is therefore not surprising that the "brain gain" has not become a major policy issue for the United States and we must turn to an analysis of the outflows from individual countries to find the reason for the widespread concern over the "brain drain."

III. IMMIGRANTS FROM INDIVIDUAL
COUNTRIES

An exact measurement of the "brain drain" requires detailed statistical information on the occupational, educational, age, and sex composition of migrants to and from individual countries. Unfortunately, such statistics do not exist because emigration from Western countries has traditionally be unrestricted and governments do not keep records of people leaving the country (except casually, by number of departures by boats and planes). This fact necessitates reconstruction of emigration data for some countries by use of the carefully kept national records of immigration by other countries. The United States has been alleged to be the major country gaining brains, and an analysis of that country's immigrants is an important first step in reconstructing global emigration statistics.

One fundamental difficulty in measuring the "brain drain" is the high mobility of professional migrants, who often reside in at least one other country before coming to the United States and who often return home after gaining professional experience. Furthermore, U.S.

[3] Source of import and government statistics: *Economic Report of the President* (1965, 1960).

immigrants recorded as being scientists or engineers may have obtained their professional training at an American university.

The best way to overcome these difficulties would be to present several empirical measures of the "brain drain." First, we would distinguish gross and net flows, that is, the difference between emigration and immigration, where the latter may be partly a reflux of old emigrants. It is quite obvious that the net figure is economically more relevant than the gross in terms of estimating a national loss resulting from free migration.

Second, we would distinguish emigrants at different levels of education, such as fully trained experienced scientists and engineers leaving paid positions, students who have just completed their formal professional education, students who are at some level of preparatory general education, and children at pre-school age who later on show the intellectual capacity to become successful professionals. While emigrants at each of these levels represent a "brain drain," the national "losses" are greater, the higher the level of education and professional expertise.

While ideally, therefore, an empirical investigation of the "brain drain" should deal with net national emigration by individuals at various levels of education (perhaps as added by the country of last residence), we have available only statistics on immigrants in science and engineering to the United States classified according to the migrants' country of last residence and by their country of birth. These data are presented in Table 2; column (1) shows the annual average number of immigrants for the period 1957–61 by country of last residence. Columns (6) and (7) show the number of immigrants for the two years

TABLE 2

SCIENTISTS AND ENGINEERS (S & E): IMMIGRANTS TO THE UNITED STATES, FIRST DEGREES GRANTED AND STOCKS IN FOREIGN COUNTRIES

	AVERAGE, 1957–61					SUM, 1962–63					RANK	
	Immigrants by Last Residence	First Degrees in S & E	Stocks of S & E	$(1)\div(2)$ ×100	$(1)\div(3)$ ×1,000	Immigrants by Country of Birth	Immigrants by Last Residence	$(6)\div(7)$	$(4)\times(8)$	$(5)\times(8)$	By Col. (4)	By Col. (10)
	(1)	(2)	(3)	(4)	(5)	(6)	(7)	(8)	(9)	(10)	(11)	(12)
Austria..........	67	526	N.a.	12.7	N.a.	83	58	1.43	18.1	N.a.	5	3
France..........	82	9,692	144,990	0.8	0.8	120	141	0.85	0.7	0.7	12	12
Germany.........	425	5,402	N.a.	7.9	N.a.	784	679	1.15	9.1	N.a.	9	9
Greece..........	64	664	12,964	9.6	4.9	172	150	1.15	11.0	5.6	6	7
Ireland..........	45	484	N.a.	9.3	N.a.	107	68	1.57	14.6	N.a.	7	5
Italy...........	71	5,628	172,600	1.3	0.4	140	123	1.15	1.5	0.5	11	11
Netherlands......	136	987	17,274	13.8	7.8	192	195	0.98	13.5	7.6	4	6
Norway..........	98	490	12,980	20.0	7.6	152	135	1.12	22.4	8.5	2	1
Sweden..........	106	1,213	21,327	8.7	5.0	113	140	0.81	7.0	4.0	8	10
Switzerland......	134	791	N.a.	16.9	N.a.	218	244	0.89	15.0	N.a.	3	4
U.K............	661	8,557	227,250	7.7	2.9	2,078	1,627	1.28	9.9	3.7	10	8
Canada..........	1,240	4,156	61,300	29.8	20.2	1,159	2,316	0.50	18.9	10.1	1	2

Source: The figures in col. (1) are simple averages of the time series found in National Science Foundation (1962). Cols. (6) and (7) were taken from National Science Foundation (1965). The data in cols. (2) and (3) are based on averaging of benchmark years found in Organization for Economic Co-operation and Development (1964, Tables 7 and 13, Annex 1). Immigration data are for fiscal years, stock and education data for calendar years.

For a precise definition of "scientists and engineers" as used in the OECD survey, see Organiza-tion for Economic Co-operation and Development (1954, pp. 21–24). The data were generated through a detailed questionnaire sent to co-operating governments. Discussion of the data-handling procedure suggests that great effort went into making the data internationally comparable. However, it appears that for some countries the available national statistics are rather deficient and only round figures were presented. For Italy it was impossible to derive stock estimates without pharmacists; thus the Italian figures are not strictly comparable to those for other countries.

1962–63, the only period when the data were available both by country of last residence and of birth.

The absolute numbers of immigrants are not particularly meaningful as a measure of loss because of the different sizes of nations. Therefore we expressed the numbers as fractions of first degrees granted in science and engineering and of the stock of people active in these fields (both are averages for the five years).

According to column (4), Canada has lost a number of scientists and engineers representing the largest percentage either of new graduates or of its existing stock of all the countries. The emigration of 29.8 per cent of first-degree earners is an economically significant amount by any standard. However, these statistics are misleading in the case of Canada since they take account neither of the reflux from the United States nor of the inflow from other countries into Canada, both of which are known to be substantial.[4]

For the countries other than Canada in our statistics we do not know the size of reflux and immigration from third countries. If these are relatively small, the losses shown will closely reflect the true losses; but final judgment on this matter must await actual empirical evidence. As can be seen from the table, there are great variations between countries. The percentage losses by Switzerland were on the average nineteen times as high as those of France, the country with the smallest losses

[4] We have made a survey of economists teaching in Canadian institutions of higher learning and have statistics on the national background of U.S. economists. There are approximately as many U.S.-born and trained economists teaching in Canada as there are Canadian-born and trained economists in teaching positions in the United States. Louis Parai (1965) has estimated that Canada is a large net gainer from migration of professionals.

according to our measure. The nations with the lowest per capita incomes in the group, Greece and Ireland, rank fairly highly and show what must be considered a substantial annual outflow of scientists and engineers to the United States, given the size of the educational efforts of these countries. We should also point out that the Common Market countries of western Europe are known to attract many workers, including skilled ones, from Greece and Ireland.

The facts that the United Kingdom ranks only in tenth place and that the percentage figure for the United Kingdom is relatively low, in spite of the concern that has been manifested about the "brain drain" in that country, illustrate the need for caution in interpreting these data. Many highly trained emigrants from the United Kingdom go to Commonwealth countries, and the migration to the United States represents only an unknown fraction of the total, so that there may really be a serious "brain drain" from the United Kingdom in spite of the facts just mentioned.

Columns (6)–(8) reveal that the natives of Ireland, Austria, and the United Kingdom have a strong tendency to migrate to other countries before coming to the United States. The most important countries of temporary residence before remigration are Canada, Sweden, and France. On the assumption that the time period of residence in another country before coming to the United States was the same in the two periods 1957–61 and 1962–63, we have applied the ratio of immigrants by residence to immigrants by birth (col. [8]) to the percentage figures of columns (4) and (5) and obtained the estimates of columns (9) and (10). These estimates express the five-year average number of immigrants to the United States as a percentage (or as a number per thousand) of the current output (or stock) of scientists and engineers in the countries in which the immigrants were *born*. While these estimates differ by as much as 50 per cent from those based on last residence, columns (11) and (12) show that the ranking of the countries is not affected significantly, a switch by two places representing the maximum change. It is difficult to decide which of the two measures is more relevant as

the five-year period. The series exhibits a distinct downward trend, which is nearly identical to that found for natural scientists. The fall in the loss rate as we measure it is due to both an increase in the number of first degrees granted and a decrease in the number of migrants. Clearly, the period under consideration is too short to permit the generalization that there has been a trend toward a reduction in the magnitude of the brain-drain problem, especially in view of the

TABLE 3

IMMIGRATION OF ENGINEERS TO THE UNITED STATES AS A PERCENTAGE
OF FIRST DEGREES GRANTED IN COUNTRY
OF LAST RESIDENCE

Country	1957	1958	1959	1960	1961	Mean
Austria...........	16.3	9.2	15.9	8.5	3.2	10.6
France............	1.5	1.3	1.3	1.3	0.8	1.2
Germany..........	15.2	9.4	9.8	7.1	5.8	9.5
Greece............	24.4	22.3	23.1	20.8	14.0	20.9
Ireland...........	26.6	22.0	11.1	7.1	10.8	15.5
Italy.............	1.8	2.6	1.9	1.5	1.0	1.8
Netherlands.......	37.4	8.8	13.7	20.3	15.4	19.1
Norway...........	26.6	31.4	26.7	18.2	17.6	24.1
Sweden...........	27.4	19.3	13.8	12.1	10.4	16.6
Switzerland........	33.2	23.8	19.6	21.2	14.8	22.5
United Kingdom...	25.9	21.8	11.3	13.4	10.3	16.5
Canada...........	60.6	45.5	47.1	44.3	31.5	45.7

Note: Source and definitions of "engineers" for both stock and immigrants are the same as in Table 2.

a measure of the "brain drain," since the data do not reveal at what age and educational level the average Austrian, for example, went to Canada, Sweden, or France before migrating to the United States.

A breakdown of the migration and degree information into the two categories of engineers and natural scientists indicates that on the average a substantially larger proportion of the annual output of engineers than of natural scientists emigrated to the United States. The data for engineers are shown in Table 3, which also shows the evolution of loss of talent, as we measure it, over

fact that the 1957–58 immigration statistics reflect the inflow of refugees from the 1956 Hungarian revolution, who had resided in another country before coming to the United States.

IV. MIGRATION OF THE SKILLED AND
GENERAL MIGRATION

When a highly skilled person leaves his current employment, the size of the resulting inefficiencies and short-run losses in production depends, first, on the extent to which other workers' output is dependent on co-operation with the emigrant's skill and, second, on the length of time required to retrain an individual to take the place of the one who has left. In an extreme case where, for example, the output of ten workers always requires the direction of one engineer, the latter's emigration leaves ten workers unemployed and unproductive until a new engineer is trained. It is clear that the short-run losses of this type will be smaller, the greater the substitutability of skills and the shorter the training period.

However, emigration would not cause

In order to gain some understanding of the absolute magnitude of such divergencies in general and their relative importance for individual countries, we have computed the index shown in column (4) of Table 4. The index was derived by dividing the percentage of scientists and engineers in all immigrants to the United States (col. [1]) by the percentage of scientists and engineers in the total population (col. [2]) in the respective countries of emigration.

TABLE 4

DIFFERENCES IN THE PROPENSITY TO MIGRATE TO THE UNITED STATES
BETWEEN SCIENTISTS AND ENGINEERS (S & E) AND TOTAL POPULATION

Country	(Stock of S & E) ÷ (Population) ×100	(S & E Immigration) ÷ (Total Immigration) ×100	Index= Col (2) ÷ Col. (1)	Rank	Rank of Migrants: (S & E by Last Residence) ÷ (First Degrees)
	(1)	(2)	(3)	(4)	(5)
Netherlands........	0.187	2.276	12.187	1	3
Canada............	.348	4.218	12.128	2	1
Sweden............	.453	4.930	10.875	3	5
Greece............	.157	1.643	10.439	4	4
Norway............	.366	3.551	9.705	5	2
U.K..............	.435	2.650	6.087	6	6
France............	.321	1.954	6.087	7	7
Italy..............	0.349	0.370	1.058	8	8

Source: For data on stock and flow of scientists and engineers see Table 2. Immigration statistics were taken from the 1964 U.S. Immigration and Naturalization Service, *Annual Reports.* Col. 5 from col. 11, Table 2.

such short-run losses even if there were zero substitutability of skills and a very long training period, if the occupational composition of the emigrants were an exact microcopy of the occupational composition of the population as a whole.[5] Alternatively, given a certain degree of substitutability between skills and an average training period, short-run losses will be greater, the greater the divergence between the skill composition of emigrants and of the population.

The results of these computations show that scientists and engineers are on the average about ten times as likely to emigrate to the United States as are people from other occupations, the incidence for individual countries being relatively about the same as it was according to the percentage of first-degree measures (cols. [4] and [5]). A most interesting result is that the value of this index for the United Kingdom is about identical with its value for France (they differ only in the fourth decimal), even though a much greater proportion of first-degree earners emigrate from the United Kingdom than from France (the

[5] We disregard all complications arising from differences in age structures, for which we had no empirical information.

proportion being 7.7 and 0.8 per cent, respectively). This result is due to a combination of factors, the most important of which are the greater number of total migrants to the United States from the United Kingdom than from France (the numbers were 27,613 and 4,487, respectively, in 1959), and the greater number of first degrees granted in France than in the United Kingdom (9,660 and 4,557, respectively, in 1959). These data suggest that the United Kingdom's problem of losing brains to the United States may be at least in part due to general migration rather than to specific disequilibria between the demands for and supplies of scientists and engineers in the two countries. While our findings are highly tentative, given the fact that the "brain drain" from Britain goes to other countries as well as to the United States, they are important and deserve further attention because of the policy implications they carry. The more the emigration of the highly skilled is simply the result of general emigration, the less appropriate are government policies directed toward holding specific professional groups. Such policies will be successful only if they create an otherwise undesirable disequilibrium in the market for the relevant skills.

It is interesting to speculate about the causes of the observation that scientists and engineers have a greater propensity to immigrate to the United States than other occupations. First, it is well known that U.S. immigration laws favor the admittance of highly trained individuals.[6]

Second, from a theoretical point of view, we would expect to find a greater

propensity among scientists and engineers than among other occupational groups to emigrate to the United States even if the immigration laws did not favor them. Scientists and engineers always have high levels of general education, which typically lead to the knowledge of at least some English, as well as a great degree of cultural openness and willingness to travel. Furthermore, the market for professionals is quite well informed internationally, so that these people often leave their country with the certainty of employment awaiting them at their destination. This eliminates the need for search of employment, which may be costly in terms of foregone earnings. In addition, other costs of moving are likely to be paid by the employers, and if not, they are a smaller percentage of basic pay of professional personnel than they are of the prospective incomes of lower-paid occupations.

The findings may, however, also be considered suggestive of more general causes of emigration, such as inadequate national demand for scientists and engineers relative to the size of the scientific establishment, which may in turn be attributable to the nature and magnitude of science and research policies followed by industry and government in the migrants' native countries. Or, alternatively, the flows could be accounted for by a disequilibrium on the demand side, such as the speeding up of scientific programs in the United States, generating demand which domestic universities are unable to fill in the short run. Unfortunately, we have no way of estimating the relative importance of any of these factors, though we believe that further research into the causes underlying the greater propensity of scientists and engineers to emigrate may yield results of great importance for future policy decisions.

[6] See National Science Foundation (1962, pp. 2–3; 1965, p. 7) for a detailed explanation of the immigration laws favoring highly skilled persons.

V. SUMMARY AND CONCLUSIONS

Our analysis in this paper has shown that the gains of the United States from the gross immigration of scientists and engineers in recent years have been equal to the annual output of about 5 per cent of the institutions of higher education in the United States. While the dollar value of the human capital embodied in these migrants represents the large sum of nearly $1 billion in 12 years, an addition of that amount to the capital stock of the United States and the increase in income resulting from it are small in relation to the large size of the U.S. economy.

For the individual countries of emigration, however, the losses from emigration of scientists and engineers to the United States represented substantial fractions of their current output of first degrees. Some countries experienced emigration of engineers equivalent to between 20 and 40 per cent of their first-degree earners in the discipline.

We have shown that scientists and engineers are much more likely to emigrate to the United States than are people from other occupations. This finding has important implications for the magnitude of the short-run frictional losses of output resulting from the emigration of skilled workers and, therefore, for national policies aimed at reducing the "brain drain."

Our analysis and data present an incomplete picture of the "brain drain" as a world problem. First, we have only statistics for U.S. gains, none for other countries. Second, our data measure gross movements and do not show the return migration of skilled people who have gained working experience and professional training in the United States; nor do they reflect inflows from third countries. Third, the data do not show where the migrants received their education. Fourth, there are no data for the less-developed countries of Asia or Africa. Fifth, the statistics cover only a short period so that it is impossible to relate recent flows to past experiences and to gain a historical perspective.

Last, and most important, our analysis has been concerned with "losses" and "gains" to the modern nation state. We have argued elsewhere (Grubel and Scott, 1966) that the most relevant unit for the measurement of the losses and gains from the migration of the highly skilled is the welfare either of the individuals they leave behind in their country of emigration or of the individuals in their country of immigration. Changes in the welfare of those individuals may be brought about by changes in their country's gross national product or military power, which enter individual utility functions as items of public consumption.

More significant to economists, however, than changes in "nationalistically" relevant variables is the effect of migration on real income per capita, an effect that includes the influence of externalities in both consumption and production. Our data, however, do not permit us to draw inferences about these most important and interesting effects.

REFERENCES

Becker, Gary. *Human Capital.* New York: Columbia Univ. Press (for the National Bureau of Economic Research), 1964.

Economic Report of the President, 1960. Washington: Government Printing Office, 1960.

Economic Report of the President, 1965. Washington: Government Printing Office, 1965.

Grubel, H. G., and Scott, A. D. "The Cost of U.S. College Student Exchange Programs" (mimeographed).

Grubel, H. G., and Scott, A.D. "The International Flow of Human Capital," *A.E.R.*, *Papers and Proc.*, May, 1966.

National Science Foundation. "Immigration of Professional Workers to the United States—1953–56," *Scientific Manpower Bull. No. 8* (NSF-58-4), 1958.

———. *Scientific Manpower from Abroad.* (NSF 62-24.) Washington: National Science Foundation, 1962.

———. "Scientists and Engineers from Abroad, Fiscal Years 1962 and 1963," *Rev. Data Sci. Resources*, Vol. I, No. 5 (July, 1965) (NSF 65-17).

Organization for Economic Co-operation and Development. *Resources of Scientific and Technical Personnel in the OECD Area.* (Statistical Report of the Third International Survey on the Demand for and Supply of Scientific and Technical Personnel.) Paris: Organization for Economic Co-operation and Development, 1964.

Parai, Louis. *Immigration and Emigration of Professional and Skilled Manpower during the Post-War Period.* (Special Study No. 1; prepared for the Economic Council of Canada.) Ottawa: Roger Duhamel, Queen's Printer and Controller of Stationery, 1965.

Schultz, T. W. "Capital Formation by Education," *J.P.E.*, Vol. LXVIII (December, 1960).

———. "Education and Economic Growth," in *Social Forces Influencing American Education.* (Yearbook of the National Society for the Study of Education, 1961, Part II.) Chicago: Univ. of Chicago Press, 1961.

U.S. Department of Commerce. "Earned Degrees Conferred: 1956." (Table 163), *Statistical Abstract of the United States, 1958.* Washington: Government Printing Office, 1958.

THE INTERNATIONAL MOVEMENT OF HUMAN CAPITAL: CANADIAN ECONOMISTS*

ANTHONY SCOTT   *University of British Columbia*
HERBERT G. GRUBEL   *University of Pennsylvania*

I / Introduction

By applying to the Canadian economics profession techniques we have developed in other papers,[1] we construct in this paper a "balance of indebtedness" between Canada and the United States. This balance arises from the contributions made by schooling in each country to the stock of academic economists in the other country. We show that, although Canada has contributed a large number of economists to the United States' stock, she has, on all assumptions about costs, gained more human capital than she has lost.

This may be surprising, because Canada is well-known as a source of American scientists and engineers,[2] and is well-known too, especially in Europe, as the destination of scientists and managers from Europe and from less developed countries.[3] Most of such impressions are based on *flow* data, of immigrant arrivals,[4] though some are based on census measures and special stock enumerations.[5] But all are extremely misleading, not simply through their inclusions

*This paper is a contraction of a longer study. Both versions have benefitted by comments from Gideon Rosenbluth and John Vanderkamp, and have depended upon the research assistance of Lawrence Brown and Christopher Poole, of the University of British Columbia, for whose active interest we are very grateful. It was supported in part by the UBC Research Fund and the Canada Council.

[1]H. G. Grubel and A. D. Scott, "The Immigration of Scientists and Engineers to the United States, 1949–61," *Journal of Political Economy*, LXXIV, no. 4 (Aug. 1966), 368–78 and H. G. Grubel and A. D. Scott, "The Cost of US College Student Exchange Programs," *The Journal of Human Resources*, I, no. 2 (fall 1966), 81–98.

[2]Grubel and Scott, "Immigration of Scientists."

[3]Louis Parai, *Immigration and Emigration of Professional and Skilled Manpower during the Post-War Period* (Ottawa, 1965), 79–83, 120–124.

[4]See the work by Sametz and others in the Department of Citizenship and Immigration. For a recent summary, see K. V. Pankhurst, "Migration Between Canada and the United States," *Annals of the American Academy of Political and Social Science*, 367 (Sept. 1966), 53–62.

[5]US Dept. of Commerce, Bureau of the Census, "Occupational Characteristics," *U.S. Census of Population: 1960*, Final Report PC (2) – 72, Table 8.

Canadian Journal of Economics/Revue canadienne d'Economique, II, no. 3
August/août 1969. Printed in Canada/Imprimé au Canada.

ANTHONY SCOTT and HOWARD G. GRUBEL

and omissions of persons, but, more important, in their arbitrary mention or neglect of the origin and value of the human capital (schooling) embodied in the migrants. This paper attempts to remedy these shortcomings by an analysis of academic economists: the number and value of native- and foreign-born Canadians who have studied abroad[6] and returned to Canada, and of foreign-born who have joined the profession in Canada. We are able to compare some of these enumerations with similar estimates about economists with Canadian birth and schooling now in the United States. This paper does not deal with the reasons for, or motives underlying, the flows.

Before proceeding, however, it is worth asking whether a study confined to economists is an adequate source of information either about Canadian professions or about brain-drain balances of indebtedness. Its representativeness of the migration rates or of foreign-born percentages in all Canadian professions must indeed be in doubt. We have collected evidence, some of it published,[7] that suggests that economists are more apt to take training abroad or to migrate than other Canadian disciplines or sciences. Hence, our economists' sums and balances may not help to predict analogous values among physicians, chemists, or professors of English.

On the other hand, economists do provide an excellent illustration of our main point: that the existence of a larger number of Canadians in the United States than of similar Americans in Canada does not indicate that the United States is "indebted" to Canada for a surplus of exported human capital. This is because many Canadian economists obtained their graduate training abroad. Human capital is credited not to the place of birth but to where education occurs.

II / The balance on the Canadian-American exchange of academic economists

In this section we estimate the values of the prior Canadian flows to the US, and of the US flows to Canada, by examining the 1964 stocks. This procedure summarizes the present situation only at some expense of sacrifice of full accuracy:

(*a*) The accompanying chart, Figure 1, is based upon the known origin of Canadian-trained economists in the US and of a sample of economists in Canada. It shows the large contribution of the Rest of the World, which, however, is excluded from our balance-sheet calculations.

(*b*) The Canadian information is based upon a sample of a universe of unknown size. We have had to guess what the total magnitude should be.

Nevertheless we think it of some value to measure the complex "debts" and "gains" which emerge when two countries as close as Canada and the United

[6]In the 1960s, about 2500 Canadians in all fields moved to the US for schooling. See *Open Doors*, Institute of International Education, 1963, 5; B. W. Wilkinson, *Studies in the Economics of Education*, Economics and Research Branch, Canada Dept. of Labour, Occasional Paper no. 4 (Ottawa, 1966) Table 4, 60, shows the number of "students" over a ten-year period, but this is certainly an understatement, being based on American visa information.
[7]A. D. Scott, "The Recruitment and Migration of Canadian Social Scientists," *Canadian Journal of Economics and Political Science*, XXXIII, no. 4 (Nov. 1967), 495–508.

International Movement of Human Capital   377

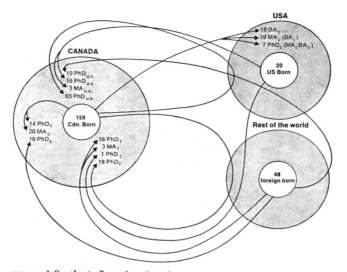

FIGURE 1 Synthetic flow-chart based on careers of 44 US academics with Canadian BAs and of 183 Canadian academics.

NOTE: This figure and the following tables are derived from:
1. National Science Foundation-American Economic Association questionnaire – used to study American economists of Canadian birth, training or experience described in H. G. Grubel and A. D. Scott, "Foreigners in the US Economics Profession," *American Economic Review*, LVII, no. 1 (March 1967), 131–45.
2. A ten per cent sample of names drawn from the directory of the American Economic Association – most of the data obtained from the sample was supplanted by the NSF-AEA questionnaire.
3. Data on salaries and qualifications of teachers in universities and colleges collected by DBS (published annually as No. 81-203).
4. The first of two sample questionnaires sent to Canadian university economics departments. It was used to establish a profile of the Canadian academic economics profession, with reference to its connections with other countries. (A second, smaller questionnaire, was used only for its income information in the original, larger manuscript).
5. *The Commonwealth Universities Yearbook, 1965*, university calendars, and correspondence with Professor M. Von Zur-Muehlen were helpful in interpreting the sample.

States in effect draw on the same labour market for the manning of university departments in a single profession. This is because in spite of the publicity given to the brain drain, and the undoubted fact that Canada has lost many valuable and important economists to the United States, the balance of our calculations is always in favour of Canada, the loss of human capital by emigration being in every calculation more than offset by the gain of human capital to those now working in Canada from training in US institutions.

Method. The method used is substantially the same as that followed in our "The Cost of the US College Student Exchange Programs."[8]

That is, we assume that each migrant, according to his age and education, embodies an amount of human capital indicated by the resource cost of his

[8]Herbert G. Grubel and Anthony Scott, "The Cost of US College Student Exchange Programs," *Journal of Human Resources*, I, no. 2 (fall 1966), 81–98.

ANTHONY SCOTT and HOWARD G. GRUBEL

TABLE I

CANADIAN CONTRIBUTION TO THE STOCK OF ECONOMISTS IN THE US IN 1964

Type of education	(1) Number of degrees	Average cost per student		Total cost—all students		
		(2) Education cost	(3) Opportunity cost	(4) (1) × (2)	(5) (1) × (3)	(6) (4) + (5)
Elementary	88	260 × 8 yrs	—	183,040	—	183,040
High School	88	538 × 4	915 × 4	189,376	322,080	511,456
Bachelor of Arts	44	1377 × 4	1800 × 4	242,352	316,800	559,152
Master of Arts	26	4143 × 2	1800 × 2	215,436	93,600	309,036
Doctor of Philosophy	7	4143 × 2	1800 × 2	58,002	25,200	83,202
TOTAL IN CANADIAN VALUES				888,206	757,680	1,645,886
TOTAL IN AMERICAN VALUES				784,586	994,708	1,779,294

NOTES

Sources and methods: Column 1. The numbers of Canadian degrees are taken from the NSF-AEA survey cards. Of the 12 individuals who left Canada before completing high school (as shown in the survey returns), it was assumed that 6 attended elementary school in Canada. Of the 88 persons who attended high school in Canada, 77 were Canadian-born and 11 were US-born. Of this latter group we assumed five took their elementary education in Canada and six did not. This gives 77 + 6 + 5 = 88 for elementary schooling in Canada.

Row 1 col. 2: From Wilkinson, Table III-10 and Appendix III Table A, 115 and 263–4. The consumer price index was used to carry Wilkinson's $253 to 1963–4 levels.

Row 1 col. 3: "US College Student Exchange," 24, and T. W. Schultz, "Education and Economic Growth" in Nelson B. Henry (ed.), *Social Forces Influencing American Education* (Chicago, 1961).

Row 2 col. 2: Wilkinson, as for Row 1 col. 2. This figure includes institutional costs but excludes incidentals such as books, supplies, and transportation, which we have deducted from Wilkinson (and Schultz).

Row 2 col. 3: Source: Wilkinson, Table III-10, gives $855 as the annual opportunity costs of a high school student in Canada in 1961–2. Wilkinson depends on Schultz's US figure and the Canadian census data on high school and university earnings. These seem a little high, as there is no adjustment for unemployment in 1961–2. In moving the estimate to 1963–4, therefore, it is raised by 7 per cent rather than the 11 per cent indicated in the DBS manufacturing earnings index.

Row 3 col. 2: Source: *Canadian Universities, Income and Expenditure, 1963-4*, DBS No. 81-212, Table 10 and p. 34. The distinction between education and research, extension, etc., costs made in "US College Student Exchange Programs" is maintained here. Basing ourselves on the percentage allocation of expenditure shown by DBS, we estimate that of the $289 million total expenditure, 61.2 per cent was direct instructional and departmental research, and of the remaining 38.8 per cent overhead, only 25 percentage points may be allocated to instruction and departmental research. (This corresponds almost exactly with the finding in "The Cost of US College Student Exchange Programs," for the US, that one-third of overhead applies to organized research and external activities, and should be disregarded.) The total, therefore, is (61.2 + 25 per cent) of $289 = $249 millions.

The overhead cost was allocated equally to graduates and undergraduates. Instructional and departmental research costs were estimated to be 4 times greater for graduates than for undergraduates (as in "The Cost of US College Student Exchange Programs"). This yields $1377 for undergraduates and $4143 for graduates. Wilkinson, p. 70, gives figures rather higher than this, chiefly because he did not reduce overhead for organized research, etc., partly because he seems to have allowed for depreciation and interest on total plant in an arbitrary way instead of using reported figures, and partly because he makes no distinction between graduate and undergraduate costs. The Canadian $1377, obtained in this way, is surprisingly higher than our $1023 for a US undergraduate year.

Row 3 col. 3: See Row 2 col. 3, above. Source here is G. Rosenbluth, *CAUT Bulletin*, (Dec.

schooling, his earnings foregone during schooling, and/or his maintenance costs at certain periods before or during schooling. His migration is a "gain" or "benefit" to the country whither he moves, which is now "indebted" to the country that incurred a "cost" or "loss" where the schooling took place. Readers who avoid our footnotes describing the calculations should, however, note the following special decisions, differing a little from our earlier paper.[9]

1. Having information on the stocks of foreign-born in both the Canadian and American professions makes it possible to look at the gains and losses from both points of view. In the earlier students' calculation, on the other hand, we had information only on the stock and flow of foreign students within the United States.

2. Opportunity cost. There are two competing assumptions about the burden of opportunity cost of study while in a foreign country: that it is borne by the home country (the student might have been working at home instead of studying abroad), or is borne in the country of study (the immigrant student might have worked instead of studying). We investigated the sensitivity of our balance-sheet to these assumptions, in view of the fact that the recent estimate by Parai on Canadian students abroad assumed that the opportunity cost is borne by Canada.

3. Self-support. Our original estimate is based upon the assumption that a very small proportion of Canadian graduate students in the US are supported by any but US sources; for the sake of clarity, we put this proportion at zero. However, it is possible that Canadian students carry with them considerable Canadian funds in the form of scholarships, earnings from past summer work, parental allowances, and so forth. We do not know. To bring out the effect of our assumption, we offer an alternative balance sheet in which the proportion of self-support is put at 50 per cent.

The Balance Sheets. We now proceed to calculate our "original" balance, as shown in Tables I and II. Each table is worked out in Canadian values and prices and the totals only are also given in American values (explained below).

Column 1 shows the numbers of students who have attained each kind of degree (for example, 88 persons now in the US attended elementary school in Canada). Column 2 shows our estimate of the 1964 resource cost of this education per student. Column 3 shows the opportunity cost of this education, per student. Columns 4, 5, and 6 then show the total of these costs for all the degrees shown in column 1.

[9]Mimeographed copies of the original study, of which this article forms a part, are available from A. D. Scott, Economics Department, University of British Columbia, Vancouver, Canada.

1965, Feb. 1966), 25, who shows earnings foregone as $2500 and summer earnings as $710, yielding our $1800. Rosenbluth uses data from DBS No. 81-520, and is rather lower than Wilkinson, who bases himself on the 1961 census.

Row 4 col. 3 and Row 5 col. 3: Opportunity costs taken to be same as for BA students. Both the lowness of opportunity costs, and the attribution of the same opportunity costs to different levels of education, are arguable but customary inputs in our, and other studies.

Row 7: American totals calculated using: Schultz, "Education and Economic Growth"; T. W. Schultz, "Capital Formation by Education," *Journal of Political Economy*, LXVIII (Dec. 1960), 571–83; Grubel and Scott, "US College Student Exchange."

TABLE II

AMERICAN CONTRIBUTION TO THE STOCK OF ACADEMIC ECONOMISTS IN CANADA IN 1964

Type of education	(1) Number of degrees	Average cost per student		Total cost—all students		
		(2) Education cost	(3) Opportunity cost	(4) (1) × (2)	(5) (1) × (3)	(6) (4) × (5)
Elementary	34 (19 × 1.8)	260 × 8 yrs	—	70,720	—	70,720
High School	31 (17 × 1.8)	538 × 4	915 × 4	66,712	113,460	180,172
Bachelor of Arts	43 (24 × 1.8)	1377 × 4	1800 × 4	236,844	309,600	546,444
Master of Arts	106 (76 × 1.4)	4143 × 2	1800 × 2	878,316	381,600	1,259,916
Doctor of Philosophy	125 (125 × 1)	4143 × 2	1800 × 2	1,035,750	450,000	1,485,750
TOTAL IN CANADIAN VALUES				2,288,342	1,254,660	3,543,002
TOTAL IN AMERICAN VALUES				1,553,486	1,725,576	3,279,062

NOTES

Column 1: These multipliers were obtained from consideration of the following information. (a) The count of US PhDs is believed to be complete. (b) The total sample is believed to be about 1.00/1.75 of the number of academic economists. (c) The sample is most deficient among colleges with proportionately few PhDs. Consequently, the multipliers were set at 1.0 for PhDs and 1.8 for BAs and 1.4 obtained for MAs by interpolation.

It can be seen that the largest total magnitudes stem from the costs of education in high school and university, the large number of years in elementary school being more than offset by the small unit costs of such education and the absence of opportunity costs at these ages.

The last line of Table II gives totals in American values, which differ from Canadian values for the following main reasons: opportunity costs of higher education in the US are estimated to be considerably higher than in Canada; and, second, the educational cost of graduate studies has been estimated to be far larger in Canada than in the United States. The first point is easily deduced from inspection of wage-rate statistics in the two countries. The second, though surprising, is confirmed by independent studies by Parai and Wilkinson.[10]

We may now confront Tables I and II. The first shows holders of Canadian degrees now in the US, and the second shows holders of American degrees now in Canada. (Thus, while there are only 7 PhDs granted by Canada in the US, there are 125 PhDs granted by US institutions now in Canada.) The balance is struck in Table III. Based on the totals in Tables I and II, it shows that, using Canadian values, the "net gain to Canada" was about $1,900,000; in US values, the "net loss to the US" was about $1,500,000.

TABLE III

"NET GAIN" TO CANADA AND "NET LOSS" TO US
FROM INTERNATIONAL MOVEMENTS OF
ECONOMISTS USING OPPORTUNITY COSTS OF
CANADIAN ECONOMISTS WITH AMERICAN
TRAINING

US contribution to training Canadian economists (Table II)	$3,543,002
Canadian contribution to training American economists (Table I)	$1,645,886
BALANCE: "net gain to Canada" (in Canadian values)	$1,897,116
BALANCE: "net loss to USA" (in American values)	$1,499,768

In Table IV, we examine the costs of training the economists in Canada at the stages enumerated in Table II by dividing these economists into Canadian-born, foreign- (non-US) born, and US-born. The purpose of this subdivision of the earlier total gross Canadian gain from US contribution to training Canadian economists is to show how much of the gain is simple US input into the training of Canadians about to return to Canada ("reflux") and how much is US input into the total education of Americans who then move to Canada (migration). The residue, foreign-born Canadian economists trained

[10]For example, a year of MA work is costed at $4143 in Canada, but only at $2437 in the US. This arises from assuming that, in Canada as in the US, graduate costs are four times undergraduate costs. Thus, the $1500 difference between the two countries is four times the difference between the undergraduate costs, for which see Wilkinson, *Studies in the Economics of Education*, Appendix 2.

We have no independent check on this four-fold ratio, but have checked that a more moderate multiplier for Canada would not change the final balance between the two countries: the Canadian favourable balance exists even at US values.

TABLE IV

AMERICAN CONTRIBUTION TO THE STOCK OF ACADEMIC ECONOMISTS IN CANADA, 1964 BY COUNTRY OF BIRTH

Type of education	Canadian-born economists with American degrees in Canada in 1964 (1)	Foreign-born economists with American degrees in Canada in 1964 (2)	American-born economists with American degrees in Canada in 1964 (3)	Average cost per student		US contribution			Total Canadian gain (9)
				Education cost (4)	Opportunity cost (5)	Total cost Canadian-born (6)	Total cost foreign-born (7)	Total cost American-born (8)	
Elementary	0	0	34	260×8	—	—	—	70,720	70,720
High School	2	0	29	538×4	914×4	11,624	—	168,548	180,172
Bachelor of Arts	9	5	29	1377×4	1800×4	114,372	63,540	368,532	546,444
Master of Arts	69	18	20	4143×2	1800×2	820,134	213,948	237,720	1,271,802
Doctor of Philosophy	80	24	20	4143×2	1800×2	950,880	285,264	237,720	1,473,864
TOTAL IN CANADIAN VALUES						1,897,010	562,752	1,083,240	3,543,002
PER CENT IN CANADIAN VALUES						54%	16%	30%	100%
TOTAL IN AMERICAN VALUES						1,673,210	502,592	1,103,260	3,279,062
PER CENT IN AMERICAN VALUES						51%	15%	34%	100%

NOTES

Columns 1, 2, 3: sample questionnaire results multiplied by the appropriate multiplier. (See notes to Figure 1 and Table II.)

in the US, is a mixed bag containing not only American citizens born outside the US but also foreigners who were only in the US long enough to acquire a degree.

From the table it can be seen that the gross Canadian gain (in Canadian funds and prices) of $3.543 million is built up as follows: 54 per cent the education of Canadian-born; 30 per cent the education of US-born; and 16 per cent the education of foreign-born. Thus, the answer to the question posed in the first paragraph is that the US contribution to the "reflux" was approximately double (54/30) the US contribution embodied in American migration to Canada. And of the overwhelming 54 per cent, the largest single part (27 percentage points) is the education of Canadian-born PhDs who subsequently returned to Canada. This is most clearly seen in column 6 line 5 of Table IV. It amounts to $950,880, a very large amount indeed. The composition of the American "gross loss," worked out in US values, is approximately the same, a slightly higher percentage being attributed to the education of US born. This is because it is only among the American-born that dearer education and opportunity costs of elementary and high school show up; Canadian-born and foreign-born economists did not go to American public schools.

III / Alternative treatments of opportunity cost

The preceding paragraphs and tables have been based on the premise that total cost of education is the sum of the resource-cost of training and the opportunity cost of using time for study rather than for production. This familiar approach to human-capital studies, applied to international movements, implies a theory that the burden of opportunity cost falls on the host country – the country where the education is taking place. But this theory can only be justified by this point of view: that the major choice open to the persons whose mobility is studied is not "In which country shall I study?", but "Being in this country, shall I study or shall I work?" Because these persons' migration is taken for granted, but their studying is not, the decision to study is consequently viewed as imposing an opportunity cost upon the host country.

When we examine the careers of the people on whom we have data, we see that there is one group at least for whom that point of view is quite inappropriate: students who go abroad to study, and then return to their own country. It is clear from their careers that the purpose of migrating was study, and that if they had decided to work instead they would have remained at home to do so. Consequently, for this group at least we must remove the host-country cost of foregone earnings and substitute for it the cost of maintenance.[11]

Fortunately for brevity, this substitution will not require a wholesale reworking of our estimates. For it does not need to be applied to Canadians

[11]This substitution makes the treatment of foreign students here similar to that in our "US College Student Exchange." An alternative would be to attribute the opportunity costs of foreign study to the home country rather than to the host; this is the procedure used by Parai (p. 122), for a rather different purpose. Wilkinson (pp. 70–9) does not consider returning students. We should record a useful suggestion by this *Journal's* reader that, instead of a two-way balance of indebtedness, a study might well utilize a three-way attribution of costs: to the migrant; to all other Canadians; and to all other Americans.

TABLE V

MAINTENANCE COST AND SELF-SUPPORT IN THE AMERICAN CONTRIBUTION TO THE STOCK OF CANADIAN ACADEMIC ECONOMISTS, 1964

Type of education	Cdn.-born econ. with US deg. in Can. in 1964	Average cost per student — Educ. cost	Average cost per student — Maint. cost	US cont. (total cost) Cdn.-born using maint. cost (1)[(2)+(3)]	Equiv. Cdn.-born econ. with US deg. in Can. in 1964 (50%) Cdn. self-support (1) × 1/2	Self-support in US values — Tuition cost	Self-support in US values — Maint. cost	Self-support in US values — Total	Net US cont. [(4) − (8)]	Cdn. cont. to train. US econ. before adding for self-support (Table I)	Self-supported students remain in US — No. of deg.	Self-supported students remain in US — Total self-support (11)[(6)] × (1.08)	Cdn. cont. including self-support (10)+(12)
	(1)	(2)	(3)	(4)	(5)	(6)	(7)	(8)	(9)	(10)	(11)	(12)	(13)
Elem.	0	—	—	—	0	—	—	0	—	183,040	—	—	183,040
HS	2	538 × 4	—	4,304	1	—	—	0	4,304	511,456	—	—	511,456
BA	9	1377 × 2	1700 × 4	110,772	5	378 × 4	2385 × 4	59,681	51,091	559,152	22	262,595	821,747
MA	69	4143 × 2	1700 × 2	806,334	35	739 × 2	2385 × 2	237,164	570,160	309,036	29	195,687	504,723
PhD.	80	4143 × 2	1700 × 2	934,880	40	739 × 2	2385 × 2	269,914	664,966	83,202	30	202,435	285,637
TOTAL				1,856,290				565,769	1,290,521	1,645,886		660,717	2,306,603

"NET GAIN" to Canada in Canadian values using maintenance cost [Table IV: (7) + (8)] − [Table V: (4)] − [Table I: (6)] = $3,502,282 − $1,645,886 = $1,856,396

"NET LOSS" to US in US values using maintenance cost = $1,450,530.

"NET GAIN" to Canada in Canadian values taking into account self-support. [Table IV: (7) + (8)] + [Table V: (9)] − [Table V: (10) + (12)] $2,936,513 − $629,910 = $2,306,603

"NET LOSS" to US in US values taking into account self-support = $224,044.

NOTES

Column 3: Canadian maintenance costs.

1. Rosenbluth, *CAUT Bulletin* (Feb. 1966), 25. Living costs are $1030. Incidental expenses are $200.

2. Canada, *DBS Bulletin*, 81–530. "University Student Expenditure and Income in Canada 1961/62'', Part II, 38. Figures for a single student living away from home, 1963/64 cost assumed the same as in 1961/62.

3. R. Rabinovitch, *An Analysis of the Canadian Post Secondary Student Population* (Ottawa, 1966), 66 and 85.

4. Since the *DBS* figures ($1030 + $200) do not include transportation costs for out-of-town students and are based on only an eight months period we have made the following adjustments: (i) added $100 for transportation; (ii) added $400 to adjust for 12 months to arrive at the $1700 figure used in column 3.

Column 6: Average tuition fees times number of years. Because self-supported students paid US Fees, these are American fees. As in "US College Student Exchange," Table 5, lines 16 and 17, graduate fees are assumed to be 28 per cent, and undergraduate fees 37 per cent, of their direct education costs. (For graduates, this percentage was also reached by a detailed examination of fees at schools apparently attended by Canadian-born economists; for undergraduates the 37 per cent is probably low, neglecting the fact that many Canadians would pay out-of-state fees.)

Column 7: Maintenance costs from "US College Student Exchange."

Column 8: Col. 5 × (col. 6 + col. 7), all multiplied by 1.08, the US-Canada exchange rate.

Column 9: Col. 4 − col. 8.

Column 10: from Table I.

Column 11: In order to find the value of self-support in tuition and maintenance it was necessary to discover the number of US degrees, the costs of which might have been "self-supported," held by Canadians now in the US. The NSF-AEA cards give some, but not all such degrees. The assumed careers are shown in the following chart, yielding 44 US BAs; 58 US MAs; and 59 US PhDs. Half these numbers are written into column 11. The reconstruction of these careers is based partly on the numbers of which these degrees are their holders' highest degrees, and partly on the distribution of careers of similar economists who returned to Canada.

going to the US and staying there, nor to Americans or foreigners coming to Canada to work as economists. For them the "gain" to their new country (or "loss" to their former country) is the earnings foregone while they were students, as shown in the estimates already explained. It need be applied only to two groups: Americans studying in Canada then returning to the US; and Canadians studying in the US then returning to Canada. The former group was so small as to be considered zero, and hence, may be neglected. The latter group, however, is large.

The reworking necessitated is shown in Table V. We have substituted for opportunity cost the maintenance costs shown in column 3. These are set at $1700 in Canada and $2385 in the United States. (The discrepancy is larger than we would have expected, but is based on evidence from two sources.) Neither figure includes international transportation, but only "domestic transport," which is thought to be large enough to cover most Canadian-American movements.

How much difference does this substitution make to the "net gains" calculated in the previous section? The new balance, adjusted for maintenance costs shows that the difference is negligible: in Canadian terms, for example, Canada still "gains" $1,856,396 (shown at the bottom of the left half of the table).

Self-support. So far, we have assumed that students going abroad to study are entirely the guests of their host country. Our discussion of the US foreign-student exchange, however, will have made clear that a final adjustment is necessary to our balance: we must allow for the fact that students going abroad do not all (or entirely) depend on the generosity of the host country, but to varying degrees "support themselves" while abroad. In our calculations,

---

NOTES TO TABLE V, continued

RECONSTRUCTION OF CAREERS OF 89 US ECONOMISTS OF CANADIAN BIRTH BY SOURCE OF DEGREE AND HIGHEST DEGREE

	UNITED STATES		CANADA
	Number of degrees	Number of highest degrees	Degree
Born		1 · 1	89 · 88
High School		44	88 · 44
BA	44 · 2 · 42	4 · 2 · 16	44 · 26
MA	58 · 12 · 46	18 · 6 · 13	26 · 7
PhD	59 · 59	66 · 7	7
TOTAL	—	89	—

Column 12: Col. 11 × (col. 6 + col. 7) all multiplied by 1.08, the US-Canada exchange rate.
Column 13: Col. 10 + Col. 12.

this adjustment must be made to the education costs imposed by two groups: Americans who have been trained in Canada, and Canadians who have been trained in the United States. (For lack of information, we neglect foreigners who trained in one of the countries then migrated to the other. We believe that their careers would change the gross totals, but not the net balance between Canada and the United States.)

The group of Americans who have been trained in Canada is so small as to be safely neglected. The group of Canadians trained in the United States must now be further sub-divided into two groups: not only those who have studied in the US and returned to Canada (who were dealt with in the previous section on maintenance costs), but also a new group, those who on completing their studies in the US, remained there. The greater the "self-support" of these two sub-groups, the smaller the net US contribution in the final balance.

As discussed already, in "US College Student Exchange," self-support can be visualized as an amalgam of three kinds of student financing: Canadians carrying Canadian scholarships and other transfers from Canadian sources; Canadians carrying their own Canadian earnings for spending in the US; and Canadians earning funds from interrupting their studies to work while in the US. We have reason to believe that all three sources are important. A little application of balance-of-payments theory shows that it does not matter whether the funds are carried from Canada or earned by Canadians in the US: in either case they reduce the net "gain" of Canada by the amount that Canada has in effect "remitted" to the US.

How great is the magnitude of this self-support? We do not know, but we do know that not only do Canadian students frequently carry grants and past earnings but also frequently depend on work as teaching assistants, research assistants, and so forth as ways of supporting themselves. Frequently regarded as "scholarships" from US sources, the latter are actually forms of self-support. Having no information on the magnitude of self-support, we have made what we regard as an extreme assumption: that one-half of tuition fees and one-half of maintenance costs are paid by self-support. We now investigate the effect of this extreme assumption on our previous net balance.

The adjustments, though laborious, are in principle simple. In Table V, columns 5–9, we take the data of columns 1–4 dealing with Canadians studying in the US and returning to Canada. Because we now assume 50 per cent self-support, one-half the tuition fees are subtracted from education cost (leaving not only the other half but the rest of education cost not covered by fees); and one-half of maintenance cost is deducted. In Canadian terms, this reduces the gross US contribution of $1,856,290 (column 4) to $1,290,521 (column 9).

For reasons already explained, we leave the education and opportunity costs of foreigners unchanged.

In Table V (columns 10–13) we turn to a set of costs that have not so far entered our balance: the education costs, *in the US* of Canadians who, after graduate training did not return to Canada. These have so far been regarded as US costs of increasing the US stock of human capital and so irrelevant to our calculations. However, it is just as reasonable to argue that these students were self-supported to the same extent as those who were subsequently attracted back to Canada. Consequently, "remittances" to them are part of the Canadian contribution to the US stock, or an offset to the US contribution to Canada.

Table I shows the distribution of Canadian degrees among the US stock of Canadians. Table V (columns 10–13) shows the total cost of their subsequent education in the US, and the Canadian contribution to their tuition fees and maintenance.[12]

IV / Summary

Our final net balance, in Canadian and US values is shown at the bottom of Table V. It is shown that our extreme assumption, that one-half tuition fees and maintenance of Canadian students abroad was paid as "remittances" from Canada, reduces the net US contribution of $1,856,396 to $629,910 in Canadian terms. Readers who believe our 50 per cent guess is too extreme may substitute their own compromise. Almost any reasonable figure will lead to the same final conclusion, that in spite of the fact that there are 89 "Canadian economists" in the US stock, as compared to only about 35 "American economists" in the Canadian stock, Canada is nevertheless "indebted" to the United States for between one-half and one million dollars in the net international exchange of persons and training.

This we believe is a striking refutation of the frequently heard suggestion that a large stock of one's nationals abroad indicates a large "brain-drain." Our human-capital approach, evaluating Canadian inputs into the US stock and US inputs into the Canadian stock, has shown that a mere counting of heads leads to the wrong conclusion.

We would suggest that the application of this kind of study to other professions and skills would be a valuable corrective to the generally accepted "brain drain" myth. While it is true that because of their mobility Canadian economists are not typical of other Canadian professions (as was admitted earlier), it is clear that even the sign of the net balance of any profession's "brain drain" cannot be guessed at without such calculations as these.[13]

Does this net balance of "indebtedness" indicate who has gained or lost in

[12]We have had to make reasonable guesses at the distribution of further education among the Canadians.

[13]Furthermore, it appears that our calculations tend to throw some shadow of doubt on the ingenious flow calculations of Professor Wilkinson, which he uses to measure the human capital embodied in all Canadian immigrants and emigrants during the years 1951–61, and which he concludes with the perfectly proper comment: "it should be evident from the above study that it is important to look beyond the absolute numbers of persons involved in international migration and consider the dollar values of the human capital flows as well. Only in this way could we hope to arrive at any realistic assessment of the dollar gains and losses involved." (p. 79)

However, he unfortunately illustrates this conclusion by showing that while emigration, in absolute numbers, amounts to only about 20 per cent of immigration, the superior human capital embodied in Canadian emigrants raises the "loss" by Canada to about 30 per cent of the value of immigrants. If Professor Wilkinson had considered also the contribution of other countries to the education of Canadians, the cost of emigration would have been reduced again, toward his original 20 per cent level. It does appear too that our technique of considering stocks may be more fruitful than his technique of considering flows in obtaining information on the characteristics of migrants.

ANTHONY SCOTT and HOWARD G. GRUBEL

the international flows? If education, maintenance and opportunity costs measured human capital prospectively as well as retrospectively, the answer must be yes. But what if the economic students who have eventually settled in the United States are, or embody, human capital superior to that of the economists who have returned to Canada? (Harry Johnson[14] and Mabel Timlin[15] can be interpreted as believing this to be the fact.) Our earlier study on the United States economic profession casts some doubt on this however, by finding no evidence in income or employment that as a group foreign economists in the US are superior to native-born.[16] This confirms that economists migrate because they increase their own capital value, not because they are better than those whom they leave, or those they join. And if Canadian migrants are not superior to US economists, why should they be assumed to be superior to Canadian economists? More research is needed, but it is so far entirely possible that the US "indebtedness" measured in terms of future productivity will be of the same sign as that measured by past costs.[17]

[14]H. G. Johnson, "Canadian Contributions to the Discipline of Economics since 1945," *Canadian Journal of Economics*, I, no. 1 (Feb. 1968), 129–46.

[15]Mabel Timlin, "Social Science Research in Canada," in A. Faucher and M. Timlin, *Social Sciences in Canada* (Ottawa, 1968).

[16]Grubel and Scott, "Foreigners in the US Economics Profession."

[17]Whether "foreign training" means anything to the quality of a country's professionals is a familiar question in other contexts. See Robert I. Crane, "Technical Education and economic development in India before World War I," in C. A. Anderson and M. J. Bowman, *Education and Economic Development* (Chicago, 1967), 167–201, and C. V. Kidd, "The Economics of the Brain Drain," *Minerva*, IV, no. 1 (Autumn 1965), 105–7, for discussion of the importance of domestic training for domestic specialists. Recent surveys in Canada by K. W. Taylor, "Economic Scholarship in Canada," *Canadian Journal of Economics and Political Science*, XXVI, no. 1 (Feb. 1960), 6–18; J. H. Dales, "Canadian Scholarship in Economics: Achievement and Outlook," an address to the Royal Society of Canada (7 June 1967; Scott, "Recruitment and Migration"; H. G. Johnson, "The Social Sciences in the Age of Opulence," *Canadian Journal of Economics and Political Science*, XXXII, no. 4 (Nov. 1966), 423–42; D. Smiley, "Contributions to Canadian Political Science since the Second World War," *ibid.*, XXXIII, no. 4 (Nov. 1967), 569–80; R. A. Preston, "Two-Way Traffic in Canadian History," *Queen's Quarterly* (Autumn 1967), 380–91. All touch on the effect of foreign standards, training or scholarship on the quality of Canadian academic disciplines.

40 - 54

THE CHARACTERISTICS OF FOREIGNERS IN THE U.S. ECONOMICS PROFESSION

By Herbert G. Grubel and Anthony D. Scott*

While the theoretical aspects of the "brain drain," the migration of highly skilled people from the rest of the world to the United States, have been analyzed recently [2] [4] [5], very few reliable statistics on the actual magnitude of the problem are available. The unavailability of the empirical information is unfortunate because as a result we cannot answer the question whether the public concern over the brain drain reflects a new trend or merely a new awareness of a flow having a long history, nor derive insights into the drain from the less developed countries of the world, nor discover anything about the "quality" of the migrants, more specifically whether the "best" in some sense are drawn to the United States.

In this paper we have tried to provide quantitative information relevant to some of these issues by analyzing the characteristics of foreigners in the U.S. economics profession. The study has become feasible through the 1964 National Science Foundation project of registering the U.S. stock of scientific and technical personnel, which recorded the life and professional histories of American natural and social scientists through surveys conducted in cooperation with professional organizations.[1]

Our analysis of the economics profession is useful even in the context of the broader question of the "brain drain" involving many other professions because economics is a science in which the transfer of foreign skills is probably about "average." On the one hand, foreign training in economics is not as readily transferable and useful in the United States as is the training of theoretical physicists. On the other hand, the tools of economic analysis are probably more uniform be-

* The authors are associate professor of finance at the University of Pennsylvania and professor of economics at the University of British Colombia, respectively. This paper was written while both authors were at the University of Chicago and it is part of a larger study concerned with the international migration of highly trained people financed by the Rockefeller Foundation and directed by Harry G. Johnson. We thank Harry G. Johnson for his intellectual and financial support and Milton Levine, Study Director of the National Register of Scientific and Technical Personnel Studies Group, National Science Foundation, for making available the data used in this study. We acknowledge gratefully comments by Zvi Griliches, J. G. Gurley, A. E. Rees and G. J. Stigler made on an earlier version of this paper.

[1] The technical details of how the survey was conducted, the response rate, etc., are set forth in [1], to which the interested reader is referred.

40

tween nations than is the specific knowledge of lawyers or historians. Also, economics is not a licensed profession, which makes it easier for economists to practice in a foreign country than, for instance, medical doctors and lawyers.[2]

Before turning to the presentation and analysis of our findings it is necessary to discuss two characteristics of the data. First, as is common experience in survey data, some respondents failed to answer some of the questions. Consequently, the sum of all observations in each of the categories discussed often fails to be as large as the total sample. Under all income classification schemes, for example, somewhere between 5 and 10 per cent of the members in each class failed to report income statistics or had no income at all. We have simply disregarded these observations in our compilations of median incomes and deciles, a procedure biasing the computed averages in an unknown direction. The unknown bias does not, however, impair the usefulness of our statistics, since we are primarily interested in comparisons between U.S.-born and foreign-born economists and there is no reason to believe that the share of nonrespondents or zero-income earners is greater in one group than in the other.

Second, we had separate information on professional salaries and on gross professional income, but decided to use only gross professional income in our analysis because the use of both would have unduly complicated the presentation of the information without adding substantially to the insights attainable by the statistic we used. Gross professional income was considered to be a more relevant measure of professional success than basic salary since the earnings from consulting, royalties, and other honorariums included in the former are an important part of many economists' incomes.

I. *Characteristics of Foreign- and U.S.-born Economists*

Table 1 was compiled from the total sample and compares the characteristics of the foreign-born and the U.S.-born. As can be seen (from columns 1 and 3 giving the absolute number, column 5 the percentage), nearly 12 per cent of U.S. economists were born abroad. However, this percentage differs for the various age-groups (see column 5). The foreign-born are relatively most numerous among the oldest age-groups, are the smallest proportions among the very young and those who are now between the ages of 50 and 60, while their share in the age-group of 30 to 45 is in between these two extremes.

[2] A study concerned with professional migration to and from Canada found that according to the 1961 census the foreign-born postwar immigrants represent 25.2 per cent of engineers, 18.5 per cent of economists, 12.6 per cent of health professions and only 3 per cent of the law profession now working in Canada. These data are from [3, Table 21, p. 63].

TABLE 1—CHARACTERISTICS OF U.S.- AND FOREIGN-BORN ECONOMISTS[a]

	Foreign (1)	Per Cent (2)	U.S. Born (3)	Per Cent (4)	Foreign Born as Per Cent of Total (5)
A. Place and Date of Birth					
1. Born before 1890	19	1.4	110	1.0	14.7
1891 1895	21	1.6	140	1.3	13.0
96 1900	67	5.0	342	3.2	16.4
1901 05	89	6.7	504	4.7	15.0
06 10	93	7.0	794	7.4	10.5
11 15	131	9.9	1,224	11.3	9.7
16 20	147	11.1	1,596	14.8	8.9
21 25	254	19.1	1,834	17.1	12.2
26 30	231	17.4	1,780	16.6	11.5
31 35	191	14.4	1,520	14.1	11.1
36 40	83	6.2	870	8.1	8.7
41 45	3	.2	41	.4	.1
Total	1,329	100.0[c]	10,755	100.0	11.9
B. Degree Information					
1. High school					
Foreign diploma	990	75.3	43	1.0	95.7
U.S. diploma	324	24.7	10,764	99.0	2.9
Total	1,314	100.0	10,807	100.0	
2. Highest degree					
B.A.	123	9.3	2,578	24.0	4.6
M.A.	384	29.0	3,727	34.8	9.3
Ph.D.	766	57.9	4,323	40.3	15.1
Other[b]	50	3.8	93	.9	35.0
Total	1,323	100.0	10,721	100.0	

	Foreign		United States		Foreign as Per Cent of Total
3. Source of highest degree					
Foreign born B.A.	28		95		22.8
M.A.	60		324		15.6
Ph.D.	184		582		24.0
Other	45		2		95.8
Total	317		1,003		24.0
3. Source of highest degree					
U.S. born B.A.	4		2,572		.1
M.A.	14		3,708		.4
Ph.D.	46		4,277		1.1
Other	9		80		10.1
Total	73		10,637		.7

[a] Subtotals differ from grand total due to information missing.
[b] This category includes economists who hold no college degrees.
[c] Percentages may not total 100.0 due to rounding.

	Foreign (1)	Per Cent (2)	U.S. Born (3)	Per Cent (4)	Foreign Born as Per Cent of Total (5)
C. Employment and Income					
1. Type of employer					
Industry	258	21.0	3,556	34.9	6.8
Academic	705	57.3	4,304	42.3	14.1
Federal government	94	7.6	1,180	11.6	7.4
State government	21	1.7	141	1.4	13.0
Other government	12	1.0	73	.7	14.1
Consulting	9	.7	72	.7	11.1
Self employed	18	1.5	174	1.7	9.5
Nonprofit organization	54	4.4	347	3.4	13.5
Other	59	4.8	333	3.3	15.0
Total	1,230	100.0	10,180	100.0	
2. Academic rank					
Dean	4	.6	18	.5	18.2
Full professor	192	31.1	1,319	35.1	12.7
Associate professor	155	25.1	842	22.4	15.5
Assistant professor	168	27.2	907	24.1	15.6
Instructor	44	7.1	319	8.5	12.1
Lecturer	23	3.7	202	5.4	10.2
Research asst. and assoc.	11	1.8	93	2.5	10.6
Other	21	3.4	57	1.5	26.9
Total	618	100.0	3,757	100.0	

	Foreign		United States		Foreign-born Income as Per Cent of U.S.-born Income
3. Gross professional income ($ thousand) Deciles:	below	6.0	below	6.9	87
		7.7		8.7	87
		9.1		9.8	93
		10.0		11.2	89
	median	12.5		12.5	100
		14.1		14.2	99
		15.9		15.9	100
		18.5		18.8	98
		22.5		23.7	95
	above	22.6	above	23.8	95

D. Characteristics of Economists with Second-Highest Degree Foreign

Classes	Birth	High School	Highest Degree	Number
1	F	US	US	3
2	F	F	US	198
3	F	F	F	134
4	F	US	F	2
5	US	F	US	3
6	US	US	F	21
7	US	US	US	39
8	All Other			9
				409

An interesting feature of these statistics is that the lowest share of foreigners occurs in the age group of people who were born during or shortly after World War I, and who were likely to have been attending institutions of higher learning during the 1930s. During this period, on the one hand, Europe experienced the tyranny of the Hitler regime which encouraged emigration of older professionals, but the United States, on the other hand, was in the middle of the Great Depression which reduced incentives for immigration, perhaps more for students than for established professionals. One interpretation of the data is

TABLE 2—FOREIGN-BORN AS A PROPORTION OF TOTAL POPULATION AND OF ECONOMISTS

Years of Birth	Foreign-Born as Per Cent of Total Population[a] (1)	Foreign-Born Economists as Per Cent of all Economists[b] (2)	General Population = 100 Index of Economists (3)
1896–1905	13.7	15.6	114
1906–1915	7.2	10.0	139
16– 20	4.3	8.9	207
21– 25	4.0	12.2	305
26– 30	3.6	11.5	319
31– 35	2.8	11.1	396
36– 40	1.5	8.7	580
41– 50	1.5	.6	40
Total	6.1	11.9	195

[a] U.S. Census of 1960, Final Report PC(2)-2D.
[b] Table 1.

that for people of university age at the time the latter factor seems to have been predominant over the former. Another explanation is that more foreigners than Americans of the relevant age groups were killed in World War II.

The secular decline in the proportion of foreign-born in the U.S. economics profession evidenced by Table 1 is put into perspective by the data assembled in Table 2. Throughout this period the share of foreign-born in the total population has fallen even more significantly (column 1) than that of foreign-born in the economics profession. Taking the proportion found in the total population as a basis (= 100) we have computed an index measuring the magnitude by which the role of foreign-born in the economics profession exceeds that in the total population. This measure shows an impressive and steady upward trend for the entire period except for the last age-group, which contains an insufficient number of observations for a meaningful interpretation. It suggests that the U.S. immigration has been selective, favoring the highly skilled or at least people capable of attaining high levels of skill.

Part B of Table 1 contains information about the level and source of scholastic degrees earned by U.S. economists. The most interesting feature of these data is that 75 per cent of the foreign-born received their high school education abroad, which means that probably no more than 25 per cent of them immigrated to the United States before the age of 18 or 19.

Section B.2 of Table 1 groups the economists according to the highest professional degree they have earned and indicates that the foreign born represent a greater share of the total the higher the degree. The next section of Table 1 reveals that fully 75 per cent of the foreign-born economists arrived in the United States before completion of their professional training abroad and enrolled in U.S. institutions of higher learning. Incorporating the information contained in Part D of Table 1 the following conclusion emerges about the extent to which the foreign born also received their education abroad: Of the 1330 foreign-born, 990 have foreign high schol diplomas, 332 have a foreign second-highest degree, 317 have foreign highest degree.

The information about degrees also reveals that a very small proportion of U.S.-born economists received some part of their training abroad. The foreign highest degree most frequently obtained by U.S.-born economists is the Ph.D., of which there are in our data 46, representing 1 per cent of all Ph.D.'s held by U.S.-born economists. Part D of Table 1 shows the extent to which U.S. economists have obtained foreign degrees other than their highest. Interesting is Class 7 which shows that 39 Americans hold a foreign degree supplementing their otherwise complete U.S. education. Of these 39 about 72 per cent, 28, count the Ph.D. as their highest degree.

Section C.1 of Table 1 reveals that the foreign born are employed in relatively greater numbers by universities, state and local government, and nonprofit organizations and are relatively under-represented in industry, self-employment, consulting and the federal government. This pattern of concentration is not surprising if we remember that academia and sometimes also the civil service have been the traditional roads for advancement of members of minority groups in many societies, since in these fields objectively measurable output and examination performance are most important for success, and language and citizenship barriers are often the least restrictive.

The interpretation of income statistics in part C.3 of Table 1 must be handled with care because the two groups under examination differ with respect to many characteristics such as employment and age, all of which tend to influence professional incomes. We turn to a closer analysis of income data in Section III below.

TABLE 3—COUNTRIES OF BIRTH—U.S. ECONOMISTS

Country or Continent	Number	Per Cent of Continent	Per Cent of Total Foreign Born	Country or Continent	Number	Per Cent of Continent	Per Cent of Total Foreign Born
			N=1287				
Africa	31	100	2	West Europe	576	100	45
U.A.R.	20	65	1	Unclassifiable	1	0	—
N. Africa	1	3	1	Scandinavia	28	5	2
East Central	1	3	—	Great Britain	97	17	8
West Central	2	6	—	Benelux	35	6	3
East South				Germany	210	36	16
Central	1	3	—	France	26	5	2
Southern	6	19	—	Austria	102	18	8
				Iberian Peninsula	6	1	—
Asia	196	100	15	Greece,			
Unclassifiable	1	1	—	Yugoslavia	50	9	4
China	82	42	6	Italy	21	4	2
S.E. Asia	6	3	—				
Indian Subcont.	44	22	3	East Europe	258	100	20
Japan	17	9	1	Russia	66	26	5
Korea	23	12	2	3 Baltic			
Formosa	4	2	—	Countries	21	8	2
Philippines	12	6	1	Poland	63	24	5
Indonesia	7	3	1	Czechoslavakia	40	16	3
				Rumania	13	5	1
Australia	19	100	1	Bulgaria	5	2	—
Australia	16	84	1	Hungary	50	20	4
New Zealand	3	16	—				
				North America	189	100	15
South America	18	100	1	Canada	160	85	12
Argentina and				Central America	6	3	—
Paraguay	7	39	1	Mexico	4	2	—
Bolivia	5	28	—	West Indies	6	3	—
Colombia	3	17	—	Bahamas	1	1	—
Ecuador, Peru	1	6	—	Cuba, Dominican			
Guiana	1	6	—	Rep.	12	6	1
Venezuela	1	6	—				

Note: "—" means less than .5 per cent.

II. *Countries of Foreign Birth and Training*

In Table 3 we present an analysis of the shares of foreign born supplied by individual countries and continents. Especially noticeable, though not surprising, are the large numbers of American economists born in Western Europe, and in Germany, Austria, and the United Kingdom especially. There are more German-born economists in the United States than there are foreigners born in any of the continents other than Europe.

However, these absolute figures are not particularly meaningful and comparisons of the importance of individual countries as well as estimates of losses from the "brain drain" require adjustments of the raw data to some common base. One adjustment factor widely used in studies of this nature, population abroad, does not appear to be useful in our context, since the level of industrialization, historic tradition in economics and other matters are the more important determinants of demand for and supply of economists. The computation of an index of adjustment incorporating these demand and supply factors requires data not now available and could not be handled in the framework of our study.

In Table 4 we have concentrated our analysis on the characteristics of economists who are both foreign born and foreign trained, focusing on holders of the Ph.D. from the major countries of Western Europe and Canada. The greatest proportion of Germans earned the Ph.D. degree in the decade of the 1920s, implying that they left Germany as young professionals during the Hitler years and that they have been expelled rather than "drained." There is a relatively large number of British, Benelux, German, Austrian, and Canadian economists who earned their degrees in the 1950s and now work in the United States. While these data could be interpreted as evidence of a "brain drain," it is quite possible that many of these men are in the United States for a period of postdoctoral training, planning to return home ultimately.

III. *Ph.D.'s in Academic Employment*

Of the 4,865 Ph. D.'s in economics for whom we have information about their place of birth and present employment, 70.5 per cent hold academic positions. We have chosen this group of most highly trained economists, all in the same type of employment, to investigate more closely the relationship between income and the country of professional training.

Such an analysis can serve two purposes. First, it serves to reveal whether the United States is attracting the "best" people, who we assume to be those who receive the highest pay for their professional services. If the United State really attracts the best foreign economists, then their incomes should be above the average of all U.S. economists since, assuming abilities to be distributed equally throughout the world, the foreigners are competitive in terms of ability only with the best of the American group. Two objections can be raised against the validity of this empirical proposition. First, foreigners may often be attracted to the United States by salaries which appear high in comparison with their domestic ones but are actually low given the U.S. scale and their ranking in ability. Second, foreigners may be very able but have training inferior to that of their U.S. colleagues. While both of

TABLE 4—FOREIGN-BORN AND FOREIGN-TRAINED U. S. ECONOMISTS

Country of Highest Degree:	Highest Degree: Ph.D.								Highest Degree: Other than Ph.D.
	U. K.	Benelux	Germany	Austria	Italy	Hungary	Canada	All Other	All Foreign Countries
Number of observations	18	11	58	37	7	13	7	33	13.2
Gross professional income ($ thousands)									
Median	16.5	17.5	15.0	13.5	17.7	10.8	14.5	14.0	12.0
Upper Quintile	25.0	23.0	20.0	18.5	37.5	17.0	20.0	22.0	19.5
Type of employer (number)									
Private industry	1	3	8	4	1	2	1	4	5.0
University or college	14	5	35	23	3	8	6	20	4.9
Federal government	—	—	4	3	2	1	—	2	.7
Nonprofit Organizations	1	1	1	—	—	—	—	2	.7
Other employers	1	1	4	7	1	1	—	10	1.0
Academic rank									
Full professor	5	2	21	7	—	5	3	7	1.4
Associate professor	6	1	5	8	2	2	1	3	.3
Assistant professor	2	2	3	2	—	—	—	2	.8
Instructor or lecturer	—	—	1	2	—	1	—	—	.8
Other	—	—	1	—	—	—	—	1	.6
Decade of birth									
Before 1890	—	—	3	—	—	—	—	2	—
1891–1900	2	—	16	5	—	1	—	3	1.2
1901–1910	2	3	19	10	4	4	3	7	3.1
1911–1920	7	2	12	11	3	6	2	11	2.1
1921–1930	6	5	7	10	—	2	2	8	3.0
1931–1940	1	1	1	1	—	—	—	2	4.3

these objections may be considered valid for the period immediately following the individual's first arrival, they lose their validity later on, as the forces of the market tend to equalize pay for equal productivity and the foreigners make up for their deficient training through study and experience.

For our empirical test we have separated our data of 3,443 observations into four groups according to countries of birth and Ph.D.: (1) U.S.-born and U.S. Ph.D. (2,870); (2) U.S.-born and foreign Ph.D. (45); (3) foreign-born and U.S. Ph.D. (416); (4) foreign-born and foreign Ph.D. (112), and computed median incomes for each decade of birth for each of the four groups. The resultant earnings-age profiles have been plotted in Figure 1. For the middle decades a rather clear picture emerges: the U.S.-born and U.S. Ph.D. group's earnings are higher than those of U.S.-born and foreign Ph.D. group, which in turn exceed those of the foreign-born and foreign Ph.D. holders. The fourth earnings profile, that of the foreign-born with a U.S. Ph.D., behaves rather differently, exceeding the U.S.-born and U.S. Ph.D. in the oldest age groups but falling behind consistently in the following decades.[3]

Albert Rees has suggested to us the use of an index which, by giving proper weights to the number of observations in each age-income cohort, allows comparison of the four categories in a more direct fashion than does the graph. The index was computed by expressing the income of each age cohort as a per cent of the U.S. income at the same age, multiplying it by the number of observations in the cohort of the respective group, adding these numbers and dividing by the total number of observations in the respective group.[4] According to this measure, the incomes of the four categories are as follows:

U.S.-born and U.S. Ph.D.	= 100
U.S.-born and foreign Ph.D.	= 95.5
Foreign-born and U.S. Ph.D.	= 94.9
Foreign-born and foreign Ph.D.	= 91.5

[3] We need to point out that the numbers of observations in the 1885 and 1935 birth-group figures are rather small, suggesting that the results are meaningful only for the middle decades. We did not employ tests of statistical significance here since we are dealing with a full population, not a sample. Median incomes are as we report them, additional observations do not exist. Measurement error is the only source of random variation and we have no way of determining the variance due to this source.

[4] The formula for the computation is:

$$I = \sum_{i=1}^{k}\left(\frac{Y_i}{YUS_i}\right) \cdot n_i \cdot 100 / \sum_{i=1}^{k} n_i$$

where I is the index, YUS_i is the income of U.S. born—U.S. Ph.D. cohort, Y_i is the income in the age cohort of the group for which the index is computed, n_i is the number of observations in the cohort and k is the number of cohorts in the group.

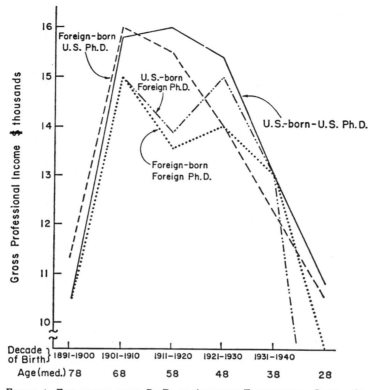

FIGURE 1. ECONOMISTS WITH PH.D. IN ACADEMIC EMPLOYMENT: INCOME-AGE PROFILES OF GROUPS DIFFERENTIATED BY COUNTRIES OF BIRTH AND TRAINING

On the basis of these findings it does not appear that the United States is attracting primarily the "best" economists from foreign countries. Also, the great melting-pot hypothesis according to which a person's place of birth has no influence on his earnings after he has been in the United States for a certain length of time does not seem to be supported by these data.

Several explanations of the income differences can be advanced, none of which, however, were we able to test any further. First, even though there is a world market for the best and the United States pays the highest salaries, other countries have nonpecuniary methods of compensating and holding their best, such as giving them prestige, power, and admiration through asking for counsel in public affairs, making them directors of institutes and bestowing official honors upon them. Second, many of the immigrants to the United States were not primarily attracted by higher salaries, but fled undesirable social and political conditions in their native countries. These motives tend to work on all people of a professional group, regardless of their abilities. Third, there may be an element of discrimination in the hiring and promoting of foreigners even by employers such as universities and colleges, which are alleged to have very cosmopolitan views on such matters. Fourth, it is possible that economists with a worldwide reputation are primarily theorists, statisticians, and mathematical economists, while those of great capacity in applied work are both less well known abroad and (by reason of their vested interest in knowledge of local institutions and situations) less mobile. If this is true, market forces would tend to draw mainly theorists and mathematicians, etc., to the United States. This situation, in turn, would explain the lower gross incomes of foreign-born economists only if it is true that "applied" economists tend to receive higher gross incomes than academic theorists. Because *gross* incomes include consultation fees, research fees, etc. from government and industry, it is not implausible that the "market" *has* drawn the best foreign economists, but only those with a theoretical specialization.

We produced an income-index like the one just discussed for groups of economists classified by the countries which granted the Ph.D.'s. The results are based on relatively few observations (see line 1 of Table 4), and should be interpreted with caution. However, they do present an interesting ranking of the value of Ph.D.'s granted by some countries.

Birth	*Ph.D.*	*Index of Income*
United States	United States	100
Foreign	United Kingdom	102.1
United States	United Kingdom	99.7
Foreign	Canada	95.8
Foreign	Austria	93.8
Foreign	Germany	89.9
Foreign	Hungary	68.1

Second, the analysis of Ph.D.'s in academic employment is relevant to the question whether the United States retains the "best" of the foreign students who have come to this country for training.

This propostion can be tested in the same way as was the previous one: The average incomes of the foreign-born with foreign secondary education but a U.S. Ph.D. should exceed the average incomes of those with a U.S. background throughout. We have grouped the foreign-born into the following four geographical areas of their high school: Canada, Western Europe, Asia, and All Other (in which Eastern Europe

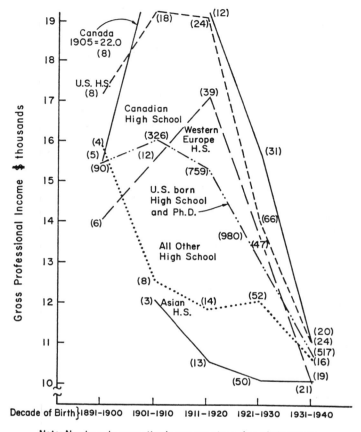

FIGURE 2. ECONOMISTS WITH PH.D. IN ACADEMIC EMPLOYMENT: INCOME-AGE PROFILES OF FOREIGN BORN U.S. PH.D., GROUPED BY COUNTRY OF HIGH SCHOOL, PLUS ALL U.S. BACKGROUND

predominates). For comparison we have also included the group of foreign-born with a U.S. high school education and a U.S. Ph.D. As can be seen from Figure 2, the income-age profiles of the Asian and "All Other" high school groups is considerably below the profile for the U.S. born and trained. On the other hand, people of all ages with a Canadian high school and those foreign born with a U.S. high school have incomes above their American contemporaries, and West European high school graduates have higher incomes than Americans during two of the decades. The numbers of observations in practically all of the categories are quite large so that the figures shown can be treated with some confidence.

The computed index provides the following summary results:

Birth	High School	Ph.D.	Index
United States	United States	United States	100
Foreign	United States	United States	111.8
Foreign	Western Europe	United States	102.8
Foreign	Canadian	United States	117.1
Foreign	All Other	United States	90.0
Foreign	Asian	United States	79.3

These computations suggest that the "quality" of Ph.D. holders of foreign birth and with a foreign high school degree is above that for U.S.-born and U.S. high school individuals for two geographical areas having a great cultural affinity to the United States and for which discrimination is likely to be smallest. The characteristics of the foreign-born with U.S. high school may be the result of well-known sociological and psychological factors common to minority groups. As for the low incomes of high school graduates from Asia and "All Other" (mostly Eastern Europe), we would suggest that they reflect discrimination rather than lower "quality," though we have no way of proving this proposition.

IV. *Summary and Conclusions*

Our analysis of the American economics profession in 1964 has revealed that the proportion of foreign-born is 12 per cent, which is about twice as high as that for the U.S. population in general. One quarter of the foreign-born arrived in the United States before high school completion, 75 per cent before acquisition of their professional degree.

Analysis by age-groups reveals that the foreign-born are a smaller proportion of the total the younger the group. But the proportion of foreign born in the economics profession is 1.1 times that for the population as a whole for the oldest age-group and is larger the younger the group. Breakdown of the foreign born by countries of origin shows that an overwhelmingly large proportion has come from Western Europe and other developed parts of the world, and only 18 per cent from Asia and Africa. Before being able to draw any conclusions about the "brain drain" problem from less developed countries in general, these data have to be put in relation to supply statistics; moreover, the economics profession may reflect only inadequately the developments in other sciences and professions.

According to the data, foreign-educated Ph.D.'s in academic employment have below-average incomes. One interpretation of this finding is that the United States does not attract the "best" economists from foreign countries, though discrimination against foreigners can also explain at least part of the income differences. The data reveal that economists with Western European and Canadian high school training who obtain U.S. Ph.D.'s and stay on at U.S. universities earn a higher income on the average than economists who were born and trained in the United States.

REFERENCES

1. COMMITTEE ON THE NATIONAL SCIENCE FOUNDATION REPORT ON THE ECONOMICS PROFESSION, "The Structure of Economists' Employment and Salaries, 1964," *Am. Econ. Rev.*, Suppl. Dec. 1965, *55*.
2. H. G. GRUBEL AND A. D. SCOTT, "The International Flow of Human Capital," *Am. Econ. Rev.*, Proc., May 1966, *56*, 268-74.
3. LOUIS PARAIS, *Immigration and Emigration of Professional and Skilled Manpower During the Post-War Period*, Special Study No. 1, prepared for the Economic Council of Canada, Ottawa 1965.
4. L. A. SJAASTAD, "The Costs and Returns of Human Migration," *Jour. Pol. Econ.*, Oct. 1962, Pt. 2, *70*.
5. B. A. WEISBROD, *External Benefits of Public Education: An Economic Analysis*, Research Rept. Ser. No. 105, Industrial Relations Section, Princeton University, Princeton 1964.

[6]

THE COST OF U.S. COLLEGE STUDENT EXCHANGE PROGRAMS*

HERBERT G. GRUBEL
ANTHONY D. SCOTT

ABSTRACT

The aim of this paper is to estimate the social resource cost to the U. S. of being engaged in a world-wide foreign college student program. The second and third sections of the study present estimates of the value of resources "invested" in foreign students in the U. S. and in American students abroad. Part IV estimates the value of students not returning to their native countries after studies in the U. S. Finally, a balance sheet is constructed of the net cost of exchanges to the U. S., and this is brought into perspective with other economic magnitudes. A *prima facie* case is made for expanding the student programs.

I. INTRODUCTION

The international exchange of college students has grown rapidly in recent years. Between the academic years 1954–55 and 1963–64 the number of foreigners studying at American universities increased from 34,032 to 74,814, while the number of American college students abroad rose from 9,454 to 17,162.[1]

There seems to be widespread agreement about the range of benefits accruing to the individual students, to the academic host institutions, and to the participating countries through the exchange programs. The

Herbert Grubel is Professor of Finance at the University of Pennsylvania; Anthony Scott is Professor of Economics at the University of British Columbia.

* This paper is part of a more intensive study of the international flow of human capital. We thank Harry G. Johnson who, as the director of a Rockefeller research project in international trade, has provided us with financial support. T. W. Schultz has given us helpful advice and counsel.
1 Institute for International Education, *Open Doors* (New York, various issues).

student's intellectual development is promoted by his contact with foreign cultures, his new social environment, and the instructional variety. The social and intellectual life on the campuses receiving foreign students is stimulated, which in turn enriches the educational experience of the domestic students. The countries from which the students come benefit both from the general development of the students and from the special skills they acquire. And, finally, the transfer of knowledge and of techniques of teaching and research made possible by the exchange programs may be very important in the development of countries now engaged in efforts of industrialization.

There are costs, however, in acquiring these largely immeasurable benefits, involving the expenditure of resources in carrying out the programs and the "wastages" arising from some students' decisions not to return to their native countries. Any rational process of deciding on the size of the U. S. foreign student exchange must therefore take into account both the costs and benefits and strike an appropriate balance between them, especially to the extent that the programs are fostered by government subsidies.

The aim of this paper is to estimate the social resource cost to the U. S. of its engagement in a world-wide foreign college student program. Such an estimate is not now available and, as we shall see, is not easy to make. The resource value represented by human education is difficult to calculate, since education has no capitalized market value and is not included in international balance of payments statistics. In addition, estimates of the cost of numerous official and private programs, such as that under the Fulbright-Hayes Act, are so diverse that it is nearly impossible to reconcile the relevant information. In this study, we shall approach the problem by using available information on the number of foreign students, their sources of support, the average cost of education for all students in the U. S., and other information which will be presented below.

One important task of estimation involves the "value" to be attached to a student's failure to return to his native country. This problem is one which not only has economic meaning, but can be measured in terms of dollars and compared with other dollar magnitudes. The extent to which the loss of an educated individual through emigration represents a loss to his country, and the precise nature of this loss, are a complicated subject, which is discussed in detail in another paper.[2] In the present inquiry we shall present two methods of estimating the dollar value of the U. S. gain from receiving an educated immigrant—our preoccupation with American

---

2   "The International Flow of Human Capital," *American Economic Review, Papers and Proceedings* (May 1966).

gains being forced upon us by the necessity of working with American price data.

Efforts have been made both by the U. S. and by their native countries to prevent non-returning students from remaining in America after their studies are completed. These efforts have not been completely successful and perhaps never will be, because rigid enforcement would require a use of totalitarian methods and a disregard of personal welfare which are incompatible with the ideals of Western culture. The alternative to such rigid laws is a continuing effort to keep non-returnees to a minimum, while at the same time considering the actual non-returnees as a part of the cost of the program, just as automobile accidents are an unfortunate but unavoidable cost of automobile traffic. Countries make every effort to keep the frequency of accidents down, but they are unwilling either to abandon automobile traffic altogether or to limit its free circulation to the extent necessary to eliminate accidents. Beyond this, however, the parallel with automobile traffic fails; for while no one benefits from an accident, the non-returning students both gain personally and become an asset to the country of their new residence, in this case the U. S.

Our use of aggregate statistics and general expenditure estimates forces us to disregard any benefits or losses due to differences in the "quality" of the foreign students and non-returnees. Though such differences may have important effects on the welfare of the countries involved, the subject of genetic and motivational characteristics is outside our area of competence.

In the next two sections of this paper we present our estimates of the value of resources "invested" in foreign students in the U. S., and in American students abroad. In Part IV we estimate the value of students not returning after their studies in the U. S. In the final section we use the data presented in the earlier parts to construct a balance sheet of the net U. S. cost of foreign student exchange. We then relate this to some other economic magnitudes in order to bring the cost estimates into perspective.

II. THE U.S. COST OF INVESTMENT IN FOREIGN STUDENTS

In an effort to clarify the nature of the annual cost to the U. S. of training a foreign student and to integrate our analysis with well known studies on human capital, we have found it convenient to distinguish four types of cost, which may be grouped in various ways to correspond with alternative concepts of cost and value. These are: (1) earnings foregone while studying, (2) direct educational costs per student, (3) maintenance and other living expenses, and (4) transportation to and from the United States. In estimating these costs we have been forced to assume that marginal and average expenses are equal.[3]

The groupings of these costs as estimates of value from various points of view are shown in Figure 1. For purposes of comparison, we show in column (1) the grouping used by Schultz and others to measure domestic human capital formation in the U. S. or in any other country: the sum of (a) earnings foregone and (b) direct educational costs. The rationale for using these two categories is explained in detail by Schultz[4] and can be summarized as follows: the resources sacrificed by giving a student an additional year of education are the earnings the student could have obtained by working instead of going to school and the services he absorbs while attending school; maintenance and other living costs are incurred whether the person goes to school or not. The loss of earnings is an expense completely borne (except for scholarships and fellowships) by the individual himself, whereas the educational costs are often borne by society through publicly financed education. In measuring the social cost of having an American citizen acquire an additional year of schooling, however, both his earnings foregone and his educational expenses are counted.

In column (1) of Figure 1 we show the types of resource cost incurred by having a foreign student fully supported from American sources attend an American university. The foreign student's foregone earnings (a) are not considered to be a cost to the U. S., though they are a private cost to the student and a social cost to his country. On the other hand, his educational expenses (b), maintenance (c), and travel (d) represent an American outlay.

Foreign students often reduce the social cost to the U. S. by paying for part or all of these expenses through remittances from home, or by working. Column (3) of Figure 1 illustrates the case of a fully "self-supported" student. We have indicated the existence of a residual cost to the U. S. even in this extreme situation because tuition charges cover only about 50% of direct educational expenditures of American institutions of

---

3   The reader who wishes to ponder the possible bias introduced by this assumption may want to know the numbers involved. In 1961, there were about 65,000 foreign students in the United States, out of a total enrollment at institutions of higher education of about 4 million. They included, of course, a much higher percentage of graduate and professional school enrollments than of general-course undergraduate enrollments.

4   "Capital Formation by Education," *Journal of Political Economy*, LXVIII (December 1960); and "Education and Economic Growth," in *Social Forces Influencing American Education*, (Chicago: National Society for the Study of Education, 1961).

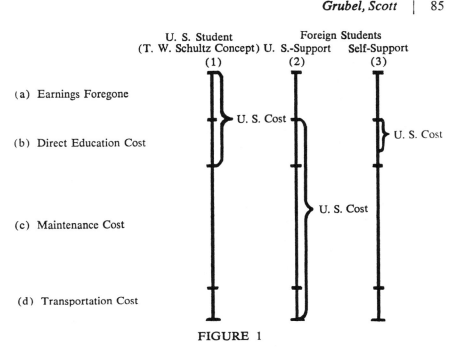

FIGURE 1

ALTERNATIVE GROUPINGS OF COSTS
AS ESTIMATES OF U.S. INVESTMENT
IN A STUDENT FROM THE U.S. AND ABROAD

higher learning. In addition, we have had to assume in our calculations that all students belong either to the category of complete "self-support" or to that of complete "U. S. support," since our source of information did not allow us to discriminate between intermediate categories.

The dollar values of the cost groupings shown in Figure 1 were estimated for each year in the following manner:

(a) *Earnings Foregone.* Since it was not necessary to estimate earnings foregone by foreign students in the United States, we shall postpone an explanation of this calculation until it becomes relevant later in the discussion of students who decide to remain in the United States.

(b) *Direct Educational Costs.* With two important modifications, we followed the method used by T. W. Schultz in his estimate of the annual cost of education per student for 1956; that is, we utilized the statistics on the expenditures and enrollment of American universities which are collected and published biennially by the U. S. Department of Health, Education, and Welfare. Our first modification was to exclude from the costs of education those expenses incurred by universities and colleges for "extension and public service, organized research and related activities and sales." Organized research usually comprises about two-thirds of these non-instructional expenditures. Our reason for excluding them is that, however appropriate it may be for such activities to be located at and supported by a university, their costs do not form a part of the expense of instructing foreign students. A part of total university overhead was also pro-rated to these non-instructional costs. As a result, our estimate of average direct educational cost per U. S. student in 1956 is about $800, considerably less than the $1,166 found in the otherwise similar estimate by T. W. Schultz.

Our second modification was to derive separate estimates for the costs of instructing undergraduate and graduate students. Information for this operation proved to be extremely scanty, however, and we were forced to rely upon evidence that the ratio of graduate to undergraduate costs for "instruction and departmental research" was 4:1.[5] We applied this ratio only to instructional and departmental research costs (which we believe to be primarily faculty salaries) and not to other university costs and overheads, assuming that such expenses are uniform for undergraduate and graduate students. As a result of these adjustments, it turns out that the direct educational cost of an undergraduate in 1961–62 was only $923, or about 42 per cent of the $2,267 cost of a graduate student. In view of the large number of graduate foreign students in the U.S., such a cost difference justifies the efforts we have made to estimate the number of students of each type and the sources of their finanical support; averages including all types of students might be extremely misleading.

It is well known that endowments, contributions, and public funds cover a large part of the educational expenditures of American universities not paid for by student tuition. In order to compute the cost of having a fully "self-supported" foreign student in the U. S. we have had to estimate the proportion of expenditures actually covered by tuition. The Digest of Educational Statistics presents median fees for undergraduates in public and in private institutions in 1962–63. We assumed that the average fee was equal to the median, and multiplied it by the number of undergraduates, thus obtaining the total undergraduate fee revenue for the year. We then subtracted this figure from the published estimate of total fee revenue received by universities to obtain an estimate of total graduate fee revenue. This estimate was, in turn, divided by the number of graduate students to produce the average graduate fee. Comparing these average graduate and undergraduate fees with our earlier estimates of the direct educational cost of graduates and undergraduates, we found that

---

5   Our chief source was estimates made by S. E. Harris and by B. Berelson, quoted by Harris, in *Higher Education: Resources and Finance* (New York: McGraw-Hill, 1962), p. 516.

the average graduate fee covered only 28 per cent of such cost, and the average undergraduate fee only 37 per cent. While these percentages correspond to the guesses made by such people as S. E. Harris, we have no independent check on their accuracy. The lack of information on this topic has made it necessary for us to attribute the same percentages to all other years in our series.

The procedure described here nevertheless suggests that in 1961–62 a "self-supported" foreign graduate student, whose education cost was $2,267, drew on U. S. sources to the extent of $1,630, while he paid $637 drawn from his savings, his family, his home government, or from part-time earnings while in the United States.

(c) *Maintenance Costs.* The third type of cost incurred in the education of foreign students is the expense of their maintenance. Since visiting students are regarded here as temporarily resident in the United States for the sole purpose of obtaining training, their maintenance and subsistence, rather than the earnings foregone because they did not enter the labor force, are the relevant measure of the cost borne by the United States economy. Students who are said to be self-supporting are assumed to obtain funds for their maintenance as well as for their fees.

We obtained an estimate of the cost of a year's maintenance by interviewing people whose administrative responsibilities include correspondence with potential foreign students and giving financial assistance to foreign students already in the country. It was agreed that the "recommended" sum needed to support a typical student from abroad was $1,800 in 1955, and $2,385 in 1964. Estimates for other years were interpolated between these two dates, producing a yearly maintenance cost for 1961–62 of $2,285.[6]

(d) *Travel Costs.* For students coming from overseas, transportation can represent a large proportion of total costs. Because the item is large, we felt obliged to make an estimate of it; but, as in the case of fees, we have no independent check on the average travel expenses of a foreign student. Our procedure was to classify the home countries of foreign students studying in the United States into regions with roughly similar air fares to this country. (After some experiment, we selected Chicago as a typical port of entry because foreign students appear to be concentrated in the middle west and on the eastern seaboard, and because air fares to Chicago and to New York from many parts of the world do not differ greatly.) It was then assumed that all students paid air fares to the United

---

6 This amount is supposed to maintain a student over twelve months, including typical transportation costs from port of entry to campus. For information on the subject we are indebted to the Chicago offices of the Institute for International Education.

States equal to the published economy (tourist) return fare from a large city in their region. For example, the fare from Sydney was used for all students coming from Oceania. Information for all years was obtained from the *Official Airlines Guide.* Because many students would have found cheaper ways to travel than by scheduled flights, our figure is probably an overestimate; however, this bias is partially offset by the fact that many students would have had to incur extra travel expenses to get to an international airport in their region. For Canadian students we assumed arbitrarily a travel expense of $100 in all years, a guess to which our final average travel cost is fairly sensitive, since about 10 per cent of foreign students come from Canada, and typical travel cost might easily be 50 per cent higher than this.

For 1961–62, our preliminary estimate of average travel cost was $848. The average annual cost depends, however, on the length of a student's stay in the U. S., which we estimate to be three years. Thus the travel cost for the stock of foreign students in the U.S. in 1961–62 would be about one-third of $848, or $283. Centering our cost in the middle year of a typical stay, we found the cost for 1961–62 to be, finally, $278.

We shall now attempt to determine who bears these costs. This part of our inquiry depends exclusively on questionnaires filled in by foreign students and summarized in the IIE publication *Open Doors.* Interpretation of this data is difficult, since the per cent of colleges covered by the survey has varied from year to year. Furthermore, within the colleges covered, the proportion of foreign students giving information about their sources of support has been variable. And finally, the question answered by the respondents has not been uniform over the years, and we have no way of knowing to what extent students who claimed to be self-supported were, for example, merely referring to the fact that they had won U. S. scholarships which covered all their costs. In the survey they would be morally justified in saying they "paid for themselves," but in our terms the cost of their education would be borne "by the United States."

In order to make the most of our information, while avoiding a spurious appearance of accuracy, we have adopted the following strategy: on the one hand, we have utilized our knowledge of the division of foreign students among graduates and undergraduates; on the other, we have arbitrarily assumed the proportion of U. S.-supported students to average 40 per cent per year. The data in *Open Doors* shows wide fluctuations from year to year, but it appeared unreasonable to consider these a reflection of actual developments.[7]

---

7 The reported percentages of U.S.-supported students between 1956 and 1964 were as follows: 41, 41, 44, 27, 26, 46, 59, 48, and 49, giving a mean of 42.2.

The numbers of "self-supported" and "U. S.-supported" students were used to derive the net U. S. costs after costs borne by the foreign students themselves have been taken into account. The latter figure came to $129 million in 1961–62. The values for the years 1954 through 1963 are shown in Table 1.[8] The net U. S. costs have risen steadily from 60 to 173 million dollars annually, due to increases both in average costs and in the number of students, as evidenced by our estimates of these factors (Table 1, items I and II).

Since the benefits from this American expenditure accrue in part to developed countries, which have large numbers of students in the U. S., it is instructive to compare these magnitudes with over-all U. S. foreign aid expenditures. In 1961 American non-military aid was approximately $4 billion,[9] so that the $129 million resource cost of foreign students amounts to about 3 per cent of this sum.

III. VALUE OF SERVICES ABSORBED BY U.S. STUDENTS ABROAD

The number of American students studying abroad is by no means negligible, though it is overshadowed statistically by the population of foreign students in the United States. In 1963, an *Open Doors* survey located 20,000 U. S. citizens in foreign institutions of higher education, of whom at least 17,000 were students. (The remaining 3,000 were U. S. faculty members, some of whom might also be studying.) The U. S. gain from having these students trained abroad cannot be estimated in the same detail as that possible in Part II above, because data on proportions of undergraduate and graduate students, sources of financial support, and length of stay are not available. In the absence of published information on these matters, we have assumed certain magnitudes for them which represent our best guesses after consulting experts and studying the relevant literature. The precise nature of our assumptions can best be explained by referring to Table 2.

Row 1 shows the number of students abroad as reported by *Open Doors*. We assumed that the ratio of undergraduate to graduate students

---

8 This time series is based on annual data from *Open Doors* and on the *Biennial Survey of Education,* with linear interpretation between survey years and with the adjustments discussed in the text.

9 *Economic Report of the President* (Washington, 1965), p. 287. If the foreign aid in the form of agricultural products is valued at world prices rather than U.S. support prices, the global aid figure is $3.2 billion. For details of this estimate, see T. W. Schultz, "Value of U.S. Farm Surpluses to Underdeveloped Countries," *Journal of Farm Economics* (December 1960).

TABLE 1

COST OF FOREIGN COLLEGE STUDENTS IN THE U. S.

	1954-55	1955-56	1956-57	1957-58	1958-59	1959-60	1960-61	1961-62	1962-63	1963-64
I. Number and Type of Students in U. S.[a]										
1. Undergraduate (UG)	20,831	21,984	24,044	26,412	27,949	27,727	29,421	31,582	34,635	40,138
2. Graduate students (GS)	13,201	14,510	16,622	16,979	19,296	20,759	23,686	26,504	30,070	34,676
3. Total Students	34,032	36,494	40,666	43,391	47,245	48,486	53,107	58,086	64,705	74,814
II. Average Cost per Student ($)[b]										
4. Educational cost, UG	676	719	777	833	856	878	906	923	973	1,023
5. Educational cost, GS	1,602	1,709	1,859	2,009	2,081	2,153	2,210	2,267	2,331	2,395
6. Maintenance cost	1,800	1,865	1,930	1,995	2,060	2,125	2,190	2,255	2,320	2,385
7. Cost of transportation	240	245	250	255	259	266	273	278	288	278
III. Total Cost, All Students ($ thousands)										
8. Educational, UG (1 × 4)[c]	14,082	15,806	18,682	22,001	23,924	24,344	26,655	29,150	33,700	41,061
9. Educational, GS (2 × 5)	21,148	24,798	30,900	34,110	40,154	44,694	52,346	60,085	70,093	83,049
10. Educational, UG + GS (8 + 9)	35,230	40,604	49,582	56,111	64,078	69,038	79,001	89,235	103,793	124,110
11. Maintenance (3 × 6)	61,258	68,061	78,485	86,565	97,325	103,033	116,304	130,984	150,116	178,431
12. Transportation (3 × 7)	8,168	8,941	10,167	11,065	12,236	12,897	14,498	16,148	18,312	20,798
13. All resources, all foreign students (10 + 11 + 12)	104,656	117,606	138,234	153,741	173,639	184,968	209,803	236,367	272,221	323,339
IV. Adjustments for Self-Support										
14. Self-Supported (Number), UG[d]	16,226	17,057	18,788	19,656	21,629	21,877	20,616	21,260	26,594	31,062
15. Self-Supported (Number), GS[d]	4,313	4,839	5,612	6,379	6,718	7,215	11,248	13,592	12,229	13,826
16. Educational cost not covered, UG (63% of 4)	428	455	492	527	542	556	573	584	616	648
17. By tuition, per student ($), GS (72% of 5)	1,152	1,229	1,337	1,444	1,496	1,548	1,589	1,630	1,676	1,722
18. Total educational cost net, UG (14 × 16)	6,945	7,761	9,244	10,359	11,723	12,164	11,813	12,416	16,382	20,128
19. Covered by tuition ($ thousand), GS (15 × 17)	4,969	5,947	7,503	9,211	10,050	11,169	17,873	22,155	20,496	23,808
V. Total, Adjusted Resource Cost to U. S. ($ thousands)										
20. Education cost not covered by tuition (18 + 19)	11,914	13,708	16,747	19,570	21,773	23,333	29,686	34,571	36,878	43,936
21. Full U. S. support (40% of 13)	41,862	47,042	55,294	61,496	69,456	73,987	83,921	94,547	108,888	129,336
22. Adjusted total cost to U. S. (20 + 21)	53,776	60,750	72,041	81,066	91,229	97,320	113,607	129,118	145,766	173,272

[a] Rows 1-3 from *Open Doors*.

[b] For explanation of figures in rows 4-7, see text, pages 000, 000, and 000.

[c] Numbers in parentheses refer to rows in this table.

[d] Rows 14 and 15 from *Open Doors*.

was 1:2, yielding the figures in rows 2 and 3. The value of a year's under-graduate and graduate education, in U. S. prices, is shown in rows 4 and 5 and was taken from our Table 1 (rows 4 and 5). We assumed that all American students abroad paid their own maintenance, travel expenses, and an annual tuition fee of $100 (shown in row 6). This assumption may be substantially correct in spite of the existence of the well-known Rhodes Scholarships and certain German government scholarships which provide American students with maintenance, etc. For such programs involve very small numbers relative to the total number of U. S. students abroad, and any errors introduced by our assumption are therefore likely to be negligible.

Given the basic data of rows 1–6 in Table 2, we arrive at the totals of rows 7–9 by multiplication. Our estimates show a steady and rapid increase in the value of educational resources absorbed by U. S. students abroad. These U. S. gains will be related to U. S. costs in Part V below.

IV. THE VALUE OF NON-RETURNING FOREIGN STUDENTS

The cost of foreign students in the U. S., presented in Part II, over-estimates the American contribution by neglecting to take account of the value to the U. S. of the students who fail to return home. An adjustment is therefore necessary, requiring the following information: first, the number of students staying in the U. S.; second, their value upon arrival; and third, the value of resources they absorbed while in the U. S. as students, which was treated as a cost in Part II.

The first of these estimates came from an unpublished study by the U. S. State Department, which set the figure of non-returnees at 10 per cent of new arrivals. The procedures for estimating this statistic are very complicated since U. S. laws and immigration statistics, which have special quotas for people with skills of certain types, do not classify separately students entering on "immigration" visas (who, incidentally, are not considered to be foreign students by the Institute for International Education) and people returning as immigrants after a mandatory stay in Canada or some other country. In the absence of any other estimates, we have used the 10 per cent figure throughout. As new evidence is accumulated, our computations will have to be revised. The numbers of non-returning students, resulting from our assumption, are shown in row 1 of Table 3 under the year in which they first entered the country.

In estimating the value of the students upon their arrival, we assumed, on the basis of the kinds of programs in which they enrolled, that the foreign students had on the average two years of undergraduate training and were 20 years old. We used two fundamentally different approaches in

TABLE 2

VALUE OF SERVICES ABSORBED BY U. S. STUDENTS ABROAD

Academic Year	1954-55	1955-56	1956-57	1957-58	1958-59	1959-60	1960-61	1961-62	1962-63
I. *Number of U. S. Students Abroad*[a]									
1. Total	9,459	9,887	12,845	10,213	13,651	15,306	19,836	16,072	17,162
2. Undergraduate students (UG)	3,185	3,296	4,282	3,400	4,500	5,102	6,612	5,357	5,720
3. Graduate students (GS)	6,272	6,591	6,813	9,101	9,101	10,204	13,224	10,715	11,442
II. *Average Values per Student ($)*									
4. Education absorbed, UG	676	719	777	833	856	878	906	923	973
5. Education absorbed, GS	1,602	1,709	1,859	2,009	2,081	2,153	2,210	2,267	2,331
6. Fees paid abroad[b]	100	100	100	100	100	100	100	100	100
III. *Total Values and Net Balance ($ thousands)*									
7. Educational resources absorbed (2× 4 + 3× 5)[c]	12,200	13,633	19,246	16,519	22,833	26,449	35,215	29,853	32,249
8. Fees paid abroad (1 × 6)	946	989	1,285	1,021	1,365	1,531	1,984	1,607	1,716
9. Net foreign contribution to U. S. students abroad (7–8)	11,254	12,644	17,961	15,498	21,468	24,918	33,231	28,246	30,533

Source: Row 1 is from *Open Doors* (various issues); rows 4 and 5 are taken from Table 1, rows 4 and 5.

[a] The ratio of UG to GS is assumed to be 1:2.

[b] Value of fees paid is assumed.

[c] Numbers in parentheses refer to rows in this table.

computing the value of such a student. In the first, called the "earnings foregone" approach, we asked ourselves what the U. S. cost of educating an American to the same level would have been. In so doing, we used essentially the cost of human capital concept developed by Schultz and illustrated in Figure 1, column (1), which holds that bringing a man to a certain level of education involves both the cost of the earnings he would have received had he worked and the direct educational expenditures on him while he is in school.

Following Schultz, we assumed that earnings foregone do not start to accumulate until after age 14, so that for our students there are six years of foregone earnings. We took Schultz's estimate of these earnings for a person in the year 1956 and derived estimates for the other years of the period by using the index of average weekly earnings in the U. S.[10] The resultant time series is shown in row 4 of Table 3.

The direct education costs for the twelve years of pre-college schooling were derived by applying a per student expenditure index for the years 1954–63 to the corresponding Schultz estimate for the year 1956.[11] For the cost of two years of college education we used our own estimates, presented above. All of these per student expenditures are shown in rows 2 and 3 of Table 3. They are multiplied by the number of students remaining in the U. S., and lead to the estimate in row 8 of the total value of non-returning students as of the year they arrive. As we can see, these annual figures have fluctuated widely from year to year, depending on the number of newly arriving students. They will be integrated with our earlier cost estimates in Part V below.

Our second approach to measuring the value of the non-returning students we have called the "maintenance cost" approach. In this concept, the value of educated immigrants to the United States is not what the cost would have been of schooling a similar American child, but what the United States saved in resources because the immigrant was educated and maintained as a child abroad before coming to America. Thus the two components of the "resources saved" by the immigration at age 20 are prior maintenance and education costs. Since our estimate of the latter is the same as that already derived, we confine ourselves here to explaining the former.

The calculation itself can be explained quite quickly. In the earlier calculation (for 1961–62) of the cost to the U. S. of investing in foreign

---

10 The index is taken from the *Economic Report of the President, op. cit.*, Table B-29, column (1), for total manufacturing. Schultz's data are found in "Education and Economic Growth," *op. cit.*, p. 65.

11 Per student expenditure from the *Biennial Survey of Education* (various issues); Schultz estimate, *op. cit.*

TABLE 3

CAPITAL VALUE OF FOREIGN STUDENTS STAYING IN U. S.

Academic Year	1954–55	1955–56	1956–57	1957–58	1958–59	1959–60	1960–61	1961–62	1962–63	1963–64
1. Number of non-returning students[a] (by year of arrival)	1,350	1,454	1,668	1,683	2,735	1,783	2,004	3,220	3,730	2,378
AVERAGE COST PER STUDENT ($)										
2. Two-year undergraduates[b]	1,352	1,438	1,554	1,666	1,712	1,756	1,812	1,846	1,946	2,046
3. Twelve years of school[c]	4,297	4,512	4,865	5,233	6,231	7,244	7,597	7,950	8,226	8,579
4. Earnings foregone[c]	7,025	7,320	7,579	7,672	8,134	8,319	8,504	8,966	9,243	9,520
5. Maintenance costs[d]	22,200	22,100	22,500	23,200	23,600	24,000	24,500	24,700	25,000	25,300
TOTAL COST ALL STUDENTS ($ THOUSANDS)										
A. *Earnings Foregone Approach*										
6. Education cost, school and undergraduate [1 × (2 + 3)][e]	7,626	8,651	10,707	11,611	21,724	16,047	18,855	31,543	37,942	25,266
7. Earnings foregone (1 × 4)	9,484	10,643	12,642	12,712	22,246	14,833	17,042	28,871	34,476	22,639
8. Total capital value (6 + 7)	17,110	19,294	23,349	24,323	43,970	30,880	35,897	60,414	72,418	47,905
B. *Maintenance Cost Approach ($ thousands)*										
9. Education cost, school and undergraduate (6)	7,626	8,651	10,707	11,611	21,724	16,047	18,855	31,543	37,942	25,266
10. Maintenance cost (1 × 5)	29,970	32,133	37,530	39,046	64,546	42,792	49,098	79,534	93,250	60,163
11. Total value (9 + 10)	37,596	40,784	48,237	50,657	86,270	58,839	67,953	111,077	131,192	85,429

[a] 10% of students entering the U. S. in the given year; from *Open Doors* (various issues).
[b] From Table 1, row 4.
[c] From Schultz; see text.
[d] Our estimate; see text.
[e] Numbers in parentheses refer to rows in this table.

students, we suggested that one year's maintenance would cost about $2,320. If the students are 20 years old, how much would their maintenance expenses total over 20 years? Obviously, the cost of a year's maintenance increases with a child's age and decreases with the size of the family or institution where he lives. On the basis of several investigations, we suggest that $24,700 would maintain a child at the appropriate standard for 20 years at 1961–62 prices.[12] This figure is considerably higher than the alternative "earnings foregone" per student discussed above. While the earnings foregone for 3,220 American students would be about $29 million in 1961–62, the U. S. resources saved on an equal number of students maintained abroad would be (3,220 x $24,700) or $79.5 million.[13]

Estimates of the total value of foreign students remaining in the U. S., covering the entire time period and following the "maintenance cost" approach, are shown in rows 9–11 of Table 3. We feel that both approaches to measuring the value of educated people immigrating to the U. S. have equal merit in terms of their logic. The widely different results may be viewed as providing us with extreme values, within which the "true" value can be found.

The U. S. cost estimate of Part II requires now another adjustment, due to the fact that the value of resources absorbed by the non-returning students was there considered a U. S. cost. Since these resources never leave the country, however, they must be subtracted from the cost estimate. The size of this adjustment will be 10 per cent of the total cost of

---

12   This estimate was actually made for 1959. It depends upon three observations: (1) a student's maintenance cost at age 20; (2) the *Monthly Labor Review* (November 1960), p. 1200, estimate of the cost of maintaining a "marginal" child in the U.S. under 9 years of age; and (3) a similar estimate for a teenager. These three figures were linked by linear interpolation and totaled for a twenty-year period. The 1959 total was almost precisely $24,000. For other years, this figure was adjusted by the *Consumer Price Index* to the appropriate level.

13   The real problem with the maintenance estimate is not the determination of the cost of child-rearing, but the conceptual problem of deciding upon the appropriate period of years. In using a twenty-year period above we imply that the U.S. resource saving should be reckoned from the birth of the future immigrant. This concept is rather far-fetched because the child cannot make the decision until he has information—say at fourteen years of age at the earliest. Neither his parents nor the United States, anxious to recruit his future services, can be certain that he will become a professional resident in the United States until about age 14 or later. Thus a good argument can be made that the maintenance cost saved should be figured only for the period during which it is *apparent* that his living abroad is actually a saving to the U.S. Without debating this conceptual difficulty, however, we can report that in order to reconcile an estimate obtained by the "maintenance cost" approach with one computed by "earnings foregone," the appropriate period for estimating both would be about 4 years— from age 16.

having foreign students in the U. S., taken *before* the adjustment for self-support. By using this gross figure we have adjusted the U. S. cost not only for the resources absorbed by the non-returning students and paid for by the U. S., but also for the resources paid for by the students themselves. In effect, the non-returning students' "self-support," to the extent that it was financed by foreign remittances, is a subsidy to the U. S. and must therefore be counted as an American gain. This final adjustment to U. S. cost, amounting to $24 million in 1961–62, is introduced in row 2 of Table 4 below.

V. THE FINAL BALANCE AND CONCLUSIONS

The various components entering into the U. S. balance on resource flows in connection with foreign student exchange were developed and explained in detail in the three preceding parts of this paper. We now turn to the task of combining them into the final balance sheet making up Table 4. All costs to the U. S. are entered with a minus sign while benefits are shown as positive entries.

The largest cost figure is shown in row 1 and represents the value of the resources absorbed by foreign students in the U. S. in the respective years and not paid for by remittances from home or from their own work. The next two rows are adjustments of this cost figure made necessary by non-returning students. Row 2 represents the value of resources spent on the non-returnees and considered a cost in the calculations of row 1, while row 3 measures the capital value of these new American citizens as of the date of their arrival. The sum of the three rows provides us with an estimate of the net cost of having the foreign students on American soil. As we can see, this figure has been growing irregularly during the ten years in question, averaging $45 million annually. Row 5 represents the value of educational resources absorbed by U. S. students abroad, and leads to our estimate of the American net balance of participating in a multilateral foreign student program. The average on this final balance comes to an annual cost of $18 million.

The second part of the table derives an alternative estimate of the U. S. balance using our upper limit on the value of the non-returning students. This figure is shown in row 3a, replacing row 3 of the previous calculation. The final balance values found in rows 4a and 6a correspond to rows 4 and 6 of the first part. According to this method of calculation, the U. S. derived an annual *benefit* averaging $16 million per year from its foreign student program.

TABLE 4

UNITED STATES BALANCE ON FOREIGN TRAINING ($ thousand)

Academic Year	1954–55	1955–56	1956–57	1957–58	1958–59	1959–60	1960–61	1961–62	1962–63	1963–64
I. Earnings Foregone Approach										
1. Adjusted total cost to U. S.[a]	−53,776	−60,750	−72,041	−81,066	−91,229	−97,320	−113,607	−129,118	−145,766	−173,272
2. Value of U. S. education of non-returnees[b]	10,466	11,758	13,823	15,372	17,364	18,497	21,227	23,637	27,222	32,334
3. Capital value of non-returnees[c]	17,110	19,268	23,349	24,323	43,970	30,880	35,897	60,414	72,418	47,905
4. Net cost of foreign students in U. S. (1 + 2 + 3)[d]	−26,200	−29,724	−34,869	−41,371	−29,895	−47,943	−56,483	−45,067	−46,126	−93,033
5. Value received by U. S. students abroad[e]	11,254	12,644	17,961	15,498	21,468	24,918	33,231	28,246	30,533	n. a.
6. Over-all U. S. balance on foreign training (4 + 5)	−14,946	−17,080	−16,908	−25,873	−8,427	−23,025	−23,252	−16,821	−15,593	n. a.
II. Maintenance Cost Approach										
3a. Maintenance saved through non-returnees[f]	37,596	40,784	48,237	50,657	86,270	58,839	67,953	111,077	131,192	85,429
4a. Net cost of foreign students in U. S. (1 + 2 + 3a)	−4,112	−8,208	−9,981	−15,037	+12,405	−19,984	−24,427	+5,596	+12,648	−55,509
6a. Over-all U. S. balance in foreign training (4a + 5)	+7,142	+4,436	+7,980	+461	+33,873	+4,934	+8,804	+33,842	+43,181	n. a.

[a] Items entered with minus sign (—) are cost to U. S.; other entries represent U. S. gain. Row 1 is taken from Table 1, row 22.
[b] 10% of Table 1, row 13.
[c] From Table 3, row 8.
[d] Numbers in parentheses refer to rows in this table.
[e] From Table 2, row 9.
[f] From Table 3, row 11.

Whichever of the two figures for the final U. S. balance one considers to be more appropriate, the importance of both estimates is that the resource cost of the program is very small indeed. Considering the high cost estimate of the two alternatives, the $17 million in 1961–62 is about .05 per cent of American imports ($28 billion), .03 per cent of U. S. defense expenditures ($50 billion), and .4 per cent of non-military foreign aid ($4 billion) in the same year. This is a very low price for the U. S. to pay for a most important part of its total aid and development effort, not to mention the more direct benefits to the American academic environment which we outlined earlier. It world-wide and U. S. benefits are as great as specialists have suggested, and if U. S. costs are as low as our final pages indicate, a *prima facie* case is created for expanding the U. S. foreign student exchange.

Excerpt from *The Immigration Dilemma* (1992), 99–127.

[7]

Chapter 5

The Economic and Social Effects of Immigration

Herbert G. Grubel

The first draft of this paper was written during the Summer of 1990 while I was Deutsche Bundesbank Visiting Professor of Finance at the Free University of Berlin. I thank Steve Globerman, Don DeVoretz, Charles Campbell, Doug Collins, Alan Jessup and seminar participants at Simon Fraser University for helpful discussions and comments.

DISCUSSIONS ABOUT POLICIES TOWARDS IMMIGRATION need a solid analytical basis to bring clarity to the likely effects of possible actions. This study attempts to provide such a basis by reviewing existing economic models which analyze the effects of immigration on output, employment, income distribution and the welfare of the population in the country of immigration.

At the outset it should be noted that this study does not discuss the effects which migration has on the welfare of emigrants or of the population in the country of emigration. This is done in order to save space and because the primary concern of this paper is immigration policies. Nevertheless, three brief points can readily be made about the problems facing migrants and the countries of emigration.

First, there is a strong presumption that migrants raise their expected future level of welfare if they move abroad voluntarily. If this were not true, they would stay at home and accept the economic, political or racial problems they encounter there rather than face the uncertain hardships and benefits from foreign residence. Second, the citizens of the country sending emigrants experience welfare effects which are analogous to those experienced by the citizens of the receiving country. All of the arguments and evidence discussed below can therefore readily be applied to the study of the effects of emigration on the welfare of residents left behind.

Third, current and past cumulative immigration into Canada are and have been large relative to the internal growth rate of the population and the total stock of Canadian born. Therefore, it is reasonable to apply the analytical structure of non-marginal flows developed below. However, the people coming to Canada represent a very small proportion of the population growth in the countries of emigration, particularly of some of the large developing countries of Asia. For this reason, the emigration flows have empirically minute effects on issues that are of central concern to Canadians, such as income distribution, the optimum growth rate and level of population and other externalities.

An immigrant has hands and a mouth

One of the most fundamental economic propositions about the effects of immigration is summarized by the idea that immigrants are both producers and consumers, or in a popular vein, each brings along hands and a mouth. This fact has two important implications for issues of great concern to the people in the country receiving the immigrants. First, it means that immigrants occupy jobs but they also add to demand for labour. When they spend their income from work they create the jobs which they fill. Second, it means that the population in the country of immigration does not suffer a reduction in income. To the contrary, the presence of new workers and consumers gives rise to the opportunity for welfare-raising additional trade and specialization among the residents of the country of immigration.

Marginal productivity theory of wages

The preceding proposition is obviously very important since it suggests that immigration must always lead to increased welfare among the residents in the country of immigration. In following sections we discuss conditions under which this proposition needs to be modified. However, because of the importance of the basic idea, it is worth considering in some detail the arguments which lead to this conclusion.

The cornerstone of the economist's model of immigration is the marginal productivity theory of wages. It states that the earnings of labour in a competitive economy are equal to the contribution which this labour makes to the output of society. The reasoning which underlies this conclusion can easily be understood with the help of the following thought-experiment.

Consider that a firm hires a given worker at a wage rate of $5 per hour. If the contribution of the worker to the output and income of the firm is worth less than the wage due, the firm loses money. It cannot pay for the capital it has borrowed and cannot provide profits for the owner in compensation for the risk involved in operating the firm. Eventually the firm goes out of business and the worker is unemployed. In the real world, firms take many precautions to avoid hiring workers at wages above their contribution to output. If a mistake is made in hiring, a worker's poor performance results in dismissal. The main point of the analysis is that competition among firms tends to assure that workers' wages are no higher than the worker's productivity.

The same forces of competition tend also to assure that wage rates are not below the productivity of workers. Consider that a person is hired for $3 per hour but contributes $5 to the net income of the firm. Word will spread about the qualities of this individual. Friends and colleagues talk about them and routine business contacts with competitors result in the exchange of first-hand information. Competitors tend to offer this individual more than $3 in order to obtain for themselves the difference between the wage rate and productivity. The incentives for such hiring by competitors cease to operate only when the wage rate is $5 and equals productivity. Often such individuals with wages below their productivity do not have to change jobs since their own employers tend to raise their wages in order to prevent them from leaving and to avoid the cost of hiring and training a replacement.

The marginal productivity theory of wages does not result in the predicted outcome at all times, not least because it takes time to establish workers' true productivity. There may also be conspiracies among employers to avoid competition for each others' workers. Individual workers may be reluctant to change jobs because of the costs and risks associated with such a move. Unions and government regulations may prevent the operation of market forces. The social value of a worker's output may be larger or smaller than the wage earned because the work or output has effects on the welfare of others which are not reflected in the market transaction. In the technical language of economics such non-market effects are called externalities. They will be discussed further below.

In spite of the many possible ways in which the marginal productivity theory of wages may fail to work, it provides the best, logically consistent and empirically supported explanation of the determination of wage rates of workers in free market economies like Canada. Most important, it provides the basis for the fundamental propositions about the effects of immigration noted above. First, immigrants do not take away jobs from the resident Canadians since their purchases create exactly the need for the jobs which they fill. Second, since immigrant workers earn a pay equal to their contribution to output of the country, when they spend their pay, they leave unaffected the income of the original residents of the country of immigration. Third, the original residents benefit to the extent that they can extend their opportunities for exchange and specialization in production.

Effects on income distribution

The preceding analysis and conclusions assumed implicitly that immigration is small enough so that it does not depress the wage rates earned by the workers in the country of immigration. In the following we discuss the case where the stock of past immigrants is so large that it results in a lowering of wages.

Consider Figure 1 in which the horizontal axis measures the quantity of labour in the country of immigration. The vertical axis measures the marginal product of labour, which is assumed to be equal to the wage rate W. The line AA' reflects the marginal productivity of labour. It slopes downward because, given the stock of capital in the economy and the ubiquitous law of diminishing returns, the marginal product of labour decreases with the addition of workers. The case of increasing returns to scale is discussed below in the context of arguments over optimum population growth rates and levels.

Figure 5-1: Non-Marginal Immigration

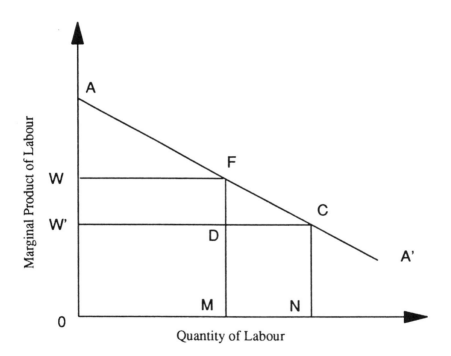

In the initial situation, the country's stock of labour is 0M and the wage rate is 0W. The total output of the economy is represented by the sum of the marginal productivities of additional units of labour and thus consists of the area 0AFM. The area 0WFM is the total income of labour. The remaining output is WAF and goes to the owners of capital. Now consider the addition of MN immigrant labour working with the given stock of capital. The wage rate falls to 0W'. Total output is now 0ACN, of which 0W'CN goes to labour and W'AC goes to the owners of capital.

For the debate over the merit of immigration, perhaps the most important conclusion of the preceding analysis is that the wage rate of the original workers falls and their total income decreases by the area W'WFD. This effect in a sense underlies the opposition of labour to large-scale immigration. This fear focuses on the loss of jobs which is the surrogate for the need to exchange high- for low-paying jobs.

The second conclusion from this analysis is that the output lost by the resident workers accrues to the owners of capital. This explains why business tends to welcome additions to a country's labour force through immigration. The third conclusion of the model is that the income of the owners of capital is increased by more than the loss of income by labour. This net gain is equal to the triangle DFC. It reflects the benefits from increased opportunities to trade created by the immigrants. It also underlies the case for immigration made by economists who focus on the increase in total output. It is clear that this analysis attaches no welfare implications to the redistribution of income between labour and capital resulting from the immigration.

Modifications of the basic model

The basic model and its conclusions have formed the views of many people about the merit of immigration, most importantly those of organized labour which opposes large-scale immigration into countries like Canada. It is based on the empirical fact that the proportion of the total labour force represented by immigrants in many industrial countries is substantial. According to Beaujot (1990) in Canada, net immigration has added about 24 percent to the labour force during the postwar years. Therefore, under the assumption that the country's capital stock had remained the same, Figure 1 is realistic and the immigrants are certain to have lowered wages of resident Canadians below the level they would have been without the immigration.

The preceding model of immigration has been discussed widely in the literature. This discussion focuses on the income redistribution effects and considers these to be equivalent to a social cost, an externality, on the grounds that welfare is lowered through a redistribution of income from labour to capital. Berry and Soligo (1969) is the most widely cited source of the analysis, though as Simon (1989) notes, there have been earlier articles by Yeager (1958) and Borts and Stein (1964), making essentially the same points. Usher (1977) and Simon (1976) used this model to estimate the size of the income redistribution and welfare effects of immigration. In essence, they made a case against immigration by arguing that immigrants "obtain benefits from capital they do not pay for, and thereby either reduce the amount of available capital per native or force natives to pay for capital to equip the immigrants." (Simon (1989), p. 143).[1]

The conclusion that immigration results in an undesirable and welfare-decreasing redistribution of income between capital and labour can be challenged on several grounds. All of these challenges introduce into the analysis essential elements of realism lacking in the basic model. The remainder of this section is devoted to this task.

The role of human capital and ownership

First, there is the question about the magnitude of the cost of the income redistribution effect in a world in which the capital stock of industrial countries consists to a very large extent of human capital in the form of education, skills and health of the labour force. An estimate by Jorgensen and Fraumeni (1987) suggests that in recent years as much as 70 to 80 percent of total US wealth consists of human capital and it is almost certain to be near this level in other developed countries like Canada.

The important role of human capital implies that the income redistribution caused by immigration largely raises the returns to this factor of production. This means in practice that immigration raises primarily the demand for and the wages and productivity of skilled labour rather than the income of owners of physical and financial capital. The wage rate depressing effects of immigration therefore tend to be concentrated on unskilled labour competing directly with immigrants. Since this segment of the Canadian labour force is rather small, the welfare effects are smaller than is suggested by the basic model. Moreover, the higher

---

1   In a personal letter, Simon pointed out that, in contrast with Usher, he does not consider this effect to be quantitatively important.

incomes of skilled workers should also be considered to have a positive effect on welfare in the views of those who deplore shifts of income from labour to capital in the standard model.

The welfare implications of the basic model are also modified by the fact that in modern industrial societies the bulk of physical and financial capital is owned by workers through pension funds and private savings. Increased returns to capital raise the wealth and income of these workers rather than those of a class of wealthy capitalists and rentiers.

In sum, the important role of human capital and the wide holding of capital in modern industrial countries like Canada implies that the redistribution of income from workers to capital raises the relative income of a very large segment of the population. However, the unskilled workers, who are also likely to own little capital through pensions, still suffer a reduction in income. Much public disagreement about the merit of immigration depends on observers' more or less subjective assessment of the welfare implications of this effect on unskilled workers. It should also rest more than it does on the assessment of the validity of the basic model from which the conclusion is derived, for there are two important modifications that need still to be made.

Immigrants bring capital

The second modification of the basic model involves the fact that migrants tend to bring along human knowledge and other capital. This extension of the analysis is shown in Figure 2, which repeats all of the elements of Figure 1 but adds a line labelled CC'. This function represents the marginal productivity of labour under the assumption that the stock of capital has been increased as a result of the immigration. Such capital growth implies that every worker is equipped with larger amounts of capital.

The size of the outward shift in the function shown in Figure 2 is such that the immigration of MN workers has left unchanged the marginal productivity of labour, original inhabitants and new immigrants combined. More precisely, it implies that the immigration induced into Canada the inflow of an amount of capital per worker just equal to the average capital per worker which would have existed without the new labour. Under this special assumption and for reasons obvious from the diagram, the wage rate of resident Canadians is not lowered by the immigration. As a result, there are none of the negative welfare effects due to income redistribution caused by immigration in the basic model.

Figure 5-2: Immigration with Capital

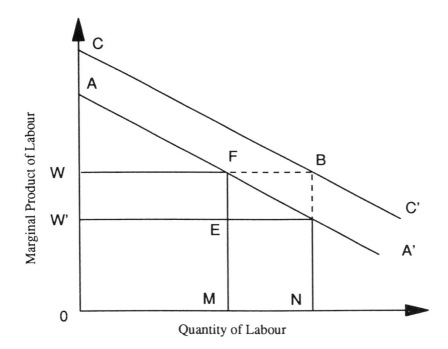

Of course, in the real world the income distribution and welfare effects depend on the actual amounts of capital brought along by the immigrants. In principle, these amounts can still result in lower wages and the implications of the basic model remain, though with less strength. The amounts could also be so great that the marginal productivity of labour is raised and there are gains for resident, unskilled workers.

There are some empirical insights available about the inflow of capital induced by immigration. Grubel and Scott (1977) estimated that the highly skilled immigrants who came to North America during the 1960s and 1970s have tended to bring along human capital just about equal in value to the average quantity of human and physical capital of a single worker in Canada or the United States. The Canadian policy which grants immigration visas to entrepreneurs able to invest at least $500,000 almost certainly raises the overall capital labour ratio in that country.

The traditional, so-called economic immigrants of the postwar years in Canada have tended to have high skill levels and some personal savings, so that the stock of capital per worker probably was lowered very little, if at all. As an example, DeVoretz (1990) has shown that the knowledge capital brought to Canada by Norwegian immigrants has raised greatly the productivity of workers engaged in fish-farming on the B.C. coast, in effect shifting outward the productivity schedule in Figure 2, just like the inflow of financial or human capital. However, for later analysis it is important to note that immigrants under the refugee and family reunion provisions of the Canadian Immigration Act are not likely to bring along amounts of human and other capital to shift outward the function by a substantial amount.

In sum, the extension of the basic model through the incorporation of the inflow of capital along with immigrants affects substantially the conclusions reached in the simpler analytical framework. The immigration of skilled and wealthy workers substantially reduces and can even eliminate the negative effect of immigration on the wages of resident unskilled workers and the distribution of income. Empirical studies suggest that this has been the case during most of Canadian history.

Induced international capital flows

The third and probably the most important modification of the basic model involves the introduction of international capital flows responsive to increased returns to capital. For analytical clarity it is important to distinguish these inflows from those discussed in the preceding section. The former are motivated by market-induced increases in the returns to capital in the country of immigration whereas the latter are tied directly to the immigration itself and would take place even if the rate of return on capital are not raised.

This extension of the model is strangely absent from the literature since in models of international finance and macro-economics, much is made of the near perfect interest elasticity of capital flows and the same assumptions can readily be applied to the present problem. With unchanged technology, constant returns to scale and an infinitely elastic supply, immigration attracts capital in an amount sufficient to keep the rate of return to investment at its initial, world level. In equilibrium after immigration and the induced capital inflows, the wage rate also remains unchanged. In effect, the capital flows endow every migrant with the same amount of capital as is used by the original residents of the country of immigration.

In Figure 2 the equilibrium with perfect international capital markets is shown by the outward shift of the marginal productivity schedule from AA' to CC'. It is due to the immigration of MN workers and leaves unchanged the wage rate at OW. In this situation, the owners of the foreign capital earn income equal to the area ACBF.

The capital inflows may be considered to have some effects on welfare. For one, nationalists in many countries object to the foreign ownership of domestic capital while Grubel (1974) has argued that the taxes paid by the foreign owners of the capital raise income in the host-country. For another, adjustments in the exchange rate may be needed to maintain balance of payments equilibrium. These exchange rate changes can involve a lowering in the terms of trade and thus a reduction in the country's welfare. However, these are separate issues, which cannot be discussed here. The most important result of the model represented by Figure 2 is that the incomes of resident workers are unchanged at 0WFM. At the same time, the immigrant workers earn a wage rate equal to that of the resident workers and a total income represented by the area MFBN.

It should be noted that the traditional model can be extended even further by considering the existence of land as a third factor of production, measured along the horizontal axis of a new diagram. The vertical axis and downward sloping function then represent the marginal productivity of immigrant labour equipped each with a quantity of capital equal to that of the resident population. In this model the immigration

110   *The Immigration Dilemma*

and capital inflow results in the traditional triangle gains from free factor movements. Most important, the usual problem of income redistribution between the owners of factors of production also takes place. In this case, the owners of land benefit at the expense of workers and the owners of capital.

In assessing the qualitative importance of this income redistribution effect, the following points are relevant. First, physical land is in finite supply on earth. However, the economically relevant supply of land services is very expandable. The intensity of land use by agriculture, industry and housing can and is being increased through the application of more and better capital. Land use for housing, for example is intensified by increasing density and raising the average height of buildings. In addition, in many countries like Canada land at the margin of economic use is taken into cultivation and converted from agricultural to other uses. Capital required for this process can be supplied through international flows accompanying immigration. The increased supply of land services affected by this process shifts outward the marginal productivity schedule of labour and capital. It thus reduces, probably significantly, the effect of immigration on the relative price of land.

Second, through widespread private ownership of housing, farms, and industrial land through corporations, the benefits of increases in the value of land are distributed widely. Losers in the redistribution of income are those who do not own land, predominantly the poor, the young and the immigrants themselves. Third, ideologically the issue of redistribution of income towards the land-owning classes does not have the same strong political bite as does income redistribution from workers to capitalist. Modern industrial countries like Canada never had an aristocratic, landed class and land ownership has always been the right and successful economic goal of people from all walks of life.

In sum, in a model which reflects the modern world of near perfect international capital movements, the welfare implications of the income redistribution effects of immigration disappear. Each migrant in effect automatically attracts a stock of capital from abroad to maintain the original wage rate and incomes of the resident workers. A further extension of the traditional model considering land as the factor in fixed supply restores the problem of income redistribution effects due to immigration. However, for a number of reasons, these effects may be considered to be less important quantitatively and ideologically than those between capital and labour considered in the traditional model.

The role of government taxation and spending

The preceding analysis abstracted from the existence of government taxation and spending programs. These programs represent one of the most important characteristics of modern industrial societies. They also are at the heart of concerns by many about immigration policies in countries like Canada. In particular, there appears to be a widely held view that immigrants raise the tax burden on residents since they are more likely to be recipients of welfare benefits and to pay on average fewer taxes than the residents of the country of immigration. How valid is this view?

Basic principles

The analysis of the effects of immigration on the tax burden of residents requires a brief discussion of the basic principles of three types of government spending programs. First, there is the provision of services which contain some elements of income redistribution but which for all practical purposes involve the substitution of government for private financing. The most important of these types of programs is education. The average family in a country like Canada pays taxes instead of private tuition to finance the education of the average number of children it has attending public rather than private schools and institutions of higher learning. The young of any generation which receive the free education eventually become tax-payers and repay their debt by financing the educational needs of the next generation. The provision and financing of government pensions involves exactly the same principles.

Seen from this perspective, the effect which immigrants have on the tax burden of residents depends crucially on the question of whether the immigrants are above or below the average of the resident population with respect to the taxes they pay and the number of children that require educational expenditures and the length of time during which they contribute to and receive public pensions.

112   The Immigration Dilemma

The second major set of government spending programs involves insurance against major hazards like unemployment, illness and general misfortunes resulting in the need for welfare payments. In the case of these programs the general principles noted above also are applicable. The payment of benefits to the average person must be equal to the taxes paid by the average resident in a country. Therefore, the crucial issue in the case of these programs is also the average propensity of immigrants to pay taxes and draw on the benefits of the programs.

The third set of government spending programs involves the provision of what is known as public goods. These consist of public security generated by the work of the police, armed forces and the judiciary. They also include transportation facilities such as roads, harbours, canals and airports for which no user-fees are charged. The basic principles about average contributions and claims are relevant for this class of government spending as in the preceding cases.

However, there is one important difference. In the case of all of the social insurance and pension programs the cost of providing government services to additional persons is near the average. In the case of public goods, on the other hand, the cost can be very low or zero. The best example of the latter case is defence. It is often cited by those who favour immigration, like Simon (1989). The strength of the security provided by defence forces to the average resident is the same regardless of the number of locally born and immigrants in the country, at least over a wide range of possible population levels.

On the other hand, in the case of practically all other public goods marginal costs are very low or zero only in the short run. In the longer run, capital projects for public goods and educational programs wear out and are expanded in response to crowding or scaled down if there is excess capacity. Since the analysis of the welfare effects of immigration should be concerned with the long run, this latter model appears to be the most relevant and we may conclude that immigrants do not provide residents with a free ride by paying for public services at unchanged levels. In the longer run they claim in services what they pay for.

Empirical evidence

There has traditionally been a strong presumption that immigrants are particularly healthy, able and well-trained individuals. The decision to leave a familiar society and face the hardships of living in a new country was not for the physically and mentally weak. Surviving the travels has tended to weed out the infirm. In addition, the immigration policies of most industrial countries during the late 19th and early 20th century reinforced these natural tendencies by refusing immigration permits to the unskilled, sick and disabled. Individuals with these natural and government-reinforced characteristics would be expected to do better economically than the average in the country of immigration. They also would be expected to be in less need of the benefits of social insurance programs.

These presumptions are reflected in almost all historic studies of the economic characteristics of immigrants to North America and Australia. There are several contributions to this volume which discuss this evidence. Nevertheless, it is worth noting here that Simon (1989) provides a summary of several studies in this tradition. Akbari (1989) has found the same for Canada in recent years. Immigrants have had lower than average incomes for short periods after arrival in the new country. Thereafter, their incomes have tended to exceed those of the resident populations, making for above-average life-time incomes. Taxes tend to be proportional to income and therefore these immigrants have tended to make above average contributions to government revenues.

The same studies also note that demands on social insurance programs by these immigrants have historically been lower than average. This is due partly to the fact that earnings and wealth of the immigrants have been above average. It is also explained to some extent by the fact that most of the immigrants in these historic studies have come from societies where traditional values of self-reliance were strong and social stigma were attached to drawing on public assistance.

The preceding empirical findings may not hold true in the future. In recent years, the immigration policies of countries like the United States, Canada and Australia have changed dramatically. Historically, the policies were designed to attract skilled labour from countries of Western Europe with relatively homogeneous cultural and linguistic characteristics contributing to their successful economic performance as found in the studies noted above.

In recent years, a complex set of political pressures have resulted in the adoption of new immigration policies alleged to be non-discriminatory and humanitarian. As a result of these policies to be discussed further below, since the middle 1970s about 75 percent of all Canadian immigrants have been refugees from persecution or close members of a family already in Canada. The bulk of these immigrants have come from countries with cultural and linguistic characteristics different from those of Canada. The economic performance of these immigrants can be studied in depth and with sufficiently large numbers only gradually, as the relevant statistical base is generated. Preliminary information collected by DeVoretz and Fagwers (1990) suggests that immigrants of the new type may have less than average incomes and have a greater propensity to draw on government programs than do the immigrants admitted under the traditional programs.

Traditional externalities

Costs imposed on residents by immigrants which are not reflected in measured market incomes, so-called externalities, underlie many of the public discussions over immigration policies. There are economic externalities like the effects of too many people on pollution and congestion and the quality of life generally. But there are also arguments about the benefits which are generated by large populations. In recent years increasing importance has been attached to what might be called social externalities. These are due to frictions among groups of residents and immigrants over discrimination and rights in housing, jobs and government grants. They also concern changes in a country's social and cultural characteristics.

These externalities will be analyzed in some detail in the remainder of this study. The current section deals with the mostly economic externalities related to population growth and levels. The following section takes on the difficult and emotionally laden subject of the social externalities.

Economic externalities—optimum population growth rates

Immigration affects the growth rate and ultimately the steady state level of the population in the country receiving the immigrants. There are several distinct types of externalities associated with different population growth rates. The first concerns the cost of government programs providing pensions, education and health care. Low or negative growth results in what is known as a costly dependency ratio. This ratio reflects the number of unproductive young and retired people who must be supplied from the output of those of working age through high levels of taxation. This taxation creates disincentives for work and investment. Immigration can be used to reduce the dependency ratio.

The second type of externalities associated with population growth involves economic adjustment costs. The nature of these costs is familiar to many from the experience of firms and similar organizations. When growth takes place, outstanding individuals can be promoted more quickly and without the need for the demotion of others. More generally, economic growth results in the more rapid introduction of new and technologically advanced machinery. As a result the average age of the economy's capital stock is lowered and its productivity is raised. Immigration can be used to increase economic growth and the opportunity to reap positive externalities of this type of externality.

The preceding suggests that positive is better than negative population growth. But what positive growth rate provides the optimum amount of benefits? We know that there is some high rate at which external diseconomies occur as a result of increasing costs from the rapid construction of social overhead facilities and private investments. In the absence of any evidence on this subject, most analysts rely on the judgement of historians who found that annual population growth rates of around one to two percent appear to have been associated with rapid economic growth without stress in Canada.

In many industrial countries, including Canada, the reproduction rate of residents is low and implies a decline in population growth during the early part of the 21st century. One estimate published in Government of Canada, Health and Welfare Canada (1989), shows that at the fertility rate of 1.7 existing in Canada during the 1980s, the population will reach a peak of 28 million in 2011. Thereafter, a slow decline sets in. After 100 years it leaves Canada with a population of about 19 million. Eventually, the population approaches zero.

The same official publication discusses the different development of the population if the fertility rate is assumed to remain the same but there is an annual net immigration of 80,000 into Canada. Under these assumptions immigration at this level does not prevent the decline of the population in the longer run since the immigrants are assumed to have the same fertility rates as Canadians have currently once they are in the country. However, the rate of decline is smaller than in the case without immigration and a stable population of 18 million is reached in the long run.

Population growth projections are hazardous since little is known about the determination of fertility rates. It may well be that Canadians would begin to have more children once population begins to decrease and the trends in the above projections will be reversed. The point of the projections is not to predict the future but to analyze the implications of recent trends for future population levels with and without immigration.

On this point the analysis is clear and persuasive. Its implications are also well understood by the public. This knowledge may well explain why in opinion surveys the aging population is considered to be the third most important factor, after unemployment and skill shortages, which should be used in setting the future level of immigration (see Reid (1989, page 10)).

Economic externalities—optimum population stock

One important problem feeding back on the choice of an optimum rate of population growth is the fact that there is also an optimum stock of population. We have seen above that with immigration at 80,000 per year the population of Canada is projected to settle at a long run level of 18 million. Other rates of immigration will result in different levels.

Analytically, the optimum stock of population is defined to exist when welfare of the population is maximized. Unfortunately, students of the question of optimum population come up with widely differing views. There is little doubt that in Canada a population consisting of a single family alone would have a low standard of living since it would have to produce all of its goods without the benefit of specialized production and trading with other Canadians and the rest of the world.

Higher levels of population bring economies of scale in production and the use of social overhead facilities. They also bring economies of agglomeration which make cities such great centres of science, technology and culture. The more people, the more geniuses there are bringing extraordinary benefits to society through their activities. On the other hand, high population levels also bring costs associated with congestion, pollution and diminished quality of life.

Because of the existence of these positive and negative influences, most people believe that there is a level of population at which additions bring gains in terms of higher productivity equal to the losses due to higher cost of dealing with crowding. At such a stock of population, productivity and living standards would be highest and population would be at its optimum level.

The widely cited and influential study by Simon (1989) did not address the question of optimum population in the way it was posed in the preceding paragraph. However, one can interpret his analysis as suggesting that he departs radically from the received wisdom and suggests that there is no such optimum level for any one country and for mankind as a whole. Or at least he may be interpreted as saying that the optimum involves such a large population that concern with it is irrelevant in the present and foreseeable future.

Simon's view is based on his interpretation of the history of population growth and the scientific and economic developments accompanying it. He believes that the growth of science and productivity are endogenous to the level of population. The more people there are the more scientific and technological knowledge is produced to overcome the problems of crowding and the scarcity of resources. This knowledge has historically permitted the industrial world to enjoy ever higher living standards. It has also resulted in great cultural achievements and higher quality of life.

Simon provides impressive evidence on the fact that science and technology have raised living standards through lowering the cost of almost all goods and services in terms of hours of labour required to acquire them, be it copper, energy or medical care of constant quality. Using life expectancy and general health as proxies for quality of life, improvements have gone along with greater population in all industrial countries.

In Simon's view, the current popular concern over pollution, global warming and other man-made catastrophes, is misplaced since progress has been made and will continue to be made to deal with these problems. In many ways, the environment in most industrial countries is cleaner and safer than it has been since the onset of the industrial revolution. At the historic and expected rate of growth of scientific knowledge it is therefore almost certain that what may be conceived to be insuperable problems of crowding, pollution and lack of natural resources will be resolved in, as yet, unknown ways by the advances in science and technology produced in growing quantity by the large populations.

Simon's conclusions may be too optimistic and are not shared by all analysts. It is conceivable that at some future point mankind will run into diminishing returns to the production of knowledge or even know everything there is to know. However, at the end of the 20th century and in the foreseeable future the prospect of this happening is not very high.

For countries like Canada the problems associated with reaching the optimum stock of population appear to be at least several generations away. This conclusion is explained by the low fertility and historic rates of immigration discussed above. Therefore the potential problems due to going beyond optimum population levels should carry very little weight in decisions about the future levels of immigration. Instead, the spectre of absolute declines in population should be one of the dominant considerations.

Social externalities

Social externalities are analogous to economic externalities. They represent effects on the welfare of some created by the actions of others which are not reflected in market prices. In the case of immigration, positive social externalities accrue to resident populations as a result of the social, intellectual and cultural enrichment of life brought about by the activities of immigrants from different cultures. The most outstanding examples are the benefits of variety of food, artistic endeavours and intellectual stimuli which immigrants from non-European cultures have brought to Canada.

Negative social externalities arise when the resident population of a country is forced by immigrants to change its culture, value systems and social structures to accommodate the new citizens. These changes are considered to be a cost. The nature and existence of the relationship between Canadian immigration and the need to make adjustments is explained by one of the contributors to this volume, Derrick Thomas (1990):

> The new ethnic and cultural composition of immigrations clearly has implications both for the integration of newcomers and for the Canadian identity. Third World immigrants diverge more radically from Canadian norms in terms of their economic, social and cultural experience than do immigrants from the traditional source areas. Many Third World immigrants also differ racially from the host population, making them visibly and permanently different from the existing majority in at least this respect. *Clearly, Canada's image of itself will change. Its culture and perhaps its social structures will also be transformed. The challenge will be to ensure that these changes occur smoothly and in a way that involves everyone—immigrants and Canadian-born"* [emphasis added].

The discussion of social externalities of immigration is a highly emotional undertaking. Nevertheless, the subject is important to many Canadians, as is revealed by casual study of the media. Certainly, any study analysing the welfare effects of immigration would be incomplete if it did not raise the issue, present some facts and summarize the different points of view.

Some facts

The type and potential magnitude of both positive and negative social externalities in Canada can readily be discerned from Figure 3.[2] Data on

---

2　The immigrants from the region "Other" have mainly been from Australia, New Zealand and the United States. Immigration from the latter country was particularly large during the war in Vietnam, when it made up a significant proportion of the total.

120   *The Immigration Dilemma*

the regional origin of Canadian immigrants are available in published form only for the years shown at the bottom of the figure. The numbers for 1956 to 1961 and 1968 to 1974 are averages. The remaining figures represent linear interpolations between the years for which the data are available. Important for the present purposes of analysis are major trends rather than precise annual figures, so that the inaccuracies of the graphic are not important.

Figure 5-3: Origin of Canadian Immigrants and Total Number of Immigrants

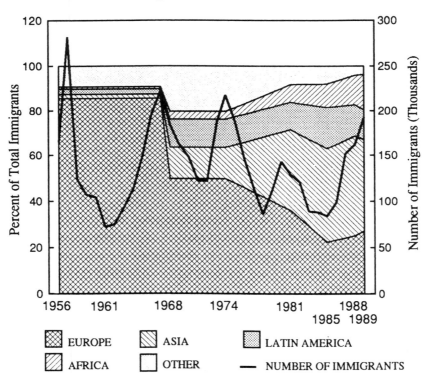

Source: Marr (1976); SOPEMI 1988 Canada
Special Tabulation for 1989; Canada Yearbook.

It may also be worth noting that the pattern of the late 1950s roughly also characterized the preceding centuries of Canadian immigration. It shows that the total annual number of immigrants has fluctuated widely between 1956 and 1989, with only a slight downward trend. Most important for the present purposes of analysis, the share of immigrants coming from different regions of the world has shown a strong and clear trend during this period.

As can be seen from the figure, during the years 1965 to 1961 about 95 percent of all Canadian immigrants originated in Europe and the United States (shown in the category "Other"). During the same period, the rest of the immigrants came from Asia, Latin America and Africa, the officially called "non-traditional" sources. The share of immigrants from these non-traditional regions has been rising since the early 1960s and reached a peak of 70 percent in 1985. The share remained at this level during the rest of the decade when a slight increase in immigration from Europe was matched by an equal sized decrease of immigration from "Other" countries.

It is important to put into perspective the influence which the changed composition of immigration flows tends to have on the characteristics of the Canadian stock of population. Let us assume that future gross immigration levels will be 250,000 per year, as was announced as the official policy in 1990, that the proportion of non-traditional immigrants remains at the recent level of about 70 percent and that immigrants once in Canada will have the same fertility rate as the rest of the population. Under these conditions, Canadians with a non-traditional family background by the year 2020 will represent only about 8 to 10 percent of the total. This result is due to the fact that annual net immigration of 200,000 represents only .5 percent of the total population. Of course, to the extent that immigrants from non-traditional origins tend to concentrate regionally, they can represent large proportions of certain areas or population centres even if they make up only a relatively small share of the total.

Problems of measuring social externalities

Unfortunately, it is impossible to use scientific methods to establish the magnitude of likely positive and negative externalities. In chapter 10, Thomas reviews the evidence which sociologists have generated. In general, such sociological studies show that immigrants in Canada have tended to integrate readily and that therefore negative and positive externalities are small and short-lived. However, there is some question about the validity of generalizing about such adjustment because in the past the ethnic minorities were very small in number whereas in the future they will be large enough to afford the construction of their own schools, places of worship and recreation and to reach a critical mass needed for the maintenance of their original culture and social value-systems.

Moreover, uncomfortable questions about the general validity of sociological findings concerning the history of immigrants' integration tendencies are raised by the persistence of problems in relations between the English-speaking majority and the natives and French-speaking minorities in Canada. In the United States, India, Lebanon, Ireland, Israel and many countries of Western Europe social, economic and religious frictions between ethnically different segments of the population continue in spite of great efforts by governments over many years to eliminate them. What have been the causes of the difficulties encountered in these countries and to what extent are they relevant to Canada in the future when there will be large numbers of non-traditional immigrants?

At any rate, Thomas notes that the analysis of the social effects of immigration lends itself to a pessimistic interpretation. This view is held by a vocal group of Canadians[3] who are urging the government of Canada to change the immigration policy such that the proportion of migrants from non-traditional sources is reduced to the levels prevailing until the 1970s and that the prominence of immigrants from Europe be restored.[4]

Persons who view the external costs of immigrants from non-traditional sources to be very large also argue rationally that if sufficient numbers of immigrants from traditional sources cannot be found, it is

---

3   See for example Collins (1979) (1987) and Campbell (1989)

4   No one knows what number of Europeans, including those from Eastern Europe, are potential immigrants into Canada. Before the opening of the Iron Curtain Collins (1979) argued that Australia faced an excess supply of immigrants from Europe, many of which would have applied for immigration to Canada.

better to reduce the overall level of immigration and accept whatever economic costs in terms of suboptimal population growth and levels this may imply. Thomas also describes the optimistic view of the social cost and benefits of having large numbers of immigrants from non-traditional sources. This view is articulated consistently by the politicians in charge of the Department of Immigration of the government of Canada. It is backed by many official departmental publications, most of which are authored by outside consultants. Most important, it is reflected in the current policies of the government of Canada.

Politics and the risks of different policies

In free countries like Canada, the government uses the political process to resolve conflicts between the views of different population groups about the desirability of certain policies. In the ideal model of democracy, therefore policies of the government reflect "the will of the people." Accordingly, the existence of the present policies favouring non-traditional immigrants implies that optimists about the social costs of such immigration represent the majority of Canadian voters.

However, two points need to be made in modification of this conclusion. First, the importance of special interest group politics has grown in recent decades with the lowering of the cost of communication and travel. Such special interest groups lobby politicians for the enactment of policies favourable to their cause in return for financial contributions and the assured delivery of votes in districts where they represent the margin of victory. At the same time, the rest of the voters are not influenced by the special interest group legislation since the costs are diffuse and often not known. According to the interest group model of government, existing policies do not necessarily reflect the will of the people as they do in the traditional models of democracy.[5] Immigrants in Canada are known to have organized effectively to lobby for the

---

5   Many scholarly works support the theory and empirical evidence on the working of special interest groups and the effect they have on economic and social policies. One of the best known of these is by Olson (1965). Brimelow (1986) discusses the relevance of the model to Canadian immigration policies developed during the 1970s.

immigration policies now in effect and some legitimate questions have been raised about the extent to which they reflect the will of the majority of Canadians.

Second, the attitudes of voters are shaped by information about the likely costs and benefits of policies. The information about the positive net benefits of non-traditional immigration in Canada are based on sociological studies undertaken when levels were low. This fact gives rise to the problem that if net benefits turn out to be negative after non-traditional immigration has continued for some time, Canadian society has to pay these costs for a long time in the future. The residents causing these difficulties cannot be expelled and reversal of the policies brings benefits only after a long lag, even if the political process makes it possible to have such a reversal. Policies which maintain the traditional composition of immigrants, on the other hand, avoid the risk of having to face the longer run costs. From these considerations follows the need to discuss whether the social benefits of non-traditional immigration exceed those of traditional immigration by a sufficient amount to outweigh the risk of the high costs associated with the former policies.

Summary and conclusions

The analysis of this study considered the economic and social effects of Canadian immigration. It showed that the economic effects of immigration on the welfare of resident Canadians tend to be positive. In Canada's market economy immigrants may be expected to earn their marginal product and thus contribute as much to output as they claim through their earnings. They do not cause unemployment and affect welfare positively as they increase the opportunity for economic exchange. The effects of immigration on income distribution considered important in the past are minimal in a world of integrated capital markets. The redistribution of income to the owners of land is likely to be small because of the ease with which the economic services of land can be augmented.

Government programs of taxation and spending can result in the redistribution of income from residents to immigrants, but only to the extent that immigrants have above average claims on services and pay below average taxes. Under the system of selecting immigrants according to their human capital and the ease of integration into the social environment, in Canada costs for the resident population did not arise. Under the new system of permitting immigration on humanitarian grounds and in disregard of likely ease of social integration, such costs are more likely to develop.

Economic externalities which are created by immigration tend to be related to optimum population levels and growth rates. While the positive and negative influences of these levels and growth rates can readily be described, they are impossible to measure and are valued differently by different individuals. Given recent trends in the fertility of resident Canadians, population growth will become negative in a few decades. Immigration levels can be chosen to obtain any desired rate of population growth and stocks. Current fertility rates and the actual level of the population suggest that by most common-sense criteria, the welfare of Canadians will be higher if immigration levels are chosen such as to assure a longer run population growth rate of around two percent per year.

Among the most important welfare effects of immigration are social externalities. These externalities manifest themselves through the possible creation and persistence of distinct groups of ethnic, racial and cultural minorities in Canada, bringing benefits as well as costs to society. Some Canadians believe that current policies favouring the immigration of non-traditional immigrants will result in positive net social benefits, others believe that these policies will create large net social costs. No universally accepted methods exist for deciding the correctness of the views of optimists and pessimists. Nevertheless, the issue is important to many Canadians and deserves further study.

One approach to this study considers the wisdom of parliament and the people who elect it to make immigration policies. A widely held view is that government policies in a democracy reflect the views of the people. Therefore, the existing policies favouring non-traditional immigrants signal that the majority of Canadians see the net benefits of such immigration to be positive. However, the special interest group model of policy making in modern democracies and the asymmetric risks of the two types of immigration policies suggest that the naive model of democratic policy formation is imperfect. At the very least, these arguments suggest that the problems of social externalities de-

126   *The Immigration Dilemma*

serves further study and public discussion.

References

Akbari, Ather S. (1989) "The Benefits of Immigrants to Canada: Evidence on Tax and Public Services," *Canadian Public Policy*, XV, 4, 424-35.

Beaujot, Roderic (1990), "Immigration and the Population of Canada," *Research Abstract*, Ottawa: Employment and Immigration Canada, March 1989.

Berry, Ronald R. and Ronald Soligo (1969), "Some Welfare Aspects of International Migration," *Journal of Political Economy*, September/October.

Borts, George H. and Jerome Stein (1966), *Economics in a Free Market*, New York: Columbia University Press.

Brimelow, Peter (1986), *The Patriot Game*, Toronto, Ontario: Key Porter Books.

Collins, Doug (1979), *Immigration: The Destruction of English Canada*, Richmond Hill, Ont.: BMG Publishing Company.

_____ (1987), *Immigration: Parliament vs. the People*, Toronto: Citizens for Foreign Aid Reform.

Campbell, Charles M. (1989), *A Time Bomb Ticking: Canadian Immigration in Crisis*, Toronto: The Mackenzie Institute.

DeVoretz, Don and S. Fagwers (1990), "Some Evidence on Immigrant Quality Decline: Foreign born versus Resident-Born Earnings Functions 1971-1986," presented at the Canadian Economics Association meetings, Victoria, B.C.

Government of Canada: Health and Welfare Canada (1989), *Charting Canada's Future: A Report of the Demographic Review*.

Grubel, Herbert G. (1974), "Taxation and the Rates of Return from some US Asset Holdings Abroad," *Journal of Political Economy*, May/June.

Grubel, Herbert and Anthony D. Scott (1977), *Brain Drain: Determinants, Measurement and Welfare Effects*, Waterloo, Ont.: Wilfred Laurier University Press.

Jorgenson, Dale and Barbara Fraumeni, "The Accumulation of Human and Non-Human Capital 1948-84," Cambridge: Harvard University, Discussion Paper.

Marr, W.L. (1975) "Canadian Immigration Policies, Since 1962," *Canadian Public Policy*, 196-203.

Olson, Mancur (1965), *The Logic of Collective Action*, Cambridge, Mass.: Harvard University Press.

Reid, Angus (1989), *Immigration to Canada: Aspects of Public Opinion*, Report Prepared for Employment and Immigration Canada by Angus Reid Group Inc., October.

Simon, Julian (1976), "The Economic Effect of Russian Immigrants on the Veteran Israeli Population: A Cost-Benefit Analysis," *Economic Quarterly*, August (in Hebrew).

_____ (1989), *The Economic Consequences of Immigration*, Cambridge, Mass: Basil Blackwell in association with The Cato Institute.

Organization for Economic Co-operation and Development (1990), *SOPEMI 1989*, Paris: OECD.

Thomas, Derrick and Strategic Planning & Research, Immigration Policy (1990), *Immigrant Integration and the Canadian Identity*, Ottawa: Employment and Immigration Canada, Immigration, November.

Usher, Dan (1977), "Public Property and Effects of Migration upon Other Residents of the Migrants' Countries of Origin and Destination," *Journal of Political Economy*, 85, 5.

Yeager, Leland B. (1958), "Immigration, Trade and Factor-Price Equalization." *Current Economic Content*, August.

102-17

[1968]

[8]

INTERNATIONALLY DIVERSIFIED PORTFOLIOS: WELFARE GAINS AND CAPITAL FLOWS

By HERBERT G. GRUBEL*

The models of portfolio balance developed by Markowitz [5] and Tobin [8] explain the real world phenomenon of diversified asset holdings elegantly and properly. The models have been criticized, extended, and empirically tested; by now their basic content has become economic orthodoxy. Strangely, however, the analysis has not yet been applied explicitly to the explanation of long-term asset holdings that include claims denominated in foreign currency.[1]

The present paper fills this gap and yields some interesting results. First, the international diversification of portfolios is the source of an entirely new kind of world welfare gains from international economic relations, different from both the traditional "gains from trade" and increased productivity flowing from the migration of the factors of production. This specific theoretical proposition is illustrated with some calculations based on empirical data drawing on *ex post* realized rates of return from investment in 11 major stock markets of the world.

Second, the theoretical model shows that international capital movements are a function not only of interest rate differentials but also of rates of growth in total asset holdings in two countries. As a result, capital may flow between countries when interest rate differentials are zero or negative and may not flow when a positive interest differential exists. Third, the analysis has some important policy implications in a growing world where monetary and fiscal policies are mixed to achieve internal and external balance.

I. *The Static Model*

Consider a world consisting of two countries, A and B, each with independent monetary and fiscal authorities and initially economically isolated from each other. Populations, income, and wealth are constant through time. There are only three forms of holding wealth: real assets, money, and bonds. The latter are issued by the government to provide investors with an interest-bearing instrument that allows bridging individuals' periods of net savings and dissavings over their lifetimes. In addition, the quantity of bonds in the market and the interest rate they

* The author is associate professor of finance at the University of Pennsylvania. The members of the University of Pennsylvania Finance Workshop have made valuable comments on an earlier draft of this paper. K. Fadner, a fellow in the University of Pennsylvania Work-Study Program, collected the data and helped with the calculations of Part II. While writing this paper the author was supported by the National Science Foundation under grant GS 1678.

[1] The importance of the real world phenomenon is exemplified by the recent report in [10].

fetch are regulated by the government in such a manner as to maintain full employment. For example, if there is unemployment, the government purchases bonds, paying for them with newly issued money. As a result of the increased money holdings and the lower yield of bonds, real assets are relatively more attractive than money and bonds and individuals try to adjust their portfolio imbalance through the purchase of more real assets, which has the desired upward effect on employment.

Assume that initially domestic portfolio balance exists at interest rates on bonds of R_A and R_B, and variances and covariances of returns of σ_A^2, σ_B^2, $\sigma_{A,B}$, where the subscripts A and B refer to the two countries and are measured from the point of view of Country A. That is R_B, σ_B^2, and $\sigma_{A,B}$ include an adjustment for exchange risk stemming from past variations in some shadow price of foreign exchange. Furthermore, assume for analytical convenience that when economic relations between the two countries are opened up only bonds and consumer goods can be exchanged so that the opening of trade does not affect the return and variance from holding real assets and money. Consequently, attention can be focused on the changes in bond holdings resulting from the opening of trade.

Before trade the expected rate of return $E(R_A)$ and risk $V(R_A)$ on the "average" investor's bond portfolio in Country A and B are:

(1) $$E(R_A) = R_A$$

(2) $$V(R_A) = \sigma_A^2$$

(3) $$E(R_B) = R_B$$

(4) $$V(R_B) = \sigma_B^2$$

After diversification a portfolio containing bonds of both Countries A and B has the following expected rate of return:

(5) $$E(R_{A,B}) = P_A R_A + P_B R_B$$

Where P_A and P_B are the proportions of bonds of country A and B respectively held in the average portfolio of Country A, P_A plus P_B must sum to one and neither may be negative. The variance of the diversified portfolio is

(6) $$V(R_{A,B}) = P_A^2 \sigma_A^2 + 2P_A P_B \sigma_{A,B} + P_B^2 \sigma_B^2$$

As the two equations show, investors have the opportunity to choose from a whole range of combinations of expected rates of return and variance by picking the appropriate sizes of P_A and P_B. Which specific combinations of risk and return they choose depends on their personal preferences, as has been demonstrated by Markowitz [5] and Tobin [8].

While the exact diversification is not important for the present purposes of analysis, it is useful to demonstrate with the help of a numerical example that diversification results in portfolios superior to one-asset portfolios of either kind of bonds.[2] Assume that $R_A = R_B = 5$ per cent. Therefore, before trade, $E(R_A) = E(R_B) = 5$. Diversification of the nature $P_A = P_B = .5$ yields an expected rate of return:

$$(7) \qquad\qquad E(R_{A,B}) = E(R_{B,A}) = 5$$

Assume that the variances of expected returns on Country A and B's properly adjusted for exchange rate fluctuations are $\sigma_A{}^2 = \sigma_B{}^2 = 10$, with a correlation between the two rates of return of $r = .3$. The variances on undiversified portfolios are $V(R_A) = V(R_B) = 10$ but the variance on the portfolio containing both assets is

$$(8) \qquad\qquad V(R_{A,B}) = 6.5$$

Thus, holding both assets does not change the expected rate of return but does reduce the riskiness of the portfolio as compared with the one-asset portfolio. By similar calculations and data it can be shown that the exchange of financial assets can lead to higher expected rates of return with equal risks and other combinations of returns and risks, all of which are superior to those from undiversified portfolios and, therefore, make the holders of wealth better off than they were without the opportunity for international diversification. The same principles apply to the residents of Country A and Country B.

The quantity of foreign bonds demanded by the residents of Country A and Country B after the opening of trade in this model depends on five primary factors. First, the size of total wealth assets held by the public: Since the variables P_A and P_B represent proportions, the absolute size of bond holdings is greater the greater the stock to which these proportions are applied.

Second, the size of the interest rate differential: Given the variances and covariance of the two-asset returns for any risk avoider, the trade-off between return and risk is more favorable the greater the foreign interest rate and, therefore, the more of the foreign asset will be held in the portfolio. Third, the size of the risk differential: For a given earnings differential and covariance of returns the foreign asset is more attractive the smaller the risk attached to it, given the riskiness of the domestic asset.

Fourth, the degree of correlation of returns on domestic and foreign assets: As can be seen from equation (6) the variance of a diversified

---

[2] The discussion of circumstances under which diversification does not take place, i.e., investors are risk lovers, domination of assets, perfect correlation of returns, etc., go beyond the scope of this paper and it is assumed that investors and assets in both countries meet the necessary requirements for diversification to take place.

portfolio is smaller the smaller the correlation of returns. Thus, given the earnings differential and variance of each asset independently, diversification reduces portfolio variance more and, therefore, is more desirable the smaller the covariance. Fifth, the tastes of the public: The combination of risk and return actually chosen from among the combinations made possible by diversification depends on wealth holders' preferences with respect to risk and return and current vs. future consumption.

Given the magnitudes of the five determinants of the demand for foreign bonds, the opening up of economic relations between the two countries is assumed to lead to a mutual exchange of bonds by the private wealth holders. Only if tastes, returns, variances and relative sizes of total wealth holdings are equal are the demands generated by each country equal. In the following analysis the empirically most relevant and theoretically most interesting assumption is made that the potential demand for foreign bonds by the residents of Country A exceeds that by the residents of Country B. The real effects of such a net excess demand are analyzed first, under the assumption of rigidly pegged exchange rates, and second, under the assumption of perfectly flexible exchange rates.

First, at pegged rates Country A's excess demand for bonds tends to depress its exchange rate and official sales of B's currency are required to keep it stable. We assume that the government of A obtains this foreign exchange from the government of B in return for its official IOU's.

When international relations are opened, the private residents of A sell off some of the bonds issued by their own government and acquire those of Country B. Some of A's bonds thus offered are purchased by residents of Country B, but under the present assumption of an excess demand for bonds by Country A, that government must purchase some of its old obligations to maintain aggregate portfolio balance and full employment. At the same time B's government issues a net supply of new bonds to the residents of A.

All of these changes in the balance sheets of governments and private wealth holders are completed a certain time after opening of international relations. The length of the adjustment depends on institutional arrangements in the bond markets and is not important for the present analysis. In the new equilibrium the excess demand for foreign exchange ceases and along with it the need for official intervention.[3] The excess demand by Country A's residents has caused the government of A to be indebted to the government of B rather than to its own citizens. B's

---

[3] The lower the risk or higher the return on bond holdings in both countries, the more likely an increase in the total demand for assets. Under these circumstances, savings will increase, causing a fall in the interest rate and requiring changes in employment policy. We neglect these effects by assuming that they are likely to be small. On the same grounds we disregard balance of payments and income problems arising from net interest payments.

government finds its obligation to A's private citizens matched by claims on A's government.

At no time between the two points of asset equilibrium did the exchange rate move and since full employment in both countries has been maintained there have been no income or price effects on the balance of trade and no real resources transferred between the two countries. The new pattern of asset holdings involves a net transfer of resources only if the interest rate on the official IOU's issued by government A and held by government B is different from that paid on the bonds issued by government B and held by the public in A, assuming equal liquidity and other service yields on each type and assuming equal taxation rates.

Second, under flexible exchange rates the net demand for B's bonds causes a lowering of A's exchange rate, the appearance of a balance of trade surplus for A, which persists until real resources equal in value to A's excess demand for bonds is realized. Then the exchange rate returns to its previous level under the present assumptions of a static world.

Assuming that neither government changes the quantity of its bonds outstanding, the net demand for B's bonds from the residents of A tends to raise the prices and lower the yields on B's bonds, inducing the residents of B to substitute real assets transferred from A for these bonds in their portfolios. There is a tendency for the return on real capital to fall in B and rise in A, reducing what *ceteris paribus* would have been the net excess demand for bonds in A. However, given the other determinants of this demand, total asset holdings and tastes, there is no necessity for this net asset demand to be moved to zero.

As long as the interest rate paid by Country B on the bonds held by the residents of A is equal to the marginal productivity of the resources transferred to B, the real income in both countries is the same as before the opening of international relations, except for the welfare gains accruing to the wealth holders from the diversification of their portfolios.

The model just presented gives rise to the possibility that real capital flows away from the country with the higher to the one with lower physical productivity of capital. Such an event occurs if the size of total asset portfolios in Country A is greater than that in Country B so that even at the initial interest rate differential in favor of A a net demand for B's bonds is created. Under flexible exchange rates these conditions result in a transfer of real resources to Country B through the process described in the preceding paragraphs.

It is clear that the welfare gains accruing to wealth holders through international diversification of their portfolios are different in nature from those known from the traditional literature in international economics, i.e., the Ricardo-Heckscher-Ohlin gains from trade and the classical gains from factors moving to higher productivity employment.

II. *Some Empirical Estimates of Potential Gains From Diversification*

In order to demonstrate the range of possible gains to American investors from international diversification of their portfolios, information on rates of return from portfolio-investment in common stock market averages of 11 major countries (see Table 1) was collected, covering the

TABLE 1—RATES OF RETURN AND STANDARD DEVIATION FROM INVESTING IN
FOREIGN CAPITAL MARKET AVERAGES
1959–1966

	Per cent Per Annum (1)	Value of $100 at End of Period (2)	Standard Deviation (3)	Correlation (R) with USA (4)
USA	7.54	178.92	47.26	1.0000
Canada	5.95	158.82	41.19	0.7025ᵃ
United Kingdom	9.59	208.00	65.28	0.2414ᵃ
West Germany	7.32	175.95	94.69	0.3008ᵃ
France	4.27	139.69	49.60	0.1938ᵃ
Italy	8.12	186.74	103.33	0.1465
Belgium	1.09	109.02	37.56	0.1080
Netherlands	5.14	149.33	86.34	0.2107ᵃ
Japan	16.54	340.21	92.52	0.1149
Australia	9.44	205.75	34.87	0.0585
South Africa	8.47	191.60	61.92	−0.1620

ᵃ Statistically significant at the 5 per cent level.
Note: For co mputational methods see text.
Sources: The share price index for the United States is Moody's industrial average of common stocks from *Moody's Indus. Manual*, June 1967. The share price index for Canada is the industrial series from the Toronto Stock Exchange Supplement Booklet No. 2, the Toronto Stock Exchange, Jan. 15, 1966.
    The share price indices for the United Kingdom, West Germany, France, Italy, Belgium, and the Netherlands are from the industrial series of the *Allgemeines Stat. Bull.*, European Economic Communities, various issues. The share price indices for Japan and Australia are industrial series from *Internat. Fin. Stat.*, International Monetary Fund, various issues. The price index for South Africa is a gold mining shares index from the *Quart. Bull.*, South Africa Reserve Bank, various issues.
    The industrial dividend yields for the United States are from *Moody's Indus. Manual*, June 1967. The dividend yield on industrials series for the United Kingdom, West Germany, France, Italy, and the Netherlands are from *Allgemeines Stat. Bull.*, European Economic Communities, various issues; for Belgium, from personal correspondence with the Dredietbank; for Japan, from *The Oriental Economist*, various issues; for Australia, from personal correspondence with the Reserve Bank of Australia; for Canada, from one published by Moss Lawson and adapted to the Toronto Stock Exchange Industrial Index, from personal correspondence with the Toronto Stock Exchange.
    The dividend yield on gold mining shares series for South Africa is from personal correspondence with the South Africa Reserve Bank.
    The exchange rates for all countries are taken from *Internat. Fin. Stat.*, International Monetary Fund, various issues.

period from January 1959 to December 1966.[4] For each of these eleven markets the following monthly observations were obtained: Indexes of common share prices (P), dividend yields on the shares in the index (Y) expressed as per cent per year, and the dollar exchange rate (X), defined as the price of one dollar. Subscripts 0 and 1 used below refer to the beginning and end of each monthly investment period; the share price index and exchange rate at the end of the current month is considered to be the price at which the next month's investment is made.

The monthly rates of return were calculated on the basis of the following considerations. The dollar price of one foreign stock market index unit is $PE_0 = P_0/X_0$. The dollar value of the investment at the end of the first month, (VE_1), is equal to the foreign currency value of dividends received $DP_1 = P_0 Y_0/12$ plus the foreign currency value of one unit of the index at the end of the month (P_1) converted to dollars at the exchange rate (X_1), i.e.,

(9)
$$VE_1 = [(P_0 Y_0)/12 + P_1]/X_1$$

The problem then becomes to find the solution value for r_1 in the equation

(10)
$$VE_1 = PE_0(1 + r)^{1/12}$$

which after some manipulation and substitution becomes

(11)
$$r_1 = \left[\left(Y_0/12 + \frac{P_1}{P_0} \right) \left(\frac{X_0}{X_1} \right) \right]^{12} - 1.0$$

A matrix of correlation among the eleven countries' monthly returns was computed and the variances and covariances were used in the subsequent calculations. Average rates of return were computed by taking the geometric mean of 95 monthly rates:[5]

(12)
$$R = \left[\prod_{i=1}^{95} (1 + r_i) \right]^{1/12} - 1.0$$

This formula, thus, computes the annual rate of return from capital gains due to common stock price and exchange rate changes, under the assumption that dividends are reinvested each month in fractional shares at current prices and that interest is compounded annually. No adjustments were made for withholding taxes on income or transactions

---

[4] January 1959 was chosen as a starting point because in December 1958 European currencies became convertible *de jure*. Common stocks rather than bonds were analyzed because of the greater variance around the average returns and across countries found in the former. The theoretical analysis can easily be modified to account for foreign stock purchases.

[5] Taking the simple arithmetic mean of the monthly rates vastly overstates the value of the capital gains between the beginning and the end of the period plus the value of the dividends. For a discussion of the biases inherent in the calculation of indices and averages see [1].

costs. It should also be noted that exchange rate variations are assumed to be the only risks attached to foreign investment. Risks on foreign investment stemming from war, confiscation and exchange restrictions could not be quantified and were disregarded. Consequently the variances used in the subsequent calculations understate foreign risk and the estimates of gains from diversification are biased upward.

The empirical calculations are unrealistic in one other important respect. Due to indivisibilities, transactions costs, and limited portfolio sizes, it is virtually impossible for anyone to hold portfolios containing all of the shares making up the indices used in the calculations. Because the portfolio variance decreases with the number of individual stocks held, the underestimate of variance available to investors implicit in the calculation procedure is smaller the more diversified portfolios are in the real world. In general, the bias may not be too large in view of the availability of mutual funds in most of the foreign markets, though more empirical information on the investment patterns, transactions costs, etc., of these funds is needed.

In Table 1, column (1) shows average rates of return calculated in the manner just discussed while column (2) shows the capital value in December of 1966 of $100 invested in January of 1959. Columns (3) and (4) report the standard deviation of monthly returns and the correlation of these fluctuations with those of Moody's industrial average of common stocks. As can be seen, the U. S. yield has been the sixth lowest, but the riskiness of the investment as measured by variance has been the fourth lowest.

Given these historic rates of return and interdependencies of the national stock markets, it is possible to compute rates of return and variances of portfolios which would have accrued to investors who had purchased foreign assets in various combinations. The most interesting of these combinations are those which for any given variance maximize the return. Portfolios which have these characteristics and are attainable with the available set of assets can be found through methods of quadratic programming, for which standard computer algorithms are available.[6]

Table 2 presents the results of two different calculations for efficient sets of internationally diversified portfolios. Part A is based on rates of return and variances of the eleven industrialized countries mentioned before, while Part B is restricted to the data of the eight countries of the Atlantic Community. The eight portfolios shown for each case are so-called corner portfolios, i.e., those at which further reduction in variance

---

[6] The program used is available in SHARE program under the code RSQPE4. It has been developed by the RAND Corporation. Finding the efficient set for 11 assets required 124 seconds on the IBM 7040. For the 8 assets the time requirement was 65 seconds.

TABLE 2—EFFICIENT INTERNATIONALLY DIVERSIFIED PORTFOLIOS

	Percentage of Portfolio Invested in Country Portfolio Number							
Part A: Eleven Industrial Countries								
Country:	1	2	3	4	5	6	7	8
United States						12.3	12.8	12.5
Canada							14.0	15.9
United Kingdom		2.4	6.3	11.9	12.0	10.7	8.4	7.6
West Germany								
France								2.7
Italy					0.2	1.7	1.7	1.5
Belgium								
Netherlands								
Japan	100.0	97.6	74.9	32.1	30.8	17.0	8.5	7.0
Australia			18.9	42.6	43.1	42.6	39.0	37.3
South Africa			13.4	13.8	15.7	15.6	15.4	
Portfolio Return	16.54	16.37	14.76	11.61	11.50	10.25	9.15	8.84
Portfolio Stand. Dev.	92.62	90.55	71.02	37.12	36.26	27.37	22.82	22.09
Part B: Atlantic Community Countries								
Country:	1	2	3	4	5	6	7	8
United States			26.6	42.9	35.7	32.1	29.5	16.4
Canada					21.3	24.9	27.3	25.4
United Kingdom	100.0	90.8	63.4	43.3	31.0	26.0	22.4	8.5
West Germany				4.7	5.0	4.3	3.6	
France						6.8	11.1	12.9
Italy		9.2	9.9	9.2	7.1	5.8	5.0	1.3
Belgium								34.4
Netherlands							1.1	1.2
Portfolio Return	9.59	9.45	8.90	8.47	7.87	7.48	7.20	4.65
Portfolio Stand. Dev.	65.28	60.63	46.67	39.76	34.49	32.23	30.96	25.10

Notes: For computational method see text.
Sources: Same as Table 1.

can be achieved only through the inclusion or omission of additional assets. The rates of returns and standard deviations for the corner portfolios are shown in the last two rows of Parts A and B of Table 2 and are plotted in Figure 1.[7] Other attainable combinations of return and standard deviations can be found by interpolation between corner portfolios, as is done by the lines drawn between the points in Figure 1.

As can be seen, diversification among the assets from the eleven countries in general would have permitted investors to attain higher rates of return or lower variance of their portfolios than they could have by purchasing a portfolio consisting of Moody's industrial average of common stocks. Which combination of assets given investors would in fact

[7] In the plotting of the data it was more efficient to use standard deviations rather than variances. Throughout this section the two terms are used interchangeably since this leaves substantive conclusions unaffected but facilitates exposition.

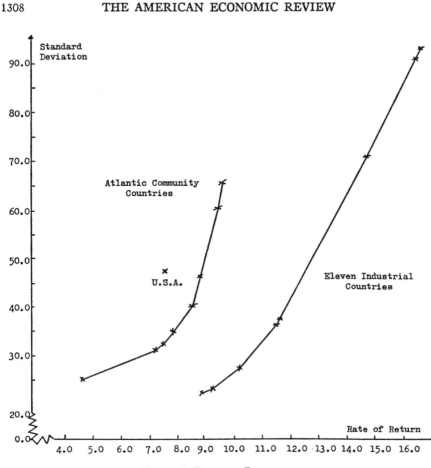

FIGURE 1. EFFICIENT PORTFOLIOS

have chosen cannot be known since it depends on their individual marginal rate of substitution between risk and return. It can be said unambiguously, however, that if an investor had wanted to maintain the same variability in return found in the New York investment, international diversification would have permitted him to earn 12.6 per cent as against 7.5 per cent, a gain of 68.0 per cent in the annual rate of return. When the opportunities for investment in Japan, South Africa, and Australia are excluded from consideration, the opportunity for gains from diversification are reduced considerably, as can be seen from Part B of Table 2, and the appropriate efficiency frontier in Figure 1. However, the increase in return attainable at the New York variance is from 7.5 per cent to 8.9 per cent, a gain of 18.7 per cent. As can be seen from

Table 2, Part B, Column 3, such a portfolio would consist of the following approximate investments: 26.6 per cent in New York, 63.4 per cent in London and 9.9 per cent in Italy.

Analogous calculations can be carried out to demonstrate the reduction in variance attainable by investing in internationally diversified portfolios with the same expected rate of return as that from investment in New York alone. Such calculations are not shown here; rough estimates can be made by inspection of Figure 1.

In general, the preceding analysis and calculations suggest that recent experience with foreign investment returns would have given rise to substantial gains in welfare to wealth holders. If past experiences are considered to be indicative of future developments, then these data suggest that future international diversification of portfolios is profitable and that more of it will take place.[8]

III. *The Dynamic Model*

Some interesting conclusions from the model of internationally diversified portfolios result from the assumption that assets in both countries are growing through time. To simplify the analysis it is assumed that growth occurs in perfect balance, i.e., that income and assets in various forms grow at the same rate r_a and r_b for countries A and B respectively, and that exchange rates are pegged rigidly. If $Q^0_{A,B}$ and $Q^0_{B,A}$ are the initial stocks of foreign assets held in static equilibrium in Countries A and B respectively, then the gross flows ($\dot{Q}^t$) at any point in time t are:

$$(13) \qquad \dot{Q}^t_{A,B} = r_a e^{r_a t} Q^0_{A,B}$$

$$(14) \qquad \dot{Q}^t_{B,A} = r_b e^{r_b t} Q^0_{B,A}$$

and the net flow from A to B ($\dot{N}^t_{A,B}$) is

$$(15) \qquad \dot{N}^t_{A,B} = r_a e^{r_a t} Q^0_{A,B} - r_b e^{r_b t} Q^0_{B,A}$$

Thus, it can be seen that the net flows of bonds between the two countries is a function of the growth rates and the size of the initial stocks in both countries. It is recalled that the initial stocks are determined primarily by the relative sizes of the two countries' wealth holdings and the existing interest rate differential.

Because of these determinants of bond flows, we have the following

---

[8] The validity of this statement depends on the interpretation of the results. One could argue that U.S. investors are in equilibrium and that the measures of risk used in the calculations represent an underestimate, which if properly accounted for would show little advantage to be gained from diversification. On the other hand, one could also argue that the calculations show the existence of a disequilibrium, that in fact U.S. investors are in the process of making stock adjustments which are taking time to accomplish. See Part V and footnote 10 for more comments on this possibility.

interesting possibilities. First, *gross* capital flows can occur between countries even if interest rates differentials are zero at all times. This is true whenever initial stocks of foreign bonds and growth rates are positive. Second, net capital flows into the low interest country (assumed to be Country A) can take place when first, $r_a > r_b$ and $Q^0_{A,B} = Q^0_{B,A}$; second, $Q^0_{A,B} > Q^0_{B,A}$ and $r_a = r_b$; third, $r_a > r_b$ and $Q^0_{A,B} > Q^0_{B,A}$; fourth, $r_a < r_b$ and $Q^0_{A,B} > Q^0_{B,A}$. In the last two cases, however, the net flow to Country A occurs only if the growth effect outweighs the stock effect or vice versa.

Under the assumed system of fixed exchange rates there are no equilibrating forces set into motion by *net* bond flows as long as the government of the country selling the private bonds is willing to accept the other country's official I.O.U.'s in the manner described in Part I. In the long run, however, these stocks of official I.O.U.'s can become very large and it is doubtful that any governments are willing to accumulate them indefinitely. Pressures for a real transfer of resources will be generated and these will bring into being equilibrating forces.

The nature of these forces can be discerned most readily in the world of perfectly flexible exchange rates, where the net demand for bonds by residents of Country A results in the transfer of real resources to Country B through the generation of a trade surplus for A. This transfer has two effects. First, the rate of real economic growth in B increases while that in A decreases. Second, the marginal productivity of capital falls in B and rises in A. Both the real growth and interest rate effects tend to reduce the gross demand for bonds in A and raise the gross demand for bonds in B. The effects persist until gross bond flows have become equalized. However, such equality does not necessarily occur when the interest rate differential is zero. The differential can be either positive or negative and gross flows can remain equal as long as the products of growth rates times stocks of foreign assets are equal for both countries.

IV. *Interest Elasticity of Capital Flows*

In this part special attention is given to the role of interest rates in the preceding models, primarily because of some interesting policy conclusions following from the analysis.

In the static model after stock equilibrium has been established bonds cease to flow between the two countries. However, the potential for flows in response to interest rate changes is always present. Thus, if for some domestic policy purpose Country A decides to lower its interest rate, foreigners will decrease their holdings of Country A's bonds and domestic wealth holders will increase their holdings of foreign bonds. The result is a net demand for bonds by Country A which leads to a transfer of I.O.U.'s to the government of B or to the transfer of real resources in the manner discussed above. However, it is important to note that in this static model the flow of capital following the interest rate change is a once-and-for-all stock adjustment, which is accomplished within a certain time period, the length of which depends on institutional characteristics of the bond market.

In the dynamic version of the model the change in the interest rate differential calls forth the equivalent of a stock adjustment flow which is superimposed on the flow due to portfolio growth. The duration of this stock-adjustment flow component depends on the institutional characteristics of the bond market, as in the static model. After completion of the stock adjustment flow, the regular transfer of bonds continues to grow at the same rate as before, but the level is different. These points can also be made with the help of the accompanying Figure 2.

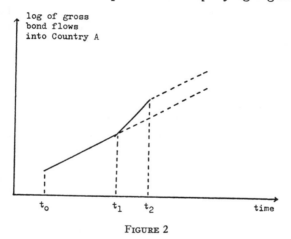

FIGURE 2

On the horizontal axis we plot time, on the vertical axis the log of gross capital flows from B to A. The line segment t_0t_1 has a slope r_a, equal to the rate of growth of wealth portfolios in Country A. At period t_1, Country A lowers its interest rate and the growth rate of foreign bond holdings in A increases, as is shown by the steeper slope of the line segment t_1t_2. After the completion of the stock-adjustment process, the rate of growth in foreign bond holdings returns to its old level r_a but the *level* of bond holdings is raised at any given moment in time by the vertical distance between the solid and broken growth lines as a result of the increased rate differential.

V. *Some Implications of the Model*

First, the classical theory of factor movements considers rates of return alone as the determinants of international capital flows. In its basic form, therefore, it cannot explain the real world phenomenon of simultaneous European investments in the United States and U.S. investments in Europe. Direct investment of this nature has been explained as resulting from the cost conditions in oligopolistic industries [2]. The present model provides an additional explanation that is especially applicable to the purchase of foreign bonds and other noncontrol conferring assets.

Second, the present model suggests that the empirical measurement of the interest elasticity of international capital movements can be improved by the inclusion of independent variables representing the growth in total asset portfolios and by studying gross flows of capital from each country. Consider, for example, the case where the interest rate differential is zero, gross flows are positive and large but net flows are zero. In our model it is possible that an increase in the rate of economic growth of one country causes the rise of that country's gross purchases of foreign assets and causes the appearance of a net flow even though the interest rate differential remained at zero.[9] A measurement of the interest elasticity of net flows would yield nonsensical results, but the measurement of gross flows and inclusion of total portfolio growth can explain the phenomenon.

Third, the model leads to the hypothesis that the large scale U.S. investments in Europe during the last decade are part of a stock adjustment phenomenon that started when European currencies became convertible *de jure* in 1958 after having been convertible *de facto* a few years earlier. If this hypothesis is correct, then there may eventually take place a slowdown in the rate of U.S. capital outflows to Western Europe.[10] However, because of the proportionately larger size of U.S. portfolios, normal growth in both continents leads to the expectation of a continued net demand for European assets. If this is so, European governments must either be willing to accept more of the U.S. government's I.O.U.'s or permit a greater trade surplus to occur if the free convertibility of the major Western currencies is to be maintained. Equalization of interest rates will be insufficient to equalize gross flows, because of the different sizes of total asset holdings in Europe and the United States.

Fourth, the portfolio model suggests that a once-and-for-all change in international interest rate differentials leads to only a once-and-for-all stock adjustment, after which gross flows return to their old levels. This implication of the portfolio model leads to an empirically important

---

[9] Harry G. Johnson has suggested a similar dependence of international capital flows on rates of economic growth in his [4].

[10] This point has also been made by J. Tobin [9, p. 168].

extension of the arguments over the proper mix of monetary and fiscal policy for the achievement of internal and external balance.

In Mundell's formulation of this argument [6] the domestic interest rate is set at such a level as to attract a quantity of foreign capital sufficient to fill the current account gap in international payments while fiscal policy is set at a level of restrictiveness sufficient to attain domestic full employment. Our model suggests that at the international interest rate differential initially chosen, there will be a stock-adjustment flow of a size that cannot be sustained beyond the attainment of the new stock equilibrium. If the external deficit on current account persists beyond this point of new stock equilibrium, then the interest rate differential has to be raised again to finance the deficit in the next period and so on until it is eliminated by some other policies. If foreign wealth holders run into diminishing returns to international diversification, then the subsequent increments to the interest differential have to be increasingly larger.[11]

Fifth, the model can be used to explain holding of foreign short-term assets as well as bonds, corporate securities, and direct investment. Continuous and growing international diversification demand for short-term assets has some interesting implications for U.S. balance of payments "deficits" under the liquidity definition. Even if the growing exchange of short-term assets between the United States and the rest of the world is perfectly balanced, the United States would show a continuous and growing balance of payments deficit since the foreign holdings of short-term dollar assets are considered to be a potential claim on U.S. reserves which the balance of payments statistics are designed to reflect. Yet, the model presented suggests that these potential liabilities are counterbalanced by U.S. holdings of foreign short-term assets and that the foreign asset demand is normal and permanent because of the continued welfare gains from holding internationally diversified portfolios. The model thus strengthens the arguments made against the use of the liquidity concept and in favor of the official-reserve-transactions concept.[12]

REFERENCES

1. L. FISHER, "Some New Stock Market Indexes," *Jour. Bus.*, Jan. 1966, *39* (1), Part II, 191–225.
2. H. G. GRUBEL, "Intra-Industry Specialization and the Pattern of Trade," *Can. Jour. Econ.*, Aug. 1967, *33* (3), 374–88.
3. ———, *Forward Exchange, Speculation and the International Flow of Capital*. Stanford, Calif. 1966.

[11] I have proved the existence of such diminishing returns to diversification in the traditional quadratic utility function [3, p. 20].

[12] These issues have been analyzed in [7].

4. H. G. JOHNSON, "Some Aspects of the Theory of Economic Policy in a World of Capital Mobility," *Essays in Honour of Marco Fanno*. Padova 1966.
5. H. MARKOWITZ, *Portfolio Selection: Efficient Diversification of Investments*. New York 1959.
6. R. A. MUNDELL, "The Appropriate Use of Monetary and Fiscal Policy for Internal and External Stability," *Internat. Mon. Fund Staff Papers*, March 1962, *9*, 70–77.
7. REVIEW COMMITTEE FOR BALANCE OF PAYMENTS STATISTICS, BUREAU OF THE BUDGET, *The Balance of Payments Statistics of the United States, Review and Appraisal*, April 1965.
8. J. TOBIN, "Liquidity Preference as Behavior Towards Risk," *Rev. Econ. Stud.*, Feb. 1958, *25* (2), 65–86.
9. ———, *National Economic Policy*. New Haven 1966.
10. "European Investors Step Up Their Purchases of American Corporate Securities," *Wall Street Journal*, Oct. 12, 1967.

Herbert G. Grubel*

Towards a Theory of Two-Way Trade in Capital Assets

The theory of intra-industry trade attempts to develop models capable of explaining the simultaneous export and import of products which are close substitutes in production, consumption, or both, and therefore are reported as being products of the same "industry." Most of these models deal with manufacturing industries. This paper develops models capable of explaining the simultaneous export and import of capital assets which is observed to take place widely among many countries during given time-periods. Some of this trade is intra-industry in the conventional sense, where the capital assets are the "products" of the financial service (or intermediation) industry. Capital assets in this category are money market instruments, bank deposits and long-term securities, bonds and equities. Models capable of explaining such two-way flows of financial claims are presented in the first three parts of this paper, building on the conventional theory of international capital flows.

In Part IV, I deal with the two-way flows of direct investment. It requires special treatment since it is not the product of the financial intermediation industry as is trade in financial claims. Yet, the simultaneous export and import of claims on real assets requires extension of conventional international capital flow theory just like the trade in financial claims. Moreover, there is the added "curious" phenomenon that the exchange of claims on real assets between two countries may involve claims on production facilities manufacturing goods that are close substitutes in production, consumption, or both. In this case we have what may be called "intra-industry trade in assets," as contrasted with "intra-financial-intermediation industry trade in assets," which is discussed in the first three parts of the paper[1].

Unfortunately, because of resource- and time-constraints I have been unable to document precisely the magnitude of two-way flows in capital

---

*Comments by participants at the conference have helped me improve this paper.

[1] In the first draft the paper carried the title "Intra-Industry Trade in Capital Assets," which evoked much criticism from conference commentators. For this reason I have chosen the new title and introduced the analytical distinction between two-way flows of financial claims and real assets.

assets in the world, even though data for such calculations are readily available. Instead, I can only report generally that the casual inspec-tion of the data reveals the existence of two-way trade in assets to be a widespread phenomenon. More precisely, reporting only one coun-try's record, the statistics show that in 1976 Germany's private long-term liabilities and assets increased by SDR millions 4,030 and 6,047, respectively[1]. At the same time, government long-term asset hold-ings increased by SDR millions 1,890. The index of intra-industry trade in long-term assets implicit in these figures and calculated on the basis of the familiar formula $B = 1.0 - |X-M| / (X+M)$ is equal to 0.99.[2] In the same year 1976 the overall absolute value of German short-term capital exports minus imports, private, official and in-cluding errors and omissions came to a net of SDR millions 324, while the sum of exports and imports came to SDR millions 7,092, giving rise to an index of intra-industry trade of 0.95.

While indices of two-way trade in capital assets for all countries and years are not always as high as the two cited for Germany in 1976, the existence of any level of two-way trade in these assets appears to deserve close analytical scrutinizing. This is so since the most wide-ly used basic models of the motives for and welfare effects of inter-national capital flows treat capital as a very homogeneous factor of production which moves from countries with low interest rates and capital productivity to those in which interest rates and productivity are high, but never in both directions.

The models to be presented and capable of explaining two-way trade in assets have been developed for other purposes of analysis and are widely known. My contribution here lies in applying them explicitly to explain motives and welfare effects of two-way flows in assets. These models do not reduce the heuristic value of the traditional, basic model of international capital flows. Instead, they are intended to enrich the basic, available theory, make it more realistic and call attention to the empirical importance of uncertainty and certain types of economies of scale, which the traditional theory assumes away. As

---

[1] These data are from IMF [1978, p. 8]. It is my understanding that the data shown reflect net changes in stocks of a country's indebtedness in the category of assets specified. In other words: in a given time-period foreign investors typically both buy and sell German long-term assets. The figure for capital import shows only the net change in the foreign ownership of these German assets. By analogy the German ownership of foreign long-term assets shown is the net of gross German purchases and sales.

[2] The properties of this index have been developed in Grubel, Lloyd [1975].

all analytical refinements of this sort, the benefits are acquired at the cost of considerable complication of the arguments, less rigor and uniqueness of predicted events and welfare effects.

The paper discusses as analytically distinct explanations of two-way trade in assets, first, speculation, second, international short-term arbitrage, third, international diversification and finally, theories of direct foreign investment. The paper closes with a summary and conclusion.

I. Speculation

One of the simplest explanations of the recorded simultaneous import and export of capital assets arises from speculation under two different circumstances. First, in a given time-period some speculators interpret events and trends as favoring the purchase of a given country's assets, while other speculators interpreting the same fact reach the conclusion that profits can be had by selling that country's assets. It is obvious that under these conditions statistics will show the observed two-way flow of capital for one country.

Second, it is possible that in one period conditions overwhelmingly favor the speculative purchases of a country's assets while in a subsequent period the determinants of speculative expectations are reversed and that same country's assets are sold. If during the period covered by the balance of payments statistics the stock of assets purchased under one set of expectations has not been liquidated, then it is possible for the statistics to show the kind of two-way capital flow under consideration here.

I do not know how quantitatively important this explanation of intra-industry trade in assets is. On the one hand, speculators are known often to form divergent views about future events, but gross figures on foreign exchange transactions are impossible to obtain. For most purposes of analysis it is net flows anyway which are of interest to policy makers and they are most apparent from the behavior of foreign exchange rates or international reserves.

The welfare effects of speculation have been discussed widely in the economics literature. It may be safe to conclude from this analysis that while the theoretical arguments are clear, it has proved to be impossible to conclude whether actual speculative episodes have increased or decreased welfare. For this reason it is also impossible to know whether intra-industry trade in assets motivated by specula-

74

tion has raised or lowered welfare in specific episodes or even on average.

II. International Short-Term Capital Arbitrage

In recent years the developments of Euro-currency markets and of a global network of multinational banks have led to the worldwide arbitrage of short-term capital funds which has been compared to the arbitrage operations of the U.S. federal funds market[1]. It enables banks and other wealthholders to lend and borrow funds on very short notice and for very short time-periods, such as a day. As such, the market makes it possible for banks to avoid the costs of being temporarily short of liquidity or central bank minimum reserves which otherwise would lead to costly portfolio readjustments or outright penalties. At the same time, lenders of these funds enjoy higher returns than they would from similar placements in purely domestic markets.

This simultaneous advantage for short-term borrowers and lenders in this market as compared with domestic markets is due to the great efficiency of the Euro-currency markets and multinational banks[2]. In this market, operations are free from taxation implicit in minimum reserve deposits and domestic exchange controls. At the same time, the banks enjoy lower operating costs because of economies of scale in dealing only with large customers and because they draw at low marginal cost on knowledge capital about the credit conditions of lenders and borrowers which the banking organisations have accumulated in the context of other business dealings.

For the present purposes of analysis the importance of the global short-term capital arbitrage arises from the following two possibilities. First, some banks within a given country may require funds while others have funds to invest within the same time-period. The efficiency of the Euro-currency market is so great that the different requirements of these domestic banks are satisfied on occasion through international channels rather than through arbitrage within the same country and the balance of payments statistics show a two-way flow of capital. Second, a country's banks may be borrowers from the international market during one period and lenders during another. If the asset holdings are not liquidated immediately upon

---

[1] This analogy has been made forcefully in the article "Stateless Money: A New Force in World Economy" [Business Week 1978].

[2] I have elaborated on these points in Grubel [1977].

reversal of the market conditions, perhaps because of transactions costs or for reasons of liquidity and portfolio balance, then it is possible for a balance of payments record covering the two periods to show growth in both foreign assets and liabilities.

The welfare effects of two-way trade in short-term assets due to the international money market arbitrage are difficult to assess. This is so because it is impossible to discover empirically whether the development of the markets is due to the avoidance of existing government regulations or whether it is based on genuine sources of comparative advantage developed as a result of recent changes in telecommunications technology. If Euro-currency markets and multinational banks were due solely to the advantages caused by the avoidance of national government regulations and taxes, then the problem of the second-best and distortions would arise. On the other hand, if these institutions predominantly exploited true economic sources of comparative advantage, then the global increase in the velocity of circulation of money would reflect a clear gain in efficiency. I suspect that probably both explanations of the causes of the global arbitrage business are valid and that, therefore, no clear conclusions about welfare effects can be reached.

In conclusion it should also be noted that the arbitrage operations may be considered to be interfering with national monetary sovereignty, increasing the difficulties encountered by national governments in their pursuit of Keynesian stabilization policies or potentially adding to the instability of exchange rates. Evaluation of the welfare cost of these influences depends on judgements about the wisdom and abilities of Keynesian policy makers and about the likelihood and cost of exchange rate instabilities caused by global short-term capital arbitrage.

III. Diversification of Security Portfolios

The theory of optimal portfolio choice in a world of uncertainty has been one of the great growth-industries in economics and finance during the last twenty years. While most of the theoretical and empirical breakthroughs in this field of study are based on the closed-economies model, basic principles of portfolio theory have been applied with some success to the explanation of international portfolio investment[1] and

---

[1] One of the first attempts in this field has been my "Internationally Diversified Portfolios: Welfare Gains and Capital Flows" [Grubel 1968]. Since then, many other studies have been published, extending the theory and

the theory of direct investment. In this section I discuss how the application of portfolio theory to investment in equities and money market paper can explain two-way flows of capital. Diversification as a motive for direct investment is discussed in Part IV.

According to the well developed and tested domestic portfolio theory, holding a maximally diversified portfolio containing the value-weighted stock-market average of a closed economy leaves investors with a minimum, non-diversifiable instability in earnings associated with the earnings level of this representative portfolio. The combination of subsets of assets available in that closed economy permits individual wealthholders only to trade off risk and return, forcing them to accept a higher risk if they wish to achieve a higher average return or permitting a lower return with lower risk. The main reason for this state of affairs is that in a closed economy the earnings of all equities are subject to sets of common, non-diversifiable macro-economic influences of the country, consisting of random shocks, such as bad harvests, business cycles and government policies[1].

In principle, the benefits from the international diversification of equity portfolios are due to the fact that foreign equities are subject to different macro-economic influences on their earnings than are domestic assets. As a result, the inclusion of foreign assets in domestic portfolios permits wealthholders to increase earnings without having to accept higher risk, to lower risk without having to decrease earnings, or to achieve both higher earnings and lower risk, as compared with the results attainable from optimal diversification within a closed economy alone.

These benefits from international portfolio diversification are available to residents of all countries. As a result, the residents of a given country can be observed to purchase foreign securities at the same time as foreign wealthholders purchase that country's securities. Modelling such a process of two-way capital flows, one can assume either that institutional barriers to the purchase of foreign securities have been removed, or that portfolios grow in absolute size and the maintenance of optimal diversification requires that foreign asset holdings grow at the same rate as the entire portfolio, holding all else constant.

---

empirical evidence. For example, Agmon, Lessard [1977], which contains additional references.

[1] This analysis is now contained in textbooks in Finance. For example, Weston, Brigham [1978, Ch. 19]. In this text can also be found references to the journal literature on the subject.

The preceding model can be made more realistic by considering that in the real world goods and capital arbitrage across countries has increased the correlation of fluctuations in earnings of all countries and therefore reduced the benefits from international diversification. However, as long as this arbitrage is not perfect, governments have the ability to pursue independent macro-economic policies and the frequency and magnitude of business cycles remain different in individual countries. Furthermore, random shocks to economies caused by nature, endogenous political developments and unforeseen changes in tastes and technology will give rise to regionally different earnings instabilities and, therefore, to benefits from international portfolio diversification even if goods and capital arbitrage were perfect.

For our purposes the main conclusion reached by the analysis of the benefits from the international diversification of portfolios is that they can give rise to the simultaneous export and import of otherwise perfectly homogeneous equities.

Portfolio diversification benefits have been shown to be available also to the managers of short-term assets and liabilities, as contrasted with the equity portfolios just discussed[1]. The benefits from this sort of activity have become particularly great since the increased exchange rate fluctuations after 1971. Managers of these short-term asset and liability portfolios of multinational enterprises especially have found that they can reduce the instability of earnings and balance sheet values expressed in the currencies of the countries in which they have to present their reports of consolidated global conditions to stockholders. This reduction in instability is achieved by selecting a judicious mix of loans and investments in different currencies. Part of this behavior is related to expected exchange rate changes, but part of it is simply defensive. One such defensive strategy is to match the value of assets and liabilities in the same currency, so that any exchange rate change leads to equi-proportionate changes on both sides of the balance sheet, leaving net worth unchanged.

The two-way flow of short-term capital arises simply from the fact that such diversification policies are pursued by firms in all countries. Furthermore, it is not unusual that a firm in one country balances its portfolio through short-term lending of sterling in London while another firm in the same country borrows sterling in London.

---

[1] For a description of business strategies based on this motive see Business Week [1978].

The welfare effects of portfolio diversification are well known from portfolio theory. They are based on the view that risk represents a disutility for wealthholders, so that any reduction in risk gained by international diversification increases the utility wealthholders derive from their holdings. It is not known how big these welfare gains have been, but judging from the magnitude of the international trade in equities and the rapid growth of the Euro-dollar business, large gains undoubtedly have taken place. Intra-industry trade in assets motivated by the desire to diversify wealthholdings reflects an unambiguous increase in welfare to wealthholders. Against these private gains should be set some negative externalities due to the economic and exchange rate instabilities which the shifts of Euro-currencies have caused. The assessment of these welfare effects is extremely difficult and the general comments made above in the context of global arbitrage apply here.

IV. Direct Foreign Investment

Direct foreign investment has been of very great empirical and political significance in recent years. Economic theorizing about the phenomenon has led to a large body of knowledge that has made it possible to assess the causes and welfare effects of direct investment.

While I have not made an empirical study, I would pass the intuitive judgement that the two-way flow of direct investment is responsible for most of the observed large intra-industry trade in overall long-term capital accounts. In the following I will sketch briefly the three main categories of motives for direct foreign investment which are found in the literature, showing how they give rise to the two-way flows under discussion here. For the sake of continuity of the analysis I will start with the diversification and exchange risk motives, even though they have a shorter history and possibly are less widely accepted than are the two other explanations based on the concept of scale economies in differentiated product markets and of the internalization of economies external to the firm.

Diversification

Rugman [1979] has argued theoretically and shown empirically that the earnings of multinational enterprises are more stable through time the more diversified their operations are internationally. Rugman's analysis emphasizes the diversification benefits derived from regionally different influences on firms' costs of production. These cost-differences arise from localized random shocks affecting the availability and cost of non-traded factors of production so that, even in a world in which goods arbitrage is perfect, fixed investment in different parts of the world has different patterns of profitability through time. As a result of more stable earnings, internationally diversified enterprises are valued more highly in the stock-market[1] than are non-diversified ones. The theory therefore explains why firms' managers have incentives to establish factories abroad, and since the incentives operate on firms in all countries, this theory provides an explanation for two-way flows in direct investment projects[2].

Differential Pricing of Exchange Risk

Aliber [1970; 1971] has argued that investors' evaluation of the risk of change of a given country's currency affects the capitalization rate they attach to earnings streams denominated in that currency. For example, if the dollar is expected to increase in value, dollar denominated assets are acceptable to investors at a lower nominal yield than are assets denominated in currencies expected to depreciate or retain their exchange value. As a result of such disequilibrium conditions, U.S. firms can borrow dollars more cheaply than their competitors and use these funds to establish direct investment facilities abroad. Under Aliber's theory, two-way flows of direct investment take place when investors' valuation of exchange risk is reversed[3].

---

[1] For evidence on this point see Agmon, Lessard [1977].

[2] However, I can see a theoretical argument similar to that made by Modigliani and Miller about the effects of leverage on the value of firms which would at the pure theory level invalidate Rugman's conclusions. The argument is that individual wealthholders can purchase foreign equities and attain the same level of international diversification as does the firm undertaking the direct investment, presumably at a lower cost than the firm. Consequently, increased firm values due to direct international investment represent a disequilibrium which private wealthholders can arbitrage away. However, as in the Modigliani-Miller analysis, the existence of taxes, transactions costs, indivisibilities and market imperfections probably can explain that direct investment is rational.

[3] This point was made by Kindleberger in his introduction to the volume he edited and in which Aliber's paper appeared. Both Kindleberger and Dunning in comments on Aliber's papers in the two respective volumes question the empirical importance of exchange risk valuation as a motive for direct foreign investment in the real world.

80

Scale Economies and External Economies

The most widely accepted theories of international direct foreign investment are by Kindleberger [1969], Caves [1971] and Johnson [1970]. In these theories, one line of arguments stresses the benefits accruing to a firm from using abroad knowledge capital in the form of product designs, technologies, advertising programs and management control techniques which were developed originally for domestic purposes and which can be used at low marginal cost abroad. The oligopolistic nature of the markets in which these firms operate makes it technically and strategically impossible for markets for this knowledge capital to exist. As a result of this specific nature of knowledge capital and the structure of the markets in which these firms operate, it pays to operate foreign subsidiaries.

A second line of argument in the theory of direct foreign investment stresses the incentives created by the existence of external economies which can be internalized through the acquisition of foreign firms. Typical of such externalities are the benefits to be had in terms of lower operating costs or greater assurance of supply which result from the vertical integration of mining, shipping, processing and manufacturing of products subject to important technological economies of scale, as in aluminium, steel and coal.

These theories are so well known that further explanations are not required here. Instead, for the present purpose of analysis, the important conclusion following from them is that the incentives for foreign investment operate on all national firms which have developed into reasonably large size before the revolution in communication and transportation took place in the 1960's and which permitted increased efficiency in the exploitation of the knowledge capital and the internalization of the externalities. As a result, two-way flows of direct investment among industrial countries have been very significant and have led to the condition where, for example, foreign ownership of German means of production in midyear 1978 was DM 50.5 billion, nearly equal to Germany's ownership of foreign direct investment assets of DM 54.8 billion [The Bulletin, 1978, p. 144].

The welfare implications of multinational enterprises and therefore of two-way flows in direct investment, whether motivated by diversification, knowledge capital or external benefits, are well understood, if somewhat controversial: the productivity of expenditures on knowledge capital formation is increased, technology is transferred, and global competition is raised. But multinational corporations also are alleged to reduce national sovereignty, exploit resources in host countries and transfer resources across borders inequitably through abuse of taxation systems and claims on government resources. In my view, the empirical evidence supports strongly that benefits outweigh costs by far. This view implies also that two-way flows of direct foreign investment are socially beneficial.

V. Summary and Conclusions

In this brief paper I have summarized known economic models which have been developed for the analysis of international short- and long-term capital flows, to show how in principle they can explain the observed phenomenon of two-way trade in financial and real assets between countries. The principal ingredients of these models are assumptions about the existence of uncertainty due to random shocks of nature and government policies, which give rise to speculation, arbitrage and benefits from diversification, and about the existence of nonmarketable knowledge capital and external economies. These elements of the analysis reflect real-world conditions which the simple models of international capital flows assume away, but which in practice play a very important role in both the investment motive and the welfare effects of foreign investment.

Unfortunately, the analysis of this paper does not permit quantification of the absolute benefits arising from markets' responses to the existence of these real world factors in investment decisions and does not permit evaluation of the relative importance of each factor. However, by pointing out how these market responses lead to intra-industry trade in assets theoretically and by indicating that such trade is quantitatively important, the paper has called attention to the potential importance of these real world determinants of foreign investment which operate together with the earnings differential motive stressed by the more basic traditional models.

82

References:

Agmon, Tamir, Donald R. Lessard, "Investor Recognition of Corporate International Diversification." The Journal of Finance, Vol. 32, New York, 1977, pp. 1049-1055.

Aliber, Robert Z., "A Theory of Direct Foreign Investment." In: Charles P. Kindleberger (Ed.), The International Corporation, A Symposium. Cambridge, Mass., 1970, pp. 17-34.

--, "The Multinational Enterprise in a Multiple Currency World." In: John H. Dunning (Ed.), The Multinational Enterprise. London, 1971, pp. 49-56.

The Bulletin, Vol. 26, Bonn, 1978, No. 23.

Business Week, New York, August 21, 1978, p. 76: "Stateless Money: A New Force in World Economy."

Caves, Richard E., "International Corporations: The Industrial Economies of Foreign Investment." Economica, N.S., Vol. 38, London, 1971, No. 149, pp. 1-27.

Grubel, Herbert G., "Internationally Diversified Portfolios: Welfare Gains and Capital Flows." The American Economic Review, Vol. 58, Menasha, 1968, pp. 1299-1314.

--, "A Theory of Multinational Banking." Banca Nazionale del Lavoro, Quarterly Review, Rome, 1977, No. 123, pp. 349-363.

--, P.J. Lloyd, Intra-Industry Trade. London, 1975.

International Monetary Fund (IMF), Balance of Payments Yearbook, Vol. 29, Washington, 1978.

Johnson, Harry G., "The Efficiency and Welfare Implications of the International Corporation." In: Charles P. Kindleberger (Ed.), The International Corporation, A Symposium. Cambridge, Mass., 1970, pp. 35-56.

Kindleberger, Charles P., American Business Abroad, Six Lectures on Direct Investment. New Haven, 1969.

Rugman, Alan M., International Diversification and the Multinational Enterprise. Lexington, 1979.

Weston, J. Fred, Eugene F. Brigham, Managerial Finance. 6th Ed., Hinsdale, 1978.

[10] N A

Excerpt from *International Capital Movements: Papers of the Fifth Annual Conference of the International Economics Study Group* (1982), 1–21.

1   The Theory of International Capital Movements

Herbert G. Grubel

When Professor John Dunning asked me to present the opening paper at the 1980 conference of the International Economics Study Group he suggested that I discuss broadly where the study of international capital movements has been and where it might go. I accepted this task happily because it seems to me that the time has come for such a broader perspective after nearly fifteen years of intensive work in the field, which may well have induced the appearance of diminishing returns and the need to move on to new fields or the search for new approaches.

The following paper is not a conventional review of the literature in the sense that I attempt a careful attribution of the discovery of ideas and empirical insights. Instead, I present a more personal view of the field in the hope that it may be somewhat less boring than more conventional reviews most often are, perhaps for some necessary reason. This paper will in fact be updating the outline of a book that has been sitting on my desk for many years and in which I hope some day to show in much more detail how the study of international capital flows has evolved from the classic explanations of the causes and effects of trade in long- and short-term fixed interest securities, to the explanation of direct investment during the last twenty years, all the while drawing on, and being enriched by Irving Fisher's concepts of human, knowledge and physical capital.

I cannot say that there is a need for, or that I have been able to find, a concept that unifies all of the many components of the existing knowledge on international capital flows, other than the obvious one that it involves the equalization of rates of return on capital in different countries. My main objective of this paper therefore is to present in Part 1 a taxonomy of approaches to the general area of study and what further fields they have encouraged or have been

1

2   *International Capital Movements*

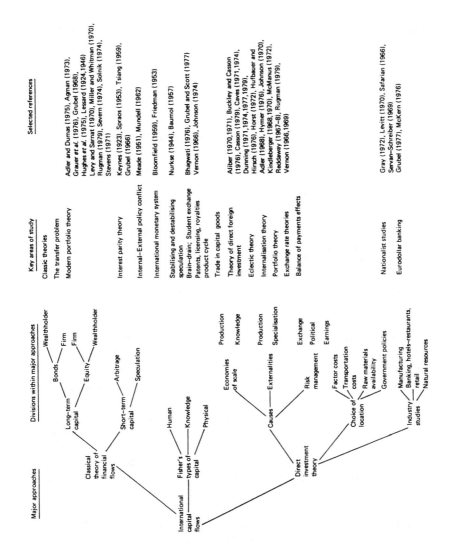

FIGURE 1.1   The theory of international capital flows

encouraged by. In the following part, I summarize briefly the main results of studies in the classic tradition (Section II), in the Fisher tradition (Section III) and in the field of direct investment (Section IV), drawing attention to what appear to me to be some remaining promising areas for further study. The paper concludes with a summary of what I think existing knowledge about the cause, nature and welfare effects of international capital flows implies for government policies.

I   KEY AREAS OF STUDY AND THEIR HISTORIC ORIGINS

The basic taxonomy for the different components of the field of international capital flows is presented in Figure 1.1. As can be seen, there are three analytically distinct approaches to the study of these capital flows. The first consists of the classic theory which deals entirely with financial flows in the form of short- and long-term securities. The theory about capital flows in the form of bonds was most appropriate for the explanation of nineteenth-century export of British capital, but it has retained its usefulness as a heuristic device for the analysis of the motives for and welfare effects of international capital flows.

The study of the other types of financial capital flows largely followed the appearance of new, real-world phenomena that were brought about by technological revolutions in communication and travel and that gave rise to important problems for policy makers. In this category we find the study of short-term capital movements in response to arbitrage incentives and in expectation of capital gains, which spawned the interest rate parity theory and modern theories of exchange rate determination as well as serving as the basis of studies of the speculative episodes of the 1930s and the merit of freely floating exchange rates.

A final component of the study of financial capital flows across borders centres on equities. Its main impetus came from the boom in US equity prices during the 1950s and 60s, which attracted foreign buyers and eventually led Americans to discover the benefits from foreign share-ownership. The area of study went through a boom period when it was subjected to the application of modern portfolio theory, which had itself caused a scientific renaissance in the study of financial markets generally. While this portfolio theory concentrated on the analysis of the motives for and welfare gains from equity investment from the point of view of wealthholders, another branch of financial theory was applied to the problem of the optimal capital structure of firms able to borrow in different countries and currencies.

The Nature of Capital Approach

One of the most insightful studies of the nature of capital was made by Irving Fisher when he distinguished human, knowledge and physical capital. This dichotomy proved useful in studying the nature, magnitude and welfare effects of the brain drain, or in more formal terminology, the uncompensated flow of human capital across international borders through the migration of highly trained persons. It is also useful to consider studies of international patents and licensing in the context of Fisher's concepts. The application of the human and knowledge capital ideas to international problems was stimulated in part by the appearance of public concern over the brain drain and technological autarchy, and in part by the study of domestic trends in productivity which started with Robert Solow's famous discovery of the X-factor in growth (1957) and is kept up by the continuing efforts of Edward Denison (1974) and many others.

Fisher's concept of physical capital permits us to place in the broader context of international capital flows, studies of trade in capital goods and equipment made for balance of payments analysis and speculation about sources and the nature of comparative advantage. It is better known in Europe than North America that two countries with consistent balance of payments surpluses in recent years, Germany and Switzerland, show a substantial and growing share of net exports consisting of capital goods and equipment while Britain and the United States have suffered declining shares in this class of export goods. A careful documentation of these trends and some theorizing about its causes and effects appears to me to be a promising field of study. I think that economies of scale in the production of capital goods are quite substantial and contribute to the virtuous circle of export success and high productivity growth domestically. Moreover, the application of investment demand models of the type produced by Dale Jorgenson (1971) for individual countries might fruitfully be developed for the world as whole.

Direct Investment Theory

The third major component of knowledge about international capital flows consists of the theory of direct foreign investment. It was developed almost exclusively during the 1960s and 70s response to an unprecedented growth in that form of foreign asset ownership, which itself was caused by the sharp fall in the cost of communication and transportation due to the revolution in the electronics and aircraft industries. These technological developments permitted the economic control of firms' global marketing, production and finance operations from a central headquarters. The identification of the activities at this headquarters that give rise to the motives for direct foreign investment was the first and exciting task of economists whose names are today associated with the development of this theory. In Figure 1.1, I show these causes as economies of scale, externalities and risk, which however cannot by themselves explain the location of the investment. For this we need to draw on knowledge of locational advantages consisting of the factor costs stressed in the Heckscher-Ohlin-Samuelson model of international trade, transportation costs, the availability of raw materials and government policies of protection, subsidies and taxation. The fact that the combination of these causes and locational factors is necessary to explain specific investments was pointed out by Dunning (1977) in support of his eclectic theory.

Figure 1.1 also shows that direct foreign investment has led to a number of studies which concentrate on specific characteristics of different types of industries, such as banking, hotels, restaurants, retail stores and natural resources and the ownership of land. While these studies tend to embody the key ingredients of the eclectic theory, they draw on other fields of study as in the case of Eurocurrency markets and multinational banking, and have been encouraged by political motives, as in the case of nationalists' concern over the ownership of land and natural resources.

After this brief overview of the taxonomy of existing knowledge, I next present the most important analytical results which were produced by each of the major categories of studies.

II   THE CLASSIC THEORY OF FINANCIAL FLOWS

In my experience of teaching international economics, the classic theory of international capital flows in all its simplicity remains the most useful heuristic tool for explaining to students the motives for, and effects of international capital movements in a world with certainty. Assuming in analogy with the pure theory of trade model that the world consists of two countries under autarchy initially and

6   *International Capital Movements*

with different rates of return to capital equal to the interest rate, the opening of trade in assets can readily be shown to lead to the equalization of rates of return and a reallocation of the world's physical stock of capital with accompanying gains in output and welfare for both countries. Figure 1.2, whose compiler is unknown to me, is an invaluable aid in establishing in students' minds these fundamental consequences of capital flows which so often are lost sight of in the discussion of more sophisticated models by economists and, very importantly, by politicians who were our former students. Because of the great value of this model I reproduce it here. Readers familiar with it can readily skip the next section.

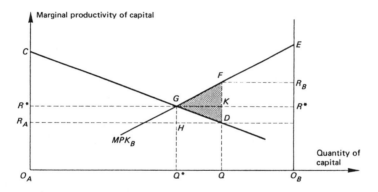

FIGURE 1.2   The marginal products of capital and capital movements

Output and Welfare Effects of Capital Flows

In Figure 1.2 the distance $O_A O_B$ measures the model's total stock of capital, of which initially and under autarchy $O_A Q$ is held by country A and QO_B by country B. The marginal productivity of capital in the two countries is measured along the vertical axis, with the marginal productivity schedules shown as $CMPK_A$ and $EMPK_B$ for countries A and B respectively. Under autarchy the world's total output of goods is measured by the areas under the two curves, $O_A CDQ$ plus$QFEO_B$. The rates of return before trade are OR_A and OR_B in countries A and B respectively.

After the removal of barriers to trade in assets, owners of capital in country A buy country B bonds for the increased yield of DF initially.

Following the purchase of these bonds exchange rate effects under a floating rate regime or exchange market influences on domestic money supplies under the gold standard lead to payments imbalances and the transfer of real resources between the two countries such that real capital is shifted from country A to country B. This process of trade in bonds and shifts in real capital continues through time as long as rates of return in the two countries differ. Equilibrium is reached when the rate of return on capital is equal in both countries at OR^*

Figure 1.2 shows dramatically the main effects of the free movement of capital. In equilibrium output of country A has fallen by Q^*GDQ and that of country B has risen by Q^*GFQ, resulting on a net world output gain equal to GFD. Country B pays Q^*GKQ of its output gain to country A holders of Q^*Q bonds yielding OR^*, and enjoys a net gain of GFK. Country A receives GKD in net reward as a result of the shift of capital.

This simple, but powerful diagram can also be used to illustrate one of the most important welfare effects of capital flows in the real world, which should dominate, but very rarely is even mentioned in discussions about the merit of direct foreign investment in many countries where ideologues concentrate on the effects of foreign capital ownership on power and income distribution. This welfare effect, stressed appropriately by Sir Donald MacDougall (1960) in his basic article, arises out of the existence of government taxation of profits and the existence of double taxation agreements among governments. In Figure 1.2 taxation at the typical rate of 50 per cent of the returns on capital by country B would mean that one half of the output Q^*GKQ remains in country B and is lost for country A. In the simplest case when country A also taxes its wealthholders at the rate of 50 per cent on profits, the owners of bonds in country A face unaltered incentives for foreign investment since the usual double taxation agreements mean that taxes paid to foreign governments can be used fully to reduce the tax obligations to the home country. In effect, the private investors don't care whether one half of their profits go to the government of either country. From a social point of view, however, the taxation system means that country A suffers a net loss in real income whenever the foreign tax payments exceed the gain in income GKD, while country B gains GFK and the tax revenue. Generalizations of this analysis of the welfare effects of taxation of foreign-owned firms as well as some empirical estimates of the effects are found in Grubel (1974).

8   *International Capital Movements*

Modern portfolio theory

One of the most important elements of realism missing from the classic model of capital flows is the existence of uncertainty in the yields on assets. The most successful method for representing uncertainty is incorporated in the mean-variance models of modern finance. However imperfect a representation of reality it may be, this model has led to many useful insights about how the world and economic policies work, though in recent years more and more intellectual effort is devoted to the solution of problems raised by the mathematical formulations of the model rather than the production of more generally useful insights about the real world.

The application of the portfolio model to the analysis of international capital flows has yielded a number of useful insights and empirical propositions. The most important of these is undoubtedly that, even in a world where rates of return on capital in different countries are equal on average, wealthholders can increase their welfare by diversifying their portfolios internationally as long as the fluctuations in the yields on assets in different countries are not perfectly positively correlated. Interesting corollaries of this idea are that uncertainty can explain the observed two-way flows of financial assets between countries and that capital flows are a function of the growth in wealth portfolios, as well as yield differentials, as wealthholders maintain balance in their portfolios.

These basic propositions have been worked out and confirmed in a number of studies, such as Grubel (1968), Levy and Sarnat (1970), Miller and Whitman (1970), and Lessard (1973). Branson (1968) and Herring and Marston (1977) have made econometric studies of financial markets and capital flows which used portfolio theory to make analytically important, but as it turns out empirically insignificant, distinctions between capital movements representing adjustment to flow and stock disequilibria. In addition, there has developed a strand of literature, perhaps best exemplified by Adler (1974) and Grauer *et al.* (1976), which deals in the international sphere with problems that have arisen mainly out of the specific mathematical formulations of the model and which therefore tend to be of less interest to students of international capital flows than those of financial theory.

One important area of finance concerns the capital structure of firms, especially the problems of leverage on equity through the issue of bonds. Severn (1974) and Stevens (1971) have used this general pattern to analyse international capital flows. The capital structure literature centres on the famous Modigliani-Miller hypothesis that firms' decisions about leverage don't matter for the capitalization of equity since individual investors can leverage their own portfolios. This hypothesis has its counterpart in the international sphere in the sense that firms need not diversify their portfolio internationally because private wealthholders can do so readily and perhaps more cheaply. In spite of writings by Adler and Dumas (1975), Agmon (1973) and Senchack and Beedles (1978), related to this problem, I believe that a paper working on the strict analogy between the leverage and diversification hypothesis would be most useful, if only to make the logical point that diversification benefits from direct foreign investment stressed in the writings of Alan Rugman (1979) are neither a necessary nor sufficient condition for direct investment. Instead, they take place only in the presence of certain capital market imperfections or of other conditions that constitute the heart of the theory of direct foreign investment.

Short-term Capital Movements

Short-term capital movements have always played an important role in the theory of the international adjustment mechanism and monetary organization. Ever since I began my studies in this field I have unsuccessfully searched for an author who explained the function of short-term capital arbitrage and speculation in models of international adjustment without governments. Instead, all of the literature I know deals with such capital as an evil that interferes with government policies designed to achieve some noble objectives. Nurkse's (1944) study did much to bring to general attention the pathology of short-term capital movements during the 1930s and probably influenced greatly the decision to permit legally the institution of direct controls on short-term capital under the International Monetary Fund Articles of Agreement. The bad reputation of short-term capital movements was further enchanced by Meade's (1951) analysis of how they interfered with the simultaneous attainment of internal and external balance in the then almost universally accepted framework of Keynesian analysis. Some theoretical models, such as Baumol's (1957), succeeded in showing that profit-making speculators may be destabilizing the exchange rate and thus further added to the ill repute of short-term capital flows.

In response to these studies of the pathology of short-term capital flows, Spraos (1953), Tsiang (1959) and others developed the theory of forward exchange rate determination, because forward exchange policy promised to provide an efficient instrument for the separation of internal and external capital markets. Mundell (1962) produced a body of analysis which showed how a suitable mix of monetary and fiscal policy could eliminate the conflict between internal and external balance. Together with the idea of a Phillips curve trade-off between inflation and unemployment, the policy mix concept may in the future be judged to have been one of the fundamental causes of the great economic problems of the Western countries during the 1970s, as it provided an intellectually respectable justification for budget deficits and the exchange rate rigidities of the parity system.

In my view, the time has come to restore the reputation of international short-term capital arbitrage and speculation as phenomena that facilitate international adjustment and economize on official reserve holdings in a world of managed exchange rates where national governments maintain stable, non-inflationary growth rates in the money supply and balance budgets over full business cycles, but where such cycles and random stocks continuously create instabilities. However, given the apparently natural tendency of economists to want to do good through social engineering, there will likely remain a strong tendency to discover, or at least articulate again, the pathologies caused by short-term capital flows and to provide ingenious cures for solving them. As a result, the knowledge of economists about the role of international capital flows that attracts public attention will continue to be useful for those who make the case of government controls on the grounds that free markets do not work.

III HUMAN, KNOWLEDGE AND PHYSICAL CAPITAL

During the late 1960s the brain drain phenomenon captured the imagination of the public and politicians, and since then the subject has attracted the attention of governments and economists periodically: Bhagwati (1976), UNCTAD (1974). The economic analysis of this problem was facilitated greatly by bringing to bear on it the concept of human capital, which had experienced a renaissance during the 1960s largely under the leadership of T.W. Schultz and the University of Chicago.

As a result of the studies in this human capital framework it has become obvious that the difference between general migration of labour, which aroused little controversy, and the brain drain, which caused such an uproar, was that the latter involved the movement of scarce human capital across international borders while the general migration involved only abundant or even surplus labour. The public concern about the emigration of this human capital is due to the fact that in most countries education is financed by public expenditures that have a high opportunity cost, so that the emigration of highly skilled persons results in the loss of something that was expensive to create and for which there was no compensation received by those who made the investment.

The human capital approach to the problem, however, also revealed that the preceding model failed to establish that the emigration of highly skilled persons reduces the welfare of those remaining behind, since the emigrants take along not only their contribution to, but also their equal-sized claim on output if they are paid their marginal product, so that those remaining behind do not suffer a reduction in their available income. Deviations of pay from marginal product occur most frequently in the case of skilled persons through the production of knowledge capital that is a public rather than a privately appropriable good. The knowledge of this type produced by the migrants in their new country of residence does return as a benefit to the people in their home country because it is essentially a free world public good. The removal of income tax payments by skilled emigrants to their home country governments also does not affect the welfare of those remaining behind since the migrants take along also their claim to government services, usually at a rate above normal just like the level of their tax obligations. By the same line of argument it can be shown that the residents of the country receiving the brain drain migrants typically enjoy no change in welfare, so that the benefits derived by the migrant himself represent the net growth in welfare arising from the phenomenon.

This price-theoretic and human capital approach to the study of the brain drain underlies Grubel and Scott (1977). Many analysts of this phenomenon consider this approach to be irrelevant and misleading, but typically they have failed to produce a refutation for it and limit themselves to the documentation of its magnitude and the alleged problems it causes for development plans.

Patents, Licensing and Royalties

Economists have developed in recent years a growing interest in the international flow of knowledge capital as a result of several developments. Firstly, the studies of the sources of productivity growth in the United States pointed to the great importance of technological improvements and the role they can play in the growth of developing countries. Secondly, science policy has undergone close scrutiny in many countries because of an alleged public dissatisfaction with the contribution of science to the quality of life in recent years. Thirdly, balance of payments analysis showed that receipts and payments on patents, licences and royalties can play an important role in a country's overall balance. And finally, theorizing about the causes and effects of direct foreign investment has pointed to the need for a better understanding of the role of proprietary technology in the decision to invest abroad as against the option of selling the knowledge as a separate package abroad.

In my view, the economic research in this field has not resulted in any important insights and policy recommendations. Perhaps this is due to the fact that there remains a cloud of mystery around the necessary and sufficient conditions for successful technology creation within countries. As several governments and large private enterprises have found out, vast resources can be used to create what appear to be the necessary conditions for the development of computer, aero-space and other glamorous high technology industries, but such expenditures do not assure success. Pinpointing and replicating the mysterious missing ingredient for the success of such ventures has not been possible, or if the Japanese have found it, they are not telling.

It may be useful to mention here the work on the product and technology cycle by R. Vernon (1966) and his research group at the Harvard Graduate School of Business as having resulted in some useful insights into the nature, determinants and effects of international knowledge capital flows. The results of this work point to the temporary value of technological innovations, how they themselves can be the primary determinants of comparative advantage and lead to direct foreign investment.

One of the major components of UNCTAD's demand for a New International Economic Order is that there should be a reform of global law under which the international flow of knowledge takes place. The ultimate objective of this reform is to lower the cost of technology for developing countries. I find the state of the debate on this issue confused and confusing. It is not clear to me whether the proponents of reform understand the nature of knowledge capital or whether they understand it but are making some empirical judgements. In my view there should be little dispute over the fact that if patent laws are changed to reduce the length of proprietary rights or to limit their applicability to certain types of countries, then the rate of knowledge-capital formation in the world will be reduced. The basic problem for which we have no empirical evidence is whether such reduced knowledge-capital formation leads to inefficiencies in the form of inequalities in the social marginal productivity of knowledge and real capital formation. While we appear to have no solid evidence on the optimality of existing patent legislation, there are indications that private firms are reasonably satisfied with current conditions and technological improvements have made a seemingly appropriate contribution to overall economic growth in the world. For these reasons, I believe that experimentation with patent laws is very risky and should not be undertaken, since it could result in the longer run in such inefficiencies in capital formation that the immediate gains of developing countries are more than offset by long-run losses. Clearly, however, we have here an aspect of the study of international capital flows that can benefit from some more research.

IV   DIRECT INVESTMENT THEORY

The basic question which the theory of direct foreign investment must answer is, why is a factory in any country owned by foreign rather than domestic entrepreneurs when efficient capital markets can be assumed to cause the financial resources to move to where the highest rates of return are available? Two subsidiary questions the theory has to answer are first, why is the foreign-owned factory located in one rather than another country and second, why is there no market for whatever ingredient provides the foreign entrepreneur with a comparative advantage over the local one?

First concentrating on the basic question, it should be noted that two apparently obvious answers have been rejected as having empirically insufficient explanatory power. Thus, capital market imperfections which lead to different costs of capital favouring the foreign entrepreneur can provide an explanation of direct foreign investment in principle. In fact, however, global financial capital arbitrage is very efficient and it just is not appealing to argue that Rolleiflex camera assembly lines in Singapore are owned by German businessmen because potential Singapore entrepreneurs face a higher cost of capital than the Germans. Clearly, cost of borrowing differences do not go to the heart of the matter. The second appealing but unsatisfactory explanation is the absence of local entrepreneurs. Again, this is simply not so. Even very rural underdeveloped countries without obvious entrepreneurs at one point in their development in the past have quickly generated large numbers of individuals willing and able to perform the functions played by entrepreneurs.

The accepted answers to the basic question were provided successfully by several economists: Hymer (1976), Kindleberger (1968), Johnson (1970), Caves (1971), Dunning (1971), Aliber (1970), Buckley (1975), Casson (1979) and Rugman (1979), just to name those that have influenced my thinking the most. These writers have analysed three causes of direct investment that can explain the phenomenon individually or in combination.

Economies of scale, broadly defined, constitute one important cause of direct investment. It is useful to distinguish analytically economies of scale in production and those that are due to the fact that the marginal cost of using already produced knowledge is near zero, though in practice the distinction may be blurred. Thus there are scale-economies in production through global advertising and the supply of automobile parts manufactured in one plant for the entire world. The development of new products, management techniques and new processes for one market gives rise to scale economies as the marginal cost of the use of the knowledge is zero. In this context arises the question mentioned above why this knowledge is not sold to foreign entrepreneurs instead of giving rise to the need for ownership of foreign production facilities.

The answer to this question is complex in detail, but rests on either of two characteristics of the product sold by the firms. Firstly, there are products like soft-drinks, drugs and cosmetics where standards of quality together with their identification by consumers are key ingredients of marketing success. Sale of the right to produce these products and market them under the creators' brand-name without control over the quality of the product is not consistent with the commercial success of these products in the long run and therefore does not take place. Secondly, there are industries like computers and automobiles, where the continuous evolution of product design and technology prevents their separate sale since the value of the whole through time is much greater than any part that can be sold separately at any given moment. In many cases, the need for the maintenance of control over quality and to assure continuity in the evolution of products and processes occur together and interact in preventing the sale of knowledge and providing the motive for direct investment.

Externalities giving rise to incentives for direct investment arise from production and specialization. Multinational enterprises essentially are vehicles for internalizing these externalities. Examples of production externalities are those which come in the form of security of supplies and markets. They accrue to multinational aluminium and petroleum industries through the vertical integration of facilities in many countries. External economies due to specialization explain the high levels of productivity found in urban centres, where demand for highly specialized skills permits them to be developed profitably. The large multinational enterprises assemble and train for their own use highly specialized and therefore efficient expertise, which is justified only because it can be used globally, while at the same time it gives rise to the comparative advantage of the enterprise. While the economies from specialization due to agglomeration tend to be general and marketable, those found within these enterprises often are firm-specific and cannot be purchased in public markets. While there appears to be a similarity between economies of scale in production and the external economies from specialization, I think it is useful to distinguish the two because empirical studies concentrating on the analysis of plant size and the indivisibility of equipment can easily miss the highly specialized technical expertise of people in the headquarters and research laboratories of multinational enterprises.

Risk management as a motive for direct investment comes in three different forms. Firstly, given the fact that goods markets are more integrated than factor markets globally, goods market disturbances affect prices and demand for products more equally in all countries than do disturbances in factor markets. Thus, a firm producing widgets in only one country and selling them throughout the world is subject to the same fluctuations in widget prices and demand as a firm with production facilities in many countries. But the former's profits tend to be less stable than the latter's because it cannot count on the stabilizing effect of less than perfectly correlated fluctuations in national factor market influences on profits. Since risk-averse investors put a premium on the stability of earnings, the internationally diversified firm enjoys a lower cost of capital and gains an advantage over non-diversified firms.

Secondly, political risks of expropriation can be lowered by a strategy for production which leaves the output from production facilities in one country worthless unless it is combined with output from other countries. For example, a plant producing automobile transmissions suitable for a specific car assembled in another country is relatively much safer from expropriation than is a plant producing complete automobiles.

Thirdly, exchange rate instabilities and temporary deviations from purchasing power parity introduce risks into lending and borrowing activities denominated in any currency, which are reflected in the average yields demanded by wealthholders on assets in different currencies. Multinational enterprises are in a position to manage the composition of their balance sheets in such a way that these risks become irrelevant and in essence they arbitrage on the average rates of return. They can therefore borrow where capital costs are low and use the funds where they are high because the market-determined cost differences apply only to undiversified firms.

Choice of Location

The preceding analysis only explains the possible sources of comparative advantage of multinational over strictly national enterprises. What remains to be explained, as Dunning argues, is why multinational firms choose to locate in one country rather than another. The answer to this problem is found at different levels of analytical abstraction. In the models of pure theory in the Heckscher-Ohlin-Samuelson tradition, location is determined by the relative factor intensity of the production process together with the relative prices of the factors of production. More realistic models introduce as determinants of comparative advantage the availability of raw materials as well as transportation costs for inputs and outputs, where the latter often is a function of the proximity of large markets. One empirically very important further element of realism is introduced by the consideration of government policies, which in developing countries especially often are an important incentive or deterrent for the choice of location.

In general, there are no great analytical problems associated with the preceding explanations of the locational decisions of multinational enterprises. However, the analysis suggests that, in contrast with the assertions of many of the more politically motivated enemies of multinational enterprises, their decisions tend to lead to the rational exploitation of sources of comparative advantage existing in individual countries, rather than involve power and motives for exploitation of people and natural resources.

Industry Studies

One fertile field of study in the area of international capital flows has been and continues to be in the application of the general principles presented above to individual industries. Thus, while most of the examples used by analysts in their discussion of scale economies, externalities and risk management are drawn from manufacturing industries, the general principles are useful also in the analysis of multinational banking and the multinational chains of hotels, restaurants and retail stores. They also are useful in the analysis of the ownership of land and natural resources by multinational enterprises. Such studies enrich not only our understanding of such important fields as Eurodollar markets and international tourism, they also can provide effective counter-arguments to nationalist and Marxist writings about the negative welfare implications of the foreign ownership of land, natural resources and the means of production.

V POLICY IMPLICATIONS OF THE KNOWLEDGE

For many economists the ultimate value of knowledge lies in its use as a guide to public policies. By this criterion the knowledge about the nature, causes and effects of international capital flows and direct investment especially accumulated in recent years is a great success. It has established firmly that foreign investment is not motivated by the political and economic aspirations of Western countries that wish to exploit the poor parts of the world through a form of neo-colonialism, as is claimed by many people. Foreign investment is the result of decentralized decisions by private individuals who are driven by the profit-motive. In the resultant voluntary exchange these individuals gain privately, but so do the people in the host-country and the world as a whole. In other words, the analysis of foreign investment has established the fact that it increases the efficiency of global resource allocation through voluntary exchange. Competition among owners of capital resources of many countries assures that there are few rents and that the global output gains are distributed according to the dictates of efficiency.

This central message of the research on international capital flows has a number of important corollaries. It implies that if national

governments interfere with the results produced by capital movements, they cannot expect to obtain great rents from the rest of the
world, but typically reduce the level of foreign investment and the
efficiency in the operation of their domestic economies. It also implies
that if foreign firms earn large rents, this is due to the absence of
competition among foreign firms which typically is caused by the
actions of governments. The accepted knowledge about foreign
investment also suggests that countries that influence the level and
composition of foreign ownership to safeguard what in Canada is
called 'the national identity' and in more Marxist terminology is
referred to as 'national independence', will find that this is achievable
only at the cost of lower levels of investment and the sacrifice of
income.

The preceding conclusions, of course, do not imply that foreign
investment yields only gains to host-countries. In the real world the
details of negotiating conditions for the construction of factories and
continuous operating decisions does not take place in well-informed,
competitive markets and in developing countries the governments
negotiating with foreign firms often are at a disadvantage. To deal
with this problem, the most effective method is suggested by the
competitive model itself and amounts to making sure that several
foreign firms bid on every project and domestic tax rates are set to
avoid generating false transfer prices. But there may also be room for
collective action through the United Nations in the form of a centre
that provides information and technical expertise needed by governments to bring their knowledge for bargaining and the surveillance of
transfer prices up to that of the multinational enterprises.

Where is the field of study of international capital flows headed?
This is difficult to predict since, as I noted already, the field seems to
have been worked over thoroughly and we may be in an era of
strongly diminishing returns. There is always room for studies involving the quantification of elasticities and the testing of the basic
theories, but data limitations are likely to prevent the generation of
any really definitive results. Studies of specific multinational industries can be expected to yield potentially useful insights into the
motives and welfare effects of their growth. Proposed policies or the
effects of policies are likely in the future to call for the application of
existing knowledge. Some useful insights might be gained by economists' efforts to understand and integrate into their own thought
structures the work of political scientists and perhaps even that of the
ideologues of the Left. In short, the field is likely to yield many more

Ph.D. theses, articles and books, but probably no Nobel prizes.

REFERENCES

Michael Adler and Bernard Dumas (1975), 'Optimal international acquisitions', *Journal of Finance* (Mar.)
Robert Z. Aliber (1970), 'A theory of direct investment', in C. Kindleberger (ed.)
―――― (1971), 'The multinational enterprise in a multiple currency world', in J. Dunning (ed.)
William J. Baumol (1957), 'Speculation, profitability and stability', *Review of Economics and Statistics*.
Jagdish N. Bhagwati, and Michael Partington (eds) (1976), *Taxing the Brain Drain* (Amsterdam: North Holland).
Arthur I. Bloomfield (1959), *Monetary Policy under the International Gold Standard* (New York: Federal Reserve Bank).
William H. Branson (1968), *Financial Capital Flows in the US Balance of Payments* (Amsterdam: North Holland).
P. J. Buckley and M.C. Casson (1976), *The Future of the Multinational Enterprise* (London: Macmillan).
Peter J. Buckley (1975), 'Alternative theories of the multinational enterprise', University of Reading Discussion Papers, No. 23 (Apr.).
M.C. Casson (1979), *Alternatives to the Multinational Enterprise*, (London: Macmillan).
Richard E. Caves (1971), 'International corporations: the industrial economics of foreign investment', *Economica* (Feb.).
―――― (1974), 'Multinational firms, competition and productivity in host country markets', *Economica* (May).
―――― (1974), 'The causes of direct investment: foreign firms' shares in Canadian and UK manufacturing industries', *Review of Economics and Statistics*, 56 (Aug.).
Edward Denison (1974), *Accounting for United States Economic Growth 1929-69* (Washington: Brookings Institute).
John H. Dunning (ed.) (1971), *The Multinational Enterprise* (London: Macmillan).
―――― (ed.) (1974), *Economic Analysis and the Multinational Enterprise* (London: Allen and Unwin).
―――― (1977), 'Trade, location of economic activity and the multinational enterprise: a search for an eclectic approach', in B. Ohlin, P.O. Hesselborn and P.J. Wiskman (eds), *The International Allocation of Economic Activity*, (London: Macmillan).
―――― (1979), 'Trade, location of economic activity and the multinational enterprise. Some empirical issues', *Journal of International Business Studies* (Winter).
―――― (1979), 'Explaining changing patterns of international production; in defence of the eclectic theory', *Oxford Bulletin of Economics and Statistics* (Nov.).

20 *International Capital Movements*

Milton Friedman (1953), 'The case for flexible exchange rates', in *Essays in Positive Economics* (Chicago: Chicago University Press).

Herbert Gray (1972), *Report on Foreign Direct Investment in Canada (Ottawa: Government of Canada)*.

Herbert G. Grubel (1966), *Forward Exhange, Speculation and the International Flow of Capital* (Palo Alto, California: Stanford University Press).

_____ (1968), 'Internationally diversified portfolios: welfare gains and capital flows', *American Economic Review* (Dec.).

_____ (1977), 'A Theory of multinational banking', *Banca Nazionale del Lavoro* (Dec.).

_____ (1974), 'Taxation and the rates of return from some US asset holdings abroad', *Journal of Political Economy* (Aug.).

_____ and Anthony D. Scott (1977), *The Brain Drain* (Waterloo, Ontario: Wilfred Laurier University Press).

R.J. Herring and R.C. Marston (1977), *National Monetary Policies and International Financial Markets* (Amsterdam: North Holland).

Seev Hirsch (1976), 'An international trade and investment theory of the firm', *Oxford Economic Papers* (July).

Thomas Horst (1972), 'Firm and industry determinants of the decision to invest abroad: an empirical study', *Review of Economics and Statistics* (Aug.).

Gary Hufbauer and Michael Adler (1968), *Overseas Manufacturing Investment and the US Balance of Payments* (Washington: US Treasury Department).

Stephen P. Hymer (1976), *The International Operations of National Firms* (Lexington, Mass.: D.C. Heath).

Harry G. Johnson (1970), 'The efficiency and welfare implications of the international corporation', in C.P. Kindleberger (ed.).

_____ (1975), *Technology and Economic Interdependence* (London: Macmillan).

Dale W. Jorgenson (1971), 'Econometric studies of investment behavior: a survey', *Journal of Economic Literature* (Dec.).

Charles P. Kindleberger (1968), *American Business Abroad* (New Haven: Yale University Press).

_____ (ed.) (1970), *The International Corporation* (Cambridge, Mass.: MIT Press).

John M. Keynes (1923), *A Tract on Monetary Reform* (London: Macmillan).

Donald R. Lessard (1974), 'World, national and industry factors in equity returns', *Journal of Finance* (May).

_____ (1976), 'World, country and industry relationships in equity returns', *Financial Analysts Journal* (Jan.-Feb.).

Kari Levitt (1970), *Silent Surrender: The Multinational Corporation in Canada* (Toronto: Macmillan).

Haim Levy and Michael Sarnat (1970), 'International diversification of investment portfolios', *American Economic Review* (Sept.).

G.D.A. MacDougall (1960), 'The benefits and costs of private investment from abroad: a theoretical approach', *Economic Record* (Mar.).

R.B. McKern (1976), *Multinational Enterprise and Natural Resources* (Sydney: McGraw-Hill).

John F. McManus (1972), 'The theory of the multinational firm', in G. Paquet (ed.), *The Multinational Firm and the Nation State* (Toronto: Collier-Macmillan).

James E. Meade (1951), *The Theory of International Economic Policy;* Vol. I, The Balance of Payments (New York: Oxford University Press).

Robert A. Mundell (1962), 'The appropriate use of monetary and fiscal policy for internal and external stability', *IMF Staff Papers* (Mar.).

Ragnar Nurkse (1944), *International Currency Experience* (Princeton: League of Nations).

W.B. Reddaway, S.J. Potter and C.T. Taylor (1967-8), *The Effects of UK Direct Investment Overseas: Final Report*, University of Cambridge Occasional Paper, No. 15.

Alan M. Rugman (1979), *International Diversification and the Multinational Enterprise* (Lexington, Mass.: D.C. Heath).

A.E. Safarian (1966), *Foreign Ownership of Canadian Industry* (Toronto: McGraw-Hill).

J.J. Servan-Schreiber (1969), *The American Challenge* (New York: Avon Books).

Alan Severn (1974), 'Investor evaluation of foreign and domestic risk', *Journal of Finance* (May).

Bruno H. Solnik (1974), 'International pricing of risk', *Journal of Finance* (May).

_____ (1974), 'An Equilibrium model of the international capital market', *Journal of Economic Theory.*

_____ (1957), 'Why not diversify internationally?', *Financial Analysts Journal* (July-Aug.).

Robert M. Solow (1957), 'Technical change and the aggregate production function', *Review of Economics and Statistics* (Aug.).

John Spraos (1953), 'The theory of forward exchange and recent practice', *Manchester School.*

Guy V. Stevens (1971), 'Determinants of investment', in Dunning (ed.).

S.C. Tsiang (1959), 'The theory of the forward exchange market', *IMF Staff Papers.*

UNCTAD (1974), 'The reverse transfer of technology: economic effects of the outflow of trained personnel from developing countries (brain drain)', a study by the UNCTAD Secretariat, TD/B/AC. 11/25 (8 May).

Raymond Vernon (1966), 'International investment and international trade in the product cycle', *Quarterly Journal of Economics* (May).

_____ (1979), 'The waning power of the product cycle hypothesis', *Oxford Bulletin of Economics and Statistics*, 41, Special Issue on Multinationals (Nov.).

[11]

The New International Banking *

One of the most striking developments in international finance during the 1970s has been the growth in foreign currency loans and deposits by the banks of almost all major Western countries. In this paper I document as a case study the growth of Canadian banks and analyse the nature, causes and welfare effects of this development. The conclusion will be reached that the growth of international banking was partly in response to technological innovations which enabled banks to provide valuable new services to their customers and to raise incomes for their shareholders. However, it is hypothesized that a significant part of the growth in foreign currency banking is the outcome of efforts to escape domestic taxation and regulation. As such it has resulted in social inefficiencies and waste which will be specified. The study concludes that through the payment of interest on required reserves these inefficiencies and waste can be curtailed.

I. The Growth in Foreign Banking

There are two basic definitions of foreign banking. First, it is defined as all lending and borrowing denominated in foreign currencies. This definition has the virtue of easy measurement, but is deficient in that it neglects Canadian dollar business dealings with foreigners and includes foreign currency dealings with Canadians. The latter is an important component of the analysis below and it will be shown that therefore its inclusion in the statistics is not necessarily a shortcoming. Second, foreign banking may be defined as lending and borrowing by Canadian banks' offices abroad. This definition is quite unambiguous,

* Some of the basic data used in this study were compiled by Barney Bonekamp when he worked as my research assistant in the summer of 1982 under a grant from the B.C. Youth Summer Employment Program. I also acknowledge gratefully support from the Center for Economic Research at SFU. Philippe Callier and John Chant made valuable comments on an earlier draft.

but it has the disadvantage of including dealings with Canadians and excluding domestic business done with foreigners. As will be seen below, these types of activities are important analytically, but there exists no published information to permit them to be separated from the data on business by offices abroad.

The two definitions of foreign banking are used in Figure 1 to put its growth into perspective and to set the stage for the following analysis. As can be seen, *foreign currency* assets as a proportion of the total have risen from 10 per cent in 1954 to 39 per cent in 1981. On the other hand, *assets booked abroad* as a proportion of total assets rose from 24 per cent in 1971 to 32 per cent in 1981. The after tax earnings data shown in Figure 1 are based on the latter definition of foreign banking. They reveal that during the period foreign relative to domestic earnings rose much more rapidly than foreign to total assets. In the terminal year 1981 for which data are available, foreign profits contributed about 47

FIGURE 1

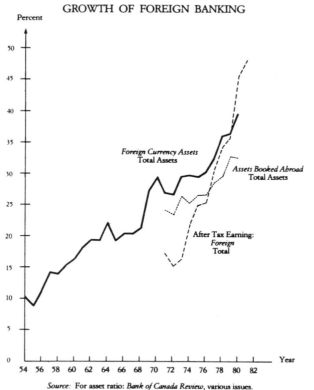

GROWTH OF FOREIGN BANKING

Source: For asset ratio: *Bank of Canada Review*, various issues.
For earnings and assets: *Bank Profits*, p. 42.

per cent of the total while assets booked abroad amounted to only 32 per cent of the total. Clearly, Canada's foreign banking and its profitability have risen sharply during the 1970s.

By any conceivable standard of comparison the data presented in Figure 1 represent remarkable developments that raise a number of questions about their nature, causes and effects. To answer these questions it is useful to consider two traditional explanations of foreign banking.[1]

First, foreign retail banking has been an historically important activity of Canadian banks. It developed during the interwar period and grew in the post-war period in the Caribbean, basing its success on the exploitation of comparative advantage in managerial and marketing knowledge developed in Canada. However, in recent years this comparative advantage has been eroded by the development of indigenous banks in those countries, partly under the umbrella of nationalistic attitudes and policies. Table 1 presents data on the regional distribution of Canadian bank branches and agencies and it shows clearly that their number is declining in the Caribbean. From a high of 197 branches in 1971-72, the number fell to 159 in 1980. Competition and regulation in these countries have, if anything, reduced the profitability of retail banking per branch, so that it is reasonable to conclude that the observed growth in foreign currency banking and profits cannot be explained by changes in this traditional type of activity.

Second, Canadian banks have historically been servicing Canadian traders, investors and tourists abroad through branches and agencies. Their comparative advantage relative to local banks stems from the intimate knowledge of Canadian customers that is developed in domestic dealings and is readily transferred abroad. The data in Table 2 document that Canada's trade defined as exports plus imports and Canada's direct investment holdings abroad did grow rapidly in dollar value in recent years. Trade grew 8.3 times and capital holdings 9.1 times. Foreign currency assets, on the other hand, grew 100 and 61 times during the periods 1954-80 and 1954-78, respectively. As a result, the foreign currency assets as a percent of trade and investment rose by almost 7 times.

---

[1] International banking and Euro-currency markets have resulted in a large and growing literature. A few of the most recent and standard books on the subject are: KHOURY (1980), DONALDSON (1979), MENDELSOHN (1980), DUFEY and GIDDY (1978), JOHNSTON (1982) and KANE (1983). Canadian multinational banking has received relatively little attention except for CLEN-DENNING (1976), RUGMAN (1979), DEAN and GRUBEL (1976). The taxonomy of types of international banking follows GRUBEL (1977).

TABLE 1

CANADIAN BANKS ABROAD 1961-80

	1961/62	1963/64	1965/66	1967/68	1969/70	1971/72	1973/74	1974/75	1976/77	1978/79	1979/80
A. Branches & Agencies											
U.S.A.	10	11	14	11	11	12	10	10	12	16	23
U.K.	10	10	10	10	12	15	15	16	16	14	14
Caribbean	91	112	154	141	172	197	168	165	170	161	159
Latin America	29	28	20	22	24	15	12	11	24	15	15
Europe			2	1	3	5	8	10	15	14	13
Asia			1	1	1	1	1	6	8	11	14
Middle East					1	1	1	5	8	8	8
Total	140	161	201	186	224	246	215	223	253	239	246
minus Caribbean	49	49	47	45	52	49	47	58	83	78	87
B. Representatives											
U.S.A.	5	6	6	10	11	13	12	13	18	19	20
Caribbean					1	1					
Latin America			1	1	1	3	5	6	11	13	14
Europe	2	3	3	4	7	9	11	9	10	11	11
Asia		1	1	2	3	7	11	12	6	15	13
Middle East					1	1	1	2	3	4	4
Australia						1	1	2	3	3	2
Total	7	10	11	17	24	35	41	44	51	65	64
C. Affiliates and Subsidiaries											
U.S.A.	1	1	1	2	2	2	2	2	2	1	1
Caribbean				1	1	4	5	6	6	7	6
Europe	1	1	1	1	2	4	4	4	5	5	5
Latin America				1	1	1	2	2	2	2	2
Middle East					1	1	1	1	1	1	1
Total	2	2	2	5	7	12	14	15	16	16	15
Overall Total	149	173	214	208	255	293	270	282	320	320	325
minus Caribbean	53	61	60	66	81	91	97	111	144	152	160

Source: *Bankers' Almanac and Yearbook,* various bi-annual issues.
Notes: 1) Caribbean includes: West Indies, Bahamas, U.S. Virgin Islands, Puerto Rico, Dominican Republic, Haiti, Cuba and British Honduras.
2) Europe includes all European countries other than U.K.
3) Middle East includes Egypt.

TABLE 2

CANADA'S GROWTH IN TRADE AND DIRECT FOREIGN INVESTMENT HOLDINGS

Trade ($ billion)	1954	1960	1970	1980
Current Receipts plus Expenditures	11.1	15.6	42.7	92.9
Foreign Currency Assets of Banks	1.1	2.7	13.7	109.9
Foreign Currency Assets as Percent of Trade	9.9	17.3	32.1	118.3
Capital ($ billion)	1954	1960	1970	1978
Direct Foreign Investment Holdings	1.8	2.5	6.2	16.3
Foreign Currency Assets of Banks	1.1	2.7	13.7	67.0
Foreign Currency Assets as Percent of Trade	61.1	108.0	221.0	411.0

From the preceding analysis of traditional foreign banking it can be concluded that the growth noted in Figure 1 is due to new and different types of activities. Table 1 provides a clue about the nature of these activities by showing that in recent years Canadian banks have opened many branches, representative offices and affiliates and subsidiaries in the United States, the United Kingdom, the rest of Europe, Asia and the Middle East, tripling their total number from 53 in 1961-62 to 160 in 1979-80. Closer examination of data on these locations reveals that these branches are concentrated in financial centers that serve as capital markets for rich hinterlands, so-called "paper centers" [2] and that together constitute the world's integrated capital markets.

II. The New International Banking

Appendix Table 1 presents the foreign currency assets and liabilities of Canadian banks by broad categories. One curious aspect of the figures in this table is that there appear simultaneously on the asset and

---

[2] Paper centers offer only a corporate presence and there are no active markets in the location. Books are kept elsewhere and serve to evade taxes.

liabilities side "bank deposits". Those on the asset side represent deposits Canadian banks made with foreign banks, while those on the liabilities side are deposits foreign banks made with Canadian banks. The data show that these interbank deposits are not just working balances of the sort domestic banks keep with each other. They run into billions of dollars and represent in recent years an average of 45 per cent of all foreign currency assets (bottom half of column 4) and about 55 per cent of all foreign currency liabilities (column 7).

The phenomenon of these large simultaneous deposits with and by foreign banks is curious for the following reason. For the business to be profitable for Canadian banks they have to charge a mark-up between the rate they pay to depositors and what they earn on their own deposits. For example, they may have to pay 9 per cent to attract depositors and earn 10 per cent on deposits with other banks. The question is why these foreign lending and borrowing banks do not get together directly and in effect save the "commission" or mark-up earned by the Canadian banks.

It is true almost by definition that the foreign banks use Canadian banks as intermediaries because they provide services that are worth the cost. Thus, Canadian banks take deposits from smaller banks in different countries and lend out the funds to smaller banks in other countries. In addition, when there are imbalances in this fundamental brokerage business, Canadian banks make deposits with or accept deposits by other large international banks that are engaged in the same types of activities. In addition, Canadian banks offer other banks the opportunity to diversify the risk of lending while at the same time they spread their own deposits among different banks to obtain the benefits of diversified asset holdings.

In Appendix Table 2 the Canadian banks' foreign currency business with other foreign banks is broken down by the location of booking and residency of the entity doing the booking. The data show in column 9 that until 1973 Canadian banks had more deposits with foreign than they attracted from foreign banks. However, thereafter the positions reversed and they became net borrowers by ever increasing amounts. In 1981 they had borrowed from foreign banks $ 78 billion and lent to foreign banks only $ 38 billion. Comparison of columns 4 with 1 and 3 shows that most of the deposits with foreign banks were booked in Canada. On the other hand, in recent years half of the liabilities were booked abroad, as can be seen from columns 5, 7 and 8. The data imply that during the 1970s Canadian banks through their offices abroad have tended to attract deposits which they relent to foreign banks through the books of their home offices, but that the amount relent in this manner became a continuously smaller fraction of the sums borrowed. Where did the excess of borrowing over lending to foreign banks go?

Appendix Table 3 shows the size of foreign currency assets and liabilities booked by other than banks. These assets consists overwhelmingly of "other loans" (see column 2 to Appendix Table 1) and represent to a large extent the loans made through the Euro-currency consortia to foreign governments and their agencies and private corporations, including Canadian. As can be seen from Table 3 in column 11, after 1976 the excess of such loans over non-bank deposit liabilities grew substantially every year. A comparison of the last columns in Appendix Tables 2 and 3 reveals that over two thirds of the growth in the excess of liabilities over assets in dealings with banks in recent years were matched by the growth in the excess of assets over liabilities in dealings with non-banks. This implies that Canadian banks in their foreign currency denominated business have become increasingly intermediaries between foreign banks as net lenders and others as net borrowers.

Appendix Table 3 in column 3 shows the magnitude of bank loans denominated in foreign currencies taken out by Canadian residents. As can be seen, these loans have risen steadily in recent years and reached $ 25.3 billion, or 23 per cent of all non-bank foreign currency loans in 1981. The foreign currency deposits by non-bank Canadian residents (column 8) do not show a trend, fluctuating around $ 9 - $ 11 billion, with a sharp drop to $ 6.8 billion in 1981.

The foreign currency deposits and loans by Canadians must be seen in the perspective of the overall bank business carried out in Canadian dollars. Thus, Appendix Table 4 reveals that after 1976 foreign currency loans to Canadians have become an ever growing percentage of regular Canadian dollar loans, rising from 6.3 per cent in 1976 to 21.1 per cent in 1981. On the other hand, foreign currency deposits by Canadians have remained around 8 per cent of total Canadian dollar deposits, with 1978 at 10.9 per cent above and 1981 at 4 per cent below the average.

The data in Appendix Tables 3 and 4 suggest that a significant and growing share of the foreign currency business of Canadian banks involves dealing with Canadian residents as both lenders and borrowers. In addition, it involves obtaining foreign currency deposits from foreign banks and lending them to Canadian residents.

In sum, the data in Appendix Tables 1-4 suggest that there has taken place a rapid expansion in foreign currency banking that may be called the new international banking. It involves Canadian banks as participants in a global interbank market and capital market as intermediaries, channelling funds across borders and offering opportunities for risk diversification. The second part of the new international banking involves Canadian residents as depositors and borrowers with the banks serving their traditional domestic intermediation role, but also providing a conduit for foreign currencies funds from foreigners to Canadians. The welfare effects of the growth of these types of the new international banking will be examined next.

III. Welfare Effects of the New International Banking

The welfare effects of the growth of the global interbank and capital market have been studied widely.[3] The benefits are increased allocative efficiency of capital throughout the world.[4] Through diversified loan portfolios and consortia international banks have been able to channel large loans to a wide range of borrowers at a scale that would have been unthinkable a decade earlier. The new international banking has been credited with the efficient redistribution of OPEC countries' balance of payments surpluses to deficit countries plagued by high costs of oil imports, thus preventing the development of great hardships for deficit countries and of a serious shrinkage of trade or the erection of trade barriers.

The welfare costs of this banking appear to consist of currency instability as large amounts of volatile funds seek to profit from expected exchange rate changes. In addition, there exists the threat of a global liquidity crisis and default risks. While it may be too early to know with certainty the magnitude of these latter risks, there is growing evidence that cooperation among banks and the assistance of governments and international organizations can prevent a major collapse of the system.

---

[3] See the literature cited in footnote 1.

[4] KINDLEBERGER (1974) has suggested that national central capital markets traditionally have served to break the monopoly of regional lenders and borrowers by bringing them together in a broad, competitive market. By analogy international centers reduce the market strength of national lenders and borrowers.

The main purpose of this paper is to call attention to two new and different sources of welfare costs associated with the new international banking. These costs have their origin in the fact that international banking represents an avenue of escape from domestic regulation and taxation.

The Escape from Regulation and Taxation

The literature on Euro-currency banking is in almost total agreement that the escape from domestic regulation and taxation has been a major driving force behind the growth of this business. This escape has contributed greatly to the reduction in the cost of intermediation so that the new international banking can pay higher interest rates on deposits and charge lower rates on loans than they can on domestic business.[5] The large average size of loans and deposits and the absence of costly retail banking services in Euro-currency markets also is responsible for lower operating costs. Unfortunately, it has not been possible to assess the relative importance of these two sources of lower foreign bank operations. However, we may consider two arguments in support of the proposition that the escape from regulation and taxation has been the major of the two causes of the new international banking.

First, the drastic reduction in the cost of communications and travel that has taken place in recent years would have made possible the global integration of national capital markets and the formation of loan consortia without the need for banks to have a physical presence abroad or even to establish separate corporate entities at home for foreign operations. In the United States the independent banks in different states are most effectively integrated into a national capital market without having offices accepting deposits and making loans in the major financial centers such as New York, Chicago and San Francisco.

Second, the seemingly minor cost of reserve requirements represents a really significant tax on the value-added of the banks' intermediation activity, as may be seen from the following analysis.

---

[5] See especially DUFEY and GIDDY (1978) and JOHNSTON (1982). The latter states: "...The necessary conditions for the development of a London market for Euro-dollar bank deposits and loans is that the sum of borrowers', depositors' and intermediaries' transactions costs should be less for at least some transactors in London than in New York". (p. 107).

Required Reserves and Taxation of Value-Added

Consider a simple model of a bank where value-added in the absence of reserve requirements V is equal to income from A dollars earning assets yielding r per cent minus the cost of servicing D dollars of deposits at the interest rate i.

$$V = Ar - Di \qquad (1)$$

In the presence of reserve requirements of q per cent on deposits the earnings assets are reduced to

$$A' = D(1-q) \qquad (2)$$

and value added becomes

$$V' = A'r - Di \qquad (3)$$

which after substitution and division by D gives value-added per unit of deposit with reserve requirements:

$$v' = r - qr - i \qquad (4)$$

From equation (1) and under the simplifying assumption that A=D, in the absence of reserve requirements, the value added per unit of deposit is

$$v = r - i \qquad (5)$$

Defining the effective rate of taxation of value-added implicit in the reserve requirement as [6]

$$t = (v - v')/v' \qquad (6)$$

after substitution it becomes

$$t = rq/(r - rq - i) \qquad (7)$$

In this simple model, if r = .10, i = .08 and q = .04, t = .25 or a tax rate of 25 per cent. In absolute values, a $ 100 deposit costs $ 8 in

---

[6] This particular formulation was chosen with the taxed value-added as a base in order to show the percentage gain available from escaping the taxation. The reason will become obvious below where it is assumed that the domestic value-added assures a normal return to capital.

It should be noted that the net gain of operating in foreign currencies in turn is constrained by the spreads prevailing for them, which in turn are determined by the respective domestic taxation. Furthermore, competition among international banks has tended to reduce spreads in Euro-currency banking such that they yield only normal returns. The resultant large interest advantages accruing to lenders and borrowers abroad represent essentially a disequilibrium situation which is slowly being eliminated by the much faster growth of Euro-currency relative to domestic banking for banks from Canada and other countries. In the discussion in the text these arguments were omitted to keep the analysis manageable and concentrating on the main point.

interest. In the absence of the reserve requirement it brings $ 10 as income for a value-added of $ 2. In the presence of the reserve requirement income is only $ 9.60 and value-added $ 1.60. The value-added per hundred dollar deposit therefore in the absence of reserve requirements is $ .40 in excess of the value-added in the presence of the reserves requirement $ 1.60. This means the tax a bank can escape by moving abroad is 25 per cent.

It is interesting to note that if *profits* constitute 10 per cent of the value-added, or $ .16 per $ 100 of deposits under reserve requirements, and if remaining components of value-added are the same in the presence and absence of these requirements, then escaping the reserve requirement raises profits from $ .16 to $ .56 or by 350 per cent. We may also note that the rate of taxation of either value-added or profits is an increasing function of the level of interest rates, given the reserve requirement q and the spread of interest rates $c = r-i$. This is intuitively obvious, but also follows from differentiating equation 7 with the result that $dt/dr = cq/(c-rq)^2 > 0$.

In support of the preceding theoretical analysis, I present Table 3 which contains evidence assembled for a 1981 Canadian parliamentary committe charged with the investigation of bank profits. It shows in the top half for the years 1977-81 the annual average prime rate, which reflects the income from short term bank loans to the banks' best clients. It is equivalent to r in the above example. The table also shows the average rate of interest paid by the banks on 90 days deposits, which is i in the above example. The difference between the two rates is shown in row three and is equal to v in the example. The implicit reserve cost is shown in row four, while the value-added after tax appears (v') in the last row. Using the definition of the implicit rate of taxation in equation (6), the value for 1981 is (1.10-.38)/(.38) = 1.89, or 189 per cent. Other years and types of loan-deposit business shown in Table 3 produce similar results.

Locational and Currency Diversion Costs

The preceding analysis of the magnitude of the effective rate of taxation of domestic value-added in banking brought about by statutory reserve requirements establishes a strong presumption, but does not prove conclusively, that a domestic distortion is responsible for a large part of the observed growth of Canadian international banking in the

TABLE 3

SEGMENTED BANK DOMESTIC INTEREST RATE SPREADS

	Prime-Related Years ended October 31				
	1977	1978	1979	1980	1981
Average Prime Rate	8.70%	9.14%	12.31%	14.08%	19.08%
Average 90-Day Deposit Rate	7.73%	8.25%	11.47%	12.64%	17.98%
Difference	0.97%	0.89%	0.84%	1.44%	1.10%
Reserve Cost [1]	(0.31%)	(0.33%)	(0.46%)	(0.51%)	(0.72%)
Net Spread	0.66%	0.56%	0.38%	0.93%	0.38%
	Consumer Years ended October 31				
	1977	1978	1979	1980	1981
Average Yield on Consumer Assets [2]	11.55%	11.24%	11.77%	12.59%	14.26%
Average Non-Chequable Savings Deposit Rate	6.53%	6.50%	9.63%	11.19%	15.13%
Difference	5.22%	4.74%	2.14%	1.40%	(0.87%)
Reserve Cost [1]	(0.25%)	(0.26%)	(0.39%)	(0.45%)	(0.61%)
Net Spread	4.97%	4.48%	1.75%	0.95%	(1.48%)

Source: Bank of Canada Review and ROYAL BANK OF CANADA, *Bank Profits* (1982).
[1] Cost of maintaining reserves with the Bank of Canada is based on the interest "give-up" on the 4% reserve required (under the old Bank Act) on these deposits. The reserve has been calculated based on the average 90-day deposit rate for prime-related and the average savings deposit rate for consumers.
[2] Royal Bank of Canada includes personal installment loans, credit card balance and mortgages.

post-war years. This distortion has resulted in the condition that there is a wedge between private and social benefits of foreign banking. There is no doubt that this new activity is privately profitable, but to the extent that it has been motivated by the taxation, it has resulted in social costs in the form of locational and currency diversion of lending and borrowing activities.[7]

The *locational diversion* arises as Canadian banks offer domestic and foreign customers special incentives to book their business abroad. Such foreign locations cause all parties to incur extra costs of travel and communication. It is highly likely that in the absence of the tax Canadian banks would have fewer branches and other offices abroad

---

[7] A general theory of the cost of such locational diversion is in GRUBEL (1982).

and that therefore they would have lower operating costs. In cases where business is simply carried on at headquarters in Canada through the books of largely fictitious branches in so-called "paper" centers, such as the Bahamas, there are wasteful book-keeping and legal expenses.

The *currency diversion* costs arise as lenders and borrowers are induced to denominate their business in foreign currencies which in the absence of the tax they would have denominated in Canadian dollars. The result is a greater amount of risk taking by some wealthholders and of forward exchange transactions to cover exchange risk by others than would exist in the absence of minimum reserve requirements.

In addition to these costs of locational and currency diversion, there are costs due to induced instability and growth of substitutes for Canadian dollar credit and demand deposits. Above we noted that Canadians have taken out increasingly large amounts of foreign currency loans which in 1981 came to 21.1 per cent of domestic currency loans. There are students of money and banking who believe that the proper management of aggregate demand should focus on managing the growth of credit. If this view is correct and foreign and domestic currency credit are close substitutes, then the growth in foreign currency credit complicates and adds to the cost of creating a stable credit environment in Canada.

By analogy, as Appendix Table 4 shows , foreign currency deposits by Canadians have averaged 9 per cent of domestic currency deposits in recent years and they have been very unstable. The Bank of Canada acknowledges that these deposits are close substitutes for domestic currency deposits by including them in the measurement of M2, along with fixed time deposits. Therefore, these foreign currency deposits influence the level and stability of the liquidity of Canadian wealthholders and complicate the task of the Bank of Canada to assure the stable growth of this liquidity.

Unfortunately, it is not possible to measure the cost of locational and currency diversion and of monetary instability caused by the new international banking, just as it is not possible to measure the benefits it has created through the global integration of capital markets and the narrowing of spreads between lending and borrowing rates for many customers. It should be mentioned, though, that just as in the case of economic integration, it is theoretically possible for the costs of diversion to exceed the efficiency gains from the partial movement to untaxed banking.

IV. Policy Implications - Interest Payments on Required Reserves

Whatever may be in practice the size of the social cost created by the discriminatory taxation of domestic and foreign banking, it seems reasonable to consider available methods for eliminating the discrimination. If the cost of such elimination is low or has other benefits, it is worth undertaking even if the costs of discriminatory policies themselves are low.

The first best solution to the problem clearly is the elimination of domestic reserve requirements. There are economists in favour of this policy in order to improve the operation of the domestic monetary system.[8] However, such a step remains highly controversial and risky because of the largely unknown consequences. It does not appear to be a realistic approach to the problems of the new international banking discussed here.

The second approach involves extending reserve requirements to all international activities of Canadian banks. One step in this direction has already been undertaken in the Bank Act of 1980 through the imposition of reserve requirements on foreign currency deposits in Canada held by Canadian residents. This policy can easily be circumvented by simply shifting these deposits to foreign subsidiaries and there are good reasons for believing that it will fail in its aim to curb the new international banking.

There have been no attempts to impose reserve requirements on foreign currency deposits in Canada held by foreigners. As Germany had experienced with such a policy, it simply leads to the flight of Euro-currency business from the country. Similarly, there have been no attempts to impose reserve requirements on deposits of Canadian banks abroad. Such a policy involves an extension of Canadian jurisdiction into foreign countries that would probably be resented and would be difficult to enforce. Moreover, it would simply put Canadian banks at a disadvantage relative to other banks and in all likelihood would force them to terminate their participation in the new international banking. U.S. government attempts to reach international agreement on the universal imposition of reserve requirements on foreign currency

---

[8] See HAYEK (1976) and HALL (1982). For a general review of the literature on private versus public money supply systems see GRUBEL (forthcoming).

deposits failed in 1980.[9] Incentives for individual, perhaps developing countries, to stay out of such an agreement are too large and if they did, locational diversion effects would become even larger.

The most rational solution to the problems raised by the new international banking involves the payment of interest on required reserves of chartered banks. It can readily be seen that under these conditions in the model above the taxation implicit in the reserve requirement would be zero or dramatically lowered, depending on the relationship between the interest rate on the reserves and investments of equal risk and liquidity. This simple policy would therefore eliminate the artificial wedge between the private and social profitability of foreign currency banking, resulting in a socially optimal level of international banking by Canadian banks. The great advantage of this policy over any other is that it can be introduced unilaterally and without the need for international agreements. In addition, Canadian banks would not oppose such a policy and some theorists have suggested that it would increase the effectiveness of monetary policy.[10]

The biggest problem associated with the proposed payment of interest on required reserves is its cost, which occurs as reduced profits of the Bank of Canada and, since they are part of general government revenue, lower tax income. At the end of 1981 the deposits of the chartered Banks with the Bank of Canada came to $ 5.3 billion, when the yield on 3-month treasury bills was about 15 per cent. Assuming that the interest rate on reserves was set at 80 per cent of treasury bill yields, the rate would have been 12 per cent and the cost for the year about $ 636 million. In that year federal government expenditures were $ 71.5 billion and the deficit was $ 7.5 billion, making the proposed tax reduction equal to .89 per cent of expenditures and 8.5 per cent of the deficit. The short run impact costs of the reduction would be reduced by temporarily increased bank profits, which taxed at the 50 per cent corporate tax rate would reduce the total revenue loss by one half. In the longer run, the excess bank profits and resultant tax revenues would be eliminated by competition through the narrowing of lending and borrowing rate spreads, but the reduced incentives to foreign banking

---

[9] See JEC hearings.

[10] See TOBIN (1960) and MITCHELL (1982). We should also note that the same incentives that reserve requirements give to foreign banking they also provide for the development of substitutes for demand deposits. Interest payments on reserves would thus also cut sharply the incentives to develop such substitutes and might result in a great stability of other monetary aggregates such as M2 and M3 and in the velocity of M1.

would result in the return of bank employees and capital from abroad and into the tax jurisdiction of the Canadian government. Lower interest rates would also reduce the loss of revenue.

There exists a political cost for any government which proposes to give a windfall gain to Canadian banks through the payment of interest on required reserves.[11] This cost can be minimized by the gradual phasing in of the payments at such a rate that the narrowing of spreads is likely to keep pace and profit rates remain normal. In addition, a publicity campaign documenting the narrowing of the spreads and resultant benefits to consumers should help lower the political cost of the policy.

It should be noted that the payment of interest on required reserves does not reduce incentives for Canadian banks to continue operating internationally in their traditional business as well as the new international banking that involves genuine economies and comparative advantage. The only and intended effect would be the elimination of inefficient incentives for the *overexpansion* of foreign currency lending and borrowing.

V. Summary and Conclusions

There are good taxes and bad taxes. Taxes are bad if taxpayers can avoid them through the incurrence of private costs that constitute social waste. Through the exogenous revolution in communications and travel technology in recent years the tax implicit in minimum reserve requirements for chartered banks in Canada has become a bad tax. The new international banking represents an innovation that permits tax evasion at great private and social cost. It has become akin to the tax on ships based on the length of the keel which Venice has imposed in the 15th century. The result of this bad tax had been changes in ship design which made them shorter and wider. While these changes saved taxes and were privately profitable they raised the social cost of transpor-

---

[11] In 1981 the government was required to launch an inquiry into banking by NDP claims of excessive profits. *Bank Profits* (1982) exonerated the banks from wrong-doing but bank profits are likely to remain a politically sensitive issue to be exploited by populist politicians at every opportunity.

tation as ships took longer in transit, they became less sea-worthy and fell prey to pirates more readily.[12]

The analysis of the growth of Canadian foreign currency banking in recent years showed that it exceeded by far the growth in its traditional, efficient determinants. The new international banking was shown to have been encouraged by very heavy rates of taxation implicit in minimum reserve requirements. From this it was concluded that it probably has grown much more than efficient participation in global integrated interbank and capital markets would have warranted. The result has been the development of locational and currency diversion costs, which are likely to be large and to be continuing to grow in the future.

The policy conclusion from the analysis of these costs is that interest should be paid on required chartered bank reserves. This policy would induce return of the new international banking to an efficient level at low financial and political costs, promising to lead therefore to valuable net social gains. While the preceding analysis was formulated in the context of Canadian banks, there is little doubt that analogous conditions hold for banks in most industrial countries and that interest payments on reserves would serve them well also and benefit the world as a whole.

Vancouver, B.C.

HERBERT G. GRUBEL

---

[12] For a price-theoretic analysis of adjustments to taxation see BARZEL (1976).

APPENDIX

TABLE 1

ASSET AND LIABILITIES BY TYPE, CANADIAN BANKS FOREIGN CURRENCIES

	Assets						Liabilities				
	(1) Call Loans	(2) Other Loans	(3) Secu- rities	(4) Dep. with Bks.	(5) Other Assets	(6) Total Assets	(7) Dep. of Bks.	(8) Other Deps.	(9) Other Liab.	(10) Total Liab.	(11) Net F.C.A.
1964	1.0	2.0	.6	1.6		5.2	.9	4.3		5.2	
65	.7	2.3	.6	1.4		5.0	1.3	3.8		5.1	− .1
66	.9	2.6	.6	1.5		5.6	1.3	4.3		5.6	
67	.7	2.7	.8	2.3		6.5	1.5	4.8		6.3	.2
68	.7	2.9	.8	3.4		7.8	2.1	5.3		7.4	.4
69	.7	3.8	.9	6.2		11.6	3.2	8.4		11.6	0
70	.6	4.7	.7	7.6	.1	13.7	4.9	8.6		13.5	.2
71	.7	5.3	.5	7.7	.3	14.5	6.4	7.8		14.2	.3
72	1.0	5.5	.6	9.5	0	16.6	8.4	8.6		17.0	− .4
73	.5	7.1	.5	14.8	.4	23.3	13.3	11.3		24.6	−1.3
74	.5	11.7	.7	14.9	.7	28.5	15.2	14.2		29.4	− .9
75	.4	14.4	.6	15.5	.3	31.2	16.3	15.1	.1	31.5	− .3
76	.5	16.5	.6	19.3	.7	37.6	20.8	17.5	0	38.3	− .7
77	.9	21.8	2.2	21.8	1.0	47.7	27.4	21.2	.1	48.7	−1.0
78	1.1	30.0	5.5	28.6	1.8	67.0	37.8	30.6	.3	68.7	−1.7
79	1.0	37.4	5.8	35.3	2.4	81.9	48.3	36.6	.3	85.2	−3.3
80	1.0	54.9	5.8	45.4	2.9	110.0	65.4	45.8	1.8	113.0	−3.0
81	1.0	94.0	6.5	38.2	7.7	147.4	78.4	65.6	8.7	152.7	−5.3
	Percentages of Total Assets						Percentages of Total Liabilities				
64	19.2	38.5	11.5	30.8		100	17.3	82.7		100	0
65	14.0	46.0	12.0	28.0		100	25.4	74.6		100	0
66	16.1	46.4	10.7	26.8		100	23.2	76.8		100	0
67	10.8	41.5	12.3	35.4		100	23.8	76.2		100	3.2
68	9.0	37.2	10.3	43.5		100	28.3	71.7		100	5.4
69	6.0	32.8	7.8	53.4		100	27.6	72.4		100	0
70	4.4	34.2	5.1	54.6	.7	100	36.3	63.7		100	1.5
71	4.8	36.6	3.4	53.1	2.1	100	45.1	54.9		100	2.1
72	6.0	33.1	3.6	57.3		100	49.4	50.6		100	−2.4
73	2.1	30.5	2.1	63.6	1.7	100	54.1	45.9		100	−5.3
74	1.8	41.0	2.5	52.2	2.5	100	52.0	48.0		100	−2.7
75	1.3	46.2	1.9	49.6	1.0	100	51.7	47.9	.3	100	−1.0
76	1.3	43.9	1.6	51.3	1.9	100	54.3	45.7		100	−1.8
77	1.9	45.7	4.6	45.7	2.1	100	56.3	43.5	.2	100	−2.1
78	1.6	44.8	8.2	42.7	2.7	100	55.0	44.5	.4	100	−2.5
79	1.2	45.8	7.1	43.0	2.9	100	56.7	43.0	.4	100	−3.9
80	0.9	49.9	5.3	41.3	2.6	100	57.8	40.5	1.6	100	−2.7
81	0.7	63.8	4.4	25.9	5.2	100	51.3	43.0	5.7	100	−3.5

Source: Bank of Canada Review, various issues, Table 15 and CLENDENNING (1976).
Note: Percentages may not total 100 because of rounding.

The New International Banking

TABLE 2

FOREIGN CURRENCY DEPOSITS WITH AND BY FOREIGN BANKS
BY BOOKING LOCATION AND RESIDENCE

	Assets = Deposits with Banks $ billion				*Liabilities =* Deposits of Banks $ billion				
	Booked in Canada		Booked Abroad	Total	Booked in Canada		Booked Abroad	Total	Net Position
	Total With Non-Residents				Total With Non-Residents				
	(1)	(2)	(3)	(4)	(5)	(6)	(7)	(8)	(9)
1966	1.5	1.5	0	1.5	1.1	1.1	.2	1.3	.2
67	2.3	2.3	0	2.3	1.1	1.1	.4	1.5	.8
68	2.6	2.6	.7	3.3	1.5	1.5	.6	2.1	1.2
69	6.2	6.2	.2	6.4	2.3	2.3	.9	3.2	3.2
70	7.1	7.1	.4	7.5	3.4	3.4	1.5	4.9	3.6
71	6.2	6.2	1.5	7.7	4.0	4.0	2.4	6.4	1.3
72	7.3	7.3	2.3	9.5	5.7	5.6	2.7	8.4	1.1
73	10.7	10.7	4.1	14.8	8.4	8.4	4.9	13.3	1.5
74	11.9	11.6	3.0	14.9	7.5	7.2	7.8	15.3	− .4
75	11.4	11.2	4.1	15.5	7.2	7.0	9.1	16.3	− .8
76	14.0	13.7	5.3	19.3	9.4	9.1	11.4	20.8	− 1.5
77	15.7	15.3	6.1	21.8	12.6	12.2	14.8	27.4	− 5.6
78	21.1	20.4	7.5	28.6	15.8	15.0	22.0	37.8	− 9.2
79	23.8	23.3	11.4	35.2	28.3	18.8	20.0	48.3	−13.1
80	34.8	33.0	10.6	45.4	30.1	28.7	35.2	65.3	−19.9
81	35.1	33.1	3.1	38.2	45.6	43.5	32.8	78.4	−40.2

Source: Bank of Canada Review, various issues, Tables 15 and 16.
Note: (4) = (1) + (3)
(8) = (5) + (7).

282   Banca Nazionale del Lavoro

TABLE 3

NON BANK LENDING AND BORROWING IN FOREIGN CURRENCIES

| | Assets – Other than Bank Deposits | | | | | Liabilities – Other than Bank Deposits | | | | | |
	(1) Booked in Canada Total	(2) With Non Res.	(3) Res.	(4) Booked Abroad	(5) Total	(6) Booked in Canada Total	(7) With Non Res.	(8) Res.	(9) Booked Abroad	(10) Total	(11) Net Pos.
1966	1.6	.5	1.0	2.5	4.1	2.9	1.3	1.6	1.4	4.3	– .2
67	1.3	.4	.9	2.9	4.2	3.4	1.4	2.0	1.4	4.8	– .6
68	1.4	.5	.9	3.1	4.5	3.4	1.4	2.0	1.8	5.2	– .7
69	1.6	.6	1.0	3.6	5.2	5.6	2.3	3.3	2.8	8.4	– 3.2
70	1.8	.6	1.2	4.4	6.2	5.4	2.2	3.2	3.2	8.6	– 2.4
71	2.0	.8	1.1	4.8	6.8	4.0	2.3	1.7	3.7	7.7	– .9
72	2.0	.9	1.0	5.1	7.1	4.1	2.5	1.6	4.5	8.6	– 1.5
73	2.4	1.2	1.2	6.1	8.5	6.1	3.1	3.0	5.2	11.3	– 2.8
74	3.9	1.8	2.1	9.7	13.6	9.2	4.4	4.8	5.0	14.2	– .6
75	5.2	2.4	2.8	10.5	15.7	9.7	5.3	4.4	5.5	15.2	.5
76	6.4	3.3	3.1	11.9	18.3	11.8	5.6	6.2	5.8	17.6	.7
77	9.8	4.1	5.7	16.1	25.9	13.6	6.1	7.5	7.7	21.3	4.6
78	16.1	4.9	11.2	22.2	38.3	22.9	11.7	11.2	8.0	30.9	7.4
79	17.5	5.9	11.6	29.1	46.6	25.7	15.8	9.9	11.1	36.8	9.8
80	22.8	8.6	14.2	41.7	64.5	30.6	19.8	10.8	17.1	47.7	16.8
81	35.9	10.6	25.3	73.2	109.1	32.1	25.3	6.8	42.2	74.3	34.8

Source: Bank of Canada Review, various issues, Tables 15 and 16.

Columns: 1: B3502; 2: B3509; 3: B3506; 4: (5)-(1); 5: B1800 - B1804;
6: B3602; 7: B3609; 8: B3606; 9: (10)-(6); 10: B1808; 11: (5)-(10).

Note: (5) = (1) + (4)
(1) = (2) + (3)
(10) = (6) + (9)
(6) = (7) + (8)
Totals may not equal sums precisely because of rounding.

The New International Banking   283

TABLE 4

LOANS AND DEPOSITS OF BANKS DEALING WITH RESIDENTS

	(1) Can $ Loans	(2) Frgn Curr. Loans	(3) $\frac{(2)}{(1)} \cdot 100$	(4) Can $ Deposits	(5) Frgn Curr. Deposits	(6) $\frac{(5)}{(4)} \cdot 100$
1966	10.5	1.0	9.5	20.0	1.6	8.0
67	11.8	.9	7.6	22.7	2.0	8.8
68	13.3	.8	6.0	26.4	2.0	7.7
69	14.9	1.1	7.4	27.3	3.3	12.1
70	15.7	1.2	7.6	29.9	3.2	10.7
71	19.3	1.1	5.7	35.6	1.7	4.8
72	23.4	1.0	4.3	40.7	1.6	3.9
73	29.4	1.2	4.1	48.6	3.0	6.2
74	35.0	2.1	6.0	58.8	4.8	8.2
75	40.4	2.8	6.9	66.9	4.4	6.6
76	49.2	3.1	6.3	76.8	6.2	8.1
77	55.3	5.7	10.3	88.7	7.5	8.5
78	62.4	11.2	17.9	103.1	11.2	10.9
79	77.9	11.6	14.9	120.7	9.9	8.2
80	93.3	14.2	15.2	134.1	10.8	8.1
81	120.1	25.3	21.1	168.1	6.8	4.0

Source: Bank of Canada Review, various issues, Tables 6 and 7.
    Column: 1 = B627; 4 = B651; 2 = B3506; 5 = B3606.

BIBLIOGRAPHY

Bank Profits, A Report by the Standing Committee on Finance, Trade and Economic Affairs, Ottawa: Queen's Printer for Canada, 1982.

BARZEL, Y., "An Alternative Approach to the Analysis of Taxation", *J.P.E.*, 1976.

CLENDENNING, E.W., *The Euro-Currency Markets and the International Activities of Canadian Banks*, Ottawa: Economic Council of Canada, 1976.

DEAN, J.W. and GRUBEL, H.G., "Multinational Canadian Banking: Its Nature, Growth and Effects on Welfare", Vancouver, B.C.: Simon Fraser University Discussion paper, 1976.

DONALDSON, T.H., *International Lending by Commercial Banks*, New York: J. Wiley, 1979.

DUFEY, G. and GIDDY, I., *The International Money Market*, New Jersey: Prentice Hall, 1978.

The Economist, "The Crash of 198?: Banks Feel the Earth Move under their Feet", Oct. 16, 1982, p. 23-26.

GRUBEL, H.G., "A Theory of Multinational Banking", in this *Review*, Dec. 1977.

GRUBEL, H.G., "Towards a Theory of Free Economic Zones", *Weltwirtschaftliches Archiv*, 1, 1982.

GRUBEL, H.G., "Is There an Important Role for an International Reserve Asset such as the SDRs?" Comment on a paper by W.M. Corden at the 1983 IMF Conference on the Future of the International Monetary System, forthcoming.

HALL, ROBERT E., "Friedman and Schwartz' Monetary Trends — Three Views: A Neo-Chicagoan View", *J. of Econ. Liter.*, 4, 20, Dec. 1982.

HAYEK, FRIEDRICH VON, *Denationalization of Money*, Hobart Paper Special No. 70, Institute of Economic Affairs, London, 1976.

JOHNSTON, R.B., *The Economics of the Euro-Market*, New York: St. Martin's Press, 1982.

KANE, D.R., *The Eurodollar Market and the Years of Crisis*, New York: St. Martin's Press, 1983.

KHOURY, S.J., *Dynamics of International Banking*, New York: Praeger, 1980.

KINDLEBERGER, C.P., "The Formation of Financial Centers: A Study in Comparative History", Princeton: *Studies in International Finance*, No. 3, 1974.

MENDELSOHN, M.S., *Money on the Move*, New York: McGraw-Hill, 1980.

MITCHELL, D.W., "The Effects of Interest-Bearing Required Reserves on Bank Portfolio Riskiness", *J. of Fin. and Quant. Analysis*, June 1982.

RUGMAN, A.M., *International Diversification and the Multinational Enterprise*, Lexington, Mass.: D.C. Heath, 1979.

TOBIN, J., "Towards Improving the Efficiency of the Monetary Mechanism", *Rev. of Econ. and Stat.*, Aug. 1960.

[12]

Excerpt from *Research Notes and Discussion Paper No. 56* (1985), 1–21.

I

INTRODUCTION

Banks have always engaged in international business. They have dealt in foreign exchange, extended credit in connection with foreign trade, traded and held foreign assets, and provided travellers with letters of credit. All this and some other types of business the banks historically have carried out from their domestic locations. There was no need for a physical presence abroad. Business that could not be carried out by mail or telecommunications was handled by correspondent banks abroad.

Some banks began to establish a physical presence abroad in the late 19th and early 20th century. This move abroad mostly was part of colonialism. Under the umbrella of the home country's colonial government, banks from Britain opened branches in the Indian subcontinent, Africa, Hong Kong, and Singapore; European and North American banks moved into the Caribbean and Latin America. These banks provided modern banking services to economies which previously had no or only a relatively rudimentary financial industry.

Multinational, also sometimes called transnational, banking is of relatively recent origin. Its development coincided and accelerated with the technological improvements and cost-reductions in international travel and communications in the post-war period. This type of banking involves the physical presence of a bank abroad.

The most prevalent and versatile legal form of this presence is a branch, which uses the home-country bank's name and organization. It is usually an independent corporate entity with limited liabilities, whose shares are owned by the parent. Other legal forms used in foreign physical presence are agencies and representative offices, which have limited legal operational authority but also limited liabilities. Subsidiaries are used if ownership is shared with other firms or individuals, mostly resi-

1

dents of the country hosting the foreign bank. These subsidiaries are mostly corporations with limited liability. In addition, of course, banks have maintained networks of correspondent banks for doing business in locations where they have no physical presence.

The theory of multinational banking explains why these banks find it profitable to have a physical presence abroad. The theory takes as given the most fundamental and important reason for any foreign investment: it raises the risk-adjusted rate of return to capital invested in the firm. The theory then develops explanations of the sources of comparative advantage, which allows a bank abroad to compete effectively with domestic banks. These domestic banks would be expected to be more familiar with local customs, laws, governments, and business firms, and to have other cost advantages. For example, their managers are locals who do not have to be paid a premium salary to persuade them to work in a foreign and sometimes relatively unpleasant environment. They do not have to co-ordinate business across borders and spend extra money on legal, translation, and communication services.

The theory of multinational banking addresses the same question as the theory of multinational enterprise generally. It is therefore no surprise to find that there is much overlap between the two theories. Both rest on the proposition that modern business generates certain assets for which there is no market except inside the firm. To exploit the value of these assets, therefore, the firm must operate abroad once it has expanded to the fullest extent domestically. Through these foreign operations it increases the return to its domestic capital above what it would have been without this move abroad. Assets giving rise to this motive are marketing and managerial know-how and information about home-country multinational manufacturing firms and tourists.

Other important motives for multinational banking are the avoidance or evasion of national taxation by customers and the escape from regulation and taxation by the banks themselves. There are also certain technical scale economies and benefits from the international diversification of business and portfolios.

In the following I discuss these motives for international banking in greater detail and then use the ideas to speculate about the welfare effects it has had. But before I turn to these topics, I present some empirical data about the magnitude of multinational banking.

2

II

SOME FACTS ABOUT MULTINATIONAL BANKING

Table 1 contains some information about the number of branches and representative offices which banks from different countries have maintained in other countries and regions of the world in 1983. These data are presented in an analytical table here for the first time. They were obtained from the country pages of the Bankers Almanac and Yearbook. The vertical list of countries is virtually complete in showing the countries of the world that have a foreign presence. The horizontal groupings were chosen in order to keep the size of the matrix manageable without loss of insights about the extent to which the world's banks have interpenetrated each others' territories.

The data show that all of the industrial countries have large numbers of branches and representative offices in other industrial countries, as well as in developing countries and the two major communist countries, the USSR and China. However, it is also noteworthy that the developing countries have banking presences in most of the industrial countries. In addition, they have networks within regions of developing countries, as in Latin America.

The United Kingdom is the home of the largest number of foreign banks, most of which are located in Africa. The United States is home to the second largest number of banks, followed by France. The latter country has a remarkably small number of foreign banks in its territory, given that it has such a large presence abroad. The Caribbean hosts the largest number of foreign banks, except for Africa, whereas the United States and the United Kingdom host a very large number of foreign banks. Remarkably large for the size of the territory and populations are the number of banks in Belgium/Luxembourg, Hongkong, and Singapore.

The growth of multinational banking may be judged by the fact that in 1968 the number of the same type of foreign banks was reported to have been 2,744 (Lees 1974). Since, according to

3

TABLE 1

The World Matrix of Multinational Banks In 1983

Country of Parent Bank	CANADA	U.S.A.	CARIBBN	LATAMER	U.K.	FRANCE	BELGLUX	NETHLDS	GERMANY	SWITZLD	ITALY	OTHEUR	AFRICA	MIDEAST	INDIASU	USSR	CHINA	ASIAPAC	JAPAN	HONGKONG	ASEAN	SINGAPO	AUSTRAL	TOTAL
										Country or Region of Foreign Presence														
Africa		1			9	4							1						1	1				18
Argentin		9	1	27	1	1			2	1	2			1					1	2		5		45
Austral		17	2	1	8				1		2	1	2	1			2	1	5	2	3	1		47
Austria		1			2														2	1		1		12
Bahrain					1																			3
Bangled					7										2									14
Belg/Lux		9	1	40	4	4		1	1	2	4	5	5	5		2			4	25	5	5	4	102
Brazil		19	10	31	7		3		4	1	2	6	5	3					2	7	2	2	1	102
Canada	3	39	44	17	9	5	1		3	1	2	2	7		2			4	6	7	5	5	5	173
Chile		3		4					1															8
China		3	1	1	3							2						3		56		3		32
Columb		2		1																				3
Denmk		4	14	2	1							2							3	2	1		1	31
Egypt			1											8										10
France	9	31	102		26	16	5		32	10	18	24	11	37	13	7	8	6	18	43	16	10	11	453
Germany	4	24	6	46	12	4					6	15	5	11	4	3	3	1	17	8	7	6	6	195
Greece	1	3			3		1		2	1	1			2								2	2	14
Hongkong		11	1	2	10	1		1	2					2	24		6	5	4	14	39	13	1	124
India	2	7	1	1	41				2				11	11	6			2	3		3	7		114
Indones		1			1														1			2		6
Israel	5	12	2	9	6		3	1	1	1	1		2			4				1	1			44
Italy	2	32	1	18	19	8		2	22	8		13	1	13			2		5	5	1	4	5	177

	Totals
Japan	384
Korea	70
Leban	6
Malays	39
Mexico	20
Nethld	150
Pakist	155
Panam	11
Parag	11
Peru	5
Phili	22
Singap	107
Spain	268
SriLan	1
Switz	133
Taiwan	9
Turkey	45
UAE	34
Urug	1752
USA	30
Venez	842
	15
Totals	9814

Totals (row): 554, 770, 159, 58, 180, 349, 90, 215, 169, 62, 241, 413, 68, 241, 186, 76, 1504, 109, 45, 160, 241, 95, 9814

Notes:

* = 1432

The regional groupings consist of the following: **Latin America:** Venezuela, Uruguay, Surinam, Peru, Paraguay, Panama, Mexico, Columbia, Chile, Brazil, Argentina; **ASEAN:** Philippines, Malaysia, Indonesia; **Other Western Europe:** Turkey, Spain, Greece, Denmark, Austria; **Caribbean:** Cayman Islands, Bahamas; **Asia-Pacific:** Taiwan, Korea, Guam; **Middle East and Egypt:** Bahrain, United Arab Emirates, Saudi Arabia, Lebanon, Israel, Egypt; **Africa:** Kenya and Republic of South Africa.

Table 1, the 1983 figure was 5,814, there has been a growth of 3,070, or 119 per cent in 10 years.

The importance of multinational banking can also be measured by the value of foreign banks' assets and liabilities, both absolutely and in relation to those of the host countries and the world as a whole. Unfortunately, data for the calculation of this measure are not available except for the United States. Here, the share of foreign banks' assets in the US total has risen from 3.6 per cent in 1972 to 9.5 per cent in 1978 (Goldberg and Saunders 1981). Since then, the share has continued to rise, but it is not certain by how much.

Finally, it is interesting that for some of the smaller countries that have become multinational banking centres, the industry has developed into a major contributor to GDP. In industrial countries, most of the banking services are attributed by national income accountants as intermediate inputs into the production of consumer and investment goods because they are purchased by domestic firms. Therefore, the amount of GDP originating from consumer spending on banking services is only about 1 per cent of GDP. In small countries with a large multinational banking sector, on the other hand, most of the services of banks are exported and therefore enter GDP as such. They have been estimated to be as high as 15 per cent of GDP for Luxembourg and undoubtedly are of similar importance for Hong Kong, Singapore and some other such multinational banking centres.

6

III

RETAIL AND SERVICE BANKING

Some international banks have branches abroad that compete with the local banks for the traditional retail banking business. Thus, we can find the large British banks in South Africa and Kenya; Canadian banks are in the Caribbean; banks from England and Japan are in California; U.S. and French banks are in some Latin American and Caribbean countries.

These banks often introduced modern banking to these countries at an early stage of economic development. Since the end of World War II and the growth of economic nationalism, these banks have been on the retreat. In some cases they were forced to close down by legislative actions. In others more subtle tax measures were used to encourage the development of a competitive, domestically owned and operated banking industry, which reduced or ultimately drove out these foreign banks.

All this history has a simple analytical explanation. At an early stage of economic development local entrepreneurs did not have the technical know-how or human capital to establish and operate modern banks. The banks in the developed countries brought this know-how and human capital from their home operations, using well established and proven managerial, marketing, accounting and other procedures. However, these sources of comparative advantage eventually became accessible to domestic entrepreneurs in the developing countries, either through education abroad, the imitation of foreign banks or purchase from consultants. At such a point, the innate advantages accruing to local entrepreneurs became dominant, and it was natural that they should eventually come to dominate the industry. In the case of some British banks, their continued operations in countries like South Africa and Kenya are British only in name. They have almost complete local autonomy and are run dominantly by local people with very limited perspectives on the global maximization of the parents' profits.

The growth of foreign retail banking in California in recent years has a slightly different explanation. Its origin stems from the ability of banks to offer differentiated packages of services appealing to specialized segments of consumers. Thus, Japanese banks in California appeal to Americans with Japanese backgrounds and others with similar tastes. In a sense, therefore, the new generation of foreign retail banks represents only an extension of the process of product differentiation which has characterized domestic banking in all Western countries. It is not likely to grow very much or become a strong force in international banking and finance.

Multinational Service Banking

In the post-war years international trade, direct foreign investment, and tourism have grown at a very rapid rate, partly because of the overall growth in income and partly because of technological innovations which lowered the cost of transportation and communication and made possible the effective global control of business operations. Banks both followed and pioneered this internationalization of business. As they followed firms and tourists, they offered services that their home-country customers had become accustomed to. In so doing they prevented them from going to foreign banks and getting used to their services. Once abroad, banks also provided information to firms in their home countries about business conditions abroad and assisted them in starting operations in other countries.

The basic economic factor enabling banks to compete with foreign banks for this type of business is knowledge. For example, a U.S. bank has daily operational contacts with a U.S. manufacturing firm. It knows the most current status of its balance sheets and income statements. It has inside information about product development and the health of its chief executive officers. It collects this knowledge routinely as necessary input into loan and other banking decisions.

This knowledge is needed in providing bank services to the foreign operations of the U.S. manufacturing firm and has two important characteristics. First, the marginal cost of its use abroad is practically zero. Second, there is no market where foreign competitors can buy it. For these reasons, the U.S. banks abroad can service the subsidiaries of U.S. based multinational trading, manufacturing and service enterprises at a lower cost than their local competitors.

8

However, the U.S. banks abroad also offer their U.S. customers a special kind of attraction. U.S. businessmen and tourists abroad find it more convenient and cheaper to deal with a bank that uses business practices with which they are familiar. The offices of American Express deliberately provide an environment that makes U.S. tourists feel at home. No foreign bank can hope to compete with those efforts, which are almost legendary among American tourists.

The growth of this service business of multinational banks has levelled off at the same time that the growth of international trade, tourism, and investment has stagnated in the early 1980s. It remains to be seen whether this development represents merely a recession or a more fundamental structural change.

9

IV

TAX EVASION, GLOBAL MONEY, AND CAPITAL MARKET BANKING

The largest proportion of all foreign bank presences is not for participation in the local retail or the international service markets. Foreign banks exist for two main reasons: the evasion of domestic taxes and regulations, and the participation in global money and capital markets. It is a striking characteristic of banks in this type of business that they are often found in the upper floors of office buildings and have only very small areas for servicing customers through tellers and other typical retail banking facilities.

During the 1960s there developed so-called paper banking centres. These are typically located on small islands with sovereign governments, such as Bermuda and the Cayman Islands. Favourable legislation encouraged foreign banks to open "brass plate" offices, which establish nothing but a legal presence there. A foreign bank would buy a licence for as little as $20,000 a year, hire a lawyer, and rent a postal box. Local lawyers represent many banks in this fashion and signify their commitment by attaching brass plates with the banks' names outside their offices. From this practice stems the name of the undertakings.

Banks keep separate books on their paper centre operations in their domestic offices. One advantage of doing this has been that the business escapes certain domestic regulations and taxes. It also assures depositors and lenders anonymity from domestic legal and taxation authorities, which the banks cannot offer otherwise. The growth of this business has been curtailed sharply by legislation in the major industrial countries, especially the United States, which deliberately was aimed at closing these tax-havens for ordinary business and the refuge possibilities for criminal dealings. Of course, it is not possible to legislate away all such activities, but the relative importance of paper centres has declined since the early 1970s.

Euro and Asian Currency Markets

The main business of multinational banks now consists of participation in global money and capital markets functioning in all of
the traditional major industrial cities of the world such as New
York, London, Paris, Frankfurt, Zurich, Milan, Tokyo, and Mont-
real. It also functions in locations that do not have the rich
industrial base as these cities, such as Panama, Luxembourg,
Bahrain, Singapore, and Hong Kong. Location of banks in all of
these centres is a necessary condition for participation in capital market transactions, where a physical presence at meetings,
proximity to transactions, and to the demanders and suppliers of
funds generate substantial information and transactions economies.

The most successful multinational banking centres have attracted the international capital market business by providing an
environment that is relatively free from taxation and regulation.
Especially the smaller centres without a large industrial base
have deregulated banking deliberately in order to create an environment attractive to foreign banks. The Singapore government,
for instance, asked the large banks of the world to prepare a
wish-list of regulatory and tax concessions needed to make them
establish a presence there. After some bargaining and strategic
decisions, many of these concessions were granted, and Singapore
today has a flourishing multinational banking industry where
previously it had none. At a time when growth of the Singapore
business was slower than had been expected, the authorities discovered that a certain local tax encouraged banks to take some of
their business to Hong Kong. This offensive tax was removed
promptly and growth resumed.

Deregulation

Probably the most important form of regulation absent from these
multinational banking centres are minimum reserve requirements.
These requirements represent a fairly heavy, implicit tax on
banking. Thus, consider a bank which obtains a $100 deposit. In
the absence of a reserve requirement it can lend out, say $90,
leaving $10 as a liquid, non-interest bearing asset. If the
interest paid on the deposit by the bank is 8 per cent and it
earns 10 per cent on its loan, the gross margin is $1 per $100 of
deposits.

Now consider the margin of this bank when the government
insists that out of every $100 deposit it diverts 5 per cent, or
$5 into a non-interest bearing deposit with the central bank. It
still has to keep the same liquid safety margin of $10, so under
these conditions it can make a loan of only $85. Assuming that

11

the bank's lending and borrowing rates remain the same, the bank's income is only \$8.50 and its interest costs are \$8, leaving a margin of only \$0.50. In other words, the innocent looking 5 per cent reserve requirement results in reduction of the gross operating margin from \$1 to \$0.50. This is an implicit tax of 50 per cent. Now if \$0.45 of the gross margin in the regulated situation is spent on labour, equipment, and rent, the profit is \$0.05 per \$100 of bank business. Under the assumption that the operating costs of the bank are the same in the regulated and deregulated environment, escape from the reserve requirement raises profits from \$0.05 to \$0.55, or by 1,000 per cent.

These simple calculations capture the essence of the reason for the growth of multinational banking since the 1960s. U.S. and other banks moved to London and have been able to accept deposits and make loans in U.S. dollars without having to maintain required reserves with either the U.S. Federal Reserve System or the Bank of England. This has been so because traditionally, domestic monetary authorities have not required such reserves on deposits denominated in foreign currencies. These deposits have grown rapidly -- world-wide and in all currencies, they amounted to over \$2,500 billion in 1985. They are usually referred to as Euro-currency deposits and Asian currency deposits, depending on the location of the banking centres. It is clear that more generally they should be referred to as geographic currency deposits, though another popular descriptive term is offshore deposits.

The growth of this business was caused by the ability of the multinational banks to offer somewhat higher deposit rates and charge somewhat lower loan rates on business transacted in these offshore banking centres. These advantages have not been great enough to attract retail and small commercial business. However, large corporations and financial institutions, as well as governments and quasi-government agencies have been able to take advantage of these favourable interest rates. The multinational banks in these centres developed to perfection the system of loan syndication in order to meet the needs of very large borrowers. These syndicated loans led to a diversification of loan risks that was very attractive to the banks. They were the vehicle by which the governments and other borrowers in developing countries were able to obtain loans so readily that they overborrowed and found themselves in the debt crisis, which rocked the world in the early 1980s.

Offshore banking was encouraged not only by the absence of reserve requirements, but also by advantageous other regulations and tax treatment. For example, withholding taxes on interest income earned by depositors are absent in all of the offshore banking centres. This gives the multinational banks in this business a big competitive edge over their domestic rivals. However, the very great importance of the reserve requirements may be judged from the fact that after the introduction of these require- ments on foreign currencies in Germany, multinational banks in that country reduced their presence substantially, and all of the Euro-currency business left the country.

Money Market Operations

However, statistics show that only about a quarter of the loans of the multinational banks are to ultimate borrowers such as govern- ments and corporations. The rest at any given moment in time are very short-term interbank loans and deposits. This business parallels the Federal Funds Market of the United States and equi- valent short-term interbank markets in other countries designed to make the most efficient use possible of the commercial banks' reserves with central banks. The multinational banks have exten- ded this business around the world.

Money in this market moves at extremely narrow margins be- tween lending and borrowing rates and in very short maturities, often just over night. The market takes advantage to some extent of the fact that the world has daylight and working hours at different periods of the 24-hour earth day. It is highly effi- cient because it involves banks that have close operating rela- tionships, which assures up-to-date information about credit- worthiness and has led to procedures that minimize transactions costs. Thus, billions of dollars are lent and borrowed on the basis of agreement reached over the telephone.

International currency exposures are an important aspect of multinational banking. As it turns out, the banks have managed to deal with these risks very effectively by simply matching assets and liabilities by maturities in every currency in their port- folio. As a result, the losses from the devaluation of a currency held are exactly matched by gains on liabilities in that same currency. The multinational banks have also succeeded in protect- ing themselves against changes in interest rates by the adoption of floating rates on both assets and liabilities. To the extent that they deal in fixed rates they have also matched assets and liabilities. However, it has not been possible to protect the business against the risk of default. The international debt crisis of the 1980s has raised this possibility, though no actual defaults of really major borrowers have taken place. This has been achieved at least in part by rescheduling of debt maturities, which in turn has increased the riskiness of the business above planned levels.

13

Other Economic Causes

The capital market business of multinational banks has been encouraged also by two other benefits. First, the multinational
banking centres have made it possible to generate large economies
of operation for the individual banks and for the industry through
externalities in the generation of information and transactions
costs. The banks in this business typically do not accept deposits smaller than $1 million and make loans only in large amounts,
though the banks in Singapore and Hong Kong have attempted to tap
a large market by accepting at one time deposits as small as
$5,000. They avoid the costs of dealing with retail customers,
such as check-clearing, cash services and instalment loans (hire
purchase agreements), which represent a large share of the cost of
doing business for domestic banks. The capital markets in the
multinational banking centres have become models of integration
and efficiency, made possible by the intensive use of electronic
equipment and the favourable legal environment. The centres have
become the heart of a web of relationships with banks in the
surrounding territory channelling funds back and forth and providing intermediation more efficiently than the regional banks ever
could.

A second benefit from participation in multinational banking
stems from the diversification of business and risks. The increased geographical spread of loans widens the types of influences affecting the banks' portfolios and since most of these
influences are imperfectly correlated, they end up stabilizing
earnings. It has been shown statistically (Rugman 1979) that the
earnings of multinational banks are more stable the greater their
international involvement. As is well known, wealthholders like
such stability and correspondingly bid up the share prices of
these banks and permit them to borrow at a lower cost.

All of these benefits from participation in the multinational
banking business have raised the profits of these institutions
during the 1970s and until the international crisis of the 1980s.

As an example of such profitability and international market
participation consider Canadian banks. During the 1970s the share
of foreign currency assets and liabilities in the total rose from
about 10 per cent to about 50 per cent. At the same time, profits
attributable to foreign operations rose to about 60 per cent of
the total (Grubel 1983). In the 1980s, however, the multinational
banks found many of their foreign loans to be non-performing, that
is, they received no interest and amortization payments. Many
should possibly be written off as non-collectible, but banks have
been reluctant to take this step. Profits from foreign operations
are down and many banks have withdrawn from offshore banking
activities. A number of U.S. banks especially have withdrawn from

London, where probably they should never have been, given the existing U.S. banking laws which severely restrict their basis of operation in the United States.

It may well be that the expansion phase of multinational banking and international capital market participation has ended. Certainly, it has become more and more difficult for new banking centres to develop in competition with existing ones. Most locations with advantageous time zones and hinterlands have been occupied, or their advantages have been pre-empted by economies of scale in others.

V

WELFARE EFFECTS

The beneficial welfare effects of multinational banking have been as follows. First, the retail and service banking activities have permitted the spreading of the fixed costs of investment in managerial control, marketing, and other know-how over a broader base. It has lowered the average cost of these investments to consumers in the home country. It has also resulted in overall lower costs of banking to consumers in the host country. Therefore the productivity of investment has been raised in the world as a whole.

In many countries domestic banking is oligopolistic and competes mostly through non-price mechanisms, such as product differentiation and tied-in sales. Through this mechanism oligopolistic rents are dissipated in real resource expenditures and even though bank profits are not excessively high, consumers face a larger spread between lending and borrowing rates than they would under greater competition. Multinational retail and service banks entering a country typically are not members of the domestic cartel and therefore can compete on price. In doing so they bring pressures on the domestic banks to do the same and the result is a more efficient system for the benefit of consumers.

Second, the global network of multinational banks and centres has integrated the world's capital markets, assuring that savings generated anywhere in the world are more likely to be used most productively in another part of the world. In addition, by causing narrower spreads, they have encouraged some lenders who would otherwise have kept their funds idle to make them available for loans. At the same time, the lower borrowing rates have encouraged some borrowers from entering the capital market who would not have done so otherwise.

Third, the benefits from diversification on the stability of bank earnings have raised the welfare of wealth-holders.

Fourth, the growth of multinational banking has forced governments to re-examine the merit of banking regulation and taxation. As a result, the regulatory and taxation system of a number of countries has been made more efficient and made consistent with the mandates of modern technology.

However, multinational banking has also had some negative welfare effects. They have arisen mainly as a result of the banks' escape from the regulatory environments that governments had established in the past for the protection of the public. Presumably, these regulations forced the internalization of externalities and led to the creation of socially useful information. It has been argued that through this escape the banks engaged in unhealthy competitive lending to developing countries, which may yet disrupt the stability of the entire world's financial system. Imperfect information about the lending of subsidiaries abroad prevented domestic bank supervisory authorities from noticing that there had developed an unhealthy concentration of loans to a few borrowers and an excess of loans over capital that had been considered prudent in the past.

Furthermore, the loss of revenue from the taxation of banking has required the raising of other taxes and possibly the development of new and more serious distortions in other sectors of the economy. Finally, the greater integration of the world's capital market means that the national monetary independence of countries has been eroded further. The multinational banking system has become a most efficient conduit for short-term capital flows which prevent national governments from pursuing monetary and fiscal policy for the benefit of their domestic economies. Moreover, short-term capital flows following speculative rather than real economic sentiments, have added to the instability of exchange rates and have made economic management more difficult.

A more subtle, rather technical criticism of the multinational banking system focuses on the fact that it makes private gains from the more efficient use of money, which in turn costs very little to produce. Therefore, banks waste real resources economizing on the use of a commodity which governments can make available at practically zero cost by an increase in commercial bank reserves and the printing of notes. Increases in the velocity of circulation and of money multipliers of national money supplies represent a very dubious social benefit.

All of these costs, however, can easily be overestimated. New theories of regulation suggest that they have reduced welfare to the extent that regulatory authorities have been captured by interest groups representing the allegedly regulated. The market solution, while not costless, may in fact be more efficient than regulation perverted from its original purpose. The transition

17

from a regulated to a deregulated environment may have presented difficulties which are likely to disappear in the longer run. The world's private banks have in fact already created the Institute for International Finance in Washington, which is charged with the task of gathering and disseminating information about loans made to individual borrowers. In the presence of such a system, a problem, such as overlending to developing countries, is unlikely to recur.

It is also worth remembering that the multinational banking system developed when the world went through a very severe economic crisis brought about by the oil price increases of 1974 and 1979 and the accompanying payments surpluses of the oil exporters and the deficits of many oil users. The banks recirculated these surpluses and probably prevented the crisis from becoming even larger than it was. Finally, the multinational banks probably added very little to the integration of the world's capital markets and therefore to the loss of national monetary sovereignty. These developments were dominated by the evolution of new technologies. The institution of multinational banking only made the new system somewhat more efficient.

VI

IMPLICATIONS FOR PUBLIC POLICY

It is obvious from the preceding list of costs and benefits from the development of multinational banking that the final word on them is not yet in. It may take years to the final assessment of the costs of the international debt crisis. The evolution of new private institutions needed for the generation of information in a deregulated environment is not complete and should continue to evolve in response to new technologies and institutions.

Judgments of the costs and benefits are also coloured by the analysts' faith in unregulated markets on the one hand and the ability of governments to improve welfare through regulation on the other. These characteristics of analysts are highly corre-lated with their political views. For this reason, the assessment of multinational banking, like that of most economic institutions, often has political overtones.

However, there is a technical and politically rather neutral policy issue concerning multinational banks. During the 1970s the U.S. Government initiated negotiations for the international, collective imposition of regulation of the industry, administered through the IMF, the Bank for International Settlements, or a similar institution. These initiatives went nowhere, as most governments correctly judged that such regulation would push the banks into other countries, which would only be too glad to open their doors to them. There exists no conceivable, voluntary mechanism that could assure that such shifting of bank activities would not take place.

A more sensible policy for the control of multinational banking would be to eliminate the distortion caused by domestic reserve requirements. Not only do these requirements result in distortions in domestic financial markets, they also represent a strong incentive for moving banking operations abroad and into foreign currencies, as noted above. The elimination of these

19

incentives does not require the abandonment of reserve requirements. It would only be necessary to pay interest on the central
bank deposits of the commercial banks. That this is so, can
easily be seen from the above numerical analysis.

The proposal has the support of a number of economists and
research departments of central banks and international organizations. It has not been adopted because the interest which central
banks would have to pay the commercial banks, under present arrangements would be lost to governments as general tax revenue.
While opposition to the proposal based on these arguments is
understandable from the point of view of democratic political
systems, it is not warranted in the light of the fact that these
revenues are very small as a proportion of total tax revenues. It
also would require only a relatively simple education campaign to
convince the public that such interest payments would raise the
profits of banks just briefly. Competition would be certain to
lead quickly to smaller spreads between lending and borrowing
rates to the benefit of domestic consumers of bank services. And
with the distorting incentive removed, multinational banking would
find its reduced, efficient level.

BIBLIOGRAPHY

There exists a very large literature relevant to the analysis of this study. The following articles contain precise references or have been mentioned in the article:

Aliber, R.Z. "A Survey of Multinational Banking". Journal of Money, Credit and Banking, 1985.

Goldberg L.G. and A. Saunders. "The Growth of Organizational Forms of Foreign Banks in the United States". Journal of Money, Credit and Banking, 1981.

Grubel, H.G. "A Theory of Multinational Banking". Banca Nazionale del Lavoro, December 1977.

————. "The New International Banking". Banca Nazionale del Lavoro, September 1983.

Lees, F.A. International Banking and Finance. London: Macmillan, 1974.

Rugman, A.M. International Diversification and the Multinational Enterprise. Lexington, Mass.: Lexington Books, 1979.

Yannapolous, G.N. "The Growth of Transnational Banking". In The Growth of International Business, edited by M. Casson. London: George Allen and Unwin, 1984.

[13]

Profitable Currency Speculation:
Service to Users or Destabilizing?

Herbert G. Grubel*

F31
D84

Introduction

The publications by Milton Friedman (1953) and Egon Sohmen (1961/ 1969) present to this day two of the most articulate and comprehensive statements of the case for flexible exchange rates. A part of this case is the proposition that in the absence of government intervention, speculators may be expected to stabilize exchange rates.

This proposition rests on two simple but powerful theorems from price theory. First, only persistently profitable speculators survive competition; persistent losers run out of equity and disappear from the market. Second, persistently profitable speculation results in the stabilization of the exchange rate, since profits can only be made by buying when the prices are low, which raises them, and selling when prices are high, which lowers them.

Towards the end of the 1950s, a number of economists challenged the general validity of the theorem that persistent profits from speculation necessarily imply stabilization. The most notable of the contributors to this literature were Baumol (1957), Telser (1959), Stein (1961), and Kemp (1963). Sohmen (1969) critically analyzed the merit of these studies. In the careful manner of a good theorist, Sohmen concluded that, in the end, the issue could not be resolved theoretically, but required real world observations. Nevertheless, he found that the models used in the counterexamples to the basic proposition were based on highly restrictive assumptions about dynamic processes and could not be considered to represent a significant argument against the presumptively stabilizing influence of persistently profitable speculation.

The currency upheavals of the 1970s that took place in the wake of the first oil-price shock elicited a number of studies that attributed the large exchange rate fluctuations to excessive speculation. Contributors to this debate were Bell (1974), who quotes a survey of the Group of Thirty

*I acknowledge the receipt of useful comments on an earlier draft of this paper by Heinz Arndt, Stephan Schulmeister, Wolfgang Kasper, and participants at the Egon Sohmen Memorial Conference.

Economists, and Kindleberger (1976). These studies are reviewed by Baillie and MacMahon (1989). These authors also endorse the view that the fluctuations have been caused by speculators. However, none of the authors in this 1970s literature discuss evidence on consistent profits earned by identifiable groups of speculators.

During the late 1980s the same topic that had been treated by Sohmen was raised again directly by Schulmeister (1988) and indirectly by Dornbusch and Frankel (1988), Frankel and Froot (1986, 1988, 1990), and DeLong et al. (1987).[1] Ironically, of course, this new challenge to the standard theorems about the stabilizing influence of profitable speculation is aimed critically at the experience with flexible exchange rates, the introduction and merit of which Sohmen had advocated so effectively.[2]

Interestingly, none of the authors in the new literature recommend a return to fixed exchange rates. Instead, they discuss corrective policies proposed by others, like the taxation of international capital flows or the introduction of dual exchange rates, only to reject them as not practical in the technologically sophisticated world of today. Nevertheless, the implications of their findings are of some importance. Schulmeister claims that the speculative profits are directly at the expense of real trade in goods and assets and that the unstable rates themselves result in costly externalities. These kinds of arguments support the army of ideological detractors from the free market system and may be expected to lay the groundwork for future interventionist reorganization of the international monetary system.

In this study I consider the merit of these new challenges to the old orthodoxy. I reach the uncomfortable conclusion that, in spite of the

---

[1] Incidentally, this new literature has no references to Sohmen's work. However, the rapid decay of citations of the work of retired or deceased economists like Paul Samuelson and Harry Johnson suggests that the explosion of knowledge has made for rapid obsolescence of past work generally and that the absence of citations to Sohmen's treatment should not be considered to be a negative reflection on its scientific merit. Rather, in my view, it reflects negatively on the new generation of economists, whose lack of historic and doctrinal perspectives often reduces the social value or their work.

[2] There are other prominent economists who advocate the adoption of exchange rate systems other than a free float. One of the most prominent and vocal of these is John Williamson (1981, 1985), who, in a number of publications, has argued for global agreements on the adoption of targets and crawling pegs. McKinnon (1988) recommends global agreement on the coordination of national monetary policies.

The recommendations for these policies are based on the perception that exchange rates are unduly unstable because there is too much speculation, according to Williamson, and too little speculation, according to McKinnon. These authors have not presented detailed evidence on excess exchange rate variability, the role of speculators, and their profits and losses. For this reason I do not deal with their arguments here. However, it is worth noting this literature as evidence of the widespread perception that speculators unduly destabilized exchange rates during the 1970s and 1980s.

availability of substantial data, empirical work did not resolve the basic issue, as Sohmen had hoped. The profession remains with assessments that in the 1990s still have to rely on the principles that underpinned the views of Friedman and Sohmen in the earlier debates.

1 The New Challenges

The clearest and most unambiguous challenge to the conventional wisdom on the stabilizing effect of persistently profitable speculation in foreign exchange markets is found in Schulmeister (1987, 1988, 1990). He notes that the foreign exchange trading departments of the major international banks are known to have made large profits from foreign currency speculation. In support of this proposition he cites profit levels found in public bank reports. In 1985, twelve large US banks earned income in their foreign exchange trading department amounting to US $1,165 million. Similar profits were reported for a large number of years. He argues that the speculation by banks has increased the volatility of exchange rates and that the profits have been earned "at the expense" of importers and exporters of goods and services.

The arguments made by Dornbusch and Frankel (1988) and Frankel and Froot (1986, 1988, 1990) are summarized most conveniently in Dornbusch and Frankel (1988, p. 165) in a section entitled: "It appears that little of the speculation that takes place is stabilising." At the same time that Dornbusch, Frankel, and Froot argue that speculation is destabilizing, they assert that banks make consistent profits, citing Schulmeister and Goodhart (1987) for supporting evidence. They also report that there is a strong demand for the services of advisors selling foreign exchange rate forecasts, especially those of chartists, which they believe to be based on nonrational models. Such firms could not be expected to prosper if they and the buyers of their services did not profit from the activities. These authors, therefore, imply that speculation in recent years has been both destabilizing and profitable.

The theoretical models and empirical evidence used by Dornbusch, Frankel, and Froot are presented and evaluated in later sections, after consideration of the possibility that speculation by banks is not consistently profitable.

2 There are no Profits from Speculation

A critical analysis of the new challenges to the Friedman-Sohmen theorem must consider the possibility that some of the factual assertions of the literature are false. One candidate for possible falsification is that banks do not make speculative profits. Dornbusch and Frankel suggest that "the reported profits are not so large that, when divided by the volume of 'real' transactions for customers, they need necessarily lie outside the normal (relatively small) band of the bid-ask spread. In other words, the profits represent the transactions costs for the outside customers" (1988, p. 168).

Dornbusch and Frankel leave this statement without further discussion. However, there is strong evidence that the high profits by banks are due to speculation. Goodhart (1987) reports the results of a survey of banks in the London foreign exchange markets. I have interviewed a foreign exchange dealer working for a Canadian bank. From these sources it appears that the foreign exchange trading departments generally follow the conservative regulations that were imposed after the failure of the Herrstatt and Franklin Banks during the 1970s. The foreign exchange trading divisions of banks cover all exchange risks that arise from the provision of services to their nonbank customers and in arbitrage operations in the interbank market.

However, increasingly since the initial institution of these rules, the trading departments have been given capital for the express purpose of exploiting profit opportunities from holding open foreign exchange positions. This capital is strictly limited, though rising, since it has yielded high rates of return. Open positions overnight are restricted to the size of the allocated capital in order to limit the risk to the bank as a whole.

Great pressures exist on the dealers, who are expected to earn a high rate of return on the capital at their disposal. Those who do not live up to expectations quickly lose their positions. Those who succeed are able to earn high personal rewards in the form of bonuses linked to the profits. The pressures of the job are such that few last for a long time.

In Grubel (1990) I have argued that the speculative profits of these banks' dealers do not occur "at the expense" of their trading customers. Instead, I have suggested that these profits are a return to the stabilization of the exchange rate which is brought about by the speculative activities of the banks. It is clear that this proposition is valid only if consistently profitable speculation is stabilizing.

2.1 Unknown Population of Losers?

It is important to note in this context a fundamental idea contained in Friedman and Sohmen and addressed in the discussion by Baillie and McMahon (1989). It is perfectly possible for a certain group of speculators to be destabilizing and lose money on average. These speculators are drawn into the business by reports of large profit opportunities and often are kept in the activity by temporary successes Eventually, such speculators lose their equity and disappear from the market. They are replaced by a new set of optimists who destabilize exchange rates by engaging in speculation that is unprofitable on average.

In the literature under discussion here, there is no mention of such a group of persistent losers in the markets of the 1980s. The control systems of banks appear to be so effective and competition among banks is so strong that no subgroup of banks can persistently lose from speculation without financial consequences and publicity in the media. The same may be said about the portfolio managers of trusts, pensions, and mutual funds.

At the same time, it cannot be ruled out that there exists a floating population of private speculators that loses regularly, destabilizes the exchange rate, and provides consistent profits for the banks, but is not known. Human nature prevents the advertisement of such behavior and I know of no systematic research on the issue. In the following I rule out this possibility not because I am confident that it is correct but because otherwise the alleged puzzle, which drives this analysis, ceases to exist. More empirical research on this issue is warranted.[3]

3 New Theory

Dornbusch, Frankel, and Froot acknowledge that it is necessary to resolve the conflict between the alleged evidence on the existence of destabilizing speculation and on the consistent profitability of this activity by banks. They attempt to do so essentially by citing theoretical articles that use mathematical constructs to generate examples of destabilizing, profitable

---

[3] More research is also warranted into the question why the daily turnover of foreign exchange in the interbank markets of the world is so high and a large multiple of transactions with nonbanks. Frankel (1988) reports that in March 1986 daily foreign exchange market transactions in the United States were $50 billion among banks and $34.4 billion among brokers and financial institutions, of which only 11.5 percent was with nonbank customers.

One aspect of the activities is reasonably clear. Not all of them involve speculative, open positions. Much of them are explained by the act of covering open positions through swaps. These swaps arise because in most centers of the world, cross rates tend to be quoted and transacted through the dollar. For example, a bank in Frankfurt deals Italian lira to a German importer paying DM by buying dollars with the DM and using the dollars to buy the lira. As a result, a transaction involving X lira tends to result in a turnover of 2X dollars in Frankfurt, all without any speculative motive.

Other transactions are motivated by arbitrage and acting on news. Someone has to make markets perfect. This topic is discussed further in Section 4 below.

speculation. They assert that "the modern theory of rational stochastic speculative bubbles has all but demolished Friedman's claim that investors who bet on destabilising expectations will lose money. In a rational speculative bubble, investors lose money if they DON'T go along with the trend" (Dornbusch and Frankel 1988, p. 165; emphasis in text).[4] They note that DeLong et al. (1987) construct a model in which there exists a class of traders who follow irrelevant noise, and "yet who prosper over time, contrary to Friedman's argument that destabilising speculators would be driven out of the market" (p. 166).

Perhaps the most comprehensive expression of this position is found in Frankel and Froot (1990, p. 184):

> Since Milton Friedman (1963), the standard argument against the importance of destabilizing speculators is that they will on average lose money, and be driven out of the market in the long run. An number of special counter-examples to the Friedman argument have been constructed over the years, most involving heterogeneous actors, (e.g., "suckers" who lose money and "sharpies" who win). The simplest counter-example would be based on the theory of rational speculative bubbles, where each market participant loses money if he DOESN'T go along with the herd. (emphasis in text)[5]

It is not possible to disprove the validity of the theoretical, mathematical arguments by which these conclusions are reached. This is so simply because these arguments involve sophisticated tautologies and the conclusions follow logically from the assumptions made. The authors of these models have selected a small number of assumptions from a very large possible set capable of constituting a simplified picture of reality. The authors of these articles, of course, typically are prepared to defend the realism of the assumptions that they have made. But there are likely to be many other models that are based on similarly defensible assumptions and that do not produce the same conclusions at stake here.[6]

---

[4] However, the authors do not provide a precise reference to the source of this conclusion, which is presented in each of the papers in which Frankel is a co-author. Presumably they assume that all readers are fully familiar with the literature on rational speculative bubbles, which may or may not be appropriate. Below I present some methodological criticism related to this issue.

[5] In the appendix I present a simple model that attempts to incorporate the essential features of the speculative bubble and various other processes, in an attempt to shed light on the consistency of the various assertions found in the literature.

[6] The best known of these is, of course, the Friedman "model" noted above. In contrast to the new models, this one has the advantage of simplicity and use of assumptions the validity and central importance of which are disputed by few economists. However, there is a puzzle why there are no articles that use sophisticated tautologies to prove that profitable speculation is stabilizing. I think that the answer to this puzzle is found in the fact that rewards in economic science tend to favor research that is "news" in the sense that it proves market failure and sheds doubt on the efficiency of free markets.

These considerations leave me with the same conclusion reached by Sohmen during the 1960s. The issue cannot be resolved theoretically. Empirical evidence is needed. This fact has been recognized by Dornbusch, Frankel, and Froot. In the following sections I discuss the empirical evidence that they have introduced in support of the basic proposition that speculation has been destabilizing exchange rates. It should be noted that this proposition is logically divorced from the question of whether it is possible to have speculation that is simultaneously profitable and destabilizing, which was addressed in the preceding sections.

The evidence produced by Dornbusch, Frankel, and Froot falls into the basic categories of macromodeling and tests of rational behavior in foreign exchange markets. The literature in these fields is vast and it is not possible to produce here a thorough, and no less a complete, review. Instead, this analysis draws mainly on the propositions found in Dornbusch and Frankel (1988) and Frankel and Froot (1990).

4 Evidence from Macro Models

One of the most important sources of information about the destabilizing effect of speculation comes from the comparison of actual exchange rates with those generated by macroeconomic models. Dornbusch and Frankel note that whereas "Exchange rates were supposed to be as stable as macroeconomic fundamentals" (p. 152), in fact, "Exchange rates move inexplicably" (p. 157). In a similar vein, Frankel and Froot report, "It is now widely accepted that standard observable macroeconomic variables are not capable of explaining, much less predicting ex ante, the majority of short-term changes in the exchange rate" (1990, p. 81).

The basis for these findings is exchange rate forecasts produced with the help of sophisticated macroeconomic models resting on different theoretical foundations like Keynesian, monetarist and rational and adaptive expectations.

The problem of poor exchange rate forecasts must be seen in the light of the fact that these models have been equally unable to perform well in explaining or forecasting other economic variables, not just exchange rates. The sources of these difficulties are well known and range from the Lucas critique and the natural instability of the estimated coefficients to the complexity of multi-equation systems and econometric estimation techniques. Perhaps most fundamentally, these models suffer from the need to estimate indirectly the nonobservable but crucial expectations held by economic agents.

Given these difficulties with macroeconomic models, it is no surprise that "economists divide into two camps" (Frankel and Froot 1990, p. 81) concerning the interpretation of the findings that exchange rates have been inconsistent with macroeconomic fundamentals.

One camp finds no evidence of destabilizing speculation. Some in this camp work with models in which exchange rates are well explained and predicted. For example, Blundell-Wignall (1986) reports on published work (Masson and Blundell-Wignall 1985) according to which the 1984 increase in the value of the US dollar is not caused by speculation but by the correct anticipation of US fiscal policy. Others in this camp work with poorly performing models. According to Dornbusch and Froot, some of these analysts attribute their results to changes in tastes and technologies in the economy which are not reflected in the models. It is clear that such a methodological stance comes close to making the theory nontestable and to assuming that the market is always right. The other camp is satisfied that the models are correct and that their poor performance is evidence of destabilizing speculation.

Authors who believe they have found evidence of irrational speculation, but especially Frankel in all of the papers cited here, tend to argue that their case is strengthened by what is known as the theory of rational, speculative bubbles. At one level of analysis this theory may be seen to be nothing more than a sophisticated way of *describing* or *naming* the deviation of actual exchange rates from those predicted by macroeconomic fundamentals in the model chosen by the author.

Specifically, the theory postulates that a substantial number of market participants expect the exchange rate to move in a certain direction because all other agents hold the same expectations.[7] As a result, it is rational to act in accordance with these expectations, and the market exchange rate is driven from the level consistent with the macroeconomic fundamentals.

The theory is deficient as a simplified description of speculative episodes because it does not explain how such bubbles get started or what makes them burst. More fundamentally, and at a methodological level, it is important to realize that such a theory cannot prove anything about the real world. Empirical tests can find evidence consistent or inconsistent with such theories and thus suggest something about their merit as a description of reality. The theory of speculative bubbles has not been tested empirically. At the same time it is not possible to use the existence of deviations of exchange rates from fundamentals as empirical evidence in support of the existence of bubbles. The theory is supposed to explain the phenomenon, and not the other way around.

---

[7] Some readers may marvel at the fact that "the theory identifies speculative bubbles with the unstable paths in a rational-expectations saddle-path problem" (Frankel and Froot 1990, p. 84).

4.1   Tests of Purchasing Power Parity

Tests of purchasing power parity represent a variant of forecasting models based on macromodels, since they postulate that the spot exchange rate is determined by relative price developments in the home country and abroad. There probably exist now literally hundreds of empirical studies of this theory, covering different exchange rates and time periods. The tests involve ever-increasing levels of econometric sophistication.

Some of the empirical studies of purchasing power parity are consistent with the goods arbitrage model of foreign exchange, some are not. In general, the longer the time period covered by the studies, the more likely it is that exchange rates conform to the development of relative price levels. The results are also strongly dependent on the starting and ending period for the analysis.

However, while there are no objective and universally accepted criteria for accepting or rejecting the validity of the theory, Dornbusch and Frankel nevertheless conclude that "not only does purchasing power parity clearly fail in the short run, but it is difficult to disprove the claim that it also fails in the long run" (p. 162).[8]

I conclude from this review of the evidence from macroeconomic models and tests of purchasing power parity that they have failed to make a very strong case in support of the view that currency speculation has resulted in significant deviations of exchange rates from macroeconomic fundamentals.

5   Nonrational Behavior

Dornbusch, Frankel, and Froot believe that there exists indirect evidence on the destabilizing nature of speculation, based on three empirical find-

---

[8] Dornbusch and Froot note that the theory of purchasing power parity was widely accepted during the 1970s and rejected during the 1980s. One of the problems of all fast-moving sciences is the short memory of researchers and a lack of historical perspectives. It is not clear from Dornbusch and Froot whether the disrepute of the theory is due to deviations that developed during the 1980s or whether new techniques of measurement and theoretical approaches have resulted in the need to revise evidence produced during the preceding centuries. I suspect that the authors must mean the former. If they do, they lack perspective on the lengthy deviations that have been observed before and that the theory is much more complex than its simple statement in textbooks is. During the early 1960s, Houthakker (1962) had used a simple purchasing power calculation to suggest that the dollar was overvalued. The resultant furore was memorable and prompted P. Samuelson (1964) to suggest that "every generation of economists needs to learn for itself the complexity of the theory."

ings. First, speculators are not rational. This proposition is alleged to follow from the results of nearly all studies of forward and actual spot rates, as well as surveys of expectations. Second, there is strong evidence that exchange rates follow random walks, which implies that the best guess about the future is that it equals the present spot rate and it makes no sense to speculate. Yet, there are speculators. Third, most market participants pay scant attention to market fundamentals. Instead, participants and especially banks, follow the advice of chartists and hold very short-term open positions.

5.1 Rational Expectations

Under the rational expectations model, regressions use the spot rate as the dependent variable and forward rates maturing at the time of the spot rate as the independent variable. The regressions are expected to have a constant and a slope coefficient with the values of zero and one, respectively. Regressions typically have not produced results consistent with this theory. However, economists are again divided into two camps about the interpretation of these results.

One camp views the results as reflecting a risk premium that forward exchange market participants are demanding for entering into contracts involving uncertain prices in the future. The other camp views the results as evidence of a systematic bias in the formation of speculative expectations, which in turn results in excessive exchange rate fluctuations. Frankel and Froot clearly belong to this camp.

5.2 Speculation in Efficient Markets is Irrational

In a static world of unchanging fundamentals and expectations, it would indeed be irrational to speculate on future price changes, since prices embody all available information about the equilibrium value of assets. However, in a dynamic and uncertain world, fundamentals and expectations change continuously. Speculators who specialize in the gathering and analysis of new information, and who act on them, make prices again consistent with the new environment. In the process, such speculators under competition earn risk-adjusted normal rates of return on their activities. Speculators who act only on the basis of past price developments, of course, do not earn profits on a consistent basis. These ideas have been worked out formally by Grossman and Stiglitz (1980). They have led Stiglitz (1983) to the conclusion that in such a dynamic world, markets cannot be completely efficient at every point in time.[9] We may conclude that it is not irrational to speculate on the effects of new developments in the presence of evidence on the efficiency of foreign exchange markets.

5.3 Acting on Chartists' Advice is Irrational

Frankel and Froot (1986, 1990) made ex post evaluations of forecasts made by professional forecasting services. These forecasts have a poor record of performance. In addition, they found that increasingly such forecasts rely on chartist principles rather than economic fundamentals. The authors interpret both the poor forecasting record and increased preponderance of chartists as evidence of destabilizing speculation. According to the authors, this conclusion is not altered materially by the fact that the quality of forecasts based on fundamentals is an increasing function of the length of the forecast.

The authors conclude that the advice of chartists leads to irrational and destabilizing speculation. In my view, this conclusion is not warranted. First, the buyers of chartist advice have at their disposal a wide range of models and forecasts. From this supply they select that which they consider to be useful, especially in the light of experience and in combination with additional information.[10] Second, the fact that chartists do not use rational economic models to justify their advice does not clinch the case. What counts is the success of the forecast. As someone once put it, it matters little whether the TV repairman believes that a component needs replacing because a little man who lives in the component has died. All that matters is that he makes the TV work again.

---

[9] The idea that efficient markets leave no room for speculative profits has been poked fun at by the following story. Eugene Fama, the premier exponent of the efficient market model, was walking along the street with a visitor from another university who pointed to a 100 dollar bill on the sidewalk and suggested that Fama pick it up. Fama answered that there could be no such bill on the ground, since someone would have picked it up already.

[10] Eugene Fama, who once was a very strong proponent of the view that past price information contains no information useful for profitable trade in securities, now believes that it is possible for some trading rules to work for some time in generating excess profits. Those with a special talent for discovering and using these rules will make profits until their activities destroy their usefulness by influencing the behavior of prices on which the rule was based, just as the theory of efficient markets implies. This revisionist thinking is based on the recognition that efficient market outcomes are not instantaneous, but, in a world in which information is uncertain and often verified only as a function of time, leaves opportunities for specialized and talented individuals to earn extraordinary profits. I have made this argument in Grubel (1979).

6 Summary and Conclusions

The large variance of exchange rates in the post–Bretton Woods era has been interpreted by some influential economists as evidence of widespread destabilizing speculation. The view is shared by politicians and the general public. The economists have supported their view by referring to theoretical models, deviations of market exchange rates from those produced by econometric models, and empirical evidence concerning the efficiency of exchange markets.

The validity of the empirical evidence on the existence of destabilizing speculation is not accepted by all specialists. Because of the nature of the evidence, it is difficult to decide its validity on rigorous, scientific grounds and choose between the competing views. However, there is strong evidence to suggest that banks have made consistent profits from speculation. According to conventional wisdom, such profitable speculation should be stabilizing. It is therefore in conflict with the evidence that there has been significant, destabilizing speculation.

The economists who believe in the existence of destabilizing speculation argue that new theories have made obsolete the conventional wisdom about the stabilizing effect of profitable speculation. The case they make is not persuasive. It is possible to construct counterexamples and theories which prove their case. However, theories by themselves can never prove such propositions in the absence of direct empirical tests. Such direct tests do not exist.

The empirical evidence adduced in support of the proposition that speculation is destabilizing is not undisputed in the literature or, as in the case of the argument about the irrationality of speculation in efficient markets, is based on static assumptions.

The examination of the evidence on the existence of destabilizing speculation presented in this paper leads me to the following conclusions. There is strong evidence that banks have consistently earned profits from exchange rate speculation and there is a strong presumption that this speculation has resulted in the stabilization of exchange rates over time, relative to the stability that would have prevailed otherwise. As a result, the profits of the banks are not earned at the expense of importers and exporters of goods and services. Instead, the profits represent the return to the service of exchange rate stabilization that the banks provided for their commercial customers.

In terms of major policy issues, these conclusions suggest that there does not exist a strong case for the introduction of taxes on foreign exchange market transactions, of dual exchange rates, or of exchange rate target zones to reduce destabilizing speculation.

Appendix

A Simple Model of Speculation Based on Chartist and Fundamentalist Motives

Consider that in the United States there are three classes of foreign exchange market participants: banks, which speculate with the help of chartist ideas and are holders of large inventories of uncovered pound balances; traders, as the ultimate users of pounds for imports and exports of goods and services; and the public, which speculates on the basis of fundamentals. Assume that the true PPP equilibrium exchange rate is 2 dollars per pound, at which trade is balanced and there are zero capital flows.

Now consider that chartists have decided that the exchange rate will go to 2.20 for a year, then to 1.80 for another year, and then return to 2. All banks go along with this view and at the beginning of the first year buy and sell pounds only at 2.20. The banks do not trade with each other at this price and therefore they do not realize any profits through this process. However, they carry the exchange on their books at the new value and at the end of the year report a profit of .2 dollars per pound.

At this new exchange rate, importers and exporters deal with banks in order to meet their obligations due to foreign trade, all of which is assumed to be billed in pounds. Since the rate of 2.20 represents a depreciation of the dollar, ceteris paribus, US trade during the year is in surplus and banks buy more pounds from traders than they sell to them. This additional stock of pounds results in losses equal to .4 dollars per pound when the market rate turns to 1.80 upon the market's acceptance of the chartists' predictions for the second year. These losses of the banks are limited to the trade imbalance that is generated by these disequilibrium rates. Under normal circumstances, these imbalances may be assumed to be small relative to the size of exchange market transactions observed in the real world and banking business generally.

The general public, which is assumed to know on the basis of fundamentals that the rate will have to be 2 in the long run, is willing to sell pounds at the 2.20 rate at which the banks are trading during the first year, expecting to repurchase the currency at its equilibrium value of two. Under these assumptions, the speculators acting on fundamentals cannot lose and may gain more than expected, since they can buy not at the expected 2 but the 1.80 rate established through the chartists' predictions.

The foreign exchange transactions in the model are reversed in the second year. Trade is in deficit and banks are forced by traders to sell pounds at 1.80 and in quantities equal to the deficit. Since these pounds were acquired at 2 initially, the banks suffer a loss, just like they did in the preceding year. Banks also lose as a result of purchases of pounds from the public, which acts on the assumption that they can sell them at 2 in the next period. Most important, the inventory of pounds carried over from the preceding period is now worth less on the books. The unrealized losses match the unrealized gains of the preceding period. Over the full cycle, gains and losses on the inventory of speculative pounds net to zero.

The most important point of the preceding analysis is that in both periods the banks as followers of the advice of chartists push the rate away from its fundamental equilibrium and destabilize it. However, they also lose money at the expense of speculators who act on the basis of fundamentals and gain nothing on the holdings of speculative funds. The variance of their earnings is increased.

In the real world, banks are alleged to profit from speculation. They therefore cannot play the role postulated in this model. Since they profit, their speculation must be stabilizing. They must be playing the role attributed above to the general public. In my view, the role of chartist advice in this outcome is not important. Perhaps banks disregard it or they act on only part of it. Or perhaps chartists are correct on average, for reasons that are not understood. In the final analysis, motives and methods used in speculation are irrelevant to the outcome and the only thing that counts is success.

References

Baillie, Richard, and Patrick McMahon. 1989. *The Foreign Exchange Market: Theory and Econometric Evidence*. Cambridge: Cambridge University Press.

Baumol, William J. 1957. "Speculation, Profitability and Stability." *Review of Economics and Statistics* 39: 263–71.

Bell, G. 1974. "Bank Speculators: Once Bitten, Twice Shy?" *The Times*, 15 May: 27.

Blundell-Wignall, A. 1986. "Understanding the US Dollar in the Eighties: Comment." *Economic Record* (Special Issue).

Borner, Silvio, ed. 1988. *International Finance and Trade in a Polycentric World*. Houndsmills, Hampshire: Macmillan.

DeLong, J.B., A. Shleifer, L. Summers and A. Waldman. 1987. "The Economic Consequence of Noise Traders." *NBER Working Paper* No. 2395. Cambridge, Mass.

Dornbusch, Rudiger, and Jeffrey Frankel. 1988. "The Flexible Exchange Rate System: Experience and Alternatives." In Borner (1988, p. 151–197).

Frankel, Jeffrey. 1989. "International Capital Mobility and Exchange Rate Volatility." Kennedy School of Government, Harvard University, Discussion Paper 175D, February.

Frankel, Jeffrey, and Kenneth A. Froot. 1986. "Understanding the US Dollar in the Eighties: The Expectations of Chartists and Fundamentalists." *Economic Record* (Special Issue).

———. 1988. "Chartists, Fundamentalists, and the Demand for Dollars." *Greek Economic Review* 10(1): 49–102.

————. 1990. 'Chartists, Fundamentalists, and Trading in the Foreign Exchange Market."
  American Economic Review, Papers and Proceedings, 80 (May): 181–185.
Friedman, Milton. 1953. "The Case for Flexible Exchange Rates." *Essays in Positive Eco-
  nomics*. Chicago: University of Chicago Press.
Goodhart C. 1987. "The Foreign Exchange Market: A Random Walk with a Dragging
  Anchor." London School of Economics, Discussion Paper.
Grossman, S.J., and J. Stiglitz. 1980. "On the Impossibility of Informationally Efficient
  Markets." *American Economic Review* 70: 246–53.
Grubel, Herbert G. 1990. "Are Banks' Speculative Profits at the Expense of Traders? A
  Comment on Schulmeister (1988)." *Banca Nazionale del Lavoro Quarterly Review* 174
  (September): 363–69.
————. 1979. "The Peter Principle and the Efficient Market Hypothesis." *Financial Analysts
  Journal*, December.
Houthakker, Hendrik. 1962. "Should we Devalue the Dollar?" *Challenge*, 11 (October).
Kemp, Murray C. 1963. "Speculation, Profitability and Price Stability." *Review of Economics
  and Statistics* 45: 185–89.
Kindleberger, Charles. 1976. "Lessons of Floating Exchange Rates." In Karl Brunner and
  Alan Meltzer, ed., *Institutional Arrangements and The Inflation Problem*. Carnegie-Roches-
  ter Conference Series on Public Policy, 3, 51–77.
Masson, P.R., and A. Blundell-Wignall. 1985. "Fiscal Policy and the Exchange Rate in the
  Big Seven: Transmission of US Government Spending Shocks." *European Economic Re-
  view* 28: 11–42.
McKinnon, Ronald. 1988. "Monetary and Exchange Rate Policies for International Finan-
  cial Stability." *Journal of Economic Perspectives* 2 (Winter): 83–103.
Samuelson, Paul A. 1964. "Theoretical Notes on Trade Problems." *Review of Economics and
  Statistics* 46: 145–54.
Schulmeister, Stephan. 1987. "An Essay on Exchange Rate Dynamics." Discussion Paper
  IIM/LMP 87–88. Berlin: Wissenschaftszentrum fuer Sozialforschung.
————. 1988. "Currency Speculation and Dollar Fluctuations." *Banca Nazionale del Lavoro
  Quarterly Review* 167 (December): 343–66.
————. 1990. "Are Banks' Speculative Profits at the Expense of Traders? A Reply to Grubel's
  Comments." *Banca Nazionale del Lavoro Quarterly Review* 174 (September): 370–376.
Sohmen, Egon. 1969. *Flexible Exchange Rates*. Revised Edition. Chicago: University of
  Chicago Press.
Stein, Jerome L. 1961. "Destabilizing Speculative Activity Can Be Profitable." *Review of
  Economics and Statistics* 43: 301–2.
Stiglitz, Joseph. 1983. "Futures Markets and Risk: A General Equilibrium Model." In M.
  Streit, ed., *Futures Markets, Modelling, Managing and Monitoring Futures Trading*. Oxford:
  Basil Blackwell.
Telser, Lester G. 1959. "A Theory of Speculation Relating Profitability and Stability." *Review
  of Economics and Statistics* 41: 295–302.
Williamson, John. 1981. *Exchange Rate Rules*. London: MacMillan.
————. 1985. *The Exchange Rate System*. Washington: Institute for International Economics.

[14]

Taxation and the Rates of Return from Some U.S. Asset Holdings Abroad, 1960–1969

Herbert G. Grubel

Simon Fraser University

The paper shows theoretically that U.S. tax laws are designed to induce equalization of private rates of return from investment in the United States and abroad but that, unless the marginal government expenditures on investment equal tax payments by the investment, there is a difference between private and social rates of return to U.S. foreign investment. Calculations covering the period 1960–69 for developed countries and U.S. holdings of bonds, equities, and direct investment in manufacturing showed that private rates of return generally were positive but that social rates of return from investing abroad rather than domestically were strongly negative, assuming zero marginal government expenditures and disregarding all externalities.

In the past the basic philosophy underlying U.S. tax laws and other regulations guiding international long-term capital flows have been to encourage the maximization of world income. The policies flowing from this philosophy by and large enabled capital to move anywhere in the world where private owners could earn highest returns.[1]

An important question facing the U.S. government and public in the 1970s is whether the internationalist philosophy that has guided past policies should be followed in the future. This question is raised by demands for change from two important sources. First, U.S. labor, which believes that foreign investment results in a loss of domestic employment

I received much assistance in the preparation of foreign rates of taxation from the International Tax Affairs Staff of the U.S. Treasury Department, headed by N. Gorden. Valuable comments on an earlier draft of this paper were made by G. Kopitz, P. Gray, H. Shapiro, M. Feinberg, G. Haberler, and other participants at a seminar at the U.S. Treasury Department, by an unknown referee of this *Journal*, and by my colleague Edward Tower.
[1] For a review of the issues surrounding the internationalist policies see Krause and Dam (1967) and Musgrave (1969). These books also provide references to the original contributions to the field.

469

opportunities and reduces the growth of wages, demands that the U.S. government "curb the substantial outflow of American capital" (Goldfinger 1971, p. 928). Second, some major foreign governments have decided that long-term capital inflows from the United States are undesirable because they lead to "takeover" of their industries[2] and induce unemployment, causing deficits on current account, or result in an unwanted increase in official dollar holdings.

In a scholarly analysis prepared for the Joint Economic Committee of Congress, Musgrave (1972, pp. 177–78) concluded: "There are sufficient doubts about the effects of foreign investment on the U.S. economy to lead to the conclusion that the U.S. tax treatment of foreign investment income should be reviewed and reevaluated. This applies especially to deferral, but consideration may also be given to limiting the present credit for foreign taxes to less than 100 per cent. Such measures would not be incompatible with opposition to trade restrictions. Indeed, they might be supportive of free trade policy."

The present paper has been stimulated by this controversy over the merits of international investment in general and the effects of taxation in particular. It attempts to shed light on the issues by presenting some estimates of the after-tax rates of return yielded by some forms of U.S. asset holdings abroad during the period 1960–69. In a rational decision about future U.S. policies, presumably such a rate of return should carry important weight.

This paper represents a pioneering effort, and its primary aim is to sort out some theoretical issues and provide a rough first estimate. No other studies of this sort seem to exist for the United States, though the broader issues of the efficiency aspects of international taxation agreements have been studied theoretically (Kindleberger 1968; Musgrave 1969) and estimates of the subsidies as dollar flows have been prepared (Musgrave 1972). The overall welfare effects of foreign investment have received a great deal of attention, and a ready set of references to these can be found in Reddaway (1968) and Dunning (1970). Jenkins (1972, chap. 4) estimates Canada's taxation gains from foreign-owned capital in Canada.

By concentrating the present study on the effects of taxation on the returns from only some forms of U.S. asset holdings, we neglect many considerations which should be weighted in the final decision about the future of international tax agreements. Thus, we disregard the effects of capital flows on the terms of trade, income distribution, externalities, the efficiency of employment policies, and the benefits from the diversification

---

[2] Significant political influence along these lines has long been felt in Canada and France. Leftist factions in developing countries have a tradition of considering U.S. investments evidence of U.S. imperialism.

of assets.[3] Furthermore, the study does not consider the returns from such U.S. assets as bank loans, investment in oil and mining, and the tax and other benefits from foreign asset holdings in the United States.

In Part I current regulations concerning foreign investments are discussed briefly. Parts II and III contain estimates of returns from foreign bond and equity holdings and direct investment in manufacturing, respectively. The paper closes with a brief summary and conclusions.

I.   The Taxation of Foreign Income

The major feature of the U.S. taxation of income from assets held abroad is the tax offset provision of international taxation agreements in existence with all major Western countries of the world. These tax provisions permit a U.S. taxpayer upon repatriation of his earnings to deduct from his tax liabilities to the U.S. government all taxes paid to foreign governments. Assuming for a moment that all earnings are repatriated during the period in which they accrue, the U.S. tax rate on foreign investment income, t'_d, is $t_d - t_f$, where t_d and t_f are the domestic tax rate on U.S. income and the foreign tax rate, respectively. In cases where the foreign exceeds the domestic rate and therefore t'_d becomes negative, the taxpayer receives no explicit U.S. tax refund on a return from that country and t'_d = 0 whenever $t_d \gtreqless t_f$. But because the taxpayer has the option of combining returns from several countries, the overpayments in some countries can be used effectively to reduce obligations for U.S. tax payment on income from other countries, and in practice a refund is provided for overpayment to some foreign governments.

As a result of the tax provision, the net private rate of return from foreign rather than domestic investment (R_P) is

$$R_P = (r_f)(1 - t_f - t'_d) + r_x - r_d(1 - t_d), \qquad (1)$$

where r_f and r_d are the foreign and domestic rates of return from foreign investment, respectively, and r_x is the nontaxable capital value change due to exchange rate revaluations expressed as an annual rate of return. Under the assumptions that $t_f \leq t_d$, implying $t_f + t'_d = t_d$, and that $r_x = 0$, the net private after-tax rate of return from foreign investment is positive $(R_P > 0)$ whenever

$$r_f > r_d \qquad (2)$$

and it becomes zero when $r_f = r_d$. These conditions are well known to be a necessary requirement for the efficient international allocation of capital, though it should be noted that, because of the offset provisions

---

[3] The classical theoretical article is MacDougall (1960). The gains from international diversification have been discussed in Grubel (1968) and Grubel and Fadner (1971).

mentioned in the preceding paragraph, if $t_f \geqq t_d$ and there are no tax credits from other countries, it is possible that $R_p < 0$ even though $r_f > r_d$ and $r_x = 0$. Therefore, the U.S. tax laws need not provide the necessary condition for the efficient international allocation of capital.

Let us now define the social rate of return from foreign investment (R_s) as

$$R_S = (r_f)(1 - t_f) + r_x - r_d + g_d, \qquad (3)$$

where g_d is the government expenditure necessitated by domestic investment but not charged to the business firm directly, expressed as an annual rate of expenditure per \$100 investment. Under the assumption that r_x and g_d are zero, the social rate of return is positive ($R_S > 0$) only if

$$(r_f - r_d)/r_f > t_f, \qquad (4)$$

which means that foreign investment is socially profitable only if the foreign rate of return exceeds the domestic rate by a percentage larger than the foreign tax rate. The analysis also implies that foreign investment is privately profitable but results in a socially negative rate of return whenever $r_d/(1 - t_f) > r_f > r_d$.

The task of the next parts of this paper is to estimate R_P and R_S using the variables shown in the right-hand side of equations (1) and (3). However, it will be impossible to provide any estimates of g_d, the savings of U.S. government expenditure realized by the location of the investment abroad, and g_d will be assumed to be zero. It is difficult to know reliably the magnitude of the bias introduced by this assumption. However, it seems clear that services provided free by governments specifically to private investment projects are a relatively minor proportion of all government expenditures, because most government services such as public utilities and judicial services are provided for a fee. At the same time, such free services as roads and public education to the work force would most often be the same with and without the existence of the investments. Final judgment of these matters must await more detailed theoretical analysis and some empirical case studies.

The preceding analysis was set out by assuming that all earnings are repatriated in the period of accrual, and in the remainder of this paper we will retain this assumption. We thus disregard the important fact that under present tax laws, whenever the foreign is below the U.S. tax rate, the payment of the remaining U.S. tax can be deferred until the profits are repatriated. The owners of foreign-reinvested profits thus enjoy the benefits of a tax-free loan. Musgrave (1972, p. 192) has estimated that the revenue loss to the U.S. Treasury from this provision came to about \$900 million in the year 1970 for the case of foreign-incorporated subsidiaries of U.S. corporations.

The arguments over the merits of this deferral provision exceed the scope of the present paper. The primary economic impact of the implicit subsidy is an inefficiently high level of foreign investment, the welfare implications of which take the form of consumer surplus.[4]

II. The Data and Rates of Return on Bonds and Equities

The empirical study of private and social rates of return to U.S. holdings and holdings abroad is based on average rates of return during the period 1960–69. This decade was characterized by the greatest degree of freedom from government restrictions in foreign exchange markets since the end of the Second World War and by rapid economic growth and capital formation throughout the world. Of course, the results of this study would have been different if any other period had been analyzed. This fact does not invalidate the calculations made, but limits the inferences we can draw about private and social profitability of foreign asset holdings over longer past periods and about the future. Dunning (1970, p. 83) has pointed to a difficulty associated with considering a period of rapid growth in foreign investments. Since it is known that investments tend to yield a lower rate of return initially than over the longer run, average rates of return during periods of rapid growth are biased downward. We have no way of quantifying this bias and will disregard it in the subsequent discussion.

Overview of Total U.S. Foreign Investment Position

Before we turn to a detailed analysis of rates of return, it is useful to present an overview of the total U.S. foreign investment position in long-term assets in order to put into the proper perspective the asset categories to which the following estimates had to be limited. For this purpose table 1 has been compiled. The upper half of the table, showing U.S. assets, reveals in column 4 that the overwhelming proportion of foreign assets held abroad is in the form of direct investment (73.7 percent) followed by bonds (12.2 percent), corporate stocks (7.2 percent), and bank loans and other assets (6.9 percent). In column 3 we see that net growth during the decade 1960–69 was greatest in direct investments (122.1 percent) and in overall investments (116.1 percent).

In the last row of the upper half of table 1 we show a rough regional breakdown of U.S. assets. Canada is the single most important location of U.S.-held foreign assets, with 33.9 percent of the total, followed by Western Europe (27.8 percent) and the rest of the world (38.3 percent). It is interesting to note that Canadian bonds and stocks represent 59 and 49

---

[4] For an excellent recent study of the welfare cost of U.S. trade restrictions using this approach and providing the relevant references to the literature, see Magee (1972).

TABLE 1

INTERNATIONAL PRIVATE LONG-TERM INVESTMENT POSITION OF THE UNITED STATES ($ MILLIONS)

	TOTAL		TOTAL PERCENTAGE		CANADA		WESTERN EUROPE		ALL OTHER	
	1960 (1)	1969 (2)	1960-69 (3)	1969 (4)	1969 (5)	% of All Countries (6)	1969 (7)	% of All Countries (8)	1969 (9)	% of All Countries (10)
Assets										
Direct investments........	31,865	70,763	122.1	73.7	21,075	29.8	21,554	30.5	28.134	39.7
Foreign bonds	5,524	11,712	112.0	12.2	6,912	59.0	607	5.2	4,193	35.8
Foreign corporation stocks	3,984	6,953	74.5	7.2	3,406	49.0	2,816	40.5	731	10.5
Bank loans and other	3,074	6,601	114.7	6.9	1,207	18.3	1,744	26.4	3,650	55.3
Total..............	44,447	96,029	116.1	100.0	32,600	33.9	26,721	27.8	36,708	38.3
Liabilities										
Direct investments........	6,910	11,818	71.0	28.8	2,834	24.0	2,659	22.5	6,325	53.5
Bonds	649	4,800	640.0	11.7	87	1.8	3,770	78.5	943	19.7
Corporate stocks	9,302	18,140	95.0	44.3	2,950	16.3	12,106	66.7	3,084	17.0
Banks and other..........	1,557	6,228	300.0	15.2	178	2.9	3,066	49.2	2,984	48.9
Total..........	18,418	40,986	122.5	100.0	6,049	14.8	21,601	52.7	13,336	32.5
Ratio of assets to liabilities	2.41	2.34	...	...	5.39	...	1.23	...	2.75	...

SOURCE.—U.S. Department of Commerce, *Survey of Current Business*, various issues.

percent, respectively, of the U.S. holdings in these classes. European corporate stocks also represent a significant 40.5 percent of the total. The rest of the world has issued a disproportionately large amount of liabilities to U.S. banks (55.3 percent of the total U.S. bank loans). About one-third of these bank loans were to Japan.

The bottom half of table 1 shows the level, composition, and growth of foreign holdings of U.S. assets. The most important conclusions from this set of data are that overall U.S. assets were 2.41 and 2.34 times the level of liabilities in 1960 and 1969, respectively. However, this average hides regional divergence, which produces a 1969 ratio of 5.39 for Canada, 1.23 for Europe, and 2.75 for the rest of the world. Of further interest is the fact that for all countries U.S. corporate stocks represent the favorite form of asset, 44.3 percent, followed by direct investment, 28.8 percent. This relationship is dominated by an overwhelming European preference of about 3:1 of stocks over direct investment. Canadians hold roughly equal shares of U.S. direct investment and corporate stocks.

The following empirical analysis is limited to the estimation of rates of return from U.S. holdings of foreign assets in the form of bonds, corporation stocks, and direct investments. This partial approach has the serious shortcoming that the results do not provide information about the social profitability to the United States of adhering to the principle of not restricting international capital flows and partaking in a worldwide system of double taxation agreements. In order to provide an estimate of this broad social profitability, it would be necessary to consider the benefits and costs arising from all forms of foreign assets and liabilities, long and short term, private and public, just as it is necessary to study all sources of income and costs to estimate the profitability of a private bank or business.

This problem of partial estimates is particularly important, since the U.S. government tax revenues lost from U.S. holdings abroad are partly offset by the U.S. taxation of foreign investment income. For these reasons, the present study must not be interpreted as providing an answer to the broad problem of U.S. benefits and costs from adhering to the internationalist principle in foreign investment policies. The empirical estimates to be presented represent merely an input, though an important input, in such a broader calculus.

Portfolio Investments

Portfolio investments are assets which do not confer control over the operation of the issuing business enterprise. Qualifying as such are bonds and equities representing no more than 10 percent of the corporation's outstanding stocks.

Calculations on the rates of return to bonds and stocks were limited to Canada and Western Europe, the major issuers of U.S.-held assets. Data on U.S. foreign portfolio holdings do not disaggregate "Western Europe" by individual countries. Average Western European rates of return were calculated by weighting individual country data by the value of U.S. manufacturing investment at the end of 1969, for which country data are available.

Bonds

The U.S. government does not possess information on the actual composition or yield of U.S. private bond holdings abroad. For this reason it was necessary to assume that the holdings consisted entirely of foreign government bonds with a maturity over 5 years and that the opportunity cost of these holdings was equal to the long-term yield on U.S. government bonds. These assumptions produce unbiased results as long as (1) the yield differentials between government and private bonds are equal in the United States and the rest of the world, (2) U.S. wealth holders purchase equal proportions of government and private bonds abroad as they would if they had invested domestically, (3) the maturity composition of foreign portfolios is the same as the domestic portfolio would have been and there are no international differences in yield curves, and (4) income from foreign government bonds is taxable at the normal rate.[5] Refinements of the estimates will have to await information on the accuracy of these hypothetical propositions about the real world.

Row 1 of table 2 shows the foreign bond yields (r_f) to have been 5.89 and 6.28 percent for Canada and Western Europe, respectively. Comparison of these yields with the U.S. yield (r_d) shown in row 8 as 4.51 percent reveals a positive net private profitability from foreign bond holdings. The foreign withholding taxes (t_f) of 15.0 and 3.2 percent (row 2) lower after-tax foreign yields to 5.01 and 6.08 percent (row 3) for Canada and Western Europe, respectively. Average exchange rate losses during the period (r_x) shown in row 4 and applied to the proportion of non-dollar-denominated bonds (row 5) reduce the gross foreign yields to 4.92 and 6.06 percent, respectively, for Canada and Western Europe (row 7). After adjustment for the domestic opportunity cost of these funds, the net social rate of return (R_s) is estimated as having been 0.41 and 1.55 percent for Canada and Western Europe, respectively.

Three brief comments regarding these calculations should be made.

---

[5] Canadian bonds issued by the provinces and municipalities especially tend to be free from Canadian taxation. This fact biases downward our estimate of U.S. rates of returns from bond holdings. Given all of the other simplifying assumptions, in the extreme, if all Canadian bonds held had been tax free, the net social rate of return would have been 1.29 rather than 0.41 percent.

TABLE 2

U.S. RETURNS FROM FOREIGN BOND HOLDINGS, 1960–69

	Canada	Western Europe
1. Average yield, government bonds, 1960–69, %/year	5.89	6.28
2. Average withholding tax, 1962–67, % of interest	15.0	3.2
3. After-tax rate of return, %/year	5.01	6.08
4. Average exchange rate change, 1960–69, %/year	−0.74	−0.46
5. Percentage of U.S.-dollar-denominated bonds 1969	88.4	96.0
6. Change of portfolio due to exchange rate	−0.09	0.02
7. After-tax, after-exchange rate adjustments, return, %/year	4.92	6.06
8. Average U.S. government bond yield, 1960–69, %/year	4.51	
9. Net social rate of return, %/year	0.41	1.55

SOURCES AND NOTES ON COMPUTATIONS:

Yield: Organization for Economic Cooperation and Development (1970, vol. 2). Fourth-quarter average long-term government bond yields were averaged over 1960–69 for each country of Western Europe. Weights for calculation of Western European average are relative value of U.S. manufacturing investment in 1969 from U.S. Department of Commerce, *Survey of Current Business* (October 1970).

Tax rate: Statutory dividend withholding tax rates compiled by U.S. Treasury International Tax Affairs Staff (Kopits 1970). Average for Western Europe weighted by U.S. manufacturing investment.

Exchange rate change: End-of-period exchange rates 1960–69 from International Monetary Fund (various years). Change in rate expressed as percentage of 1960 rate. European rate is average weighted by manufacturing investment.

U.S. bond rates: 3–5-year U.S. government issues (U.S. Government 1971, p. 264, table C57).

First, the exchange rate adjustment would be much more unfavorable if the December 1971 currency realignments had been within the period covered in this study. However, the net effect on the foreign rates of return would not have been mitigated considerably by the fact that nearly 90 percent of all foreign bonds held by U.S. residents are denominated in dollars.

Second, the U.S. bond yield shown is unadjusted for the theoretical fall in the U.S. rate that would have occurred if the funds invested abroad had been used to purchase U.S. bonds. This adjustment seems unnecessary in light of the fact that the total value of bonds in circulation in the United States at the end of 1969 was $495 billion, of which the $7.5 billion of foreign bonds represent only 1.5 percent.

Third, it is customary to assume that market interest rates reflect expected rates of inflation over the life of financial assets. The risks of unexpected changes in the price level and the resultant wealth redistribution are shared equally between lenders and borrowers, assuming that expectations on the average are correct. However, when unexpected inflation does occur and is biased in favor of foreign borrowers, the resultant wealth gain accrues to non-U.S. residents.[6] One may wonder

[6] Aliber (1973) has shown that during several years of the post–World War II period interest rates typically failed to reflect exchange rate changes.

JOURNAL OF POLITICAL ECONOMY

TABLE 3

U.S. RETURNS FROM FOREIGN CORPORATION STOCK HOLDINGS, 1960–69

	Canada		Western Europe
1. Average dividend yield, 1960–69, %/year ..	3.4		3.9
2. Average capital gain, 1960–69, %/year	9.6		2.7
3. Total yield: (1) + (2)	13.0		6.6
4. Average withholding tax, % on dividends..	15.0		7.6
5. Average capital gains tax, %	0.0		11.3
6. Net after-tax yield, %/year	12.5		6.0
7. Average exchange rate change, 1960–69, %/year	−0.74		−0.46
8. Yield after tax and exchange loss	11.7		5.5
9. Average U.S. dividend yield, 1960–69, %/year		3.2	
10. Average U.S. capital gain, 1960–69, %/year		6.7	
11. Sum (9) + (10)......................		9.9	
12. Net social rate of return: (8) − (11).......	1.8		−4.4

SOURCES AND NOTES ON COMPUTATIONS:

Dividend yield: Annual yield for Canada, United Kingdom, France, Germany, Italy, the Netherlands, Norway, and Sweden from Organization for Economic Cooperation and Development (1970); each country's annual rate is averaged for the decade. Western Europe average weighted by book value of U.S. direct investment in manufacturing in 1969 (from U.S. Department of Commerce, *Survey of Current Business*, October 1970).

Capital gains: Based on stock market indices of all countries in sample. Source same as dividend yield. Western Europe average weighted like dividend yield figure.

Withholding tax rate and exchange rate changes: see table 2.

U.S. dividend and capital gains: Standard and Poor's 500 stocks (Organization for Economic Cooperation and Development 1970, pp. 162–65). Last month of each year averaged over 10 years for dividend yield. Percentage gain of price, end of 1960 to end of 1969 for capital gains.

to what extent the average nominal bond yields shown above can be assumed to have reflected fully anticipated rates of inflation during the period.[7] However, it is analytically not useful to consider that investors consistently over a decade are injured by unexpected inflation rates, and the data presented above will not be corrected for any inflation losses.

Equities

The estimation of foreign rates of return on equities is nearly identical to that undertaken for bonds. In the absence of any information on yields of actual holdings, the yield figures of rows 1–3 are based on the assumption that U.S. holders owned portfolios equal to the "averages" of the individual markets, with Western European holdings weighted by the share of U.S. direct investment. As can be seen from table 3, private rates of return from Canadian stocks were equal to 3.4 and 9.6 percent from dividends and capital gains, respectively. The analogous rates for Europe were 3.9 and 2.7 percent. After application of the withholding and capital

[7] During the period 1960–69, when the U.S. consumer price index rose 23.8 percent, analogous percentage rises in some of the major countries in this study were: Canada, 26.7; United Kingdom, 40.0; Germany, 25.7; France, 42.5; Italy, 40.3 (International Monetary Fund, various years, country statistics).

gains taxes (rows 4 and 5), the after-tax yields were 12.5 and 6.0 percent for Canada and Europe, respectively. Adjustments for exchange rate losses yielded the final figures of 11.7 and 5.5 percent for the two regions.

One theoretically very difficult problem I have been unable to solve concerns the choice of an appropriate U.S. opportunity cost for the funds invested in foreign equities. There appear to be two extreme theoretical possibilities. On the one hand, we may consider that the purchase of domestic rather than foreign equities would have affected only the stock of U.S. financial wealth in the form of equities in the portfolios of the public; there would have been no induced new equity flotations, corresponding real capital formation, and profits taxable at the corporate income tax rate. Under these assumptions and given that foreign equity holdings are but a minute fraction of the stock of U.S. shares held by Americans, the proper opportunity cost of foreign equity purchases is the returns from U.S. stock market investment. Rows 9–11 in table 3 show the dividend yield and capital gains of stocks in Standard and Poor's 500 share index. They total 9.9 percent and imply that the holdings of Canadian shares resulted in a positive net social rate of return of 1.8 percent per year during the decade. The corresponding figure for Western Europe was a negative 4.4 percent.

The other extreme treatment of the opportunity cost of foreign equity purchases considers them to have come fully at the expense of real capital formation by existing or potential new firms. In order to produce after-tax profits for dividend distribution and reinvestment equal to the 9.9 percent annual yield on equity shares, these firms would have had to earn a pretax rate of return of 16.6 percent, assuming the corporate tax rate to be 40.4 percent (see table 4, row 4 and note h). While the preceding arguments contain many hidden assumptions about the operation and efficiency of capital markets and the role of taxes and depreciation, the resultant estimate of the rate of return on real capital formation is close enough to other data available (see table 4, row 3, last column, and note h for the source) to provide a reasonably reliable benchmark for our purposes of calculation. Use of the preceding assumptions leads to the conclusion that the average annual rates of loss from U.S. equity holdings during the decade were 4.9 and 11.1 percent for Canada and Europe, respectively.

Without much further empirical and theoretical analysis, which would lie outside the main objectives of this paper, we cannot decide which of the above two theoretical models describes the real world most accurately. However, the ranges calculated under the two extreme assumptions indicate that foreign equity investments during the period probably yielded a negative rate of return, though a very small positive yield from Canadian equity holdings cannot be ruled out.

TABLE 4

AVERAGE RATES OF RETURN FROM DIRECT MANUFACTURING INVESTMENT, 1960–69

	Canada	U.K.	Belgium and Luxembourg	France	Germany	Italy	Netherlands	Denmark
1. Book value, 1969, $ million	9,389	4,555	700	1,518	2,750	716	656	58
Before-tax rates of return on:								
2. Book value	16.4	21.6	23.5	14.3	26.7	17.0	15.3	20.1
3. Equity	22.6	28.1	30.1	18.6	34.3	22.1	19.9	26.1
4. Effective corporate tax rates	45.0	45.4	31.2	37.0	33.0	44.2	24.4	13.9
After-corporate-tax rates of return on:								
5. Book value	9.0	11.8	16.2	7.6	17.8	9.5	11.6	17.3
6. Equity	12.4	15.3	21.1	9.9	23.1	12.4	15.1	22.5
7. Ratio of dividends/earnings	0.48	0.56	0.37	0.46	0.60	0.72	0.63	0.97
8. Tax rate on dividends	15.0	0.0	15.0	15.0	15.0	5.0	0.0	5.0
9. After corporate and dividend taxes rate of return, equity	10.8	15.3	19.4	8.6	20.0	11.6	15.1	21.2
10. Exchange rate adjustment, % per year	−0.7	−1.4	0.0	−1.4	1.2	0.0	0.4	−0.8
11. Gross social rate of return, (8) − (9)	10.1	13.9	19.4	7.2	21.2	11.6	15.5	20.4
12. Net social rate of return, (10) − 19.3%	−9.2	−5.4	0.1	−12.1	1.9	−8.3	−3.8	1.1
13. After adjustment for royalties and fees	−6.3	−0.3	5.2	−7.0	7.0	−3.2	1.3	6.2

Table 4 (*Continued*)

	Norway	Spain	Sweden	Switzerland	Australia	South Africa	Sum or Average	U.S. Domestic
1. Book value, 1969, $ million	62	295	179	380	1,567	374	23,199	...
Before-tax rates of return on:								
2. Book value	15.6	12.9	23.3	21.4	23.7	27.2	19.5	19.3
3. Equity	20.3	16.8	30.3	27.8	30.8	35.4	25.5	40.4
4. Effective corporate tax rates	32.1	30.3	48.5	15.8	39.3	25.8	40.7	...
After-corporate-tax rates of return on:								
5. Book value	10.6	9.0	12.0	18.0	14.4	20.2	11.5	11.5
6. Equity	13.8	11.7	15.6	23.4	18.7	26.3	15.1	...
7. Ratio of dividends/earnings	0.00	0.66	0.92	0.46	0.49	0.55	0.52	...
8. Tax rate on dividends	5.0	15.0	5.0	5.0	15.0	7.5	10.9	...
9. After corporate and dividend taxes rate of return, equity	13.8	10.0	14.2	22.8	16.4	24.8	13.7	...
10. Exchange rate adjustment, % per year	0.0	-1.7	0.0	0.0	0.0	0.0	-0.3	...
11. Gross social rate of return, (8) – (9)	13.8	8.3	14.2	22.8	16.4	24.8	13.4	...
12. Net social rate of return, (10) – 19.3%	-5.5	-11.0	-5.1	3.5	-2.9	5.5	-5.9	...
13. After adjustment for royalties and fees	-0.4	-5.9	0.0	8.6	2.2	10.6	-0.9	...

SOURCES AND NOTES ON COMPUTATIONS:
a) Book value from U.S. Department of Commerce, *Survey of Current Business* (October 1970), p. 23.
b) After-tax rates of return on book value are equal to "earnings" divided by preceding year's end "book value" (U.S. Department of Commerce, *Survey of Current Business*, various years).
c) Equity is equal to book value divided by book value minus liabilities to parent (from U.S. Department of Commerce, *Foreign Affiliate Financial Survey*, 1966–69 [1970, pp. 23–33, tables III and IIIb]).
d) Effective tax rates from U.S. Treasury Department (1969, p. 143, table 24).
e) Tax rate on dividends supplied by U.S. Treasury Department.
f) Exchange rates from International Financial Statistics (various years).
g) Dividends are equal to "income" from direct foreign investment (U.S. Department of Commerce, *Survey of Current Business*, various issues).
h) U.S. domestic rates of return on manufacturing investment from U.S. Government (1969), p. 283, table C74). Tax rate calculated from given rates.
i) Royalties and fees from U.S. Department of Commerce, *Survey of Current Business*, various issues.
All rates of return for individual countries are simple average of period 1960–69. World average is weighted by 1969 value of direct investment.

III.   Direct Investment in Manufacturing

United States statistics on direct foreign investment are much more complete and reliable than the statistics on stocks and bonds. For this reason, in row 1 of table 4 we show U.S. holdings by individual countries, the sum of which represents 78.8 percent of all U.S. direct manufacturing investment abroad in 1969.

United States direct investment holdings at the end of 1969 were 41.6 percent in manufacturing, 8.0 percent in mining and smelting, 28.2 percent in petroleum, and 22.2 percent in other industries. The present study is limited to manufacturing investment for two reasons. First, because the profitability of investment in mining and petroleum is so dependent on the availability of natural deposits, it is impossible to establish reliably what the domestic opportunity cost of the foreign investment would have been. Second, special treaties with foreign governments about royalties, special accounting, and depreciation rules governing these nonmanufacturing industries abroad and in the United States makes it impossible to estimate rates of return which would be theoretically appropriate for the present purposes of analysis.

The U.S. government publishes regularly "earnings" and the "book value" of U.S. manufacturing enterprises abroad. Earnings are defined as "the sum of the U.S. share in net earnings of foreign corporations and branch profits after foreign but before U.S. taxes." Book value is defined as "equity of, plus liabilities to, parent."[8] The published U.S. statistics on rates of return from foreign investment simply represent earnings per year as a percentage of book value at the beginning of that year. A 10-year average of these rates of return (1960–69) is shown in row 5 of table 4. In the following we will discuss the adjustment made on these figures to derive the estimates of net social rates of return shown in rows 12 and 13 of table 4.

Earnings and Foreign Income Taxes

In order to compare properly U.S. and foreign business income tax rates, it is insufficient to use statutory rates because in each country definitions of income, expenses, depreciation allowances, etc., are different. Fortunately, there exists a U.S. government study of effective foreign tax rates based on the U.S. definition of corporate income and depreciation rates (U.S. Treasury Department 1969). These tax rates were estimated from data submitted to the Internal Revenue Service for the fiscal year 1961–62 by calculating for each corporation its income according to U.S. laws and expressing the actual income taxes paid to foreign governments as a fraction of this income. As can be seen from row 4 of table 4, these tax

---

[8] For an updated and clear definition of terms employed in U.S. government statistics on the U.S. foreign investment position see U.S. Department of Commerce, Survey of Current Business (October 1971, pp. 37–38).

rates vary widely between countries, but the weighted average of 40.7 percent is only 0.3 percent above the domestic U.S. rate.

As a result of the absence of foreign tax rate data on years other than 1961–62, it was assumed that these rates were in force throughout the decade under study, and the average before-tax rates of return for the period were calculated by inflating the average after-tax rates of row 5. The results are shown in row 2 of table 4. The weighted average of before-tax returns on book value is 19.5 percent per year.

Book Value versus Equity

However, before domestic and foreign rates can be compared, it is necessary to adjust the foreign rates so that they reflect return to equity rather than book value. The liabilities to parent, which represent the difference between foreign equity and book value, are loans or other extensions of credit, which do not share in the risks accruing to equity investment. The earnings on these nonequity U.S. assets should be considered as a separate category of U.S. foreign assets but will be disregarded here. In this study we will adjust the book value by taking advantage of a recent publication (U.S. Department of Commerce 1971) of the financial structure of U.S.-owned corporate manufacturing affiliates abroad. It shows liabilities to parents to have been 27.3 and 23.1 percent of book value for affiliates in Canada and the rest of the world, respectively, during the period 1966–69. Under the assumption that this financial structure is representative of the full population of U.S.-owned foreign corporations and branches[9] and for the full decade 1960–69, we estimated average annual rates of return to equity by multiplying the rates of return on book value shown in rows 2 and 5 by 1.376 and 1.30 for Canada and the remaining countries, respectively. The results are shown in rows 3 and 6 of table 4. In the remaining parts of table 4 all further adjustments on rates of return will be made on the equity base, which is the theoretically proper one for the comparisons with U.S. domestic rates of return.

Dividend Withholding Taxes

United States income from foreign manufacturing investment is subject to double taxation in the same way as income from domestic corporations. First, the government taxes the corporation's income directly, which calls for the adjustments already made. Then the dividends distributed by the corporation are subject to a dividend withholding tax. In row 8 of table 4 we show the rate at which foreign governments withhold dividends.

However, the second form of taxation takes place only on that portion

[9] According to U.S. Department of Commerce, *Survey of Current Business* (October 1971, p. 38), earnings of foreign corporations and foreign branches were $6.3 and $2.5 billion, respectively, in 1970.

of earnings that is distributed rather than reinvested. In row 7 of table 4 the average 1960–69 ratio of distributed to before-income-tax earnings is shown. For all countries (next to last column of table 4) the average of 10.9 percent withholding tax (row 8) applied to the 52 percent average distributed earnings (row 7) is seen to lower the after-corporate-income-tax rate of return on equity of 15.1 percent (row 6) to 13.7 percent (row 9). Therefore, the average withholding tax rate is effectively equal to 1.4 percent of equity per year.

Exchange rate changes over the period under study increased or decreased the capital value of the foreign investment holding in terms of U.S. dollars at the annual rate shown in row 10 of table 4. Row 11 contains the rates of return after taxes and exchange rate adjustments, which are the theoretically relevant base of comparison with the domestic opportunity cost of the resources, the pretax rates of return on U.S. domestic manufacturing investment of 19.3 percent during the decade (see note *h* of table 4 for the source of the 19.3 figure). Row 12 of table 4 presents the net social rates of return of investing abroad rather than domestically as defined in equation (3).

As can be seen, the all-country average shows a negative yield of -5.9 percent per year. Positive yield of 0.1, 1.9, 1.1, 3.5, and 5.5 percent were achieved only from the investments in Belgium and Luxembourg, Germany, Denmark, Switzerland and South Africa, respectively.

Royalties and Fees

The theoretical literature on the determinants and welfare effects of direct foreign investment[10] stresses the comparative advantages accruing to multinational corporations from the use of research, management, and marketing skills, which are developed at high initial cost for the domestic U.S. market but which can be applied at relatively low marginal private cost in the operation of foreign subsidiaries. In their accounting conventions, these corporations charge their subsidiaries the average cost of developing the production, management, and marketing knowledge, and the U.S. government reports the value of income from these sources as "royalties, license fees, and rentals" and "management fees and charges," royalties and fees for short.

In the reporting of the balance of payments it is theoretically unobjectionable to include royalties and fees in "income from foreign investment," along with dividends and distributed profits,[11] on the grounds that without the foreign direct investment this financial flow would not have taken place. However, in the present analysis we are concerned with the productivity of resources, not financial flows. From this point of view the

---

[10] See Kindleberger (1968), Johnson (1969), and Caves (1971).

[11] The U.S. balance-of-payments statistics report income from foreign investment as the sum of dividends and distributed profits plus royalties and fees to subsidiaries.

full value of royalties and fees represents a net increase in the productivity of U.S. knowledge capital only if the marginal cost of providing these services is genuinely zero. More generally, the social income from royalties and fees charged foreign subsidiaries is equal to the difference between the average cost at which they are billed and the true marginal cost.

Unfortunately, there exists no evidence on the relationship between marginal and average cost of these services, and in our calculations we had to assume that the marginal cost was zero.[12] As a result, the estimate of the return from foreign investment is almost certainly biased upward, since it is highly unlikely that the marginal cost is zero. However, as one of the important findings of this paper is the negativity of the net social rates of return from foreign investment, the bias introduced by our assumption is in the proper direction.

During the period 1960–69, the value of royalties and fees averaged 2.1 and 3.9 percent annually of the book value of foreign investment in Canada and Europe, respectively. These figures were adjusted for the equity base, and we assumed that Australian and South African rates were the same as those for Europe. The resultant increase in rates of return, which is not subject to any forms of foreign taxation, was added to the net social rates of return shown in row 12 of table 4. The results are presented in row 13 of table 4 and indicate that the overall, all-country average was −2.7 percent compared with −6.4 percent without the adjustment for royalties and fees. Positive adjusted rates of return are shown for Belgium and Luxembourg (5.2), Germany (7.0), the Netherlands (1.3), Denmark (6.2), Switzerland (8.6), Australia (2.2), and South Africa (10.6). The overall average (−0.9) is dominated by the proportionately large investments in Canada (−6.3) and the United Kingdom (−0.3). France (−7.0) and Spain (−5.9) retained their substantial negative rates.

Confiscation

In the past, U.S. investments in many countries of the world, but especially in Cuba, Eastern Europe, China, and some Latin American countries, have been lost to private investors and to the U.S. economy as a result of confiscation or inadequate compensation by foreign governments. In

[12] Theoretically, the opportunity to earn further income on the knowledge capital originally produced only for domestic use should increase the yield from this knowledge capital relative to other forms of capital formation. Therefore, the opportunity to charge foreign subsidiaries for a share of these costs should induce increased expenditures. Once such an expansion has taken place, it is theoretically appropriate to charge foreign subsidiaries the full share of the average cost and inappropriate to consider income from royalties and fees as representing a net social gain acquired at zero or even very low marginal cost. In the long run all fixed costs are variable, and the analysis should reflect this fact. For this reason the adjustments to the rates of return on row 12 must be considered as introducing a theoretically very strong upward bias to the results.

principle, these losses should be averaged and incorporated into the present calculation of net social rates of return from foreign investment. Unfortunately, no ready data are available to carry out such calculations, and the necessary adjustments of our estimates are not undertaken. Consequently, the results presented above are biased upward. In spite of this upward bias, however, the rates still average out to negative.

IV. Summary and Conclusions

The analysis presented in this paper must be considered exploratory. Future studies may well lead to important revisions of the main conclusions that during the decade 1960–69 U.S. holdings of foreign bonds were socially profitable while some of the equity and direct manufacturing holdings resulted in a social loss. Extensions of the analysis in future studies may profitably take place along the following lines.

First, an attempt should be made to estimate returns to total U.S. asset holdings abroad, including short-term assets, bank loans, direct investment in forms other than manufacturing, government holdings, etc. The effect of investment in mining and oil on U.S. terms of trade should be analyzed carefully.

Second, the U.S. holdings should be considered as part of a global system which results in foreigners also holding U.S. assets taxable by the U.S. government. For example, at the end of 1969 the nonliquid, private, long-term U.S. investment position showed $96 billion assets abroad and $41 billion liabilities to foreigners. Foreign investment in the United States probably results in net U.S. gains which can be considered as offsetting the losses discussed above.

Third, the externalities and government expenditures associated with asset holdings of various forms should be explored further. As an entity, U.S. taxpayers receive government services that tend to be equal in value to all of the taxes paid. The relevant question about the welfare effects of foreign direct investment therefore is the extent to which tax payments by corporate or other business entities can be considered as being in return for a government service that can be eliminated in the United States and has to be undertaken abroad because of the U.S. capital export.

Until these lines of analysis have been explored further, the results of the present paper on the social nonprofitability of many foreign investments should be used with the proper caution in any policy decisions about restrictions on and taxation of U.S. asset holdings abroad. However, the evidence is sufficiently reliable to conclude that the export of capital from the United States for direct investment in manufacturing and the internationalist policies guiding the taxation of income from this capital do not clearly raise U.S. welfare and probably lower it.

References

Aliber, R. "Tests of Fisher's Expectations Hypothesis." Paper presented at the Royal Economic Society Conference of Specialists in International Monetary Economics, Ditchley Park, England, January 1973.

Caves, R. "International Corporations: The Industrial Economics of Foreign Investment." *Economica* 38 (February 1971): 1–27.

Dunning, J. *Studies in International Investment.* London: George Allen & Unwin, 1970.

Goldfinger, N. "A Labor View of Foreign Investment and Trade Issues." In *Williams Commission Report.* Washington: Government Printing Office, 1971.

Grubel, H. G. "Internationally Diversified Portfolios: Welfare Gains and Capital Flows." *A.E.R.* 58 (December 1968): 1299–1314.

Grubel, H. G., and Fadner, K. "The Interdependence of International Equity Markets." *J. Finance* 26 (March 1971): 89–94.

International Monetary Fund. *International Financial Statistics.* Washington: Internat. Monetary Fund, various years.

Jenkins, G. "Analysis of Rates of Return from Capital in Canada." Ph.D. dissertation, Univ. Chicago, 1972.

Johnson, H. G. "The Efficiency and Welfare Implications of the International Corporation." In *The International Corporation,* edited by C. P. Kindleberger. Cambridge, Mass.: M.I.T. Press, 1969.

Kindleberger, C. P. *American Business Abroad.* New Haven, Conn.: Yale Univ. Press, 1968.

Kopits, G. F. "The Industrial Economics of Foreign Investment: A Comment." Mimeographed. Washington: Treasury Department, 1970.

Krause, L., and Dam, K. *Federal Tax Treatment of Foreign Income.* Washington: Brookings Inst., 1967.

MacDougall, D. "The Benefits and Costs of Private Investment from Abroad." *Econ. Record* 36, no. 73 (March 1960): 13–36.

Magee, S. "The Welfare Effects of Restrictions on U.S. Trade." Working Paper no. 18. Chicago: Graduate School of Business, University of Chicago, December 1972.

Musgrave, P. *United States Taxation of Foreign Investment Income.* Cambridge, Mass.: Harvard Law School, International Tax Program, 1969.

———. "Tax Preferences to Foreign Investment." In *The Economics of Federal Subsidy Programs,* pt. 2. Washington: Joint Econ. Committee of Congress, June 11, 1972.

Organization for Economic Cooperation and Development. *Financial Statistics,* vol. 2. Paris: Org. Econ. Cooperation and Development, December 1970.

Reddaway, W. B., et al. *Effects of U.K. Direct Investment Overseas.* Cambridge: Cambridge Univ. Press, interim report 1967, final report 1968.

U.S., Department of Commerce. *Survey of Current Business,* various years. Washington: Dept. Commerce.

———. *Foreign Affiliate Financial Survey, 1966–69.* Washington: Dept. Commerce, July 1971.

U.S., Government. *The Economic Report of the President.* Transmitted to Congress February 1971. Washington: Government Printing Office, 1971.

U.S., Treasury Department. *Internal Revenue Service, Statistics of Income, 1962, Supplemental Report: Foreign Income and Taxes Reported on Corporation Income Tax Returns.* Washington: Government Printing Office, 1969.

by Herbert G. Grubel

The Peter Principle
and the
Efficient Market Hypothesis

▶ While Paul Samuelson concedes that "perhaps there are managers who can outperform the market consistently," he questions why academic investigators have been unable to find any evidence of their existence. Professor Grubel suggests that the answer may lie in the Peter Principle.

When a portfolio manager has investment success with a particular portfolio, it often presents him with opportunities to manage different and larger portfolios. So long as he continues to succeed, he will continue moving from one portfolio to another, larger portfolio. Ultimately, he will confront a portfolio so large that his talents are taxed to the limit; having reached his level of "incompetence," he will no longer be able to achieve above-average returns.

In a world in which recognition for success comes rapidly, portfolio managers rapidly reach their levels of incompetence and tend to remain there for some time. Thus, at any given moment, only a small proportion of all portfolio managers will be earning consistently above-average returns. And they will move through the successful portfolios of their careers so quickly that their existence will not really be visible to the tests of academics.

If this hypothesis is correct, a successful portfolio manager should produce longer runs of above-average returns if he persists in managing small portfolios than if he moves on to larger portfolios. More generally, because the successful portfolio manager tends to change jobs frequently, any proper test of his existence requires analysis of the performance history of the manager, rather than the performance history of the portfolio. ▶

Herbert Grubel is Professor of Economics at Simon Fraser University, Burnaby, Canada.

He thanks Stephen Easton, John Herzog and his former colleagues at the Finance Department of the University of Pennsylvania, Pao Cheng, Arthur Zeikel and Paul Samuelson for their helpful comments.

THE efficient market hypothesis, together with the empirical tests establishing its validity, represents one of the most important achievements in finance during the 1960s. The theory has received widespread public attention and has undoubtedly influenced the behavior of many investors. In fact, evidence suggests that investors who believe in the efficient market hypothesis are less willing to follow professional investment advice, avoid turnover of their holdings and entrust less of their wealth to paid managers of mutual funds and other imperfectly diversified portfolios.[1]

Analysts and portfolio managers, having seen the great prestige and incomes they enjoyed during the 1960s fall dramatically during the 1970s (though principally for other reasons), have engaged in many debates about the merit of the efficient market hypothesis with its proponents from the academic world. The academics tended to win these arguments easily by pointing to the strong evidence that mutual funds on average earned a rate of return that was only equal to that of the market as a whole, and that individual funds traced through time did not succeed in earning above-average rates of return for more than a very few years.

Against these statistics, members of the investment community can offer only casual evidence and a belief that some professionals, who are better analysts than others, produce above-average yields for the portfolios they manage. This view has been spelled out by Arthur Zeikel: "In any group of people . . . some will exhibit the capacity to recognize and use information faster than others, and that capacity puts them at a competitive advantage. Professional portfolio managers are paid to exhibit that capacity on behalf of clients and customers." It follows that "the

1. Footnotes appear at end of article.

market is not totally efficient in its response to new developments. New and important information simply is not available simultaneously to all who might recognize or use it. Not all who recognize it are able to use it efficiently."[2]

Paul Samuelson concedes that "perhaps there really are managers who can outperform the market consistently—logic would suggest that they exist." But he goes on to ask why investigators—like Irwin Friend, William Sharpe, Fischer Black and Myron Scholes—have been unable to find such managers."[3] This article argues that investigators have not found evidence of especially talented professionals outperforming the market consistently in part because they have not asked the correct questions and have used false data.

Talented investment analysts who can consistently outperform the market typically have high job mobility, appropriate a large share of their talents in the form of rent and, more or less quickly, become victims of the Peter Principle.[4] To discover the statistical existence of exceptional investment talent, one must analyze the performance records of individual managers through their professional careers, rather than portfolio performances divorced from the records of individual managers.

This article does not include any empirical evidence on the performance of individual investment managers through time simply because the necessary data were unavailable. (In fact, my hope is that people with access to the relevant data will make them available to me or undertake the empirical analysis themselves.[5]) The article begins with a general description of the special talents that would characterize gifted portfolio managers, then explains why conventional studies have not been able to discover evidence of the existence of such managers. It concludes with a description of a more abstract model and suggestions for testing it.

A Description of Peter's Ability

To describe precisely the characteristics of a financial analyst with special abilities, whom we may call Peter the Wizard, assume that financial analysts other than Peter operate at a standard level of ability and operate efficiently, as implied by the most common form of the efficient market model. In such a world, the price of Polaroid stock at all times would be efficient. For example, announcement of plans to market a new, improved camera would impel analysts to invest in research about past sales of cameras and film, general economic conditions, key personnel and many other elements considered relevant to the estimation of investment value. These analysts would very quickly reach a consensus about the proper implications of all this information for the value of the firm's shares and

would act upon it. The resulting share price of Polaroid would be efficient in the usual sense that past price behavior contained no systematic clues about future prices and in the broader economic sense that no analyst could invest in further research and expect the benefits to exceed his costs.

Enter Peter the Wizard, who has special talents in interpreting information. According to the story related to me as true by a Wall Street analyst, Peter had an intuition about the amount of film bought by the average new owner of the camera. With the proper amount of secrecy, he invested in the commission of a consumer survey of the buying habits of new camera owners. This survey revealed that the market price of Polaroid stock was too low. Consequently Peter, who was managing a portfolio that was not yet large, purchased a number of shares, influencing the market price only marginally but increasing the return on his portfolio significantly above average, since the consumer survey eventually proved to be correct, and Polaroid's earnings and the price of the stock rose to the level predicted by Peter.

Peter's Ability and Conventional Efficient Market Tests

Episodes similar to the one above are, of course, not inconsistent with the efficient market hypothesis; it is an observed fact that, in every time period, some portfolios show above-average rates of return. The efficient market model assumes, however, that such successes are the result of luck and represent random events.[6] Peter, according to the efficient market hypothesis, should not be able to repeat his performance for a statistically significant number of successive periods. Empirical studies of individual portfolios through time apparently support this view.

In its simplest version, the new model I propose suggests that Peter can and does use his wizardry to produce above-average yields for a statistically significant number of periods in succession, but that his successes do not show up in conventional empirical tests for two reasons. First, Peter's very success continuously exposes him to offers to manage different and larger portfolios, hence he tends to change jobs frequently. The proper test of Peter's existence therefore requires analysis of the performance of portfolios managed by him through his lifetime. Second, as Peter's reputation increases, so does his compensation and the size of the research staff he directs. These outlays represent a cost of managing a portfolio and are deducted from the portfolio's gross earnings to derive the net income that underlies most studies of the efficient market model. This suggests any analysis of the performance of portfolios managed by Peter should be based on yields before, rather than after, adjustment for expenses.

We can extend this basic notion by applying the original Peter Principle. Peter the Wizard probably started out showing exceptional talents as a broker working for some large firm and dealing with customers coming into the office on their own. When his advice turned out to be better than average, he acquired a growing number of regular clients, and the value of the total assets he directly or indirectly managed increased. As his reputation and income continue to grow, he will be offered jobs managing institutional portfolios of increasing size.

Finally, however, Peter must confront a portfolio so large that his talents are taxed to the limit and the number of situations where he can successfully invest additional research funds for above-normal yields becomes too small to permit above-average returns for the entire portfolio. In other words, Peter sooner or later reaches his level of "incompetence." In a world where the process of reaching this level is rapid, and tenure in the equilibrium position long, we would expect to find at any given moment only a small proportion of all managers on their disequilibrium path, earning consistently above-average returns.

This may explain why, as Samuelson put it, these exceptional talents are "remarkably well hidden."[7] Proponents of the efficient market model would argue that rare investment talent tends to be discovered quickly and, in the terminology used here, moves through a disequilibrium path to equilibrium so quickly that its existence is not really visible. But the existence of the talent and its rate of movement should be susceptible of empirical demonstration.

Samuelson explains why Peter's movement towards his level of incompetence is not instantaneous:

> "From the nature of the case, there must always be a measure of uncertainty and of doubt concerning how much of one's money one can entrust to an adviser suspected of having an exceptional talent. . . . It is a mistake to think that *so much money* will follow the advice of the best talents inevitably, as a *matter of the logic of competitive arbitrage alone*, to leave . . . every security with the same expected variability and with the same expected return."[8]

The reasons for the uncertainty are fairly obvious. Even under efficient market conditions some portfolio will show performance above the average. But the investor has no way of knowing whether this performance is due to the random luck of a Peter in equilibrium or to the talent of a Peter on a disequilibrium path. Only time and experience can tell.

History does provide examples of rare talents enjoying persistent investment succees. Bernard Baruch and J.M. Keynes are outstanding examples from an era when institutions were not set up in such a way that talented investors rapidly reached their Peter limit. In the real world, of course, investment analysis talent is likely to be normally distributed, like all other talents, and persons whose names have entered history books represent the upper end of the distribution and can be expected to be rare.

In sum, the efficient market model can accommodate the possibility that portfolio managers differ according to their abilities to discover investment opportunities, with some producing consistently above-average yields on the portfolios they manage; but such managers are discovered quickly, and the resultant flow of funds into their portfolios, together with increased costs associated with increases in their research expenditures, occur so rapidly that empirical studies have been unable to identify them. This article maintains, however, that there are good reasons for believing that the discovery of and reaction to such exceptional investment talent is not instantaneous, hence that properly designed research should be able to establish the existence of such individuals.

Some Ideas on Testing

The preceding analysis can be made more rigorous with the help of a diagram suggested to me by Pao Cheng. In Figure I, the vertical axis measures portfolio returns and the horizontal axis portfolio size. The rate of return R_m is that of the market average. The line PP', which we might call Peter's Path, shows the functional relation between size and average performance of portfolios managed by Peter. With a portfolio of size A, Peter is able to earn on average a (risk-adjusted) return equal to R_p. As portfolio size increases, however, Peter's Path approaches the market average.

The line JJ' shows John's path, reflecting the investment analysis talents of another wizard. As drawn, John's abilities are superior to those of Peter,

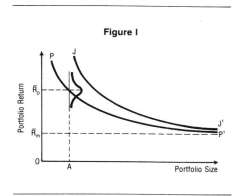

Figure I

since at any given portfolio size, he is able to produce a superior performance. The paths of John and Peter are representative of a whole family of varying investment talents, talents that, like most human abilities, will be normally distributed. While the paths may not all be parallel or asymptotic to the market path, it will probably be convenient to assume that the family of paths has some statistically convenient properties.

Given the life histories of a number of portfolio managers, particularly information about their incomes and the returns, variances and sizes of the portfolios they have managed, a random walk model would permit specification of the length of runs of risk-adjusted returns above normal that normal individuals could expect in an efficient market. Then, if the data show persons who have produced runs longer than those expected from a purely random process, we would accept the hypothesis about the existence of wizards. Indexes of wizardry could be developed to test whether the distribution of talent is indeed normal. The importance of portfolio size could also be tested. If our hypothesis holds, a person of a given quality of talent should produce longer runs of above-average yields if he persists in managing small portfolios than if he moves into larger portfolios.

Of course, most of the arguments presented here are empirically unverified, although writings support the theoretical approach and imply that, ultimately, the existence of investment wizards can be an empirical question. Given my inability to discover or generate data for such an empirical study, this article remains basically a theoretical exercise. But it is open to empirical testing by someone with the relevant data. As Samuelson said, in the contest between academics and practitioners over the validity of the efficient market model, the ball is in the court of the practitioners. It is up to them "to dispose of the uncomfortable brute fact [of empirical evidence that markets are efficient] in the only way that any fact is disposed of—by producing brute evidence to the contrary."[9] ∎

Footnotes

1. Arguments along these lines have been made by Fischer Black, "Can Portfolio Managers Outrun the Random Walkers?" *The Journal of Portfolio Management*, Fall 1974. He argues that portfolio managers should attempt less to forecast prices than to diversify portfolios to achieve optimally desired leverage and risk.

2. A. Zeikel, "The Random Walk and Murphy's Law," *The Journal of Portfolio Management*, Fall 1974, p. 21.

3. P.A. Samuelson, "Challenge to Judgment," *The Journal of Portfolio Management*, Fall 1974, p. 17.

4. The Peter Principle in its original formulation states that individuals in any job who produce work of outstanding quality tend to be candidates for promotion to positions of higher responsibility demanding greater skills. Such promotion continues until individuals have reached positions in which their capacities are taxed to the limit so that they perform no more than average quality work. As a result of the operation of this principle we find that most jobs in the world are performed by persons who are just competent to do average quality work. This, in the view of the authors of the Peter Principle, often implies that the work is done "incompetently." See L.J. Peter and R. Hull, *The Peter Principle* (New York: W. Morrow and Company, 1969).

5. My colleague John Herzog and I have made some efforts to generate a data base through a survey of Canadian portfolio managers. However, preliminary results are discouraging because the data requested are very personal and involve confidential relations with wealthholders, which many people apparently are unwilling to reveal for personal reasons or because of potential loss of confidentiality. However, there may exist somewhere a set of biographic data collected by a professional association or a government agency that could be used for the purpose of the proposed study. Alternatively, some such institution may be encouraged to add relevant questions to one of its routine surveys. It would seem very much in the interest of the investment industry to test the proposed model and to attempt a scientifically designed reconciliation of the broadly held views of the members of the industry with the evidence on the efficient market hypothesis produced by academic investigators.

6. P. Samuelson has dealt with the problem that prices of assets are, according to economic theory, determined by real forces in a theoretically predictable way. Therefore, their movement through time cannot follow entirely a Martingale process, since this implies that asset prices essentially would be indeterminate and independent of real economic forces. In "Is Real-World Price a Price Told by the Idiot of Chance?" (*Review of Economics and Statistics*, February 1976) Samuelson summarizes and extends earlier work showing that prices anticipated properly according to real factors still fluctuate randomly. Yet, the fact that prices in the longer run are determined by real forces does seem to give rise to the opportunity for earning extraordinary profits from the correct forecasting of the influence of such real factors on prices, even though tests of short-run fluctuations show them to be random.

7. Samuelson, "Challenge to Judgment," p. 17.

8. Ibid., p. 19. (Italics in original.)

9. Ibid.

[16]

I. SERVICES AND THE CHANGING ECONOMIC STRUCTURE

Herbert G. Grubel
Michael A. Walker

Canada

L80

Modern Service Sector Growth: Causes and Effects

1. Introduction

The growth of service-sector employment and GDP in industrial countries has been significant in the 20th century and has reached levels which have given rise to all kinds of theorizing and speculation about its causes and effects. Figures 1 and 2 illustrate this development for Canada in terms of employment, showing that service-sector employment has grown from near 35 per cent to over 70 per cent of the total between the census years 1911 and 1981. Employment in the service sector has exceeded that in goods production since 1958. Very similar developments have taken place in other industrial countries and with respect to the growth in GDP, as is documented below.

In this study, we review briefly the existing body of knowledge relevant to an explanation of the causes and effects of this growth of the service sector. Part 3 presents a taxonomy of service industries and a pioneering approach to the estimation of consumer, government and producer services. The determinants and welfare effects of these services are discussed in Part 4.

2. Review of the Literature

Hill [1977] discusses definitions and conceptual issues surrounding the service sector. While these issues are interesting and important, in this study we approach them pragmatically. The service sector is what the UN system of national accounts and most national statistical offices record as such in terms of employment and GDP. The possible develop-

2

Figure 1 - Historic Employment Shares for Canada (census years)

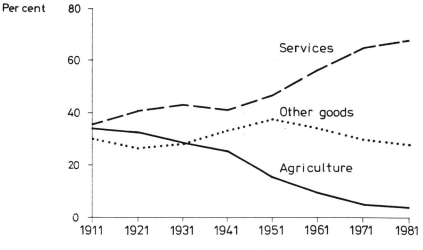

Source: Government Printing Office [1983].

Figure 2 - Employment in Canada by Industry Groups

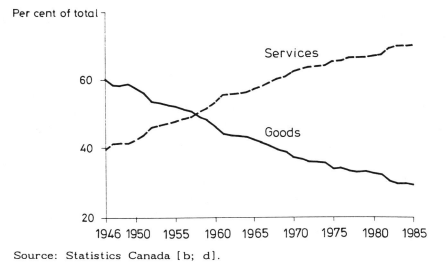

Source: Statistics Canada [b; d].

ment of new and better data in the future may require adjustments to our theories and results.

In a large and growing literature, the causes and welfare effects of the historic growth in the service sector are being analysed. At the risk of oversimplification, this literature may be divided into five classes.

Firstly, Adam Smith and other classical economists considered the production of services to be unproductive. This notion was based on their concept of exchange value and the perception that services are performed by servants for individuals. Such services, once produced, cannot be exchanged for money or other goods in the manner in which material goods can be. While modern value theory has discredited the validity of the view that the production of services involves an unproductive use of resources, the basic idea still pervades much public thinking in the West. In the Soviet Union's national income accounts personal services are not recorded as part of national output. In the 1950s, the United Kingdom imposed special taxes on personal services in order to discourage their production.

Secondly, the now classic studies by Stigler [1956], Baumol [1967] and Fuchs [1968] explained the growth of services as the result of a high income elasticity of demand for, and the low rate of productivity growth in the production of consumer services. The analytical focus of these studies has been on the implications of these characteristics on overall productivity growth and inflation. The conclusions of this analysis have entered the economics literature as the widely-known "Baumol Effect".

Thirdly, Fisher [1939] developed a model of primary (agricultural and other natural resource industries), secondary (manufacturing) and tertiary (service) sectors. Modern economic development in this model was seen to generate growth in output and productivity in the primary sector which, given the saturation of demand, led to the shrinking of this sector's share of employment and output. The labour released from this sector moved into the manufacturing sector. Eventually, manufacturing employment was expected to experience a relative decline for the same reasons that resulted in the shrinking of the primary sector. The surplus labour was then expected to find employment in the tertiary industries.

4

Literature of recent origin such as Shelp [1981], Bell [1979], Blackaby [1978] and Bluestone and Harrison [1982] builds on this model by Fischer. Broadly speaking, these authors argue that the service sector is encountering the same problems of saturation in demand that have befallen the primary and secondary sectors before. However, there is the new problem that labour not needed in this sector has nowhere to go. There is no corresponding fourth sector that expands and satisfies new types of demand.

This literature has attracted much attention among politicians and some economists since it offers an innovative explanation of the high unemployment rates and the balance-of-payments problems of the United States of the 1980s. It has given wide publicity to the concept of "de-industrialization", the existence of which is considered evidence of a fundamental pathology of free market systems and creating the need for industrial planning. In addition, this literature decries the growth of the service sector since it is alleged to reflect "doing each other's laundry" (with a zero gain in real output) and to result in a "bi-modal income distribution" (services requiring waiters at low wages and computer experts at high pay with a decline of the middle-income occupations and pay). These phenomena are also considered to create a need for industrial planning.

Fourthly, Riddle [1986], Ott [1987], Tatom [1986], Kutscher and Mark [1983] and Kravis [1983] have developed analytical models and empirical evidence largely in response to the arguments made by the most recent critics of service-sector growth. Their main findings are that recent trends are a continuation of past developments, especially the growth in demand for consumer services and that there is no reason for public intervention to prevent de-industrialization or any other allegedly undesirable developments.

For example, Ott [1987, p. 13] presents recent statistics and notes "The shift in output has reflected a relative shift in consumer demand toward services". Riddle [1986, pp. 218; 229] notes in the concluding section of her book entitled "Services and the Quality of Life" that "services are the housekeepers of the world".

The fifth set of studies like Gershuny and Miles [1983], Swan [1985] and Radwanski [1986] build on the preceding literature but add as an innovation a special emphasis on the role of producer and government services in the growth of the service sector.

The current study is in this tradition. Its main contribution lies in the quantification of the relative size of consumer, government and producer services. It will be shown that in Canada during the post-war years at least, the share of GDP originating with producer services has been twice that of consumer and government services. The share of the last two sectors has remained nearly constant in real terms since the 1950s and almost all real growth in Canada has come from producer services. Similar results have emerged from estimates made for other countries, though there are some interesting differences in the growth rates of the different sectors in the United States, Japan, Greece and Sweden, as will be seen below.

3. The Basic Taxonomy

The purpose of this section is to give a more precise definition of the analytical classes of consumer, government and producer service sectors and to present estimates of the size of each for a number of countries.

a. Consumer Services

Consumption expenditures are one of the cornerstones of the Keynesian models of the economy. Traditionally, they distinguish between spending on durable and non-durable goods and services. Here, we are concerned with spending on services which consist of the output of restaurants, hotels, financial and insurance firms, retail outlets, amusement and recreation facilities, personal service facilities for hair, clothing, shoes, automobiles and household goods and communication and public transportation systems. This list is not exhaustive and its precise statistical coverage is specified in the original sources of time series presented below.

6

b. Government Services

Government services are generated by the incurrence of exhaustive expenditures required in the administration of education, health, welfare, defence, justice and general government programmes. It is clear that under this definition government services exclude money spent in transfer payments, though they include the cost of carrying out these transfers.

We assume that all exhaustive government expenditures are made available free of charge to citizens and that they result in public consumption, except for real capital formation. This assumption results in an overestimate of total government service consumption if some government spending is used by producers, some education and health expenditures go towards net human capital formation and spending on defence is considered to be a form of investment in national security. It also leads to an over-estimate of government service consumption if there are charges to consumers and they are included in the category of service consumption spending discussed in the preceding section.

c. Producer Services

Producer services, which may also be called intermediate input services, are all those services not bought by private individuals or provided by governments. They consist of the output of industries known as Business Services, comprising computer, accounting, advertising, personnel, protection and similar industries. However, they also include a part of the output of several industries that are often better known as sources of supply for consumer services. These are the financial, insurance, real estate, transportation, engineering, legal, storage, communication, hotel, restaurant and many other service industries.

Several studies noted above have dwelled on the very rapid growth of Business Services in recent years. While this sector has experienced the most rapid growth of all service sub-sectors, in 1985 it still represented a relatively small proportion of total employment in Canada.[1] Below, we provide empirical information which reflects the increased use of business as well as the other producer services.[2]

d. Estimation Technique

The estimation of the relative size of the three service sectors has been dictated by the absence of any time series on producer services and the availability of the following three basic statistical time series in nominal and real terms. Firstly, the most basic is the series on GDP at factor cost for the sum of all service-producing industries. Secondly, there are time series on gross expenditures on services by consumers, and thirdly, exhaustive expenditures by government. Estimation of the value of producer services basically involves the subtraction of consumer service spending GDP and of exhaustive government spending from the total value of service GDP. The residual is equal to the value of producer services.

The estimation procedure required some minor adjustments to the basic time series data. Government spending was reduced by expenditures on government capital formation on the grounds that this involves mainly spending on construction of roads, schools and similar projects. However, no adjustment was made to eliminate material inputs from the remaining government services. These data thus count as service GDP

---

[1] The level of employment in Canada in Business Services in 1985 was 498 thousand and therefore less than that in Health and Welfare with 979 thousand, Education with 745 thousand and Accommodation and Food Services with 632 thousand (Statistics Canada 71-001, February 1986).

[2] Space limitations prevent us from discussing here the role of international non-factor trade in services. However, we should note that available statistics on Travel, Freight and Shipping, Business Services and Other tend to be weighted heavily in favour of producer services, since the only consumer services are virtually those absorbed by tourists. For more on the nature and magnitude of trade in services, see Grubel [1986; 1988], where it is argued that the bulk of services are traded internationally after they have been embodied as producer services in material substances or they have been produced or absorbed by persons or goods during temporary stays abroad.

8

the goods used up in the production of the government services, such as paper and computers.[1]

A second adjustment is based on the fact that the value of consumer service expenditures include the values of intermediate material inputs, such as the food served in restaurants.[2] The ratio of value added to gross output of these consumer service industries was about 0.6 for Canada during the 1970s. This figure was used to deflate the gross service consumption data for all of the countries in this study and for all years since the correct figures could not be obtained from available data sources. This procedure is likely to create a relatively small bias in the comparison of intertemporal developments within each country, since the consumer service industries are relatively labour intensive and have experienced little technological change. For the same reasons, comparisons of different countries should be subject to relatively small biases.

In sum, the estimating procedure derives producer services as a residual: Total Service Expenditure and Product minus Government Provided Services minus Consumer Service GDP equals Producer Service GDP.

---

[1] If the material inputs used by the government (and consumer service producing industries) are not deducted from the gross expenditures, it is possible in principle for the sum of these service expenditures to exceed the total GDP of the service industries measured through output. Therefore, the failure to deflate government exhaustive spending for material intermediate inputs results in an underestimate of the size of the demand for producer services. The same bias results from the failure to deduct the intermediate service inputs purchased by governments from exhaustive government spending. However, this treatment probably creates a relatively minor bias given the adjustment made for capital formation and the labour intensity of most government services. The exception, in this is spending on defence, which in the case of Canada is relatively minor (3 per cent of GDP). It should also be noted that if the proportion of material and intermediate service inputs used by governments in the provision of their services has remained constant, then there will be a relatively unbiased estimate of the rates of growth of the share of producer services in GDP.

[2] Use of the GDP of consumer service-producing industries eliminates from gross production figures not just material but also intermediate service inputs bought by the industry. These intermediate service inputs are thus attributed to the producer service sector, which is the intention of the exercise.

e. Empirical Results

At the end of 1987, Statistics Canada produced a revised set of statistics on real GDP at factor cost in 1981 prices for the years 1961-1986. These data were used to develop Figures 3 and 4 which show the shares of consumer, government, producer and total service expenditures as a percentage of GDP for those years in nominal terms, real terms and as an index to highlight changes in the size of shares. Required basic data for analogous estimates could be found in OECD National Accounts publications only for the years 1970-1984 and for a small set of countries. Estimates of the size of the different service sectors for some of these countries are contained in the appendix tables and only the changes in the index are presented in figures.

f. Results for Canada

Figure 3 shows the shares of nominal GDP represented by output of the total and different sub-sectors of the service industries. The growth of the total share closely parallels that of the growth in the employment share shown in Figure 2. It is also clear that consumer and government services in recent years have been about equal size and each have been slighly more than half the magnitude of producer services.

Estimates in terms of constant prices are shown in Figure 4. They reveal that in throughout the period as a per cent of GDP consumer and Government services have been of about equal size while producer services have been about 40 to 50 per cent greater as a share of GDP. The representation of the shares in terms of levels hides some interesting developments of the shares through time which are brought out effectively in Figure 4. Most notable in this representation is that producer services have grown, somewhat cyclically, 20 per cent as a share of GDP during the 25 years under observation. Consumer services, on the other hand, have represented a declining share of GDP between 1961 and 1973 but recovered their 1961 levels by 1986. Government services kept pace

10

Figure 3 - Shares of Different Service Sectors in Canada's Nominal GDP, 1947-1983

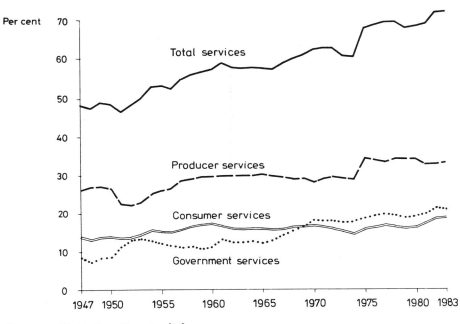

Source: Statistics Canada [a].

with the growth of the producer services until 1982. Thereafter, their share fell to the level they had occupied in 1961.[1]

g. *Some Thoughts on Prices*

The preceding results depend heavily on the quality of the price data used in the construction of the series. It is well known that price and productivity data present particularly severe problems for statis-

---

[1] The finding on the relative decline of the government share points to the importance of transfer payments in total spending. However, this decline may also be a statistical artifact. See the next section for more details.

ticians in the case of government services. These problems are mostly
due to the absence of market prices and often units of output, as in the
case of defence. To overcome these problems, statisticians assume that
the real quantity of output is strictly proportional to real expenditures
on inputs by governments.

Figure 4 - Shares of Services as a Percentage (1981 dollars)

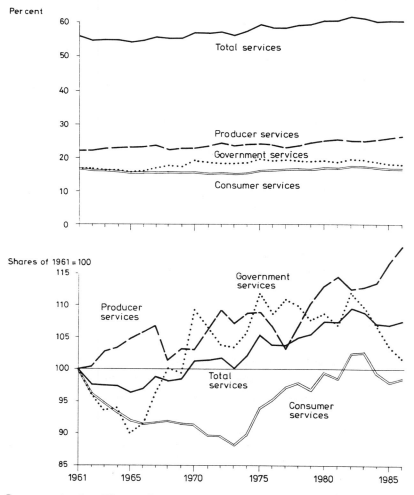

Source: As for Figure 3.

For example, a doubling of employees issuing pension cheques is assumed to result in a doubling of real service output. This procedure neglects the fact that the number of cheques issued may have grown more than 100 per cent through the simultaneous introduction of computers and the doubling of employees. Under such a condition the real quantity of government services produced has more than doubled while official statistics show only a growth of 100 per cent. By analogy, deterioration in the quality of services, such as the incidence of misdirected cheques, should be reflected as a factor lowering the real quantity of government services produced.

There is only inconclusive empirical evidence on the real quantity of output by governments adjusted for changes in productivity and other inputs. One may surmise that computers, word-processors and modern means of communication and travel have probably increased the productivity of civil servants and soldiers. On the other hand, Read [1983] has produced evidence on the decline of productivity in Canada Post, in spite of large increases in capital per worker.

There are also problems associated with the measurement of price and quality changes in privately-produced services. The bias in the data resulting from these problems appears to be less severe than that stemming from the measurement of government service output.

In the absence of reliable information, we have to accept the results reported above as the best systematically available. However, we can note, that if there is a systematic underestimate of productivity increases in the government sector, then the consumption of real government services has been greater than is indicated by current data. In other words, Canadians have been provided with pension cheques and defence at rates growing more rapidly than is implicit in Figure 4. Under these assumptions, the share of real government services in GDP has declined less or may even have increased. Most important, it is logically possible that, under these assumptions, the real share in producer services has remained constant or has fallen.

Below, we assume that bias in the measurement of real service production is sufficiently unsystematic and small to preserve the validity of the main findings: producer services represent about one half of all service output, consumer and government services one quarter each in nominal terms. The growth of real service output is dominated strongly by the growth of producer services.

h. Some Preliminary Evidence on OECD Countries

The OECD publication of the National Accounts of member countries contains the information needed to estimate the level and real growth rates of consumer, government and producer services for a number of countries. In the appendix tables, we present the shares of total services GDP made up of these components for the years 1970-1985 for these countries. From the analytical perspective of our study, the most important result emerging from these tables is that, in recent years, in both nominal and real terms the level of producer services has been somewhere between 28 and 33 per cent of all services. Canada is the outlayer with 41 per cent. The great similarity is remarkable in the sense that the sample covers such diverse countries as the United States, Japan, Norway, Sweden and Greece.

The proportion of consumer services has been around 15 per cent of the total for all countries except Sweden and Norway, where it has been roughly one half that size. The explanation for this is likely to be found in the much larger government service sector in these latter two countries.

For the purpose of theorizing, we have prepared Figure 5. It presents the time trend of the share of real producer services in total GDP for each of the countries in the sample (the data in the appendix give percentages with total service GDP as the base of 100). The data show an interesting similarity of the size of the share for the United States, Greece, Sweden and Japan, all of which have remained unchanged during the 15 years of observation. Canada stands out as the country with a rapid and consistent growth in the producer service sector. Norway, on the other hand, is notable for the consistent decline in this share.

A detailed analysis of this data cannot be presented here. However, it is tempting to suggest that in Norway, Sweden and Greece the very rapid growth and high level of government service spending may be due to the rapid growth in producer services put out by the government which in the other countries tend to be produced in the private sector.

14

Figure 5 - Producer Services as a Per Cent of GDP (constant prices)

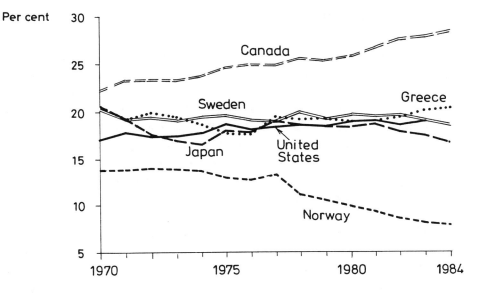

Source: OECD [various issues].

If this hypothesis is correct, then the main point of our basic model is reconfirmed by the international evidence. The bulk of the growth of service-sector GDP is due to the increased output of producer services. Obviously, these propositions need further investigation by a detailed analysis of the composition of government spending or correlation analysis between the growth rate of government and producer services. Also, constancy of the producer service-sector share in the United States and Japan, which has been unaccompanied by a growth in government services, needs to be explained.

In sum, the evidence on the levels and growth rates of different service sectors in different countries is presented here more for discussion than in definitive support of our model.

4. The Economics of Individual Sectors

a. *Consumer Services*[1]

The demand for individual goods and services in the budgets of consumers has been studied by Houthakker and Taylor [1966] and Prais and Houthakker [1971] in their path-breaking application of econometrics and the use of computers. Schweitzer [1969] and Tulpule and Powell [1978] have made similar studies for Canadian and Australian consumers respectively. Bernstein and Geehan [1988] used translogarithmic expenditure functions to estimate demand functions for Canada.

These and other studies have found that the income elasticity of demand for services ranges between 0.6 and 2, with an average of slightly above 1. The income elasticity of demand is high for some services, such as fancy restaurant meals and other traditional luxury services. On the other hand, for a wide variety of personal, household and recreation services, the income elasticity is quite low because modern technology has produced substitute goods such as appliances for household services and modern electronic devices for entertainment outside the home. Bernstein and Geehan [1988, p. 331] found an income elasticity of demand for insurance services of about 1.5.

The importance of the aggregate consumer services used in the preceding section suggests that it might be interesting to consider the demand for the sum of all consumer services, something which has been given little attention before. Only very recently Summers and Heston [1988] have studied total service consumption spending in 60 countries. They found that "service expenditures are somewhat income elastic with respect to consumption when allowance is made for relative prices" [ibid., p. 16]. Bernstein and Geehan [1988, p. 331] have found the demand for non insurance services in Canada to be about 1.25.

Below, we present data on Canada, though the application of the model to conditions in France and the United States has produced very

---

[1] The analysis in this section draws heavily on Grubel and Hammes [1987].

16

similar results. [1] Using aggregate data, a standard demand equation for total Canadian consumer spending on services for the 1961-1985 period was estimated[2] with the following results:

[1] $\ln(S) = -1.175 + 1.172\ln(TE) - 0.39\ln(PS)$
          (-8.6) (16.81) (-2.48)

where S is the real service expenditure per capita, TE is total real consumption expenditure per capita and PS is the relative price of services, ln means natural logs and the values in parenthesis are t-values. The number of observations is 25, R' is 0.989 and the uncorrected Durbin-Watson statistic is 0.42.

As can be seen, the estimated income elasticity in this equation is statistically significant, has the theoretically-expected sign and is consistent with that found in other studies. The price elasticity coefficient is significant and has the expected sign. However, the level of the Durbin-Watson statistic suggests the omission of a variable.

In the search for this omitted variable, we constructed a model of household behaviour in which changes in the female labour force participation rate is an exogenously-given, driving force. According to this model, the movement of women into the labour force reduces the production of certain types of services in the household and increases their purchase in the market. Accordingly, changes in the female labour force participation rates are hypothesized to result in shifts in the demand

---

[1] Grubel and Hammes [1987] and Hammes, Rosa and Grubel [forthcoming] contain results for the United States and France respectively. Trivedi [1988] used the basic model to estimate the demand for consumer services in India. In place of labour force participation rates for females he found the rate of urbanization to be a theoretically and empirically strong shift parameter for the demand function.

[2] The data were taken from Statistics Canada, CANSIM matrix 6708, series D 10131 and D 10147, both series as revised in 1986. Further information on prices, other independent variables, econometric techniques and a theoretical model of household behaviour is given in Grubel and Hammes [1987]. However, we should note that the demand equation is identified as a result of the assumption that the supply of consumer services is perfectly elastic. This assumption seems reasonable in the light of the fact that the consumer service industry is relatively small and most of the factors of production it requires, mostly notably labour, are good substitutes in use in other industries.

function for services and change the total expenditure and relative price coefficients in the estimating equation. The results of our calculations are:

[2] $\ln S = 1.009 + 0.348\ln(TE) + 0.703\ln(F) - 0.007\ln(PS)$
        (6.86)   (6.09)   (15.42)   (-0.13)

The symbols are defined as before, F is the female labour force participation rate, the numer of observations is 25, R^2 is 0.999 and the uncorrected Durbin-Watson is 2.07. These results are consistent with our model and basic postulates of consumer behaviour. They imply that the income elasticity of demand for consumer services is well below one and that the growth in demand for them has been driven by the growth in the female labour force participation rate. At the mean, for every one per cent increase in the participation rate, the demand for consumer services has increased to 0.7 per cent.[1]

For our general analysis of the service sector, these estimates have three important implications. Firstly, they imply that the rise in the female labour force participation rate from 28.7 per cent in 1961 to 54.4 per cent in 1985 has been responsible for 63 per cent of the increased demand for consumer services. Secondly, this demand growth reflects a shift from unrecorded household production into the recorded formal sector by an amount equal to 16.4 per cent of the growth of GNP per capita during this period. Thirdly, if and when there is a change in the female labour force participation rate, the demand for consumer services and rate of measured economic growth may be expected to change correspondingly and by substantial amounts.

----

[1] The validity of our model finds support in the findings of Scarfe and Krantz [1988, p. 47] that, in econometric equations estimating the demand for restaurant meals in Canada, there is a significant difference in determinants of low (Chain) and high-priced (Independent) restaurants. The elasticity of demand with respect to total family expenditures is low for the former and high for the latter while the former shows statistically significant correlation with female labour force participation rates while the latter does not.

18

b. Government Services

During the immediate post-war period the dominant theory of the determinants and effects of government spending was that articulated most persuasively by Musgrave [1959], who, in turn, drew heavily on Pigou. This theory perceived government spending to be the outcome of a detached, rational calculus and administration by agents without any self-interest. It was postulated to involve the meeting of merit wants, the internationalization of externalities and the provision of public goods, all of which resulted in increased social welfare attainable with given resources.

The validity of Musgrave's public finance theory was challenged by the public choice model of Buchanan and Tullock [1962] and others. According to this view, government spending has been motivated predominantly by the efforts of politicians to secure votes from special interest groups that benefit from these expenditures. It is therefore likely to decrease rather than increase overall social welfare.

The spending data on Canada presented above lend some support to the public choice models. While government spending in total has been claiming ever increasing shares of GDP, most of the growth has been in transfer payments rather than exhaustive expenditures. As the data show, the latter in real terms actually represent a 20 per cent smaller percentage of GDP in 1986 than in 1961. According to the public choice approach, this is due to the fact that transfer payments can be aimed very well at special interest groups whereas real government services cannot.

The data on other countries, however, suggest that generalizations on this matter are difficult. US trends resemble those in Canada, especially if the growth of the 1980s in exhaustive expenditures were adjusted properly for increases in defence spending. Exhaustive spending in Japan fluctuated widely, but has been level for the period since 1971. Greece and Sweden, on the other hand, have experienced large growth in spending.

The future of government service production is difficult to predict. In North America, tax revolts have limited the ability and willingness of politicians to raise taxes while transfer payment programmes have a built-in growth. As a result, exhaustive expenditures are likely to shrink further in real terms. On the other hand, the deterioration of social overhead capital and real services may so reduce the quality of life and efficiency of the economy that pressures for increased spending will mount. Whether or not these pressures will succeed will depend significantly on the ability to bring under control the internal dynamics of transfer payment programmes and the tendency of politicians to buy votes by the initiation of new programmes for their constituencies. Undoubtedly, conditions in every country are different and we are not qualified to speculate on those.

c. *Producer Services*

According to neo-classical economic theory, growth in output per capita is an increasing function of society's ratio of capital to labour, where the former consists of real, human and knowledge capital. One of the ideas of the Austrian School of Economics expressed in the writings of von Boehm-Bawerk [1932] and found in Wicksell [1901] is that this capital-deepening involves increases in the "roundaboutness" and specialization of the entire production process.

Robinson Crusoe increased the roundaboutness of fish production when he constructed a fishing net. He did so because it enabled him, over the technical life of the net, to catch more fish than he could have through the use of the labour spent in making the net and the use of the same fishing effort without the net.

In a more complex society, fishing nets are produced by specialists who use machinery, human skills and scientific knowledge are produced by further specialists. All of these production processes increase roundaboutness and the "distance" between ultimate consumers of final output such as fish and the activities of these producers of intermediate inputs. The prices of these intermediate inputs must be high enough to earn producers at least normal returns. At the same time, these intermediate inputs must yield a positive net return to their users. Otherwise there is no market for them.

We think that it is useful to consider the providers of producer services to be one important set of specialists in this process which generates ever-increasing roundaboutness, specialization in production, capital-deepening and increases in labour and other factor productivity. It is difficult to generalize about the factor inputs and other technical characteristics of producer service industries.

Baumol [1984] has shown that some service industries have high capital-labour ratios, as for example the telecommunication industries and utilities. On the other hand, many firms providing producer services use workers with high levels of training, employ sophisticated techniques but have low levels of physical capital. These firms may be said to operate with high levels of human-knowledge capital per worker. Examples in this field are the computer and communications consulting firms that have developed since the electronic revolution of the 1970s. Birch [1979] shows that many of these firms are small and run by Schumpeterian entrepreneurs, but that there are also the large and more traditional firms in the financial, legal, accounting and engineering service industries. Finally, there are highly labour-intensive, low-tech producer services, such as janitors and retail clerks.

d. *Schumpeterian Process*

Seen in this perspective, the relative growth of the producer service sector can continue for as long as technological innovations maintain a marginal rate of return to capital greater than the rate of interest. In a market economy, this innovation is generated to a significant degree by Schumpeterian entrepreneurs. Of these, a large proportion fails, another large segment earns only normal rates of return, but they all are driven by the expectation of large, if temporary, returns, which accrue to only a few. As long as an environment favourable to these entrepreneurs is maintained, they venture into business with innovative technology, processes and services nd the dynamic process of accumulation and service-sector growth continues.

e. *Productivity*

One important implication of our model of the producer service sector is that its effect on the productivity of labour and other industries can be indirect but still very important. For example, consider the above model of fishing and capital-deepening through the use of nets. Assume that the net-making industry is without technological advances and that labour productivity in this industry is constant. Assume also that technological advances increase the effectiveness of nets in catching fish. Finally, consider that the fishing industry finds it profitable to increase the quantity of nets per worker. During the postulated period of innovation and capital-deepening, the price of fish may fall and demand increase sufficiently so that more workers are needed. Alternatively, the quantity of workers employed may fall. In either case, during the period under consideration the productivity of labour in the net-producing industry is unchanged but that in the fishing industry is growing since each worker catches growing numbers of fish in every new time period during which technology improves.

Computer, telecommunications, financial and similar service industries are much like the industries producing fish nets in the preceding example. They may be experiencing low or zero productivity gains,[1] but their inputs generate productivity increases in the industries purchasing their output. For example, productivity may have been constant in the firms which wrote the programmes required for the operation of the automated bank teller machines which were introduced in the banking sector in recent years. However, there is little doubt that the use of these teller machines raised the output of financial service industry workers in terms of cheque cashing transactions per time period.[2]

In modern economies, productivity gains generated by service industries may not even show up because of deficiencies in measurement procedures. For example, a town may initially be served by one shopping centre located at one end of town and operating at a certain level of productivity. Now consider that competition results in the establishment of a second shopping centre at the opposite end of town. In the new equilibrium, both centres operate profitably, each serving half the

---

[1] The validity of the following analysis is independent of the assumption about productivity developments in the service sector. We have chosen the present assumption because it is widely considered to be correct, although there is much argument over the validity of current measurement techniques [see Mark, 1982] used in arriving at this view.

[2] We owe this example to Chant [1988].

town's population. Under these conditions, it is easily possible that by traditional measures productivity in the retail sector serving the town has decreased, average retail margins have increased while at the same time there is genuine equilibrium in that all firms earn normal returns and the efficiency of household production has increased sufficiently to create an increase in overall welfare. [1]

f. Trade in Services

Our approach to the study of services in modern economies has some interesting implications for international trade in services, which have been discussed at greater length in Grubel [1988]. However, it is worth noting here two implications of the overwhelming importance of producer services in the economy.

Firstly, producer services are likely to play a significant role in the determination of comparative advantage. This is not a new idea since it is now widely accepted that the omission of human and knowledge capital underlies the Leontief paradox. These forms of capital enter the production process largely through the activities of producer service industries. More recent work in international economics by Krugman [1979] and Brander and Spencer [1983] have pointed to the potential role of comparative advantage played by industrial strategies in the development of new products and industries. In almost all of the examples used in this literature, but especially automobiles, computers and aircraft, these strategies require the use of high technology and other inputs which are typically provided by producer service firms.

Secondly, producer services are traded to a small degree by the temporary movement of delivery agents, as when professional consultants move abroad temporarily to provide a service. [2] There is also some pro-

---

[1] We owe this example to Acheson and Ferris [1988]. In some theoretical models the welfare gains from such locational differentiation are ambiguous. See, for example, Eaton and Wooders [1985].

[2] The permanent establishment of foreign operations by firms in the service sector involves international capital and therefore factor service flows. These are not the trade in services which has attracted the concern of policy makers and theorists in recent years. However, it

ducer service trade carried on by the temporary stay of capital equipment abroad, as in the case of leased drilling platforms and aircraft selling transportation to foreigners. The rest of the producer services are
traded after they have been embodied in material substances.

According to Iococca [1984], Chrysler automobiles embody medical
services worth more than the steel used in their construction. Of
course, the steel in turn embodies many types of services and so on for
the inputs used in steel production, in patterns which can be established
through the use of input-output tables. Many producer services are embodied in paper, electronic storage devices and electronic signals. [1]

Our model of services implies that much theorizing about service as
a special type of trade is unwarranted and that the standard theoretical
treatment of services as essentially non-tradeable deserves to be retained. At the same time, the model invites theorizing about and
measurement of embodied service trade.

5. Summary and Policy Implications

The main contribution of this study consists of the development of a
taxonomy and measurement of consumer, government and producer services. The measurement technique, which can be applied in all countries
with modern national income accounting systems, showed that in Canada
about one half of all service GDP is used by producers, one quarter is
consumed directly and one quarter is produced by government mainly for
domestic consumption.

Our model of the demand for consumer services points to the importance of the monetization of household production as a driving force of

---

should be noted that service firms abroad tend to generate direct service trade to the extent that they generate income from patents, royalties, copyrights and other knowledge capital. Unfortunately, these
sources of comparative advantage of foreign subsidiaries are not normally captured by existing balance-of-payments accounting procedures,
as has been discussed by Rugman [1987].

[1] Some consumer services are traded in this manner after embodiment in
such a form as life assurance contracts, but we believe this type of
trade to be relatively unimportant.

demand. It also implies that the income elasticity of demand for services by consumers is much lower than suggested by the existing literature.

For economic policy, the most important finding is the relative importance and growth of producer services in the economy. The phenomenon falls readily into conventional theories of capital accumulation and specialization in production and suggests that the growth of the service sector will continue for as long as this accumulation continues.

Seen from this perspective, service sector growth is not a drag on economic development, as is implied by models which assume that consumer and government services dominate the sector and its growth. On the contrary, producer services are probably an important source of the productivity gains in the goods-producing sector. This may well be so in cases where productivity in the producer service industries proper is stagnant or even falling. In addition, producer services are part of the endowment which determines comparative advantage. Through embodiment in material substances generally and goods in particular, indirect trade in producer services is a source of gains from trade and specialization much like real capital and natural resources.

Our findings imply that it is inefficient to base development strategies on the subsidy of goods-producing industries at the expense of taxes on the service sector. In a growing and efficient world, much of the capital deepening is in the form of human and knowledge capital, which constitutes the main productive factor in the dynamic producer service industries. In a free market, marginal returns to investment in producer services and goods production tend to be equalized. Taxing one sector to benefit the other therefore may be presumed to reduce rather than raise income and welfare.

Appendix Tables

Table A1 – Proportions of Various Segments of Service Sectors in Nominal and Real Terms for Canada, 1970–1984

Year	Per cent in nominal terms				Per cent in real terms				Per cent in real terms set at 1970=100			
	G	C	P	T	G	C	P	T	G	C	P	T
1970	15.53	13.88	35.23	64.64	16.03	13.96	34.54	64.53	100.00	100.00	100.00	100.00
1971	15.33	14.06	35.87	65.26	15.33	14.06	35.87	65.26	95.58	100.76	103.85	101.13
1972	15.34	13.87	36.04	65.26	14.96	13.92	36.15	65.04	93.31	99.76	104.66	100.78
1973	15.01	13.23	34.84	63.07	14.75	13.47	36.28	64.50	92.01	96.51	105.02	99.95
1974	14.94	12.82	34.65	62.40	14.73	13.52	36.65	64.90	91.87	96.86	106.09	100.56
1975	16.16	13.35	33.97	63.48	15.14	13.97	37.22	66.33	94.44	100.08	107.74	102.78
1976	16.43	13.74	34.57	64.74	14.61	13.97	37.78	66.35	91.13	100.07	109.36	102.82
1977	17.08	14.04	34.02	65.14	14.82	14.08	37.52	66.42	92.44	100.88	108.62	102.93
1978	17.09	14.13	33.73	64.96	14.62	14.14	38.24	66.99	91.15	101.28	110.70	103.81
1979	16.57	13.87	32.58	63.01	14.37	14.16	38.14	66.67	89.62	101.45	110.41	103.31
1980	16.77	14.04	31.83	62.64	14.28	14.54	38.40	67.22	89.06	104.20	111.17	104.17
1981	17.11	13.95	32.83	63.89	14.16	14.35	39.46	67.97	88.31	102.83	114.22	105.32
1982	18.15	14.72	33.81	66.68	14.75	14.91	39.86	69.51	91.96	106.82	115.39	107.72
1983	18.45	14.80	33.69	66.95	14.54	14.72	40.29	69.55	90.71	105.43	116.64	107.77
1984	18.26	14.67	33.50	66.43	13.99	14.33	41.00	69.32	87.27	102.68	118.68	107.41

Note: G = Government provided services, C = Consumer service GDP, P = Producer service GDP, and T = Total GDP of the service-producing sectors. – Real terms variables are in 1971 prices.

Source: OECD [various issues].

Table A2 - Proportions of Various Segments of Service Sectors in Nominal and Real Terms for the US, 1970-1983

Year	Per cent in nominal terms				Per cent in real terms				Per cent in real terms set at 1970=100			
	G	C	P	T	G	C	P	T	G	C	P	T
1970	16.74	16.65	29.08	62.47	17.35	16.16	27.91	61.42	100.00	100.00	100.00	100.00
1971	15.93	16.85	30.54	63.31	16.38	16.26	28.96	61.59	94.42	100.59	103.76	100.28
1972	16.25	16.84	30.02	63.11	16.26	16.25	28.66	61.17	93.73	100.53	102.72	99.60
1973	15.57	16.58	29.85	62.00	15.39	16.12	28.83	60.35	88.73	99.74	103.31	98.25
1974	16.16	16.95	29.79	62.90	16.20	16.66	28.87	61.73	93.36	103.08	103.44	100.50
1975	16.80	17.34	29.46	63.60	16.80	17.34	29.46	63.60	96.83	107.30	105.55	103.55
1976	16.83	17.50	29.06	63.38	16.63	17.33	28.95	62.91	95.84	107.21	103.75	102.43
1977	16.48	17.62	29.03	63.13	16.18	17.20	29.57	62.95	93.29	106.42	105.95	102.50
1978	15.88	17.58	29.49	62.50	15.70	17.18	29.98	62.86	90.53	106.29	107.42	102.35
1979	15.77	17.75	29.45	62.97	15.76	17.38	29.61	62.75	90.85	107.49	106.12	102.17
1980	16.46	18.35	29.02	63.84	16.31	17.89	29.72	63.92	94.00	110.67	106.51	104.07
1981	16.59	18.43	28.50	63.52	16.34	17.75	29.97	64.05	94.18	109.78	107.39	104.29
1982	17.68	19.58	28.04	65.30	17.41	18.65	28.88	64.95	100.37	115.37	103.50	105.74
1983	17.78	19.86	28.68	66.31	17.17	18.70	29.36	65.23	98.97	115.70	105.19	106.20

Note: G = Government provided services, C = Consumer service GDP, P = Producer service GDP, and T = Total GDP of the service-producing sectors. - Real terms variables are in 1975 prices.

Source: As for Table A1.

Table A3 - Proportions of Various Segments of Service Sectors in Nominal and Real Terms for Japan, 1970-1984

Year	Per cent in nominal terms				Per cent in real terms				Per cent in real terms set at 1970=100			
	G	C	P	T	G	C	P	T	G	C	P	T
1970	3.11	13.12	31.04	47.27	5.01	15.26	36.55	56.82	100.00	100.00	100.00	100.00
1971	2.93	13.74	31.93	48.59	4.35	15.64	33.82	53.81	86.84	102.48	92.55	94.71
1972	2.69	14.11	32.12	48.92	3.49	15.62	33.75	52.86	69.75	102.38	92.34	93.05
1973	2.64	13.76	31.28	47.68	3.06	15.81	33.00	51.87	61.16	103.61	90.29	91.30
1974	3.90	13.65	32.19	49.75	4.30	16.33	31.85	52.48	85.91	106.99	87.15	92.37
1975	4.75	14.82	32.53	52.10	4.53	16.78	32.98	54.29	90.45	109.95	90.24	95.55
1976	4.70	14.91	32.60	52.20	4.59	16.28	33.23	54.11	91.72	106.70	90.93	95.23
1977	4.29	15.39	33.84	53.53	4.00	16.23	34.80	55.02	79.76	106.38	95.21	96.85
1978	3.54	16.10	34.06	53.70	3.31	16.54	34.56	54.41	66.05	106.36	94.57	95.76
1979	3.37	16.59	34.14	54.10	3.29	16.85	34.29	54.43	65.66	110.42	93.83	95.80
1980	3.70	16.49	34.21	54.40	3.66	16.50	34.19	54.36	73.13	108.16	93.56	95.68
1981	3.86	16.53	34.43	54.82	3.73	16.39	34.54	54.66	74.45	107.43	94.51	96.21
1982	4.12	17.16	34.11	55.39	3.86	16.75	33.57	54.18	77.12	109.74	91.85	95.36
1983	4.47	17.58	34.11	56.16	4.06	16.87	32.96	53.89	81.04	110.54	90.19	94.85
1984	4.79	17.53	33.63	55.95	4.25	16.59	32.02	52.86	84.78	108.73	87.61	93.03

Note: G = Government provided services, C = Consumer service GDP, P = Producer service GDP, and T = Total GDP of the service-producing sectors. - Real terms variables are in 1980 prices.

Source: As for Table A1.

28

Table A4 - Proportions of Various Segments of Service Sectors in Nominal and Real Terms for Greece 1970-1984

Year	Per cent in nominal terms				Per cent in real terms				Per cent in real terms set at 1970=100			
	G	C	P	T	G	C	P	T	G	C	P	T
1970	8.08	12.91	36.18	57.17	8.08	12.91	36.18	57.17	100.00	100.00	100.00	100.00
1971	8.40	12.92	35.08	56.39	8.39	13.08	34.66	56.13	103.87	101.38	95.80	98.19
1972	7.41	12.61	35.46	55.48	7.26	12.99	35.72	55.97	89.93	100.63	98.73	97.91
1973	6.99	11.54	34.09	52.63	7.72	12.82	35.20	55.75	95.61	99.36	97.30	97.52
1974	10.18	12.12	32.41	54.71	10.49	13.27	33.15	56.90	129.87	102.83	91.61	99.54
1975	11.02	12.17	33.69	56.88	10.60	13.06	33.36	57.03	131.32	101.23	92.21	99.76
1976	11.39	11.98	33.11	56.48	11.17	13.05	33.10	57.32	138.27	101.14	91.49	100.27
1977	12.18	12.11	33.65	57.95	11.57	13.23	33.58	58.38	143.25	102.51	92.82	102.13
1978	12.71	12.17	32.93	57.81	11.82	13.18	33.06	58.07	146.43	102.14	91.38	101.58
1979	13.10	11.77	33.17	58.04	12.21	13.32	33.11	58.64	151.18	103.21	91.53	102.58
1980	13.69	12.15	30.66	56.50	12.42	13.68	32.51	58.61	153.84	106.00	89.85	102.52
1981	14.17	12.64	29.27	56.09	12.74	13.91	32.75	59.40	157.79	107.77	90.51	103.90
1982	15.70	12.32	29.52	57.54	13.74	14.10	32.28	60.12	170.18	109.23	89.21	105.16
1983	15.83	12.05	30.85	58.73	14.26	14.23	32.88	61.37	176.57	110.30	90.87	107.35
1984	15.22	11.96	31.61	58.79	13.55	14.41	33.35	61.32	167.85	111.69	92.19	107.27

Note: G = Government provided services, C = Consumer service GDP, P = Producer service GDP of the service-producing sectors. - Real terms variables are in 1970 prices.

Source: As for Table A1.

Table A5 - Proportions of Various Segments of Service Sectors in Nominal and Real Terms for Norway, 1970-1984

Year	Per cent in nominal terms				Per cent in real terms				Per cent in real terms set at 1970=100			
	G	C	P	T	G	C	P	T	G	C	P	T
1970	12.46	9.32	38.06	59.84	13.64	9.14	37.31	60.09	100.00	100.00	100.00	100.00
1971	13.21	9.26	37.56	60.03	13.57	9.09	37.33	59.99	99.49	99.49	100.04	99.83
1972	13.06	9.41	37.82	60.28	13.11	9.00	37.58	59.69	96.09	98.54	100.72	99.34
1973	13.50	9.30	38.28	61.09	13.56	8.91	37.45	59.93	99.41	97.56	100.38	99.73
1974	13.68	9.04	37.70	60.42	13.60	8.73	37.30	59.62	99.67	95.54	99.96	99.22
1975	14.51	9.16	34.88	58.56	13.78	8.80	36.21	58.78	100.99	96.25	97.04	97.82
1976	15.19	9.06	34.97	59.21	14.00	8.61	35.97	58.58	102.66	94.21	96.41	97.49
1977	15.30	9.25	35.46	60.02	14.17	8.69	36.57	59.43	103.85	95.11	98.01	98.90
1978	15.40	9.25	33.87	58.52	14.14	8.60	33.75	56.49	103.68	94.12	90.45	94.01
1979	15.19	8.89	32.66	56.74	14.43	8.53	32.76	55.72	105.76	93.33	87.81	92.72
1980	15.09	8.32	31.59	55.01	14.74	8.32	31.94	55.01	108.08	91.09	85.61	91.54
1981	15.57	8.73	30.73	54.66	16.00	8.44	31.08	55.51	117.26	92.34	83.30	92.38
1982	16.25	8.66	30.11	55.02	17.01	8.53	29.75	55.29	124.69	93.40	79.73	92.01
1983	16.40	8.89	29.39	54.68	16.96	8.56	28.86	54.37	124.30	93.72	77.33	90.49
1984	15.80	8.77	29.13	53.70	16.55	8.52	28.60	53.67	121.36	93.25	76.64	89.32

Note: G = Government provided services, C = Consumer service GDP, P = Producer service GDP, and T = Total GDP of the service-producing sectors. - Real terms variables are in 1980 prices.

Source: As for Table A1.

30

Table A6 - Proportions of Various Segments of Service Sectors in Nominal and Real Terms for Sweden, 1970-1984

Year	Per cent in nominal terms				Per cent in real terms				Per cent in real terms set at 1970=100			
	G	C	P	T	G	C	P	T	G	C	P	T
1970	16.40	9.82	33.62	59.83	20.72	9.47	32.39	62.59	100.00	100.00	100.00	100.00
1971	17.93	9.83	32.43	60.20	21.49	9.58	31.18	62.25	103.72	101.10	96.25	99.46
1972	18.54	10.06	33.11	61.71	21.86	9.66	31.09	62.62	105.52	102.01	95.97	100.05
1973	19.00	10.03	32.16	61.19	21.96	9.58	30.75	62.29	105.98	101.15	94.91	99.52
1974	19.62	9.75	28.50	57.87	22.13	9.63	30.99	62.75	106.81	101.70	95.66	100.26
1975	20.49	9.37	29.06	58.92	22.82	9.62	30.92	63.37	110.14	101.59	95.46	101.25
1976	21.66	9.43	28.87	59.96	23.54	9.69	30.20	63.42	113.59	102.31	93.22	101.34
1977	23.95	9.72	29.20	62.87	24.46	10.03	29.87	64.36	118.04	105.87	92.21	102.83
1978	24.23	10.01	30.40	64.64	24.57	9.96	30.84	65.37	118.59	105.10	95.22	104.45
1979	24.69	9.93	29.94	64.56	25.09	9.78	30.17	65.04	121.10	103.20	93.13	103.91
1980	25.28	9.75	30.30	65.33	25.28	9.75	30.30	65.33	121.99	102.96	93.53	104.38
1981	25.87	10.10	30.08	66.05	26.18	9.95	29.76	65.88	126.35	105.00	91.87	105.27
1982	25.98	10.48	30.18	66.64	26.36	10.05	29.68	66.09	127.20	106.08	91.63	105.59
1983	25.51	10.38	30.25	66.14	25.96	9.96	29.61	65.54	125.31	105.12	91.42	104.72
1984	25.07	10.22	30.55	65.84	25.81	9.77	29.04	64.62	124.59	103.09	89.65	103.25

Note: G = Government provided services, C = Consumer service GDP, P = Producer service GDP, and T = Total GDP of the service-producing sectors. - Real terms variables are in 1980 prices.

Source: As for Table A1.

Bibliography

ACHESON, Keith, Stephen FERRIS, Retail and Wholesale Trade Services in Canada. Fraser Institute Service Sector Project, Vancouver 1988.

BAUMOL, William, "Macroeconomics of Unbalanced Growth". The American Economic Review, Vol. 57, 1967, pp. 415-426.

--, Productivity Policy and the Service Sector. Fishman-Davidson Center for the Study of the Service Sector, Discussion Papers, 1, April 1984.

BERNSTEIN, Jeffrey, Randall GEEHAN, The Insurance Industry in Canada. Vancouver 1988.

BELL, David, The Coming of Post-Industrial Society: A Venture in Social Forecasting. New York 1979.

BLACKABY, Frank (Ed.), De-Industrialization. London 1978.

BLUESTONE, Barry, Bennett HARRISON, The Deindustrialization of America. New York 1982.

von BOEHM-BAWERK, Eugen, Capital and Interest: A Critical History of Economical Theory. (Ist edition 1884.) Reprinted New York 1932.

BRANDER, James A., Barbara J. SPENCER, "International R&D Rivalry and Industrial Strategy". Review of Economic Studies, Vol. 50, 1983, pp. 707-722.

BUCHANAN, James M., Gordon TULLOCK, The Calculus of Consent: Logical Foundations of Constitutional Democracy. Ann Arbor 1962.

CASSON, Mark, The Firm and the Market. Cambridge, Mass., 1987.

COASE, Ronald, "The Nature of the Firm". Economica, Vol. 4, 1937, pp. 386-405.

CHANT, John F., The Market for Financial Services: The Deposit Taking Institutions. Fraser Institute Service Sector Project, Vancouver 1988.

EATON, Curtis, Myrna WOODERS, "Sophisticated Entry in an Address Model of Product Differentiation". Rand Journal of Economics, Vol. 16, 1985, pp. 282-297.

FISHER, Allan G.B., "Production, Primary, Secondary and Tertiary". Economic Record, Vol. 15, 1939, pp. 24-38.

FUCHS, Victor, The Service Economy. National Bureau of Economic Research, New York 1968.

GERSHUNY, Jonathan I., Ian MILES, The New Service Economy: The Transformation of Employment in Industrial Societies. New York 1983.

GINZBERG, Eli, George J. VOTJA, "The Service Sector of the US Economy". Scientific American, Vol. 244, 1981, pp. 48-55.

GOVERNMENT PRINTING OFFICE, Historical Statistics of Canada, Series D8-55. Ottawa 1983.

GREY, Rodney de C., Services and Intellectual Property Rights. Institute for Research on Public Policy, Discussion Paper Series on Trade in Services, Victoria, BC, March 1988.

GRUBEL, Herbert G., "All Traded Services are Embodied in Materials or People". The World Economy, Vol. 10, 1986, pp. 319-330.

--, "Direct and Embodied Trade in Services: Or, Where is the Service Trade Problem?". In: Chung LEE, Seiji NAYA (Eds.), Trade and Investment in Services in the Asia-Pacific Region: An Emerging Issue. Boulder 1988.

--, David L. HAMMES, Household Service Consumption and its Monetization: Or, How Much of Each Other's Laundry Are We Doing? Fraser Institute, Discussion Papers, 4, Vancouver 1987.

--, Michael A. WALKER, The Canadian Service Industries. Fraser Institute Service Sector Project, Vancouver 1989, forthcoming.

HAMMES, David, Jean-Jacques ROSA, Herbert G. GRUBEL, "Consumer Demand for Services". Kyklos, forthcoming.

HILL, T.P., "On Goods and Services". Review of Income and Wealth, Vol. 23, 1977, pp. 315-338.

HOUTHAKKER, Henrik S., Lawrence D. TAYLOR, Consumer Demand in the United States, 1929-1970, Analysis and Projections. Cambridge, Mass., 1966.

IOCOCCA, Lee, Iococca: An Autobiography. Toronto 1984.

JONES, Ronald, Frances RUANE, Appraising Options for International Trade in Services. Institute for Research on Public Policy, Discussion Paper Series on Trade in Services, Victoria, BC, March 1988.

KUTSCHER, Ronald E., Jerome H. MARK, "The Service Producing Sector: Some Common Misperceptions". Monthly Labor Review, Vol. 106, April 1983, pp. 21-24.

KRAVIS, Irving B., Services in the Domestic Economy and World Transactions. National Bureau of Economic Research, New York 1983.

KRUGMAN, Paul, "Increasing Returns, Monopolistic Competition and International Trade". Journal of International Economics, 1979, pp. 469-479.

McFETRIDGE, Donald G., Douglas A. SMITH, The Economics of Vertical Disintegration. Fraser Institute Service Sector Project, Vancouver 1988.

MARK, Jerome H., "Measuring Productivity in Services". Monthly Labor Review, Vol. 105, June 1982, pp. 3-8.

MOMIGLIANO, Franco, Domenico SINISCALCO, "The Growth of Service Employment: A Reappraisal". Banca Nacionale del Lavoro Quarterly Review, Vol. 142, 1982, pp. 269-306.

MUSGRAVE, Richard, The Theory of Public Finance. New York 1959.

ORGANISATION FOR ECONOMIC CO-OPERATION AND DEVELOPMENT (OECD), National Accounts - Detailed Tables. Paris, various issues.

OTT, Mack, "The Growing Share of Services in the US Economy - Degeneration or Evolution?". Federal Reserve Bank of St. Louis Review, Vol. 69, 1987, pp. 5-22.

PRAIS, S.J., Henrik HOUTHAKKER, The Analysis of Family Budgets. Cambridge 1971.

RADWANSKI, George, Ontario Study of the Service Sector. Ministry of Treasury and Economics. Toronto 1986.

READ, Lawrence M., "Canada Post: A Case Study in the Correlation of Collective Will and Productivity". In: Donald J. DALY (Ed.), Research on Productivity of Relevance to Canada. Ottawa 1983, pp. 129-136.

RIDDLE, Dorothy I., Service-Led Growth: The Role of the Service Sector in World Development. New York 1986.

RUGMAN, Alan M., "Multinationals and Trade in Services: A Transactions Cost Approach". Weltwirtschaftliches Archiv, Vol. 123, 1987, pp. 651-667.

SCARFE, Brian L., Murray KRANTZ, The Market for Hospitality. Fraser Institute Service Sector Project. Vancouver 1988.

STIGLER, George J., Trends in Employment in the Service Industries. Princeton 1956.

SHELP, Ronald K., Beyond Industrialization: The Ascendancy of the Global Service Economy. New York 1981.

SUMMERS, Robert, Alan HESTON, The International Demand for Services. University of Pennsylvania, Discussion Papers, 32, January 1988.

SWAN, Neil M., "The Service Sector: Engine of Growth?". Canadian Public Policy, Vol. XI, 1985, pp. 344-350, supplement.

SCHWEITZER, Thomas T., Personal Consumer Expenditures in Canada, 1926-75. Economic Council of Canada, Ottawa 1969.

STANBACK, T. M., Jr., Services: The New Economy. Montclair, NJ, 1981.

STATISTICS CANADA [a], GDP at Factor Cost by Industry. Series 13-531, 61-213, Occasional Papers, 15-001.

-- [b], GDP by Industry. Cat. No. 61-213, 1981, 1986 for years after 1971.

-- [c], The Labour Force, Cat. No. 71-001, February 1986.

-- [d], National Income and Expenditure Accounts, Vol. I, The Annual Estimates 1926-74. Cat. No. 531, Occasional Papers, 1976 for years up to 1971.

TATOM, John A., "Why has Manufacturing Employment Declined?". Federal Reserve Bank of St. Louis Review, December 1986, pp. 15-25.

TULPULE, Anthony, Alan A. POWELL, Estimates of Household Demand Elasticities for the ORANI Model. University of Melbourne, Impact Project Research Centre, Preliminary Working Papers, OP-22, 1978.

TRIVEDI, Vish, The Service Sector in India. Dissertation, Simon Fraser University, Burnaby, BC, 1988.

WILLIAMSON, Oliver, "Transactions Cost Economics: The Governance of Contractual Relations". Journal of Law and Economics, Vol. 22, 1979, pp. 233-261.

WICKSELL, Knut, Lectures on Political Economy. London 1901.

[17]

The Dominance of Producers Services in the US Economy *

The rapid growth of US service sector employment and output has attracted the attention of a number of studies, most of which considered the effect to be detrimental to the well-being of Americans and often saw in it the need for the adoption of industrial strategies. The most recent and widely cited studies in this tradition have been by Bell, Shelp and Bluestone and Harrison,[1] who did much to popularize the concepts "de-industrialization" and "post-industrial society" and related them to the growth of the service sector.

The ideas of these authors are surrounded by a model of historic determinism with wide appeal. This model, very popular during the 1930s, postulates the existence of development cycles which take countries from primary to secondary and tertiary stages. The second and third stages were initiated as productivity growth and consumer satiation in agriculture and manufacturing, respectively, pushed labour into the next highest sector. The chilling prospect for our age is where will the workers go after computers have raised productivity in the tertiary sector and consumer demand reached its limit? The model took on a seemingly special relevance as an explanation of the high unemployment rate during the recession of 1981-82 and the subsequent shrinkage of industries in the rust belt of the United States.

---

* The paper applies to US data a methodology which was developed in the context of a major research project dealing with the service industries in Canada. It was financed by the Government of Canada and administered by the Fraser Institute. Further elaboration of the ideas in this paper is found in HERBERT G. GRUBEL and MICHAEL A. WALKER, *The Canadian Service Industries*, Vancouver: The Fraser Institute, 1989.
    [1] The references to these writings are: DAVID BELL, *The Coming of Post-Industrial Society: A Venture in Social Forecasting*, New York: Basic Books, 1973; BARRY BLUESTONE and BENNET HARRISON, *The Deindustrialization of America*, New York: Basic Books, 1982; and RONALD SHELP, *Beyond Industrialization: The Ascendancy of the Global Service Economy*, New York: Praeger Special Studies, 1981.

BNL Quarterly Review, no. 176, March 1991.

Blustone and Harrison[2] also authored a study of the income distribution effects of the service sector growth and in it developed the concepts of "the vanishing middle class" and the "bimodal income distribution", again attributing much of the phenomenon to the growth of the service sector.

Troughout modern history, the service sector has been identified as the cause of economic troubles. Adam Smith considered it to involve the non-productive use of resources, an idea which was picked up by Marx and Lenin. It resulted in the exclusion of personal service industry output from the national income accounts of the Soviet Union and other socialist economies. As late as the 1960s a British Labour government imposed a special tax to discourage the growth of the industry.

The more recent work of Baumol and Fuchs[3] influenced the thinking of generations of economists with theorems about the low productivity growth of the sector, the resultant upward bias on prices generally and the cost of government in particular. Browne[4] discussed the widespread notion that much of the service sector growth involves "taking in each other's laundry". According to this model, women entering the labour force reduce production in the traditional household and replace it with the same output produced in the market. This process involves an overstatement of economic growth because national income accountants record the increase in the market production but do not note the decrease in the output of households.

In all of these studies, the analysis has concentrated on services for consumers, bought in the market or supplied by government. The most memorable of the analysis by Smith deals with the work done by personal valets and actors. Baumol's widely cited model involves the unchanged productivity of quartets playing the same piece of music through the centuries. Bell, Bluestone and Harris draw heavily on the image of the modern fast food service restaurants. The government supply of education, health and welfare services for public consum-

---

[2] BARRY BLUESTONE and BENNET HARRISON, *The Great American Job Machine: The Proliferation of Low-Wage Employment in the US Economy*, Washington: Joint Economic Committee, 1986.

[3] WILLIAM BAUMOL, "Macroeconomics of Unbalanced Growth", *American Economic Review*, 57, 1967, pp. 415-26; VICTOR FUCHS, *The Service Economy*, New York: National Bureau of Economic Research, 1968.

[4] L.E. BROWNE, "Taking in Each Other's Laundry – The Service Economy", *The New England Economic Review*, July/August 1986.

ption is documented and discussed in many studies, supporting the widely held belief in the importance of government services in the overall growth of the service sector.

Interest in producer services is a relatively new phenomenon and is found most notably in the recent studies by Ginzberg and Vojta, Gershuny and Miles; and Riddle.[5] In general, the relative importance of this service sector is inferred from the very rapid growth of the industries called Business Services. Momigliano and Siniscalco[6] in a pioneering study evaluated the quantitative importance of all producer services in the output of the goods sector. Using input-output tables, they measured the direct and indirect input of producer services in the Italian economy and showed that they represented a very large and growing part of the entire service sector.

In this study we measure the level and growth of producer services in the US economy, using an innovative technique which avoids the use of complex input-outpt calculations. The technique permits us to overcome a basic problem of existing government statistics. These statistics only show the total production of financial, insurance, architect, computer, communication, transportation, restaurant and many other services which are purchased by both consumers and industry. Only that share of these services bought by industry can properly be considered to be producer services.

I. The definition and measurement of consumer, government and producer services

The national income accounts of the United States contain a long and consistent time series on the *total size of the service producing sector* of the economy, as measured by its value-added or GNP. This basic time series is shown as the top line in Figure 1. It has produced the 50 percent figure noted in the opening sentence and provoked much of the recent discussion in the literature.

---

[5] J.I. GERSHUNY and I. MILES, *The New Service Economy: The Tranformation of Employment in Industrial Societies*, New York: Praeger Publishers, 1983; ELI GINZBERG and GEORGE J. VOJTA, "The Service Sector of the US Economy", *Scientific American*, 244, 3, March 1981, pp. 48-55; DOROTHY RIDDLE, *Service-Led Growth: The Role of the Service Sector in World Development*, New York: Praeger Special Studies, 1986.

[6] MOMIGLIANO, FRANCO and DOMENICO SINISCALCO, "The Growth of Service Employment: A Reappraisal", in this *Review*, September 1982, pp. 269-306.

FIGURE 1

TYPES OF US SERVICES
(1982 Dollars, Percent of GNP)

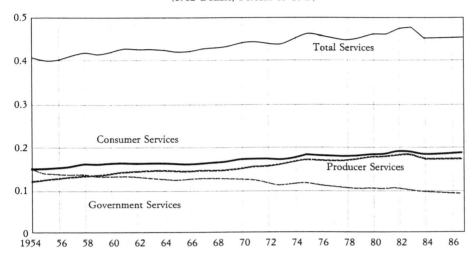

In recent years national income accountants and scholars have been reflecting on the measurement principles and techniques which underlie these figures. However, progress on these matters is slow. The analysis thus far promises to result in marginal improvements only. As a result, revisions based on new data and concepts lack urgency and are not likely to be available for a long time, if ever. The data used here, therefore, are the best available.

Data on the purchase of *consumer services* are available from national spending surveys. These data are reliable and consistent since they serve as the raw data for the calculation of consumer price and expenditure statistics and contain very detailed records on hundreds of goods and services bought by consumers. They provide estimates of spending on such services as finance, insurance, communication, transportation, computers and restaurants.

These data cover expenditures and therefore include the goods components of the final price. Included in expenditures on restaurants, for example, is the cost of the food. To eliminate this goods component and make the series consistent with the GNP concept of the overall service sector output, it is necessary to determine the value-added of these service industries. For this purpose we drew on data from a major study of the service industries in Canada, where we had estimated the ratio of value-added to gross output of these service industries to be .6. We assume that this figure is the same for US and Canadian service industries and that it has not changed during the period under study. The bias introduced by this assumption is unknown but unlikely to affect the main findings of this analysis.

To obtain information on *government services* it is necessary to divide government expenditure into its two main components, transfer payments and exhaustive spending. The former involves pensions, welfare and unemployment insurance payments. Exhaustive expenditures go for the provision of education, health, defence, justice and general government services, including the administration of the pension and welfare transfers, at all levels of government. The value-added of the government sector as published by the US government is used in this study to measure the value of national product devoted to the provision of government services of this type.

Producer service output is estimated by the subtraction of the consumer and government services from the total service sector output. Producer services therefore contain the output of the industries obviously producing intermediate inputs, like Business Services and Wholesale Services. Importantly, they also include as a residual the output of all those industries widely viewed as serving mainly consumers, like finance, restaurants, hotels and transportation. A large fraction of the output of these industries is used by business and government as input into the further production of goods and services.

It is important to note a likely downward bias in the estimation of producer services. Many of the services produced by government are used as inputs by business. The most obvious are the output of the Departments of Agriculture and Commerce, but most other government departments serve both consumers and business. Unfortunately, it is not possible to determine the relative magnitude of the two. By not allocating any of the government service output to the category of producer services, our procedure biases downward the estimate of the latter.

II. The size and growth of the types of service industries

In Figure 1 the size of the total service sector and its three components are shown as a percentage of GNP and in constant 1982 dollars, for the years 1954-1987. The top line shows the clear upward trend in the basic series. Small fluctuations around the trend are correlated with business cycles. Traditionally these cycles have resulted in greater swings in goods than in service industries' output, which explains why the 1981-82 recession shows the service industries' share at its postwar peak.

Figure 1 indicates that in 1954 consumer and government services each represented 15 percent of GNP while producer services held the smallest share at 12 percent. Since then, the share of government services has been on a rather steady downward trend to a 1987 level of slightly less than 10 percent. Producer and consumer services trended upward and by the end of the period had reached 18 and 19 percent, respectively.

For the purposes of the present analysis, greatest interest lies in rates of growth rather than levels of the types of services. Relative growth rates are brought out effectively in Figure 2, which uses the information contained in Figure 1 but expresses the share of GNP of each sector in 1954 as an index of 100 and traces the development of this share through time. According to this figure, government services during this period have dropped by one third, total services have risen by 17 percent and consumer services by 32 percent, all expressed as a share of GNP. The growth in the share of producer services by about 52 percent has been the most rapid by a large margin.

III. Causes and effects of changes in share by sector

What have been the causes and welfare effects of these trends in the share of output of the three sectors?

Government services

The decline of the value-added by the government service sector appears to be inconsistent with the widely accepted view that the

The Dominance of Producers Services in the US Economy   63

FIGURE 2

GROWTH OF SERVICES
(Percent of GNP; 1982 Dollars; 1954=100)

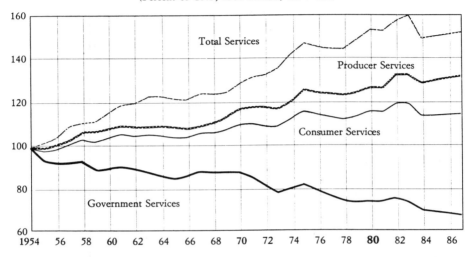

share of government in the economy has been growing rapidly, even during the administrations of President Reagan. The main explanation of the puzzle is found in the fact that transfer payments have increased very rapidly. This development is consistent with the modern theory of government spending associated with the publications of James Buchanan, the 1984 winner of the Nobel prize in economics. It is much easier to target transfer payments rather than exhaustive expenditures to benefit interest groups which repay politicians by voter loyalty and financial contributions. Moreover, transfer payments are determined by existing laws while much of the exhaustive expenditure requires new and politically difficult legislative initiatives.

We can only speculate on the welfare implications of this decline in exhaustive expenditures. On the one hand it may be seen to be desirable since the private sector is capable of supplying most of these services more efficiently than the government. On the other hand, it is also possible that the decline has reached an inefficiently low level, given the more than normal complaints from many users in recent years about the adverse consequences of reduced supplies of education, health, justice, police, patent administration, basic science, defence, airport safety and many others.

We cannot assess here the relative merit of the two views on the decrease in the supply of government. A consensus on this issue has not emerged even among well-informed economists. The main reasons for this are inadequacies in factual knowledge, along with differences in ideological perceptions of the role of government.

However, there are two relatively technical matters which should enter into any debate over the supply of government services. First, the decline in the supply of government services shown in the graphs may be overstated by the way in which government services are measured. By accounting convention it is assumed that output of the sector is proportional to the amount of labour used. As a result, the data do not account for changes in the productivity of this labour. This means that if, for example, administrators of the social security system have become more efficient in the issue of pension checks through the use of computers, the volume of government services supplied has increased more than the data show. There may well have been productivity gains in defence and health care and other services, which bias downward the estimate of supply. On the other hand, reductions in the efficiency of government services production lower the size of this bias. In spite of substantial efforts to quantify productivity in the government sector, no reliable and consistent data are available to correct for the bias in the existing statistics.

Second, the contracting out of government services at all levels has increased the efficiency of production. For example, it is well documented that workers in privately owned garbage collection firms remove about 94 percent more tons per crew person per hour than do workers employed in the public sector.[7] Generalizing from this example suggests that the trend towards privatization generally biases downward the estimate of the quantity of government services supplied. Unfortunately, no estimates of the precise magnitude of this bias are available. However, the public's assessment of the success of privatization may well have an important influence on the future growth of the government service sector employment and output as measured traditionally.

---

[7] See, for example, MICHAEL A. WALKER, editor, *Privatization: Tactics and Techniques*, Vancouver: The Fraser Institute, 1988.

Consumer services

The demand for consumer services is influenced by two op-
posing forces. On the one hand, the demand for consumer services is
an increasing function of family incomes. The rich are spending larger
proportions of their incomes on entertainment, restaurant services,
recreation, education, health and similar services.

On the other hand, increases in average income through time
have not generated increases in demand for these services which
might have been expected from the cross-section evidence. One
reason for this is found in the so-called Baumol effect. According to
this model, many types of services by their nature require personal
contact and therefore productivity of supply cannot be increased
significantly by the use of technology. Important examples of such
services are entertainment, bus transportation and taxis, barbers and
private education and health care. The cost of these services has been
rising because the labour needed has to be paid wages that are
competitive with those paid in industries in which the application of
technology has increased productivity of labour and resulted in increasing wage rates. The increases in the relative prices of these
services have a negative influence on demand. The development of
new products has made possible the consumption of substitutes for
these services. For example, TV and musical recordings have substituted for the services of live entertainers, vacuum cleaners and
washing machines have taken the place of domestic workers.

The relatively low growth rate of the share of consumer service
demand shown in the graphs represents the net of influences of the
growth in average incomes, the rise in relative prices of services and
the development of substitutes. However, in a recent study of the
demand for consumer services by Hammes *et al.*,[8] the female labour
force participation rate has been identified as an important influence
on the demand for these services. Econometric results suggest that
about 40 percent of the increase in the demand for consumer services
has been attributable to this change in behaviour, which in turn has
been driven by increases in educational attainment by women and
exogenous changes in social norms. The effects of the increases in the
female labour force participation rates on the service sector may be

---

[8] DAVID HAMMES, JEAN-JACQUES ROSA and HERBERT GRUBEL, "The National Accounts, Household Service Consumption and its Monetization", *Kyklos*, 1989.

seen from the finding by Scarfe and Krantz[9] that the demand for high priced restaurants is functionally related to family incomes whereas demand for the output of fast food restaurants is a function of the female labour force participation rate.

The future of the demand for consumer services will be determined by developments which are difficult to predict, such as the introduction of technological substitutes and changes in the female labour force participation rates. However, if the past is any guide for the future, the growth of the demand for consumer services will remain constrained. We may be reasonably confident that its growth, and that of government services, will not embrace an overwhelmingly large proportion of the country's productive capacity. The US economy will not become de-industrialized and face the problems which many have predicted to arise in the wake of such a development.

Producer services

A large and most rapidly growing proportion of producer services are sold by firms which employ persons with high skill levels, such as finance, accounting, legal, advertising, science, engineering, architecture, computer, communications and training of personnel. There are also business services requiring low skills, like janitorial, personnel, wholesale, retailing and personnel services. All of these producer service industries draw on a growing stock of knowledge in the natural, engineering, social and managerial sciences.

It is through the increased use of human and knowledge capital, along with physical capital, that economic development and increasing productivity are achieved. The overwhelming importance of human and knowledge capital in this process has been discovered in the 1960s by Solow, who was awarded the 1986 Nobel prize for this work. The finding was confirmed and strengthened in recent work by Jorgensen and Fraumeni[10] who claim that as much as 80 percent of US wealth consists of human and knowledge capital.

How are these forms of capital introduced into the production process? Why has the accumulation of this capital not resulted simply in an increase in the number of highly skilled workers by manufac-

---

[9] Brian Scarfe and David Krantz, *The Accommodation, Food and Beverage Industry in Canada*, Vancouver, B.C.: Fraser Institute Service Sector Project, 1988.

[10] Dale Jorgenson and Barbara Fraumeni, *The Accumulation of Human and Non-Human Capital 1948-84*, Cambridge: Harvard University, 1987.

turing firms, where they would be counted as working in the goods producing sector? The answer to these questions may be found in the ideas of Austrian school of economics. This school made much of the proposition that increases in the quantity of physical capital per worker are associated with increased specialization of the production process, which they labelled increased roundaboutness. We now postulate that this same process of specialization accompanies increases in the stock of human and knowledge capital per worker.

Experts in finance, advertising, entertainment, law, science, engineering and similar fields are becoming increasingly specialized. Their expertise tends to be so specialized that it is not needed full time by even the largest manufacturing concerns. However, they can be employed fully by a firm catering to customers throughout a region, country or even the world. Importantly also, there has been the development of specialized firms with producer service expertise which cater primarily to smaller firms in more localized markets which previously have tended to do without them. It is clear that such specialization has been encouraged by technological improvements in communications and travel. The main point here is that the human and knowledge capital deepening and the accompanying patterns of specialization have resulted in a growth in the demand for the services of such firms by the goods producing sector, governments and other producers of services.

An understanding of the phenomenon of producer service growth may be aided by considering the idea that these services end up embodied in goods, where they constitute an ever increasing fraction of the final price of a product. For example, Lee Iacocca[11] has noted in his biography that a larger part of a Chrysler car's costs now consists of spending on medical services for workers than spending on steel. In addition, of course, all of the material inputs used by automobile manufacturers embody growing amounts of producer services, as for example in the many electronic devices. The phenomenon is general. Its manifestation in the extreme is found in the case of computer disks which hold a sophisticated program. This product is counted as the output of the goods industry but the value of services embodied in such a disk may easily represent 90 percent of the market price of the good. At the same extreme end of goods with high amounts of embodied services we find modern medicines and complicated machinery like typewriters, assembled in fully automated factories.

---

[11] Lee Iacocca, *Iacocca: An Autobiography*, Toronto: Bantam Books, 1985.

IV. Summary and policy implications

In sum, the preceding consideration lead us to the following, central postulate. The growth in the share of producer services shown in the statistics above is due to the process of human and knowledge capital accumulation and increased specialization in the producer service industries. It has resulted in the phenomenon of ever increasing shares of embodied services in the market value of US goods and the output of government and other service industries.

The implications of this analysis are important for a number of public policy issues. First, the growth of the services sector does not imply the de-industrialization of America in the sense that goods production will cease or even decrease dramatically. The number of people employed by the goods producing sector may continue to fall, but there is no theoretical limit, short of 100 percent, of the proportion of market value of goods accounted for by the workers in the producer service sector. There will not be high unemployment levels because of productivity gains in the service sector and the satiation of consumer demand for services.

Second, while producer service industries typically do not show rapid increases in productivity, they are one of the main sources of productivity gains in the goods producing sector. Third, goods are an effective vehicle for international trade in embodied services. They will permit continued exploitation of the sources of comparative advantage among nations and there is no need to worry that US goods producers will be wiped out by competition from cheap labour in newly industrializing countries. Fourth, there will be no problem with a bimodal income distribution and the vanishing of the middle class. The future middle class is likely to be recruited from workers employed in producer service sector. It will grow more rapidly and offer jobs that are more highly paid and require higher technical skills than the consumer service sector.

Burnaby,
Vancouver

HERBET G. GRUBEL - MICHAEL A. WALKER

[18]

KYKLOS, Vol. 42, 1989, Fasc. 1, 3–15

The National Accounts, Household Service Consumption and its Monetization

DAVID L. HAMMES, JEAN-JACQUES ROSA and HERBERT G. GRUBEL *

I. INTRODUCTION

There is much interest in statistics coming from systems of national income accounts. National income data calculated through the accounts allow comparisons across countries of national income levels, both in the aggregate and on a per capita basis, as well as allowing comparisons of rates of changes in these measures. Such comparisons are often used to rate the relative performances of economies around the globe.

Dissatisfaction with using statistics such as gross national product (GNP) or GNP per capita as a measure of comparing welfare or well-being across economies is well known and much discussed[1]. Questions of the dispersion of income, omissions from GNP and the composition of output all focus on the weakness of such measures when used to make inter-country welfare comparisons or intra-country comparisons over time. While these problems are well known it is the case that imperfect, but consistent, measures have been revealed preferred to no measure at all, hence their frequent use.

* Respectively Assistant Professor of Economics, the University of Hawaii at Hilo, USA, Professor of Economics, Institut d'Etudes Politiques de Paris, France, and Professor of Economics, Simon Fraser University, Vancouver, Canada.

This work was initiated while HAMMES was at the Fraser Institute, Vancouver, Canada.

The views expressed are the authors' alone and not the aforementioned organizations.

1. While we use the concept of gross national product for illustrative purposes our discussion is aimed also at any of the national income accounting measures, including gross domestic product (GDP) and the net measures of national and domestic products.

3

DAVID L. HAMMES, JEAN-JACQUES ROSA AND HERBERT G. GRUBEL

One area of admitted weakness in the national accounts is the omission of work performed in the household that is not marketed through formal markets. Common examples are the labour services of housewives and neighbours trading gardening and home or car repair services. There has been much recent work attempting to quantify the size of these non-marketed activities in addition to the work quantifying 'underground' or unreported economic activity in an economy[2].

These studies generally conclude that once omissions of legal and illegal activity are accounted for in measures of national products inter-country differences, on a per capita basis, in the national accounts magnitudes are much reduced. The studies also show that, for a given country, the measured changes in the per capita magnitudes as calculated from the national accounts may be biased downward by the growth of unreported activities[3].

Omissions from the national accounts as well as illegal and unreported activities all understate the actual levels of national products and incomes. Other than descriptive accounts there are few, if any, discussions of how the national accounts may be systematically overstated[4].

This is unfortunate as we believe that social trends since 1960s and current national accounting conventions lead to the systematic overstatement of national incomes and product. The nature of the overstatement we discuss is that which is caused by a reduction in the level of omitted economic activity relative to total economic activity[5]. As

2. See FEIGE [1984], HAWRYLYSHYN [1978] and SWINAMER [1985].

3. This growth may be for many reasons. For example, rising marginal tax rates on personal incomes may raise the proportion of economic activity in non-reported sectors relative to reported sectors. As a result, total incomes may remain virtually the same, but measured national income will fall.

4. These descriptive accounts of how the national accounts system overstates incomes and products usually revolve around the failure in national accounting to include the negative externalities inherent in producing measured national income. See NORDHAUS and TOBIN [1972].

5. This was first done by GRUBEL and HAMMES [1987] and the formal analytics of the theory that follows is presented in that paper. GRUBEL and HAMMES refer to the process of moving economic activity from an omitted to included market as monetization' and, for want of a better word, we continue that usage.

4

NATIONAL ACCOUNTS, HOUSEHOLD CONSUMPTION AND MONETIZATION

activity previously omitted from the national accounts is captured in formal market national income figures will rise ceteris paribus *even though* there has been no real increase in total economic activity, incomes or product.

More concretely, since the middle of the 1950s in the U.S. and Canada and since the early 1960s in France, there has been the social phenomenon of women entering or re-entering the labour forces in those countries at a steady rate. This may be for many reasons. We mention two. First, following the second World War, family formation and child-bearing and rearing activities kept many women out of the formal work force. As children reached school age mothers' entry into the labour force became less costly and therefore increased. Secondly, women's investment in human capital, especially in the 1970s continuing into the 1980s, has increased their opportunities in the market relative to the home.

As the labour force participation rate of women rises women have less time to devote to economic activity in the home. Given that there is not a desired measurable decrease in the standard of cleanliness and quality of life in the home, services previously provided by women and omitted from the national income accounts will now have to be provided through the market. Consequently, measured national income rises[6]. But, because women's work in the home is omitted from the national income accounts in the first place, there is no corresponding decrease in national income reflecting women's decreased home production. Therefore, we argue much of the rise in national incomes due to monetization is illusory.

This illusory overstatement, if statistically verified, is important for the following reason. Discussions of the growth in national in-

---

6. Assuming the labour force participation rates of men to be invariant to this shift.

The increase in measured national incomes consists of two components, the first is the statistical illusion of a rise due to the transfer of activity from the omitted markets to the included markets. The second and very real increase is due to the re-allocation of resources through specialization to their highest valued uses. Assuming the utility of the two jobs equal, labour will only switch from the omitted to included markets when the wages available in the formal market dominate those implicitly available in the home. Consequently, one is able to join the labour force, pay for house cleaning services and have purchasing power left over. National income has therefore risen.

DAVID L. HAMMES, JEAN-JACQUES ROSA AND HERBERT G. GRUBEL

come aggregates may be seriously flawed if account is not taken of the monetization of activity. We provide here the results of such a statistical analysis for the U.S., Canada and, for the first time, France[7].

Figure 1

Real and Nominal Expenditures on Services as a Proportion of Real (1971 constant dollars) and Nominal Total Consumption Exp.

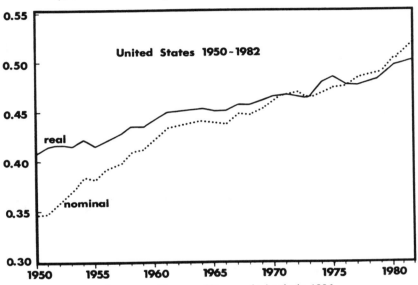

Source: U.S. Dept. Commerce/Bureau of Economic Analysis, 1986

7. These calculations provide 'truer' price and income elasticities for services as well.

There is another interesting reason to study this problem. Discussions in political economy regarding inter-country comparisons often show the more 'socialized' western countries with the highest measured per capita incomes relative to the more 'market oriented' economies. However, this may be a phenomenon of the statistical illusion we discuss above. Countries which provide more social services, child care and the like will have higher rates of female participation in the formal work force. This is because the opportunity costs of leaving the home are lowered by state subsidized services. The lower levels of economic activity falling into the omitted markets relative to the formal markets – what we would refer to as higher levels of monetization – in these economies will be captured by national income accountants and as a result the measured national incomes and products will be higher. We provide first estimates for the U.S., Canada and France and leave this topic for further research.

6

NATIONAL ACCOUNTS, HOUSEHOLD CONSUMPTION AND MONETIZATION

Figure 2

Real and Nominal Expenditures on Services as a Proportion of Real
(1971 constant dollars) and Nominal Total Consumption Exp.

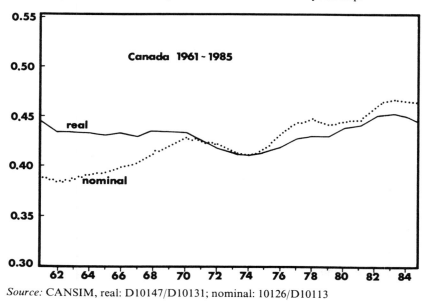

Source: CANSIM, real: D10147/D10131; nominal: 10126/D10113

II. PRICES, INCOMES AND SERVICE EXPENDITURES

In order to formally estimate the magnitude of the upward bias inherent in national income accounts due to the monetization
phenomenon we assume the following. In the household monetization is the replacement of own-produced economic activity by the
market purchase of *services.* While it is undoubtedly true that some
goods have replaced own-produced effort in the home we argue that
in the main marketed services, cleaning, child care, gardening, car
care and the like, replace omitted own-produced services. Consequently, if our hypothesis is true, we expect real expenditures on
services as a proportion of total consumption expenditures to *rise*
with increases in the labour force participation rates of women. As
can be seen in *Figures 1, 2* and *3,* for the U.S., Canada and France

7

DAVID L. HAMMES, JEAN-JACQUES ROSA AND HERBERT G. GRUBEL

Figure 3

Real Expenditures on Services as a Proportion of Real
(1971 constant dollars) Total Consumption Expenditures

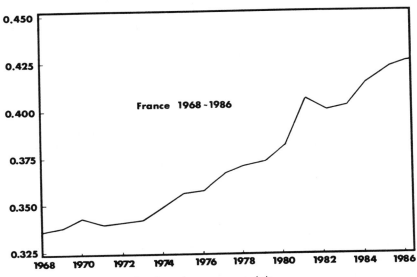

Source: Inséé, Consommation des ménages par produit.

respectively, this pattern holds in two of the three cases[8]. Working against the rise in the proportion service expenditures are relative to total consumption expenditures is the fact that relative prices of services have risen in all three countries over the relevant time periods. This may explain the almost constant fraction of real total expenditure devoted to services in Canada.

8. The time periods looked at in the three countries vary. In the U.S. we consider the period 1950 to 1982; in Canada the period runs from 1961 to 1985, and in France, 1968 to 1986. These differences are due to data limitations. In Canada, recently revised data has become available, but the revisions were extended back only to 1961. In France, a consistent set of data on services was only available post-1968.
    Sources for the data: U.S.: U.S. Department of Commerce/Bureau of Economic Analysis, *The National Income and Product Accounts of the United States, 1929–1982, Statistical Tables,* Washington D.C., 1986; for Canada: Statistics Canada, CANSIM Matrix 6708, series D10131 and D10147; and for France: Insee, *Consommation des ménages par produit.*

8

NATIONAL ACCOUNTS, HOUSEHOLD CONSUMPTION AND MONETIZATION

Finally, the impact of rising real incomes must be separated from the effect of monetization. It may be claimed that a rising proportion of real service expenditures reflects nothing more than the presumed highly income elastic nature of the demand for services[9]. Therefore, we include in our modelling real income as a separate variable in order to keep the two influences, monetization and real income, separate.

III. THE MODELS AND ESTIMATION

We are attempting to measure the impact of real income, relative prices and monetization on the demand for real consumer services. Following earlier work on the demand for services we use real total consumption expenditures as a proxy for real total income and put all relevant variables on a per capita basis[10]; following from the discussion in Section I above, we use the female participation rates for women as a proxy variable for the degree of monetization[11], and use price indices of services divided by price indices of goods as the relative price variable.

As a starting point, we use traditional analysis and attempt to explain the demand for services as a function of prices and incomes alone. The consumption of services (S) is an increasing function of total expenditures (TE), both expressed in real terms and per capita, and a decreasing function of the relative price of service in the consumption basket (PS). Assuming that the supply of services is infinitely elastic at observed prices assures that we are estimating the proper demand elasticities.

9. However, in earlier treatments of the demand for services this monetization variable was omitted. Therefore, it is highly likely that the elasticity of the included income variable is overstated in previous estimates as monetization and income are positively related.

10. The standard references are HOUTHAKKER and TAYLOR [1966], PRAIS and HOUTHAKKER [1971] and PHILIPS [1974].

11. *Sources:* for the U.S.: U.S. Government Printing Office, *Economic Report of the President, 1986,* Table B-34, page 292. For Canada, Statistics Canada, Series CS11-516E Cat. No. 71-529. For France, Insee as noted in footnote 8.

9

DAVID L. HAMMES, JEAN-JACQUES ROSA AND HERBERT G. GRUBEL

We estimate in the natural logarithms of the variables in order to evaluate the coefficients as elasticities directly. The equation estimated is:

$$Ln(S) = C + Ln(TE) + Ln(PS). \qquad (1)$$

The results for the three countries are shown in *Table 1*.

Table 1

Income, Prices, and the Demand
for Market Services

Variable	C	Ln(TE)	Ln(PS)	R^2(Adj.)	DW
US	− 1.651	1.092	0.25	.998	1.64*
	(− 3.3)	(18.62)	(2.98)		
Canada	− 1.175	1.172	− 0.39	.989	0.42
	(− 8.6)	(16.81)	(− 2.48)		
France	− 5.16	1.44	− 0.297	.993	2.04*
	(− 3.61)	(9.55)	(− 1.97)		

Student's t-statistic in parentheses
* Cochrane-Orcutt correction for first order autocorrelation

The income elasticity of the demand for services is 1.1 or greater in all three cases and the price elasticity of demand has the expected sign in two of the three cases.

First order autocorrelation was evident in all three countries and we leave the Canadian case uncorrected as an example. Existence of autocorrelation indicates the omission of at least one explanatory variable.

We now add the female labour force participation rate as an explanatory variable in order to estimate the degree to which the demand for services is a function of monetization. The equation for estimation becomes [12]:

$$Ln(S) = C + Ln(TE) + Ln(PS) + Ln(F) \qquad (2)$$

The results appear in *Table 2*.

12. We retain the assumption that the supply of services is infinitely elastic.

10

NATIONAL ACCOUNTS, HOUSEHOLD CONSUMPTION AND MONETIZATION

Table 2

Female Participation
and the Demand for Market Services

Variable	C	Ln(TE)	Ln(PS)	Ln(F)	R^2(Adj.)	DW
US	1.049	0.639	− 0.06	0.446	.999	1.74*
	(1.08)	(8.45)	(− 0.89)	(3.47)		
Canada	1.009	0.348	− 0.007	0.703	.999	2.07
	(6.86)	(6.09)	(− 0.13)	(15.42)		
France	− 4.20	0.953	− 0.338	0.982	.994	2.00*
	(− 1.38)	(2.73)	(− 2.61)	(2.57)		

The inclusion of the female participation rate has the expected sign and, in the Canadian case, eliminates the first order autocorrelation. In all cases, as expected, the income elasticity of the demand for services is lowered when the monetization effect is accounted for. In all cases this elasticity is lower than one indicating that the demand for services is income inelastic. While the relative price effects are statistically insignificant in the U.S. and Canadian cases, the sign is as hypothesized in all cases and statistically significant for France.

IV. SUMMARY AND ECONOMIC IMPLICATIONS

We argued in Section I and II above that the omission of household economic activity in the national income accounts would lead to an overstatement of national incomes and their growth rates as economic activity shifted from the unrecorded household sector into the included market sector. This growth in GNP we argued would be a statistical illusion and inter-country and intra-country comparisons made upon published data may yield spurious results. Our estimates imply the following.

In the U.S. the female labour force participation rate rose from 33.3 percent to 52.7 percent between 1950 and 1982. This is a rise of 58.25 percent. In *Table 2* the elasticity of demand for services due to monetization (for the U.S.) is estimated at 0.446. This means a one percent rise in the participant rate leads to a 0.446 percent rise in the demand for services. Taking the 58.25 percent rise in the female

11

DAVID L. HAMMES, JEAN-JACQUES ROSA AND HERBERT G. GRUBEL

labour force participation rate over the entire period we estimate that monetization accounted for 26 percent (0.5825*0.446) of the growth in real service consumption in the U.S. During this period real service consumption averaged 27.5 percent of real GNP. Therefore, our results imply that 7 percent (0.26*0.275) of the increase in real GNP per capita was due to the monetization of economic activity. As expenditures on services as a fraction of GNP was higher in the later years this effect will be larger in those years.

In Canada we find similar results. The participation rate rose about 89 percent from 1961 to 1985 [13]. The elasticity of demand for services due to monetization is (from *Table 2*) 0.703 implying that 63 percent of the increase in consumption of services by Canadian households has been due to the demand-driven portion of monetization. The proportion of market services consumed by households has remained roughly constant at 26 percent of GNP implying that 16.4 percent of the increase in Canadian GNP per capita is due to the monetization of household services demand.

In France the results are similar again. Participation rates rose 19.2 percent from 1968 to 1986 [14]. The monetization elasticity of demand for services is 0.982. These results imply that 18.8 percent of the growth in real service consumption is due to monetization over that period. Service consumption average 23 percent in France over the 1968 to 1986 period [15]. Therefore, on average, 4.3 percent of the growth in real GDP per capita is due to the effects of monetization in France [16].

13. 28.7 percent in 1961 to 54.4 percent in 1985.

14. 38.6 percent in 1968 and 46 percent in 1986.

15. Again, as in the U.S., the fraction rose in France over the period in question. Service consumption expenditures were 19.8 percent of GDP in 1968 and 28.4 percent in 1986.

16. While the relative size of the monetization effect looks smaller for France than for the U.S. and Canada readers should note three things. First, the estimated elasticity of demand for service consumption through monetization (as shown in *Table 2*) is higher in France than for the other two countries; second, France had a much lower rate of growth in the female labour force participation rate; and third, the differing length of the time periods used in estimation affect the results. Interestingly, the proportion of total consumer expenditures per capita devoted to service consumption is very similar in all three economies.

NATIONAL ACCOUNTS, HOUSEHOLD CONSUMPTION AND MONETIZATION

One interesting implication of our findings concerns the expected growth in demand for marketed consumer services. Since the female labour force participation rates are higher in the U.S. and Canada relative to France more room for overstatement of national accounts exists for French national accounts in the future.

Another implication is that as the rates of female participation slow the conditions for growth in the demand for consumer market services will be slower than in the postwar years we examined here.

A final implication of our econometric results relates to the existing literature on the demand for services [17]. Our econometric estimates of the total expenditure elasticity of demand for household-bought services of 0.64 for the U.S., 0.35 for Canada and 0.95 for France are in strong contrast with the estimated elasticity of over one in the first set of equations (reported in *Table 1*) and the conventional wisdom that the income elasticity of demand for such services is high.

The idea that the income elasticity of demand for services is high stems from early budget studies by ENGEL and others. During the period from which the data for these studies was drawn, services were provided by servants for persons with high incomes. In recent times, on the other hand, it is quite possible that the income elasticity of demand is low since many efficient and low-priced substitutes in the production and consumption of services have been developed.

REFERENCES

FEIGE, E. L.: 'Microeconomics and the Unobserved Sector', in: BLOCK, W. and WALKER, M. A. (eds.), *Taxation, An International Perspective,* Proceedings of An International Symposium, The Fraser Institute, Vancouver, B. C., 1984.

FUCHS, V. R.: 'An Agenda for Research on the Service Sector', in: INMAN, R. P. (ed.), *Managing the Service Economy,* Chapter 12, Cambridge: Cambridge University Press, 1985.

In the time period in question the fact that the female participation rate grew most slowly in France accounts for the difference in results. Based on the elasticities, for a given percentage change in female participation rates, the impact can be expected to be greatest in France relative to the U.S. and Canada.

17. See FUCHS [1985]; INMAN [1985] and SUMMERS [1985].

DAVID L. HAMMES, JEAN-JACQUES ROSA AND HERBERT G. GRUBEL

GRUBEL, H. G. and HAMMES, D. L.: 'Household Service Consumption and Its Monetization', Service Project Discussion Paper 86-5, The Fraser Institute, Vancouver, B. C., revised 1987.

HAWRYLYSHYN, O.: *Estimating the Value of Household Work in Canada, 1971,* Statistics Canada, Cat. No. 13-566 Occasional, 1978.

HOUTHAKKER, H. S. and TAYLOR, L. D.: *Consumer Demand in the United States, 1929–1970, Analysis and Projections,* Cambridge: Harvard University Press, 1966.

INMAN, R. P.: *Managing the Service Economy,* Cambridge: Cambridge University Press, 1985.

NORDHAUS, W. and TOBIN, J.: 'Is Economic Growth Obsolete?', in: *Economic Growth,* NBER, Fifth Anniversary Colloquium V, New York, 1972.

PHILIPS, L.: *Applied Consumption Analysis,* Amsterdam, New York, Oxford: North-Holland, 1974.

PRAIS, S. J. and HOUTHAKKER, H. S.: *The Analysis of Family Budgets,* Cambridge: Cambridge University Press, second impression, abridged, 1971.

SUMMERS, R.: 'Services in the International Economy', in: INMAN, R. P. (ed.), *Managing the Service Economy,* Chapter 1, Cambridge: Cambridge University Press, 1985.

SWINAMER, J. L.: 'The Value of Household Work in Canada', *The Canadian Statistical Review,* March (1985).

SUMMARY

National account statistics typically omit some non-marketed economic activity. Over time, if non-market activity declines relative to total economic activity, national accounts estimates of output and income and their changes will be overstated. This overstatement affects comparisons of growth for a single country through time as well as affecting comparisons among countries.

Using labor force participation rates as a proxy for the move from non-market production to market production this paper finds and provides empirical measurements of the systematic overstating of national accounts output data for the United States, Canada and France in the post World War II period.

14

4210
4220
6350

OECD

OECD
180
F14

290 - 301

[1987]

[19]

All Traded Services are Embodied in Materials or People

Herbert G. Grubel

⚟HE LITERATURE and public policy discussions on international trade in services are badly in need of some conceptual simplification based on unifying principles from economic theory.[1] I attempt to present such a simplification in this article by first discussing the nature of services and providing some definitions. Then I set out a taxonomy of ways in which trade in services takes place. Through this taxonomy it is shown that services can cross international borders only if they are embodied in either material substances or people.

SERVICE TRANSACTIONS DEFINED

In a well-known article the British economist T.P. Hill, now at the Organisation for Economic Cooperation and Development in Paris, provided some key insights about the nature of services by contrast to that of goods.[2] He showed the irrelevance of such attributes as intangibility (at final consumption all consumption involves intangible benefits) and non-permanence (car-repair services have some permanence) and proposed a definition which may be summarized as follows: A service is an economic transaction between two agents which leads to a change in the condition of a person or a good.[3] Of further central relevance for the present analysis is the characteristic that 'services are consumed as they are produced in the sense that the change in the condition of the consumer unit must occur simultaneously with the production of that change by the producer'.[4]

The acceptance of the proposition that the production and consumption of a service take place as the producer transforms the condition of a person or a good has the following two implications for the nature of international transactions in services. First, they take place when persons, capital or goods deliver services or absorb services that transform them in some way after they have crossed an

HERBERT G. GRUBEL: Professor of Economics at the Simon Fraser University, Burnaby, in Canada, and director of the Canadian service industries project at the Fraser Institute, Vancouver; author of *Free Market Zones* (1983) and *The International Monetary System* (1985) and co-author of *Intra-industry Trade* (1976).

international border for a temporary stay abroad. Or, second, they take place when international borders are crossed by material substances that embody in them services.

The first type of service trade has been identified by several other economists. [5] It includes tourism, transport, consulting, education, capital, labour and a wide range of other services. Its nature will be discussed further in the next two sections. The importance of identifying separately this type of service trade stems from the fact that it can be restricted only by limiting rights of individuals and firms to cross borders themselves or to ship goods across borders for the purpose of providing or absorbing service operations abroad.

The second type of service trade involves what Jagdish Bhagwati calls 'splintered services' and the Australian economists Gary Sampson and Richard Snape refer to as 'separated services'. [6] Such services are splintered or separated from their original production as they are embodied in goods for separate sale. Examples of such splintering are the recording of musical performances and the transmission of engineering consulting services through correspondence. Trade in these types of services is discussed in the fourth section. It will be seen to involve border crossings of material substances which differ from ordinary goods only in the magnitude of the value added by domestic service industries relative to the value added by domestic manufacturing industries.

PEOPLE, CAPITAL AND FIRMS MOVE ACROSS BORDERS TO ABSORB AND PROVIDE SERVICES

In this section are discussed the basic characteristics of the type of trade in services which requires that individuals or capital move across borders in order to absorb or deliver services.

People Move Abroad to Absorb Services

The following balance-of-payments categories involve the absorption of services in one country by people from another country.

Tourists from the home country A consume housing, food, transport and other goods and services while visiting country B. This consumption is reported in the balance-of-payments accounts of country B and A as service exports and service imports respectively. For many countries, international tourist expenditures are quantitatively important items in the balance-of-payments accounts.

Students from country A attend universities, technical colleges, hospitals, conferences, workshops and similar activities primarily to generate increases in their human capital. They consume country B educational resources and, coincidentally, housing, food, personal and other goods and services. They generate some benefits to the residents of country B through the internationalization of the education process. In principle, the balance-of-payments treatment of international student exchange is quite clear. The value of the educational resources (at long-run average cost?) and the value of the locally-consumed other services are exports of country B and imports of country A. At the time that the students return to their home country, there should be a balance-of-payments entry recording the flow of human capital into A, for that country's capital stock is raised and its domestic production would have required an investment in human capital through the use of resources with a corresponding opportunity cost. Country B, on the other hand, experiences no change in its capital stock through the departure of these students and therefore there does not need to be an entry in the balance-of-payments accounts. The volume of international trade in educational services is poorly documented and quantitatively it is not very important in relation to national educational efforts or other trade flows. It concerns policy makers periodically after reports about the departure of a brainy migrant appear in the media and the current concern with trade in services has stimulated some interest. [7]

Medical patients from country A go for treatment in country B. They consume primarily health care but also transport and similar services. The value of the medical and other services should be recorded as exports for country B and imports for country A. Trade in this service is unimportant for most countries as a proportion of total domestic health care or of total trade. But it is important for some countries where there is a potential for much growth in this trade as expensive specialization in skills and equipment continues to increase. There are already large medical service industries serving foreigners in Switzerland and London. In addition, regional centres for health care may develop in developing parts of the world. [8]

Film producers from country A use country B's environment, film support and transport, housing and other such services. Their activities result in service exports for B and imports for A. Trade in this business has been growing as the technical quality of filming equipment has freed producers from the need for studio lighting and sound conditions. [9]

Military personnel from country A use country B's environment to absorb services. Perhaps the best example of trade in this category involves the stationing of NATO military personnel in Canada where they engage in training exercises requiring large thinly populated areas and special climatic conditions. The services absorbed by the foreign military in Canada represent an export for Canada.

People and Capital Move Abroad to Produce Services

Individuals and firms move abroad to produce services that consist of either pure labour or the combination of labour and human capital. It is important to note the conceptual and practical difference between temporary and permanent migration of service-producing individuals. National-income accountants consider the value of the services provided by these individuals to involve trade in services only if the stay abroad is three months or less *and* if the individual is paid by a foreign firm. If the individual stays longer than three months or is on the pay-roll of a local firm (domestic or foreign-owned), or both, the services delivered are not considered to be imports. Instead, they are considered to be outright contributions to gross domestic product, as if they had been made by a citizen of the country.

Labour services in their purest form are provided by workers employed by construction companies abroad. For example, Pakistani workers are providing much of the construction labour in Saudi Arabia. Korean construction firms and workers are engaged in major construction projects around the world. Guest workers in the Federal Republic of Germany and other West European countries who are on temporary work permits generate labour-service imports into these countries.

Teachers and academics from country A engage in a wide range of activities abroad, such as giving seminars, reading papers at conferences, lecturing in regular university programmes, teaching company courses and doing research at institutes and universities. The value of these services represents an export for the home country of these experts and an import for the country in which they deliver the service. In principle, there should be accounting for the consumption of housing, food and other goods and services while living abroad, but the small value of these service exports provides little incentive to national statistical offices to set up surveys capable of measuring them. [10]

Artists, entertainers, musicians and people with similar skills from country A give rise, through their performances in country B, to service exports for A and service imports for B. These are counted normally in 'Miscellaneous Accounts' and should in principle be offset by consumption of housing, food and other goods and services.

Soldiers and military advisers from country A stationed in country B to provide defence against foreign aggression represent an export of services from the former to the latter. American soldiers in Western Europe and the Republic of Korea are the best-known examples of such trade in services. There is offsetting consumption of services locally. Except in cases where there are explicit contracts between the governments involved in these transactions, it is difficult to value these services for balance-of-payments purposes and they are usually subsumed in accounts that record government transactions.

Foreign investment in the form of financial capital or direct investment from country A to country B usually leads to the flow of factor services from the former to the latter country. In the case of services delivered by foreign investment abroad it is important to distinguish between genuine factor-service income in the form of interest and dividends, on the one hand, and income that represents payment for services provided by parent companies to their foreign subsidiaries, on the other.

The Canadian economists Alan Rugman and James Markusen have argued in two recent studies that the modern theory of direct foreign investment implies that much of what statisticians consider to be capital factor-service income does in fact represent payment for the export of services.[11] Factor-service flows involving capital are important for many countries and have received much attention from economists. They will not be discussed further here.

In general it should be noted that the present taxonomy makes it possible to dispense with a different analytical treatment for factor and other services, as appears in most other studies of trade in services. One of the main advantages of the present analytical approach is that it shows the close similarity of the policy issues surrounding international flows of capital and trade in services. Both focus on the right to sell in a foreign country a service which requires the physical presence of the service-delivering agent or, as it is often referred to, the right of establishment.

GOODS MOVE ABROAD FOR TRANSFORMATION AND
PROVISION OF SERVICES

International trade in services that depends on the border crossing of goods consists of two distinct categories, one where goods are transformed abroad and the other where the goods provide services to foreigners.

Goods Shipped Abroad for Transformation

In order to give rise to service trade rather than conventional merchandise trade, goods must be shipped across borders for a limited period, during which they are subjected to repair, assembly or some other transformation that does not change them significantly. During this period the goods typically remain the property of foreigners.

This type of trade takes place because it is cheaper to have the work done abroad than domestically. In this sense, the motives for transactions considered in this category are identical to those which make for the purchase of ordinary goods abroad. Standard models of international trade theory can be used to explain the determinants of trade flows. Some illustrative examples of this type of service trade are as follows.

Repairs in country B of ships, aircraft, motor vehicles, computers, paintings, furniture and similar goods owned by residents of country A result in exports and imports of services for B and A respectively. Trade in these kinds of services is not important for most countries, but some countries, such as Singapore and Malta, have been able to use their locations at crossroads of major commercial routes to sustain major ship and, in recent years, aircraft repair industries.

Packaging, husking, shelling, cleaning, storage and wholesale activities in country B of goods owned by residents of country A involve what has historically been known as entrepôt trade. It results in service exports for B and service imports for A. International trade statistics from before World War II show entrepôt trade as a category separate from conventional trade in goods. Since the end of World War II countries have increasingly abandoned this distinction because of the declining importance of entrepôt activities. For regional commercial centres, such as Singapore, however, it is still a significant source of export earnings.

Assembly and finishing in country B of electronic equipment, garments, toys and similar goods owned by residents of country A have become increasingly more important activities in recent years. Very similar in character is the practice of having data recorded on documents in writing and owned by residents of country A entered into electronic storage devices by residents of country B. The essence of international transactions in this category is that the goods being transformed must remain the property of the foreign owner and that the value added by the process must be a small proportion of the total value of the good. The declining costs of transport and communication have made it economical to have these typically labour-intensive activities performed in countries with low labour costs. The development of special export-processing zones with low levels of regulation has further encouraged the growth of this service trade. [12] According to the taxonomy presented here the assembly and finishing of goods should result in labour-service exports for B and labour-service imports for A. In practice, however, most countries subsume it in statistics on trade in goods. The components appear as imports and the assembled goods appear as exports. At best, the trade is shown separately as entrepôt trade by the service-exporting country.

Goods Shipped Abroad to Provide Services

Certain goods are shipped across borders for limited periods to perform certain specialized tasks. They remain the property of foreigners and typically are machinery or transport equipment on lease or rented out. The owners of such goods generate a service export for their home country A while country B imports these services.

The motivation and source of comparative advantage for this type of activity may be financial, as in the case of aircraft leasing, or it may be based on the joint provision of specialized engineering, geological and repair services, as in the case of drilling rigs and sophisticated industrial equipment. The sale of transport services owned by residents of one country to residents of another is quantitatively an important component of the balance-of-payments accounts of many countries. It arises in connection with tourism and business travel. In the shipping of goods its importance has been influenced heavily by the existence of flags of convenience.

Of some quantitative importance in recent years has also been the rental or leasing of ships, aircraft, motor vehicles, computers, oil-drilling rigs and other industrial equipment. Leasing arrangements for large passenger jets have been important elements of non-price competition for major aircraft manufacturers. Generally, however, the importance of arm's-length leasing and renting has been over-shadowed by the practice of firms establishing foreign subsidiaries to exploit non-financial sources of comparative advantage embodied in these types of goods.

MATERIAL SUBSTANCES EMBODYING SERVICES
MOVE ACROSS BORDERS

In all countries, statistical offices have identified industries producing goods and industries producing services. Using such a national taxonomy and an input-output table it is possible to estimate the value of non-factor services entering final domestic consumption. It is also possible to estimate the value of non-factor services which are used as an input in the further production of goods and services. Thus it is possible to establish the direct and indirect requirements for non-factor service inputs of individual goods-producing industries. Most important for the present analysis, such calculations lend themselves to the estimation of the value of non-factor services embodied in the goods exported and imported by a country.[13]

Much can be gained by considering that all international trade consists of material substances that have non-factor services embodied in them, the exception being the trade which requires the temporary movement of people, firms and goods as discussed in the previous two sections. Splintered or separated services, which are considered by Professor Bhagwati and Dr Sampson and Professor Snape to give rise to trade in services, need to be embodied in goods like records, books or telegraphic messages. The 'embodiment approach' to trade in non-factor services presented here thus embraces the splintering phenomenon that is the cornerstone of the most widely-used alternative approach to the problem.

Splintered Services are Embodied Services

Goods embodying these splintered services are no different from other traded goods which are recorded in merchandise accounts. All of them have embodied in them certain amounts of non-factor service inputs. What distinguishes trade in services and trade in goods is the relative proportion of the price of the traded substance which can be attributed to value added by service industries and by manufacturing industries. Trade in splintered services is characterized by a very high ratio of non-factor service value added to manufacturing value added.

Outstanding examples of such goods with a high proportion of service value added are (i) letters, books and reports containing customized scientific, engineering and other intelligence data, (ii) letters devoted to legal documents granting patent and franchising rights, (iii) electronic discs containing computer programmes or data and (iv) films and tapes storing motion pictures. Income from the sale of these material devices abroad is traditionally recorded as service income. The arbitrariness of this dichotomy is seen most readily by considering that the sale of a computer chip is taken to represent the export of a manufactured good, even though the value added provided by the traditional production process may be only a very small fraction of its total, the main part having been provided by engineering, scientific and marketing services. It can easily happen that the ratio of service value added to manufacturing value added in a computer chip is greater than that ratio for a musical recording.

Invalid Existing Distinctions

The above reasoning and examples suggest that existing statistical and analytical distinctions between trade in services and trade in goods are undesirable on logical grounds. Abandoning them results in greater logical consistency of existing practices and has another important advantage. It points to the fact that free trade in goods automatically assures free trade in non-factor services. There is no need for a special treatment of trade in services under the General Agreement on Tariffs and Trade (GATT), or in bilateral or any other trade negotiations.

Are Electronic Signals an Exception?

International trade in telecommunication services directly and the transmission of splintered services through such means appear to represent a special case since they do not require embodiment of the service in a good. This is not correct though if one substitutes the words 'material substances' for 'goods' in the above contexts. All international trade involving electronics results in the crossing of borders by material signals that in principle are recordable and measurable, much like books, letters and floppy disks.

The case of international transmission of electronic signals raises the general issue confronted by customs agents and statisticians in registering and in assessing the value of services that are embodied in material substances. In principle, registering of the trade should not give rise to special difficulties, for it can be monitored whenever the substances cross borders. Electronic signals represent a special problem for such monitoring, but it is one which can be overcome. If one may judge from the fragmentary evidence available about the electronic-surveillance activities of national secret security agencies, the technical problem has been solved and it is merely a matter of cost of use for commercial purposes.

The value of such trade can also be established in principle since it is always accompanied by invoices. There may be problems in preventing misrepresentations of the true value of services, especially in the case of intra-firm trade of multinational enterprises. This problem is no different in nature, although it may be in degree, from the general problem faced by customs agents in assessing the value of goods. Distortions and such problems are a decreasing function of barriers to free trade. At any rate, differences in the degree of difficulty in assessing the true value of transactions are not a good ground for claiming a dichotomy between trade in services and trade in goods which otherwise does not have an analytically valid foundation.

Economic Growth and Embodied Services

Abandonment of the distinction between trade in services and trade in goods and the analytical emphasis on trade in embodied services have one other important advantage. They put to rest fears expressed by a number of analysts who believe that the growing share of service industries in advanced economies results in a lack of competitiveness, unemployment and ultimately an inability of these countries to pay for the imports of goods required for a high standard of living.[14] In the analytical perspective presented here, the growth of service industries is, to a very large extent, due to the growing requirements for non-factor service inputs of goods-producing industries. Most of these services stem from human, knowledge and cultural capital which is being formed and applied in the continuous process of capital deepening and 'roundaboutness' of production. These processes do not result in a loss of competitiveness. On the contrary, they shape and maintain comparative advantage. There is no limit to the extent to which non-factor services can be embodied in goods and thus traded internationally.[15]

SUMMARY AND POLICY IMPLICATIONS

International trade in services occurs in two categories.

The first category requires that people, capital, firms or goods temporarily move across borders. There, people absorb foreign services like tourism, transport, education and medical care and goods are repaired, assembled or transformed in some other way. Alternatively, people abroad provide services to foreigners, as do business consultants, bankers, lawyers, teachers, insurance specialists and military personnel. Firms provide services of pure capital and other capital assets and goods deliver services like transport and drilling of oil wells.

The second category of trade in services, that involving non-factor services, takes place when goods embodying such services are traded internationally. All manufactured goods in modern economies contain some embodied non-factor services and all trade in services requires embodiment of the service in a good, except for cases considered in the first category. Under current statistical and analytical conventions, letters, books, reports, contracts, electronic signals and other material substances are considered to give rise to trade in non-factor services if they are produced by so-called service industries like business, engineering, computing or entertainment services. On the other hand, items like computers are considered to result in merchandise trade, even though the value of non-factor services embodied in them may be as high, or higher, relative to the cost of manufacture as it is in items giving rise to service trade.

The main analytical conclusion reached by this article based on this model is the following. There is no valid distinction between trade in goods and trade in non-factor services. International negotiations on the liberalization of trade in services are about two traditional issues. First, they are about the right of people and firms to produce and sell services abroad, which is known as the right of establishment. Second, they are about the liberalization of trade in goods. If this last is achieved it results automatically also in freer trade for non-factor services.

The main policy implication of the analysis is that there is no need for the establishment of a new international institution like the GATT in which negotiations would focus on the liberalization of trade in services. Instead, efforts should continue to be focussed on negotiations in the well-established tradition of aiming for free trade in goods and assuring rights of establishment for firms and service-producing individuals.

The preceding analysis does nothing to make me hopeful about the chances that much progress is likely to be made in assuring free rights of establishment. There are good reasons for slow progress in liberalization in this field in the past — reasons that are mostly outside the realm of economic analysis. Restrictions on the licensing of professions similarly have a long tradition and have generated powerful interest groups that are likely to oppose vigorously the granting of licences to foreign practitioners.

In the field of financial, insurance, transport and similar services most countries have erected pervasive nets of regulation to deal with what have been perceived to be serious externalities arising from the free operation of markets. These regulations typically restrict all competition. Keeping out foreign competitors by denying them the right of establishment or the right to sell goods that embody services is merely a by-product of such general restrictions. Interest groups which have benefited from this regulation have opposed, more or less successfully, sweeping de-regulation in many of these industries. They have done so in spite of a persuasive body of evidence that de-regulation would result in an increase in total welfare. This same political and economic power held by interest groups will be mobilized to prevent international capital flows and migration that would create more competition in these regulated service industries.

In spite of, and perhaps because of, these obstacles to free international capital flows, migration and trade, it seems important not to confuse the issues on negotiating tables by referring to them as issues involving trade in services. They are, plain and simply, issues of free trade in goods and the right of international investment and operation in service industries by foreigners.

---

1. This article is a revised version of a paper presented at the annual meetings of the American Economic Association held in New Orleans, December 1986. It was written while the author was director of the Canadian service industries project at the Fraser Institute in Vancouver. The project is financed by the Department of Regional Industrial Expansion of the Government of Canada.

2. T.P. Hill, 'On Goods and Services', *Review of Income and Wealth*, New Haven, December 1977.

3. After providing examples of services, Professor Hill notes in a key section of his article: 'In every case [of the services described], some change is brought about in the condition of some person or good, with the agreement of the person concerned or economic unit owning the good. Secondly, the change is the result of the activity of some other economic unit. These two points provide the key to the concept of a service. A service may be defined as a change in the condition of a person, or of a good belonging to some economic unit, which is brought about as the result of the activity of some other economic unit, with the prior agreement of the former person or economic unit' (*ibid.*, p. 318). Professor Hill makes much of the point in this definition and his discussion of the fact that in an economic sense one cannot do a service for oneself. In my definition I have taken account of this aspect by using the term 'economic transaction'.

4. *Ibid.*, p. 337. Professor Hill uses 23 pages of printed text to analyze the validity of the statements in the light of an almost exhaustive list of what most people would accept as economic service activities. Many points of qualification are found. For example, if the change in the condition of a good is too great then we refer to manufacture rather than a service transaction. Thus one would refer to automobile repair services, but the manufacturing process of rebuilding automobile engines (my example). Obviously Professor Hill's qualifications cannot be discussed here.

5. One of the first and clearest statements of this position is found in Jagdish N. Bhagwati, 'Splintering and Disembodiment of Services and Developing Nations', *The World Economy*, London, June 1984. The point is also presented in Gary P. Sampson and Richard H. Snape, 'Identifying the Issues in Trade in Services', *The World Economy*, June 1985, in Robert M. Stern and Bernard M. Hoekman, 'Issues and Data Needs for GATT Negotiations on Services', *The World Economy*, March 1987, and in Chung H. Lee and Seiji Naya, 'The Internationalization of US Service Industries', mimeograph, Department of Economics, University of Hawaii, 1986. In this last, the authors say: 'Trade in services generally requires providers or receivers to move between countries, whereas trade in goods . . . does not require their movement' (p. 18). Some special problems arising from the temporary migration of service-delivering people have recently been discussed in Bhagwati, *International Trade in Services and its Relevance for Economic Development*, Xth Annual Lecture of the Geneva Association (Oxford: Pergamon Press, for the Services World Forum, 1986), and Bhagwati, 'Barriers to International Trade in Professional Services', *University of Chicago Legal Forum*, Chicago, 1986.

6. For precise references, see the above note.

7. The topic of balance-of-payments accounting for student exchange and human capital flows is intricate in detail and complicated by many institutional peculiarities, such as the existence of host-country scholarships and the under-pricing of educational services. There is also the problem that students often work in the foreign country where they are studying. This activity is in effect an import of labour services for the host country and an export for the home country, but statistical procedures of most countries do not capture this trade. Similar labour-service trade may take place

in the case of tourists. These topics cannot be pursued here. For a detailed theoretical and empirical analysis, see Herbert G. Grubel and Anthony D. Scott, *The Brain Drain: Determinants, Measurement and Welfare Effects* (Waterloo, Ontario: Wilfrid Laurier University Press, 1977).

There has also been a flurry of interest in the topic in Australia, where scholars and government representatives have been discussing the possibility of deliberate policies for the development of education as an export, particularly to the developing countries of South-east Asia. The United Nations Conference on Trade and Development (UNCTAD) has investigated the possibility of having an international accounting system for the flow of human capital and embodied educational resources across borders.

In the report *Trade in Services: Exports and Foreign Revenues* (Washington: US Government Printing Office, for the Office of Technology Assessment, United States Congress, 1986), it was estimated that in 1983 the revenues of the United States from the sale of educational services to foreigners were between $1.6 and $2.4 billion. In the same year, outlays of the United States on educational services abroad were between $100 and $300 million.

8. Singapore has deliberately developed the health care industry for export to residents from neighbouring countries in South-east Asia.

9. In Canada, the government of the province of British Columbia has been very successful in attracting Californian film makers, partly because of the scenery and partly because of the low cost of support services expressed in American dollars. The future of the trade is influenced by two different developments. On the one hand, it will grow further as the demand for film entertainment continues to rise in response to the availability of more and specialized electronic entertainment technologies around the world. On the other hand, the industry expects the development of an electronic system which uses twice the number of dots per inch than do current television screens. The sharpness and colour quality of the recordings in experimental sets have been found to be as great as those of conventional films based on chemical processes. The adoption of this technology is likely to increase the efficiency of film production since the outcome of all photographic efforts can be assessed immediately. This will lower the cost of production, but it will also reduce the time spent in foreign countries and consuming services.

10. I do not know how technical experts sent abroad by international organizations, such as the International Monetary Fund (IMF) and the United Nations, are treated in national accounts. Consider an Indian citizen on the pay-roll of the United Nations who is resident in New York and providing a consulting service in Kenya. Presumably that activity would be considered to give rise to a Kenyan service import. But which country is credited with supplying the export?

11. See Alan Rugman, *A Transaction Cost Approach to Trade in Services*, Dalhousie University Discussion Paper (Halifax: Dalhousie University, 1986); and James R. Markusen, *Service Trade by the Multinational Enterprise* (Vancouver: Fraser Institute, forthcoming).

12. The economics of such zones are discussed in Grubel, *Free Market Zones* (Vancouver: Fraser Institute, 1983).

13. There is, of course, a strict analogy between this calculation and that pioneered by Wassily Leontief in his efforts to measure the labour and capital content of the trade of the United States. Richard Harris and I are working on a paper to estimate the value of services embodied in Canada's exports and imports. In a preliminary study, I have used some simple assumptions to allocate service industry output to final and intermediate uses and, at a very aggregative level, I have found that Canada has a strongly positive balance of trade in embodied services. See Grubel, 'Direct and Embodied Trade in Services: Where is the Service Trade Problem?', in Lee and Naya (eds), *Trade and Investment in Services* (Honolulu: East-West Center, forthcoming).

14. Examples of the literature in this tradition are Frank Blackaby (ed.), *De-industrialization* (London: Heinemann, for the National Institute of Economic and Social Research, 1979), and Barry Bluestone and Bennett Harrison, *The De-industrialization of America* (New York: Basic Books, 1982).

15. The ideas about the nature of services and their role in economic growth are developed further in Grubel and Michael Walker, *The Canadian Service Industries* (Vancouver: Fraser Institute, forthcoming).

20

Liberalization of Trade in Services: A Taxonomy and Discussion of Issues[1]

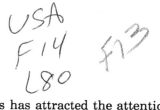

International trade in services has attracted the attention of policy-makers and economic analysts as a result of two main developments over the last decade. First, the large U.S. trade deficits during the 1980s have generated a search for fundamental explanations. One of these is based on the realization that during this period over 70 per cent of employment and national output of the U.S. economy stemmed from the service sector. As a result, a process of "de-industrialization" was believed to be taking place. According to this model, a large part of the balance of payments problems of the 1980s has been due to de-industrialization and the disappearance of traditional goods export industries.[2] The problem was expected to become worse with the expected continued growth of the service sector industries.

At the same time that most service industries' output is not tradable, the output of those which can be traded economically has been subject to a wide range of restrictions by foreign governments. These restrictions are especially harmful to the United States since these tradable services are seen to require the use of relatively large amounts of human and knowledge capital, factors of production in which the country is considered to be well endowed.

---

[1] The analysis draws heavily from a major study of Canadian Service industries undertaken during 1987-88 at the Fraser Institute in Vancouver and sponsored by the government of Canada. This fact explains why Canadian practices are used as illustrations. Their use is not to imply that Canadian policies on service trade are in any way exceptionally numerous or harsh.

[2] For this line of analysis see Blackaby (1978), Bluestone and Harrison (1982), and Shelp (1981).

1

Second, coincident with the development of these ideas was a growing chorus of complaints to the U.S. Government by American business. They decried the lack of protection of intellectual property rights abroad and charged that service industry exports were hampered by discrimination in foreign countries. In particular, intellectual property rights violations through the copying of computer software, medicines, records, films, video-cassettes, and branded consumer goods were seen to have resulted in large losses of revenue and damage to the marketing and quality control investments of firms. These violations took place on a large scale because some governments refused to enforce existing national laws concerning the protection of such rights. Singapore and the other Little Dragons were identified as some of the worst offenders in this field. Some other violations were due to the deliberate actions of governments, like that of Canada, which had legislation that enabled Canadian firms to copy U.S. medicines without proper compensation to their designers.

Discrimination against U.S. banks, securities dealers, insurance companies, and sellers of software for telecommunications was found to hamper the export of these services to many countries. The Japanese Government and publicly owned enterprises were singled out for their discriminatory practices, mainly perhaps because that country enjoyed large and growing bilateral merchandise trade surpluses. However, many developing countries, especially in Latin America and Asia, were subjected to the same criticism.

As a result of these developments, the U.S. Government decided to launch a major diplomatic initiative aimed at a global liberalization of international trade in services. This initiative was taken in the framework of negotiations for a new round of trade talks under the auspices of GATT at Punta del Este. After hard rounds of bargaining, the liberalization of service trade was entered into the agenda for the upcoming Uruguay Round of negotiations. However, these talks will be taking place separately from those concerned with the liberalization of merchandise trade. The main consequence of this procedure is that concessions made by countries in merchandise trade cannot be linked officially to concessions made in services trade. This approach represents a compromise of the U.S. demands for a linking of the negotiations and of the demands of an alliance of developing countries led by Brazil and India, which wanted services trade to be excluded altogether from the agenda of the Uruguay Round.[3]

---

3   For a report on the Punta del Este negotiations see Hindley (1989).

2

The following presents a taxonomy of types of service trade around which will be organized a discussion of the main issues which will be on the agenda of the upcoming negotiations.

I. WHAT IS SERVICES TRADE?

The taxonomy of service trade presented in Table 1 is designed to simplify thinking about service trade.[4] It is needed because this trade is a complex phenomenon which involves several categories, each of which is different in some essential ways important for the negotiations. For example, most of the

TABLE 1

A Taxonomy of Service Trade, Canada-U.S. Bilateral Flows, 1983

Type of Services	Exports + Imports/Canada GDP
Factor Service Trade	
Returns from financial assets, direct investment	4.0
Fees and royalties	.3
Labour	nd
People and Goods Service Trade	
Travel and transportation	2.0
Other private services (business services, banking, insurance, computers)	.3
Embodied Service Trade	10.0

political attention during the Punta del Este negotiations has been focused on intellectual property rights and business services, as discussed above. Yet, by far the largest amount of service trade in the balance of payments of the United States and most other countries is in factor services.

---

4   Similar taxonomies have been produced by Bhagwati (1984) and Sampson and Snape (1985).

3

The taxonomy is useful also by permitting the introduction of some fundamental insights about the nature of the domestic service industries, which greatly simplify the discussion of the issues. The main conclusion of this analysis will be that services cannot be traded directly, that instead they require either the movement of people or prior embodiment in material substances.[5] Free trade in services thus is assured through the freedom of people to move abroad temporarily in order to sell their services and through the unrestricted movement of material substances across borders. The achievement of the latter objective has been the traditional task of GATT.

In the last column of Table 1 the bilateral imports and exports under each category of service trade are summed and expressed as a percentage of Canada's GDP in the year 1983.[6] Exports and imports are summed to indicate properly the relative importance of the different categories while avoiding distortions due to bilateral imbalances. It is clear that if the same dollar values were expressed as a percentage of the U.S. GDP, they would be approximately one tenth of the size shown, though the relative sizes would remain unchanged.

According to Table 1, the first category of service trade involves income from the basic factors of production, financial capital, and direct investment; knowledge capital in the form of fees and royalties; and labour. Capital services flowing from assets held for the long term are recorded as interest and dividends. It can be seen that these amount to 4 per cent of GDP and are quantitatively by far the most important category of service trade found in the balance of payments statistics. On the other hand, the politically important trade in fees and royalties is quite small. It amounts to .3 per cent of GDP and thus is equal to only about one tenth of the traditional capital service flows.

---

5   The analysis documenting the role of producer services in the domestic economy is found in Grubel and Walker (1989). The new taxonomy of international trade in services was first presented in Grubel (1987).

6   It may be worth noting that for the United States this bilateral trade expressed as a percentage of U.S. GDP is roughly one tenth of the magnitude shown in the table since the U.S. economy is about ten times the size of the Canadian economy. It may also be worth noting that large unilateral surpluses in factor service and travel and transportation trade between the two countries in favour of the United States in 1983 were cancelled by a large surplus in embodied service trade in favour of Canada. The two countries thus had a balanced exchange of services.

4

Trade in pure labour services is entered in Table 1 as a reminder of its existence. An estimate of its size is missing since neither the U.S. nor the Canadian Governments are keeping records of this type of trade. It is not clear whether this is so because the size of this trade is negligible or because there are no institutions for collecting the relevant information. For some countries like Mexico, Turkey, Pakistan, and Korea the export of temporary labour generates significant balance of payments income. For countries that are important buyers of foreign labour services, like Singapore, Germany, and the United States, payments for this labour are significant debits in the balance of payments statistics.

People and goods service trade shown as the second major category in Table 1 takes place predominantly when tourists, students, and medical patients go abroad to absorb services and when teachers, doctors, business consultants, and other professionals deliver services during a temporary stay abroad. There are analogous imports absorbed by capital equipment, as when ships and planes are repaired and maintained abroad. Capital goods produce service exports when they carry foreign passengers and freight and provide oil drilling services abroad. The table shows that the subcategory "travel and transportation" in the balance of payments statistics has amounted to 2 per cent of Canadian GDP in 1983, half that of the asset incomes and payments. The category, "other private services", which is heavily weighted by professional and business services like finance, management consulting, marketing, accounting, insurance, education, and health, came to only .3 per cent of GDP.

Embodied Services

Embodied service trade shown in Table 1 has been specified and estimated especially for this analysis. As can be seen, it is the largest entry in the trade and represents 10 per cent of Canadian GDP. Embodied service trade is not found in any official balance of payments statistics or scholarly publications. Underlying this concept is the proposition that trade in services can take place in only two ways. The first is when deliverers or consumers of the services move abroad physically, in ways noted and measured above.

Alternatively, the service has to be embodied in a material substance before it is transmitted abroad. This important idea requires some elaboration. Consider an economist in Singapore who does a market survey report for a Japanese company. The results of this survey can be transmitted to the Japanese company only through a written document, be it a letter, pamphlet or book, or an electronic device, be it telephone, fax, or a computer disc. It matters little for the present purposes of analysis that customs agents and statisticians have great troubles monitoring and valuing this trade. The basic fact is that if letters, packages, and electronic signals can flow freely across borders, then there is freedom in the kind of service trade generated by economists, bankers, lawyers, accountants, engineers, and similar professionals.[7]

In this analytical perspective, service trade is the same as goods trade since goods also have services embodied in them. It is useful to view internationally traded goods as lying along a spectrum according to the amount of direct and indirect services embodied per dollar of final sale. At one end of the spectrum are standardized commodities like wheat, which has embodied in it the scientific services of the hybrid seed grower and insecticide producer, transportation, accounting, management, and marketing services. The sum of all of these services may amount only to 5 per cent of the market price of wheat. In the middle of the spectrum we find automobiles. Lee Iacocca (1985) noted in his autobiography that Chrysler spends more on medical services for its worker than it spends on steel. Both expenditures have to be recovered in the final price of cars. The health, science, engineering, and business services embodied in cars represent an ever increasing proportion of the total costs while the use of these services results in ever decreasing requirements for steel.

It is only an historic coincidence that a product further along this spectrum of service intensity, a computer program disc, is considered to be a good. The value added made up of the traditional manufacturing process represents a very small amount relative to the spending on the programming, scientific, marketing, and management services. On the extreme end of the spectrum of service contents we can find the electronic message through which

---

7   Richard Snape has pointed out to me that this statement is not entirely true since domestic agents may be prohibited from doing business by mail with foreigner. One example of such a prohibition has been by U.S. authorities on the purchase of Irish Sweepstake tickets. It has been nearly impossible to enforce this rule. However, I do not know of any prohibitions on service trade through the mail between the United States and Canada. In both countries the sale of insurance and land by mail is heavily regulated but to the best of my knowledge, this regulation does not discriminate against foreign countries. It is aimed at the protection of consumers against fraud generally. This topic will be discussed further below.

a lawyer provides services to a client abroad. The cost of producing the material substance in the process is a tiny fraction of the total of the export .

Embodied services trade can be measured by the use of input-output tables and the calculation of the direct and indirect services required per dollar of final sales for individual industries. Through the application of this statistic to exports and imports by industries it is possible to calculate the value of embodied services trade quite precisely.[8]

The estimate in Table 1 is based on the use of a simpler and less precise method. It involves estimation of the amount of producer services in the Canadian economy. This is done by taking the total service industry GDP and subtracting the GDP originating with consumer service industries and the exhaustive expenditures of the government. The residual is the GDP of producer services, which is expressed as a per cent of total goods production and goods trade.[9] In studies made of Canadian trade the two approaches generated very similar results.

II. ISSUES CONCERNING FACTOR SERVICES

The analysis now uses the preceding taxonomy to discuss outstanding policy issues concerning trade in services.

Direct Foreign Investment

The liberalization of direct foreign investment in services will be an important agenda item during the Uruguay Round of negotiations. It is important to note that this is so in spite of the fact that direct foreign investment involves capital flows, which should be considered in the capital account of the balance of payments and which traditionally have not been the subject of GATT negotiations. Since most of the issues to be discussed have more in common with other direct investment restrictions than services, they would more

---

[8]   This has been done for Canada by Cox and Harris (1989) and for India by Trivedi (1989).

[9]   For a detailed discussion of this calculation see Grubel and Walker (1989)

appropriately be discussed in entirely new types of negotiations over direct investment policies generally.

However, given the Uruguay agenda, we expect that the negotiations over the liberalization of investment in service industries will focus on the removal of legislation limiting foreign ownership. This legislation owes its existence to the view that many service industries, but especially those in the financial service sector, are crucial to economic development, planning, and stability.

The demands for the liberalization of foreign service investment will be formulated under the principle that every foreign firm should have "the right to establishment under national treatment". This principle means simply that foreign investors have the automatic right to establish a business if they meet the same conditions imposed on domestic investors.

Most emphatically this principle does not mean that a country loses the right to regulate its industries in ways it considers to be in the national interest. For example, a government may strongly regulate its banking industry and have a separation of commercial and investment banking, specific capital and liquidity requirements, and mandated lending and borrowing rates. The setting of these and other rules remain an undisputed exercise of national sovereignty, however much they may conflict with market ideologies or interfere with efficiency.

Not permitted under the principle are rules and regulations which apply only to foreign-owned enterprises. Many countries have such rules in place. For example in Canada the assets of foreign-owned banks may not exceed a certain proportion of the sum of all assets of Canadian-owned banks. Other countries exclude foreign-owned banks from certain types of business like government bond dealing. Under the principle of national treatment, such discriminatory practices are prohibited.[10]

---

[10] There have also been complaints about discriminatory practices used by publicly owned enterprises in the selection of suppliers of certain services by foreigners. Best known here are the tendencies of national postal and telecommunications authorities in Japan and Western Europe to rig the bidding mechanism for orders such that foreign firms are effectively excluded. The liberalization of such practices should be covered under the subject of preferential state purchasing practices in the conventional GATT negotiations. There is nothing special about telecommunications services in this context.

Economic principles suggest that the universal applicability of national treatment to foreign investment increases efficiency since only commercial competitiveness determines success of enterprises. Its operation also increases competition since actual or potential entry by foreign firms limits the strength of domestic oligopolies. Such limitations tend to give rise to especially large benefits in industries in which the regulated environment has given rise to opportunities for collusion and the dominance of regulatory bodies.

The adoption of the principle of right to establishment and national treatment will be opposed strongly by some governments which will argue that the right to exclude foreign owners is one of the most important prerogatives of national sovereignty. They will point to the fact that even countries like the United States and Germany have violated the principle of non-discrimination in the treatment of foreign investment, even though they profess a strong commitment to liberal foreign investment policies. They will recall that recently when direct foreign investment appeared to threaten the national interest, the governments of these countries acted to protect it. For example, during the heyday of OPEC it was made quite clear that legislative barriers would be used to prevent the foreign take-over of U.S. firms important for defence production, like IBM and McDonnel-Douglas. In Germany the government prevented the purchase of a large block of Mercedes Benz Company shares by Arab interests, which would have given them a significant control over the operation of that firm.

From the preceding discussion it is clear that there will be much hard bargaining before the world will have a code of liberalization of foreign service sector investment which is acceptable to and adopted by all countries. Overcoming conflicts between efficiency and ideology in political, democratic environments is never easy. The difficulties may be expected to be even greater in an international forum involving many countries with different cultural traditions and economic systems.

Labour

The liberal treatment of foreign labour by both the exporting and importing countries might similarly be codified during some international negotiations in the future. Such a code might protect the human rights of foreign workers and the stability of countries, the economies of which are exposed to severe disruptions by the sudden expulsion or recall of foreign workers. However, there are no plans for the formal discussion of these issues during the Uruguay Round.

Intellectual Property Rights

One of the two most important issues on the agenda for the Uruguay Round concerns the protection of foreign-owned patents and copyrights. The issues are clear in principle.[11] In the modern industrial world much of current and future productivity is due to the use of scientific, engineering, and commercial knowledge. This knowledge is costly to produce and easily devalued through copying by competitors. The production of adequate amounts of knowledge in market economies requires that creators of knowledge enjoy legal protection from competitors through patents and copyrights.

Economic theory suggests that efficiency is attained when the protection of knowledge producers is so long and secure that the creation of knowledge capital results in the equality of the marginal productivity of all forms of capital, in particular real and knowledge capital. While the formal theoretical efficiency conditions are clear, unfortunately empirical information on its attainment in the real world has not been produced. However, most analysts agree that the efficient length is neither zero nor a very long period like 100 hundred years. In fact, most countries have enshrined in national legislation patent protection of between ten to fifteen years. In the absence of more solid information it may be best to consider that these national laws were put into effect after a careful weighing of costs and benefits to the public interest and that they come close to achieving it.

For the present purposes of analysis it should also be noted that little is known about the reduction in incentives and the rate of knowledge capital formation, which results from the refusal of some governments to provide foreign owners of knowledge capital the same protection that they provide to their indigenous owners. It is theoretically possible that existing national protection generates too much knowledge capital in the world so that reduced incentives from such behaviour moves the global stock lower and closer to efficiency. However, it is also possible that such behaviour produces the opposite effect. The preceding arguments and lack of knowledge may well be used by some governments in the Uruguay Round discussions to defend their discrimination against foreign owners of intellectual capital.

---

11   For a discussion of the issues see also Grey (1987).

Another argument likely to be used for this purpose involves the basic theorem from neo-classical economics that in efficient equilibrium the price of any good or service is equal to the marginal cost of producing it. Since the marginal cost of using existing knowledge like a pharmaceutical formula is zero, the efficient price for its use should also be zero. Accordingly, the efficiency of the world economy would be increased if countries would use foreign-owned knowledge without compensation to its owners.

This argument neglects the difference between short- and long-run marginal cost. The resultant error becomes readily apparent when we consider that the theorem also implies that empty seats in movie-houses and planes should be given away free whenever they are not sold to paying customers. Under such an arrangement the supply of movie-houses and planes would vanish quickly. In the longer run, free use of commercial and industrial knowledge similarly would reduce the stock and rate of production of new knowledge, possibly by a large amount. As a result, countries which have benefited from the free use of the knowledge in the short run can easily be made worse off in the longer run.

Some intellectuals and politicians, especially those from developing countries with a strong preference for socialist ideology, will argue at Uruguay for the right to use foreign intellectual property without compensation on the grounds that their peoples are poor and deserve charitable treatment. They will remind politicians from industrial countries that this form of charity is politically very convenient for them since it can be hidden readily from the scrutiny of the voting public. It is difficult to reply to this argument except on the similarly moralistic grounds that poverty is not a sufficient justification for the theft of intellectual and commercial property.[12]

In sum, from the preceding it is apparent that negotiations over the protection of intellectual property rights will be difficult. The difficulties will be reduced only somewhat by the creation of the common analytical and knowledge base sketched in the preceding paragraphs. They will also be reduced somewhat by the acceptance of the basic principle that the primary

---

[12] In most Western law codes there are no penalties when persons steal to save their lives. However, this situation is hardly applicable to developing countries. Even under the best of circumstances, the amount of resource transfers generated by adherence to likely international intellectual property rights treaties is negligibly small for most developing countries.

11

objective of such international negotiations is to assure the creation of an efficient trading system, not the redistribution of wealth.

III. PEOPLE SERVICE TRADE

I know of no countries which have restrictions on the sale of tourist, medical, and education services to foreigners. Some countries have regulations to assure that such temporary visits are not used to overcome more stringent laws on permanent immigration. Others regulate the use of socialized medical and educational services by foreigners to protect the financial integrity of the system. These regulations are designed to protect the integrity of important national programmes. They do not create inefficiencies in the international economy and are not subject of formal criticism in the international community.

On the other hand, many governments have restrictions on the freedom of their citizens to travel abroad for the absorption of tourist, medical, and educational services. Most of these restrictions are part of a system of import licensing and economic planning.[13] Their liberalization is best considered in the Uruguay Round session concerned with the use of import restrictions for balance of payments reasons.

Since restrictions on people service imports are relatively few and small, have little quantitative impact, or belong into another agenda, they are likely to be discussed little, if at all, at the Uruguay Round.

People Service Exports

People move abroad to deliver services under two institutional arrangements. First, their business is headquartered in the home country. People go abroad only to do whatever is needed to provide the service to the foreign customer.

---

13   Singapore is familiar with the effects of a sudden change in such regulations when some years ago the government of Indonesia imposed a high departure tax on its citizens and sharply curtailed tourism and medical service purchases in Singapore.

For example, engineering consultants from Singapore go to China to inspect locations and gather information necessary to design a plant. Most of the design work on the project is then done at the Singapore base of the firm. Other trips by the consultants may be necessary, as during construction of the plant, but Singapore is the home base of the engineers.

Under the second arrangement firms in the service industries have subsidiaries or branches abroad. It is well known from the theory of direct foreign investment that the success of such foreign operations depends crucially on the maintenance of effective management control and of the corporate culture. These objectives can be achieved only by staffing of the foreign operations with persons who have been trained at headquarters and who work there periodically for prolonged periods of time.

Many countries have severe restrictions on the temporary immigration of persons who wish to deliver services under both of these arrangements for the delivery of people services. For example, Canadian immigration authorities are known for enforcing very stringent conditions and lengthy and costly procedures before they issue temporary work permits to foreigners. U.S. immigration authorities in recent years have begun to ask for work permits even from Canadian academics who deliver lectures or seminars for which they are paid.

It is clear that the liberalization of service trade requires the ready issue of temporary work permits to the foreign deliverers of the services. The value of liberalized direct investment in services is diminished by restrictions on the issue of such work permits.

Negotiations over the removal of such restrictions are likely to be difficult in the Uruguay Round again because the policy interferes with the exercise of national economic sovereignty, manpower policies in this case. The basic conflict is between efficiency gained through the use of the least cost providers of the service from abroad and the loss of employment opportunities for citizens. Citizens who can be identified as the losers of jobs through the liberalization, of course, have effective interest group lobbying, while foreigners do not. At the same time, potential gainers of jobs in the service export fields typically are not represented by political lobbies. All of these elements are the ingredients of much hard bargaining at the Uruguay Round.

13

IV. EMBODIED SERVICES TRADE

Embodied service trade may enter the Uruguay Round of negotiations in the following ways. First, there may be demands for the removal of restrictions on the sale of services from abroad, such as Irish Sweepstake tickets, which require the presence of neither a foreign firm or person. It should be noted that in this case again liberalization does not mean that countries have to change domestic regulations. If the sale of sweepstake tickets is prohibited because all gambling is illegal, then this policy need not be changed. Similarly, if the sale of insurance requires registration and prudential supervision of firms, then foreign companies which do not follow this regulation can legitimately be prohibited from selling insurance through the mail.

Second, the existence and quantitative importance of embodied service trade suggests a strong link between negotiations for free trade generally and free trade in the services. The unrestricted movement of mail and electronic signals embodying services may have to become an explicit item for the traditional GATT negotiations.

Third, one of the important problems likely to confront the negotiations arises even if there is complete acceptance of the principle of right to establishment under national treatment. The problem arises from the fact that national regulations in many countries are anti-competitive and anti-trade. Some governments will attempt to use moral suasion and appeals to self-interest to achieve changes in this environment, but it may be doubted that such exhortations will produce many results. Under these conditions, gains from trade in the direct foreign investment in service industries will be limited. Many of the fears of the effects of de-industrialization on international trade will remain.

The realization that a very large and growing proportion of the service sector consists of producer services which end up embodied in goods and influence competitiveness suggest that concerns over de-industrialization are unwarranted. Even if U.S. service sector firms cannot expand strongly abroad, their effect on domestic goods production and competitiveness will assure that the country has sufficient goods for export to pay for the imported goods demanded.

14

V. SUMMARY AND CONCLUSIONS

This study has attempted to sort out the issues over the liberalization of international trade in services which are likely to be discussed in the upcoming Uruguay Round. It was argued that one important focus of the discussion will be on the right to establishment of foreign service industries under the condition that they meet all of the regulatory requirements imposed on domestic firms in the industry. Most emphatically, the adoption of this principle does not mean that signatories have to change their domestic regulatory environment in any other way.

The second important focus of negotiations will be patents and copyrights. The economic issues in this field are difficult conceptually and little is known empirically about optimal rates of protection of knowledge capital producers. There are clear trade-offs between benefits from the global, collective protection of these rights in the short and the long run. These issues are also clouded by ideological arguments and notions of equity. The resolution of existing conflicts promises to be difficult.

Trade in people services gives rise to the need for international agreement on the conditions under which temporary work permits are issued to the deliverers of services abroad. Granting the right to establishment and national treatment for service industries loses much of its value if the issuance of such permits is not established simultaneously.

The regulation of national service industries will not be subject to negotiations at the Uruguay Round, except for the rules discriminating against foreigners. As a result, even after successful negotiations of the issues noted above, there are likely to remain many regulations which in effect reduce the level of trade and investment. The concept of embodied service trade suggests that these conditions will not do great harm to industrial countries with large and growing service sectors. The producer service industries will assure that the remaining goods industries are competitive internationally and that their output enters into international trade after embodiment in goods.

As in other trade liberalization efforts under GATT in the post- war years, the negotiations will be difficult and proceed slowly because of conflicts between efficiency and the pursuit of ideological and other policy goals by governments. The difference is that service industries, particularly finance,

15

have been considered traditionally to involve the national interest more strongly than goods production. In addition, because of the high labour intensity of many service industries, they have above average political interest group power to block deregulation.

References

Bhagwati, Jagdish N. "Splintering and Disembodiment of Services and Developing Nations". *The World Economy* 7, no. 2 (June 1984): 156-79.

Blackaby, Frank, ed. *De-industrialization*. London: Heinemann Educational Books, 1978.

Bluestone, Barry and Bennett Harrison. *The Deindustrialization of America*. New York: Basic Books, 1982.

_____ . *The Great American Job Machine: The Proliferation of Low-Wage Employment in the U.S. Economy*. Washington: Joint Economic Committee, 1986.

Cox, Donald and Richard Harris. "The Service Content of Canadian Trade". In *Topics in Service Sector Research*. Vancouver: The Fraser Institute, forthcoming 1989.

Giersch, Herbert, ed. *Services in World Economic Growth*. Tuebingen: Moor, forthcoming 1989.

Grey, Rodney C. "Services and Intellectual Property Rights". Paper prepared for the Institute for Research in Public Policy, Victoria, B.C., 1987.

Grubel, Herbert G. "All Traded Services are Embodied in Materials or People". *The World Economy* 10, no. 3 (September 1987): 319-30.

Grubel, Herbert G. and Michael Walker. *The Canadian Service Industries*. Vancouver: The Fraser Institute, forthcoming 1989.

Hindley, Brian. "The Uruguay Round and Trade in Services". *In* Giersch (1989).

17

Iacocca, Lee *Iacocca. An Autobiography.* Toronto. Bantam Books, 1984.

Sampson, Gary P. and Richard H. Snape. "Identifying the Issues in Trade in Services". *The World Economy* 8, no. 2 (June 1985): 205-24.

Shelp, Ronald K. *Beyond Industrialization: The Ascendancy of the Global Service Economy.* New York: Praeger Special Studies, 1981.

Trivedi, Vish. "Aspects of India's Service Sector". Ph.D. dissertation. Department of Economics, Simon Fraser University.

Name Index

Economists of the Twentieth Century

Monetarism and Macroeconomic Policy
Thomas Mayer

Studies in Fiscal Federalism
Wallace E. Oates

The World Economy in Perspective
Essays in International Trade and European Integration
Herbert Giersch

Towards a New Economics
Critical Essays on Ecology, Distribution and Other Themes
Kenneth E. Boulding

Studies in Positive and Normative Economics
Martin J. Bailey

The Collected Essays of Richard E. Quandt (2 volumes)
Richard E. Quandt

International Trade Theory and Policy
Selected Essays of W. Max Corden
W. Max Corden

Organization and Technology in Capitalist Development
William Lazonick

Studies in Human Capital
Collected Essays of Jacob Mincer, Volume 1
Jacob Mincer

Studies in Labor Supply
Collected Essays of Jacob Mincer, Volume 2
Jacob Mincer

Macroeconomics and Economic Policy
The Selected Essays of Assar Lindbeck, Volume I
Assar Lindbeck

The Welfare State
The Selected Essays of Assar Lindbeck, Volume II
Assar Lindbeck

Classical Economics, Public Expenditure and Growth
Walter Eltis

Money, Interest Rates and Inflation
Frederic S. Mishkin

The Public Choice Approach to Politics
Dennis C. Mueller

The Liberal Economic Order (2 volumes)
Gottfried Haberler
Edited by Anthony Y.C. Koo

Economic Growth and Business Cycles
Prices and the Process of Cyclical Development
Paolo Sylos Labini

International Adjustment, Money and Trade
Theory and Measurement for Economic Policy, Volume I
Herbert G. Grubel

International Capital and Service Flows
Theory and Measurement for Economic Policy, Volume II
Herbert G. Grubel

Unintended Effects of Government Policies
Theory and Measurement for Economic Policy, Volume III
Herbert G. Grubel

The Economics of Competitive Enterprise
Selected Essays of P.W.S. Andrews
Edited by Frederic S. Lee and Peter E. Earl